# ANOREXIA NERVOSA AND RELATED EATING DISORDERS IN CHILDHOOD AND ADOLESCENCE

# Anorexia nervosa and related eating disorders in childhood and adolescence
## 2<sup>nd</sup> Edition

edited by

### Bryan Lask
*St George's Hospital Medical School, London, UK,
and Huntercombe Manor Hospital, Berkshire, UK*

### Rachel Bryant-Waugh
*Great Ormond Street Hospital for Sick Children, London, UK*

## Psychology Press
a member of the Taylor & Francis group

Copyright © 2000 by Psychology Press Ltd, a member of the Taylor & Francis group
All rights reserved. No part of this book may be reproduced in any form, by
photostat, microform, retrieval system, or any other means without the prior
written permission of the publisher.

Psychology Press Ltd, Publishers
27 Church Road
Hove
East Sussex, BN3 2FA
UK

**British Library Cataloguing in Publication Data**

A catalogue record for this book is available from the British Library

ISBN 0-86377-803-8 (hbk)

Cover design by Leigh Hurlock. Illustration of *Felicity's Food Flower* taken from Chapter 11
of this book. Copyright © 2000 Psychology Press Ltd.

Typeset by Graphicraft Ltd, Hong Kong
Printed and bound in the UK by Biddles Ltd, Guildford and King's Lynn

# Dedication

This book is dedicated to our own families: Judith, Gideon, and Adam; Alexander, William, Annelies, and Joseph. They have patiently and sympathetically tolerated our devotion to manuscripts and word-processors. Our devotion to them for all they have given us prevails.

# Contents

# Acknowledgements

Many of our colleagues, past and present, have not contributed directly to this book. None the less, their ideas, creativity, support, encouragement, enthusiasm, and hard work are reflected throughout.

The Medical Research Council, the Garfield Weston Foundation, the Child Growth Foundation, and the Gordon Carlton Memorial Fund have all contributed generously to our Research Programme. Without their support, much of our research could not have been carried out.

We are inordinately grateful to Johanna Richardson, our Editorial Assistant, who brought order to chaos, and Katie Ellis, who laboured long and hard with diligence and humour, to compile the subject and author indexes.

# Contributors

**Marianne Bentovim**, The London Child & Family Consultation Service, 234 Great Portland Street, London W1N 5PH, UK.

**Rachel Bryant-Waugh**, Consultant Clinical Psychologist, Department of Psychological Medicine, Great Ormond Street Hospital for Children, Great Ormond Street, London WC1N 3JH, UK.

**Deborah Christie**, Consultant Clinical Psychologist, Adolescent Services, North House, Middlesex Hospital, Cleveland Street, London W1N 8AA, UK.

**Morag Close**, Chartered Physiotherapist, Huntercombe Manor Hospital, Huntercombe Lane South, Taplow, Berks SL6 0PQ, UK.

**Rose de Bruyn**, Consultant Radiologist, Department of Radiology, Great Ormond Street Hospital for Children, Great Ormond Street, London WC1N 3JH, UK.

**Jacqueline Doyle**, Research Psychologist, formerly of Department of Psychological Medicine, Great Ormond Street Hospital for Children, Great Ormond Street, London WC1N 3JH, UK.

**Isky Gordon**, Consultant Radiologist, Department of Radiology, Great Ormond Street Hospital for Children, Great Ormond Street, London WC1N 3JH, UK.

**Tara Haggiag**, former patient.

**Peter Honig**, Family Therapist, Phoenix Centre, NHS Eating Disorders Service for Children and Adolescents, Ida Darwin, Fulbourn, Cambridge CB1 5EE, UK.

**Bryan Lask**, Consultant Psychiatrist, Department of Psychiatry, Jenner Wing, St George's Hospital Medical School, Cranmer Terrace, London SW17 0RE, UK; also SW London & St George's Mental Health NHS Trust, and Huntercombe Manor Hospital, Taplow, Berks SL6 0PQ, UK.

**Maryann MacDonald**, parent.

**Jeanne Magagna**, Consultant Child & Adolescent Psychotherapist, Department of Psychological Medicine, Great Ormond Street Hospital for Children, Great Ormond Street, London WC1N 3JH, UK; also Joint Co-ordinator of Centro Studi Martha Harris di Firenze Child Psychotherapy Training, Florence, Italy.

**Marc Neiderman**, Huntercombe Manor Hospital, Huntercombe Lane South, Taplow, Berks SL6 0PQ, UK.

**Dasha Nicholls**, Clinical Lecturer, Institute of Child Health, London, UK; also Research Fellow, Department of Psychological Medicine, Great Ormond Street Hospital for Children, Great Ormond Street, London WC1N 3JH, UK.

**Wendy Sharman**, Clinical Nurse Specialist, St George's Eating Disorder Service, St George's Hospital Medical School, Cranmer Terrace, London SW17 0RE, UK; also Hebdon Lodge, Springfield University Hospital, Glenburnie Road, London SW17 7DJ, UK.

**Anna Tate**, Teacher-in-charge, Mildred Creak Child and Adolescent Psychiatric Unit, Department of Psychological Medicine, Great Ormond Street Hospital for Children, Great Ormond Street, London WC1N 3JH, UK.

**Beth Watkins**, Research Psychologist, Department of Psychiatry, Jenner Wing, St George's Hospital Medical School, Cranmer Terrace, London SW17 0RE, UK; also Huntercombe Manor Hospital, Taplow, Berks SL6 0PQ, UK.

**Shelagh Wright**, Southampton Eating Disorders Service Juniper Centre, Exford Avenue, Harefield, Southampton, Hants SO18 5DJ, UK.

# Prologue

In the prologue to the first edition of this book we raised the question of why there should be yet another book on eating disorders. We justified the first edition on the basis that it was the first book to deal with early onset eating disorders, i.e. eating disorders occurring in people below the age of 16. This is a distinct population, quite different in many ways from those who develop eating disorders in their late teens or adult life. Obviously some of the issues are similar, but many are different. In various important respects the aetiology, clinical presentation, phenomenology, and treatment all differ. Further there is a wider range of eating disorders in the younger age group.

The first edition was set in the context of a recent increase in dieting behaviour in children (Hill, 1993; Hill, Oliver, & Rogers, 1992). This was clearly a cause for concern, particularly because dieting is a risk factor for the development of eating disorders (Wilson, 1993) and the prevalence of diagnosable eating disorders in a specific population is likely to be directly proportional to the prevalence of dieting behaviour in the same population (Hsu, 1990). At the end of the 20th century, eating disorders, including those of early onset, have become a major public health issue. Referral rates continue to increase and the need for more and improved services has been manifested by the expansion in specialist services for this population.

Our own experience and knowledge have been greatly enhanced by both the passage of time and concerted research endeavours. We believe that now is an appropriate moment to offer a distillation of current information about eating disorders in this younger population. The contributors to this book are all people with whom we have worked on the eating disorders programmes at

Great Ormond Sreet Hospital for Children and at Huntercombe Manor Hospital. Between us we have tried to convey our knowledge, perception, and understanding of these problems, and to share our clinical experience of assessment and treatment.

Part 1 of the book opens with a chapter written by Tara Haggiag, now a young adult but many years ago a patient of ours. She vividly describes her childhood experience of anorexia nervosa, her torment and suffering. Tara clearly demonstrates that anorexia nervosa is only superficially about weight, and far more about inner distress.

The next chapter is by Maryann MacDonald, the mother of a child who had anorexia nervosa. Her chapter movingly conveys the mother's view of her child's illness and, just as importantly, her view of the health care system and the treatment process. Further, she has sought and incorporated the views of many other parents whose children were treated in other centres. We have made no editorial adjustments to this chapter, for, although it makes painful reading to those of us who believe we do our best, and certainly work with the worthiest of intentions, it is clear that we, "the professionals", have much to learn. Hopefully we have indeed learned, for, with exception of MacDonald's chapter, all the other chapters in this second edition are completely new or have been thoroughly revised and updated.

The rest of the book is divided into two further parts. Part 2 deals with the clinical presentation, both physical and psychological, of early onset eating disorders, their epidemiology, aetiology, and outcome. Part 3 is determinedly practical and devoted to clinical issues. Following chapters on psychosocial and physical assessment and an overview of management issues, there are chapters on family-oriented treatment, cognitive-behavioural therapy, psycho-dynamic psychotherapy, inpatient work, physiotherapy, group work, schooling, and finally legal and ethical issues.

Here are a few technical points.

(1)   We have made frequent use of case illustrations, and many of the children are referred to in different chapters. For obvious reasons we have changed the children's names, but we have kept the pseudonyms constant throughout so that readers may cross-refer should they so wish.

(2)   For ease of reading, and because far more girls than boys experience eating disorders, we have referred to the children as girls, unless we are specifically discussing boys.

(3)   The age group represented in this book ranges from about 8 to 15. There is no totally satisfactory term to cover this group. In consequence we have used various terms such as "children", "young person", and when appropriate "adolescent". It seems difficult to get it right and we hope that we will be forgiven if we have appeared condescending or inappropriate in our terminology.

We hope that readers will find what follows of interest and value. Although we do not expect agreement with all that we say, we trust we have conveyed some of the fascination and challenge that we have experienced in working with these children and their families.

Bryan Lask and Rachel Bryant-Waugh<br>
April 1999

## REFERENCES

Hill, A. (1993). Pre-adolescent dieting: Implications for eating disorders. *International Review of Psychiatry, 5*, 87–99.

Hill, A., Oliver, S., & Rogers, P. (1992). Eating in the adult world: The rise of dieting in childhood and adolescence. *British Journal of Clinical Psychology, 31*, 95–105.

Hsu, G. (1990). *Eating disorders*. New York: Guilford Press.

Wilson, G. (1993). Relation of dieting and voluntary weight loss to psychological functioning and binge eating. *Annals of Internal Medicine, 119*, 727–730.

# Personal experiences

# CHAPTER ONE

# The broken jigsaw:
# A child's perspective

**Tara Haggiag**

Recently my sister, Alexandra, visited a friend with anorexia nervosa in hospital. Hearing about my sister's university acceptance, Laura, her friend, suddenly grimaced. Her face contorted into a sarcastic smile and she laughed mockingly. Laura's natural disposition had always been friendly and open and her jealous behaviour was a surprise. At that moment my sister experienced an uncannily clear flashback. She was transported back to our local hospital where I was being treated for anorexia nervosa twelve years ago. I was 9 years old, she was 7. Alexandra remembered calling out, "Tara, I love you!" but the door slammed shut in her face as I shouted, "Go away! I hate you!" During the time I had anorexia nervosa Alexandra was completely shut out of my life. Resentful, I felt that somehow my parent's love had been transferred from myself to her.

My sister's sad memory filled my eyes with tears. I could only say, "I am so sorry. Can you ever forgive me? I feel so badly for the way I acted towards you while I was anorexic". I realise there is no going back. My own memory of what occurred over those years is like the broken pieces of a jigsaw puzzle that never quite fit. There are chunks of memory which have been amputated from my mind, censored because they were too painful. Nevertheless, certain things remain crystal clear, never to be forgotten.

At 5 years old I began to suffer from compulsive behaviour. This meant that I would take my socks on and off up to four or five times before I was satisfied. When walking along the pavement it was imperative that I avoided the cracks. This obsession with ordinary habits meant that I was late for everything and often my parents would leave me behind as a punishment. This early disorder was a signal that something was wrong. Psychiatrists advised my mother to ignore my "negative behaviour" and reward "good behaviour". As a result I felt rejected and loved only for the "good" me.

When I was 8 we visited my grandfather in Tuscany, and a chance remark deeply affected me. I shall never forget sitting on the grass and looking out at the glistening ocean as I experienced the last few moments of childhood innocence. My grandfather strolled past with my father and remarked, "Tara is a cute little girl, but when she loses her puppy fat she will be really beautiful". Presumably my grandfather meant well, but he was unaware of the power his poisonous words were to have. I was sensitive and remember desperately wanting to be perfect in every way.

Before reaching my ninth birthday I had begun dieting. Along with a drastic reduction in my food intake were some rather unusual habits. I started drinking from a baby bottle and using a baby knife and fork. I found clothes from my early childhood in the attic and began wearing them. This baby syndrome was a desire to be a loveable baby again, like my brother who was a year old and loved by everyone. I was the eldest child and felt that somehow I was also the bad child. With my younger sister and brother to take care of, it was difficult for my mother to divide her time equally between us. The younger children required much of her attention and, not fully understanding the situation, I began to feel increasingly left out.

In school during lunch a child in my class tormented me: "Every bite of food you eat is making you fatter," he teased. Dieting fads filtered all the way down to the playground. Parents who slimmed passed a "thin is best" message to their children, encouraged by the media. It is no coincidence that I obtained the starring role in my school play in the midst of my weight loss. The more I suffered from anorexia nervosa the more determined I became to be the best.

Sensitive to the dynamics between my parents, I felt protective towards my mother and tried to prevent my parents from arguing. Refusing food was a way of gaining control over my life. It seemed to distance me from family pressure and made me feel independent. I ate alone, making myself small portions of food in the kitchen, sometimes substituted by a handful of sunflower seeds or a piece of fruit. When anyone mentioned my unusual eating patterns I retaliated with hostility. As time went on my weight fell rapidly and the situation became out of control. Not knowing who to ask for help my mother took me to our local GP. He informed her that it was simply a phase that I would grow out of.

Next we visited a nutritionist who lectured me on the fat and protein content of foods. This encouraged my obsession and increased my growing list of "bad foods" to eliminate from my diet. I began to keep a diary of the few foods I ate, from half a Rivita to a bite of apple, and counted each calorie. The diary kept a record of my weight each morning. The goal was to continue losing weight each day. If I maintained my weight, that was acceptable; if I lost weight I was satisfied and relieved. But if I put on even a fraction of a kilo, I was miserable and would restrict myself even more the next day. The result was that I ended up eating just three pieces of fruit a day.

I remember my father chasing me up the stairs of our family house in a rage. I knew how to push all his red buttons at once and he was not always able to restrain himself. On these occasions he seemed to lose his adult mind and become an 8-year-old child, like me. Household articles would fly around as we bulldozed through the house leaving behind broken objects and a stream of tears and misery while my mother tried to mend all the shattered pieces.

"She's just a little girl!" my mother cried as we scrambled past. "She needs discipline and authority, she must know who the real boss is in this family!" my father yelled back. One time, on being chased upstairs for a spanking, my head accidentally hit the corner of the bedside table. As the blood poured from the wound all I can remember feeling was relief. My father and I clashed because we shared a very similar temperament. We were both stubborn and opinionated.

My rage forced him to confront his own rage, so frightening he struggled to keep it locked away. In my relationship with my father I never felt I had the space to be angry without attracting negative attention. This in turn led me to feel insecure and unloveable. I continued unconsciously to provoke him, waiting impatiently for the day when he would love me unconditionally for the real me, however bad I was. My mother reacted very differently when faced with my resentment. She closed up emotionally, seemingly detached and uninvolved. In moments when I felt I needed her most I would come up against what seemed like a blank wall. During this time I wrote a short poem describing the isolation I felt:

> I feel as though I'm in a box with a lid shut as tightly as can be, open and shut, open and shut, but the lid never opens for me.

My mother was angry at my father for putting his work first. He often stayed late hours at his office while we all waited for him and dinner became cold. My father never had what could be called a family upbringing. By the age of 3 his parents had divorced and by 10 he was packed off to boarding school in a foreign country. He had no model of fatherhood to follow.

Anorexia nervosa was a downhill struggle. I was convinced that the thinner I was the more loveable I would be to the rest of the world. Fashion spreads filled the walls of my bedroom and the emaciated figure of the average fashion model became the god I worshipped. The films *Flashdance* and *Footloose* starring skinny women had an affect on my attitude towards food. The protagonist in *Flashdance* lives on Diet Coke and cigarettes while spending the rest of her time dancing and working out. I made a silent vow to myself that I would become like her. The stick-thin fashion models I saw daily in magazines and on the television increased my determination. I insisted that I was eating—it just happened to be when no one was around. When the school doctor weighed me I stole some kilogram weights and hid them in my pocket.

My first experience of being treated for anorexia in our local hospital haunts my mind. I was diagnosed as the bad child because the good child ate what her parents fed her. The bad child refused. The treatment was similarly black and white. The hospital was unaccustomed to dealing with anorexic children and it seems that my case was part of an experimental treatment. I shall never forget a particular family therapy session. Chicken flew across the room as my parents were directed by the head psychiatrist to grab hold of me and force feed me. Above us a video camera recorded the entire scene as other professionals stood watching the episode through a one-way screen. It was the epitome of humiliation for a family that was already falling apart.

My parents felt labelled as the bad parents whose sin could only be absolved through keeping a tighter rein over their unruly daughter. The mistake made by this psychiatric team was damaging. My father's quick temper was encouraged in a continued attempt to "control Tara". It was like fighting fire with fire, and as a result of this therapy I became even more angry and frightened. I ran, kicked, and screamed around all doctors and figures of authority. I tried to escape from the confinement of the hospital and from my parents whenever the chance arose. What I needed to know was the reality: that my parents truly loved me and were on my side doing everything they could to ensure my survival. Instead, the power struggle continued.

The therapy that I was subjected to, with its isolation chamber and brutal system of punishment and reward, is something that continues to scar me to this day. I was left alone in an empty room with everything I owned confiscated. The only time I saw the nurses was during meals. My mother was not even allowed to visit me. She wept alone in the hallway while I sat numbly by myself in bed. I continue to wonder how this treatment was ever meant to give me the will to live? The notion that I was the black sheep, a devil child that had to be fixed in order to be loved, continues to haunt me.

My worst memory comes back to me like a nightmare. I am being grabbed by three nurses and a doctor. They pull me forcefully into a white room where my clothes are stripped off and I am covered by a blue cloth. Then I am held down as a gastric tube is pushed up my nostril and into my stomach. The pain is nauseating. This punishment is not for refusing to eat, but for not finishing my food within a time limit. The tube was never used on me at Great Ormond Street Hospital. On the rare occasions that it was imperative for others it was never used forcefully or as a "punishment".

In between admissions to the local hospital, on a winter ski holiday with my family, I described my inner struggles:

> I came out of hospital half a year ago. Now I'm at the end of a snowy Swiss holiday. Nothing is going right for me. I'm sad all the time. Me and the family are just not getting on at all. I feel really bad because I stole some money off my parents! My walkman has run out of batteries and Dad refused to buy me new batteries! I really need them badly. I need a little more LOVE from my parents. Pop and break dancing music can't do all of the trick. I need some love. REAL LOVE. Help me someone.

I believe that love is the key word in the recovery from anorexia nervosa. Inside I loathed myself and not eating was a way of expressing my inner feeling of unworthiness. The outer anger that I expressed came as a result of the inner torment that rattled daily within my mind. I did not know how to love myself and did not believe that anyone could possibly love me the way I was. More than anything I needed to be hugged and reassured by my parents that they loved me but I didn't know how to ask and the distance between us simply continued to grow. The stolen money was an attempt to steal back the parental love I felt deprived of. Feelings of rejection turned into isolation. My anger turned inward against myself and ate me up.

> As I'm skiing down the slopes I hear strange voices. And then thoughts run past my mind. I'm scared . . . What should I do? Do I really want to live anymore? Well not with therapy! I'm scared of eating again. Help me Help me Help me.

Secretly, I wanted to please my parents and make them happy. But my inner voice of negativity always seemed to win me over and eventually I felt powerless, only able to express myself accurately through writing. There was a huge gap between my inner feelings and the negative outer expressions that continued to show themselves. I was bad and my efforts to be good and loveable always failed:

> The world seems to be closing in behind me. Like when you see a beautiful flower open and give you joy just to smell and look at it. And then you realise its leaves are going brown and it is going to close and die soon. Well I expect that is how it is for me and my mum and dad. I am the bud or flower or whatever and they have to watch me going backwards.

I wished my mother would take me in her arms and hold me, telling me over and over how much she loved me. Sometimes she exclaimed "I don't understand why you feel so unloved". Malnourishment had shattered my nerves and my reactions were unpredictable. In reality I was by no means the easiest child to love. Yet underneath was just a frightened little girl needing reassurance. My worst enemy was myself and my own unconscious; a negative voice that constantly affirmed my unworthiness. It is something I struggle with to this day.

The local hospital seemed convinced that if my parents could learn to force feed me and, if the hospital could ensure my weight gain, then everything else would work itself out. Anorexia nervosa is not that simple. At Great Ormond Street Hospital, where I was transferred after many months of unsuccessful treatment, they understood that my neurosis had to be treated at its roots. This had less to do with food and more to do with family relations. By this advanced stage in our crisis positive rebuilding was crucial to enable the family to find the hope and strength to recover.

The way forward only emerged when I entered Great Ormond Street. I went into long-term treatment and lived there for 10 months. My parents came in for meals and family therapy. Great Ormond Street insisted that the family eat meals together. During these meals my parents practised working as a team. This was a major change from previous meals, which were filled with arguments and anxiety. They learned how to listen and communicate when there was tension. Weekends were spent at home where the skills we had learnt during the week were practised. Because I was a child my parents were able to keep me at Great Ormond Street and in retrospect that was incredibly lucky.

The goal treatment was particularly effective. If I behaved and ate properly I would achieve my goal in the form of a special treat. Outings involved anything from visiting the zoo to challenging the shoots at the Richmond water slides. These activities were not only essential as an incentive to get better, they revived my enthusiasm for living. Another aspect of Great Ormond Street, essential to my recovery, was the love and support I felt from members of staff. No one was on a power trip to exercise their authority over the children. In contrast my personal helpers showed true compassion that seemed miles away from the sterile theories tried and tested on me at the local hospital.

From the beginning of my hospitalisation I had individual therapy sessions. I drew pictures from a box filled with crayons and pens. For a long time I simply drew but said nothing. It took a while before I trusted my therapist enough to speak. Sometimes I felt frustrated by the long lapses of silence. I often wished that we could have a real conversation together not based on theory. Apart from gaining intuition about my anorexia, I needed to get away from dwelling on negativity and concentrate on the positive aspects of my life. Therapy became a constant and stable part of my life and continued throughout the four years later spent at boarding school. I came home from boarding school every weekend to have therapy. By the time I was in boarding school I had learnt the skill of articulation and therefore spoke frequently. The time spent in therapy was an important back-up in times of anxiety and stress, inevitably encountered at school.

Luckily the environment at boarding school was a positive experience. Inherent was a structured life within a caring community. At age 11, one year after being discharged from Great Ormond Street, my ability to express myself had developed. This can be seen in a letter written to my parents from boarding school:

17.2.88

Dear Mom and Dad,

I don't know how to explain myself in words, but letters are something else. I feel badly because I feel I do everything wrong sometimes and I don't know what to do about it. Sometimes I feel as though I embarrass or upset you, but why I do not know. I want so much for you to understand me but sometimes I think you cannot. That's why I would like to spend more time with you so that you can understand the way I think. I'm sorry if I've caused you any inconveniences. I hope you don't think I'm just a stupid spoilt brat. I'm sorry if you think this letter is stupid. I love you both more than words can say. If I don't live up to your standards please let me know.

Love Tara.

P.S. Please don't be angry with me whatever the reason I'm sorry.


Today I rarely think about the time I spent overcoming anorexia. Yet situations do occur that shock me into the realisation that the mindset of anorexia is like a contagious drug. It captures its innocent victims early on in a neurosis that continues to spread rapidly. Seemingly innocent Barbie, for instance, can have a traumatising effect on a young child. I thought little of the impact Barbie had on me until recently something happened while babysitting Amy, a 5-year-old girl, which brought it all back.

Amy was playing in the bathtub with seven Barbies. Suddenly she shot up out of the water, "Look at my tummy!" she yelled, pointing to her child-shaped stomach. "It's not at all like Barbie's! Her waist goes in and mine sticks out . . . that means I'm fat!" I empathised with her and felt sad.

In September 1996, Nicki Pope, the medical correspondent of the *Daily Express*, published an article called "Sindy the Slim Sinner". The subtitle read, "Waif-like doll blamed for causing anorexia in girls as young as nine" This immediately caught my eye as it was the precise age I became anorexic. In her article, Pope relates Sindy to models like Jodie Kidd and suggests that such extreme thinness contributes to the rise of anorexia in young girls. "Supermodels such as Jodie Kidd, Kate Moss and Trish Goff have been blamed for spreading the cult of ultra-thinness. But now experts say Sindy and her arch rival Barbie also play a key role in reinforcing the body-image message." The article explains how Sindy's once doll-like figure in the early 1960s has been transformed to become "pointedly thin".

So, what does cause anorexia nervosa in children? It seems to me that there are a variety of contributing factors: parental relations, school pressures—including academic expectations and relationships with other children, media images that are often absorbed unconsciously, and an extremely negative self image. As an anorexic child I struggled daily with intense feelings of negativity that seemed to confirm my unworthiness. In my mind I was not valuable enough to be fed properly. From personal experience I believe that one of the greatest needs during anorexia is reassurance and the continual confirmation that the sufferer is loveable and worthy.

Skilled treatment at Great Ormond Street enabled my family and I to gain the communication skills and confidence to relate positively towards each other again. Slowly the relationship with my parents improved. On difficult days, when feeling imperfect, I try to remember that buried within is a little girl who still needs support to live each day without punishing herself. It takes strength to love oneself. Luckily I was supported by my parents and the staff at Great Ormond Street in my time of need, which is why I am here today. Recently a family friend asked; "How did you ever recover from anorexia?" I replied without hesitation, *"It was through love."*

CHAPTER TWO

# Bewildered, blamed and broken-hearted: Parents' views of anorexia nervosa

**Maryann MacDonald**

*Editors' Note*

*This chapter has been written by the mother of a child who had anorexia nervosa, treated in our Eating Disorders Clinic. We believe it important to include a parent's view in this volume as families' experience of living with such illnesses and treatment offered are often overlooked. We have not edited the content of this chapter in any way, as to do so would not be in keeping with our aim to give parents a free voice. The author bases her text on her own experience, but includes the views of a number of other parents whose children received treatment for an eating disorder from a wide range of different resources around the country. Together, these parents are at times highly critical of current clinical practice, yet they offer many constructive suggestions for improvement. We have found Mrs MacDonald's chapter so moving and instructive that we have decided to place it near the beginning of our book. We have benefited greatly from her contribution and we hope that in turn so will the children and families we see.*

What is it like to be the parent of a child with anorexia nervosa? It is to ask yourself all day and half the night what went wrong. It is to read everything you can find on anorexia nervosa to try to understand and help your child and to learn from your reading that it is your fault that your child is ill. It is to be blamed by no one more than yourself.

It is to reach out for life when you want to die, knowing that you do so to survive and help your child survive, but knowing also that for doing so you will probably be accused of being callous and uncaring. It is to have everything about you rejected by your child—your food, your body, your personality, your

11

achievements. It is to wonder long after your child is "well" if you have caused her harm in some way that is so grievous that she will never recover.

These are some of the descriptions of the experience I have gathered from parents of anorexic children. Being the parent of an anorexic child affects one profoundly and irrevocably. My own daughter suffered from anorexia nervosa when she was 12 years old. When I was asked to write this chapter on a parent's view of the illness, I was not sure how much just one parent could contribute. After all, the book was to include sections on treatment of the illness by international experts. All I had to comment on was my own experience of living with an anorexic child for less than a year, and a half-dozen or so family-therapy sessions which had left me confused. When I asked whether I could examine our family's records to gain further insight for purposes of this chapter, I was told that this would not be possible. This made me feel that though my views were being nominally sought, as the parent of an anorexic I was not really trusted. Also, when I looked at the proposed contents of the book, I noted that "A Parent's View" was handwritten in, an afterthought, perhaps, as the last topic in the book before the conclusion.

Still, I felt that parents' views of the illness ought to be included in the book. After all, it is parents who have lived with and observed the anorexic child from birth, and who have had to deal with the anorexic child's problems first-hand, 24 hours a day. So I met with several parents of former anorexics to obtain their ideas. We decided the most useful course of action would be to gather as much reaction from other parents as possible. Together we prepared a questionnaire. It was mailed to parents who responded to an advertisement in the Eating Disorders Association newsletter, and given directly to parents of anorexics known personally. Altogether, responses were obtained from 30 families.

These responses were heartbreaking. I found myself reading them with tears rolling down my face. I feel a tremendous responsibility to speak for these varied parents, most of whom put much time and thought into their answers. It is clear that these people feel they need to be heard and have never before been asked. Many had covered every available space on the questionnaire with lengthy answers to the questions asked, striving to express every detail of their experience. Wherever possible in this chapter, I will try to quote the parents' own words, and allow them to speak for themselves.

## MOTHERS AND THEIR DAUGHTERS

First of all, I think it is significant that not a single questionnaire was returned by a father. They were without exception completed by mothers. Mothers are those most intimately involved in the day-to-day difficulties of living with an anorexic child. Mothers feed children, from birth onwards, and anorexia nervosa is a refusal to be fed. The mother of an anorexic has the bitter experience of having her love and nurturing, symbolically herself, rejected. In the great majority of cases, anorexia nervosa is an illness that affects girls, often at the onset of adolescence. Why is this so? Why do these girls feel such a strong need to reject their mothers and their own female bodies?

I am convinced that the answer to this question lies in society's view of women. Women are the "second-best" sex. They are no longer respected in their traditional roles as housewives and mothers, and often find it difficult to succeed in pursuits outside the home, partly because of discrimination and partly because of the difficulties of balancing their work with their domestic responsibilities. If they do work, they are most often expected to fulfil all their traditional functions as well.

One of the most constant of a mother's responsibilities is to make sure that her family is fed. She must shop, cook and wash up every day of her life. But at the same time, she must be careful not to overeat herself. She must not get fat, for above all, society despises a fat woman. A woman can be forgiven for being "just a housewife", but she cannot be forgiven for being fat. Her obligation is to be slim and attractive to men. So she must take care of and feed everyone but herself.

This imposes a strain on a woman's life. A little girl growing up, playing with her impossibly-proportioned Barbie doll, may not see this strain. But as she moves into adolescence, she begins to look her biological destiny in the face, and what does she see? Her mother. Her mother, whom she may always have loved, she now sees with new eyes. She may, because of her love, be unable to bear the sight.

Most probably, her mother's attractiveness has begun to fade. She may, in middle age, have become somewhat overweight. She may or may not work outside the home. If she does not, her daughter, like the rest of society, cannot respect her. If she does, she no doubt experiences a greater or lesser degree of difficulty in balancing her career with her continuing need to look after her family.

This coincides with her daughter's growing awareness that she, too, will be expected to be both successful in the world and, simultaneously, feminine, sexual, and a self-denying mother. It is all too much. The daughter feels pain for her mother's life and anger that the same will be expected of her. She resolves never to be "stuck" like her mother. And the stage is set for her to begin to work compulsively to achieve in the world and to keep her body as thin and non-maternal as possible.

But what is it that makes the difference between the girl who is prepared to diet to be slim and to outstrip her mother's achievements and the girl who is prepared to starve herself to the point of emaciation and to work obsessively for success, never satisfied with her accomplishments?

Some mothers remarked on worrying characteristics in their children which pre-dated their eating disorders. My own daughter was always extremely anxious. As a baby, she never wanted to be held and cuddled. She would squirm out of my arms, seemingly restless and impatient for activity. As she was my first child, this was disappointing for me. I found myself taking her for endless walks to keep her happy and amused. She seemed always to be anxious and unsettled. Her father and I hoped that when she started school she would be busier and therefore happier, but she didn't seem to like school much at first, and often cried and did not want to go. Although she was very bright, we deliberately made a point of not making demands on her to achieve any particular grades, and in fact changed her school after several years to one that was more relaxed in the hope that she would feel less pressured. But no matter what we did, she remained nervous, constantly sucking her thumb and biting her nails. When I once discussed this with a wise and experienced teacher of hers, he remarked: "Your daughter may not be pressured by what you do or say but by who you are," implying that perhaps my child felt her parents' success in life was a hard act to follow.

Another mother, in listing factors that may have contributed to the development of anorexia nervosa in her daughter, also mentioned severe anxiety.

> [She had] irrational and unexplained fears: fear of being poisoned, fear of death, fears that she was not a perfect Christian (she had become fanatical about religion although we are not religious ourselves).

Another whose "socially precocious" daughter became anorexic at the age of $8\frac{1}{2}$ remarked:

> She was very highstrung and became jealous and aggressive when her sister was born. We probably didn't handle it very well, but the constant tantrums and rebellious behaviour were exhausting. Her domineering personality seemed to manipulate the entire family. By the time she was five years old, she refused to get dressed for school and said that voices told her not to do what we asked her to do. Her behaviour became disturbed and obsessional and I took her to see a child psychiatrist. Behavioural therapy was all that was offered, so I tried to reward her for good behaviour and ignore the bad . . . It didn't work, and I think confirmed her darkest fears that she wasn't as good or lovable as her little sister.

Intense jealousy of siblings was a common element mentioned by parents in discussing factors that may have led to their children's illness. A mother of six said:

> I realize that she was crying out for attention . . . Her eldest sister was only 18 months older than her, tall, naturally slim, and has plenty of confidence in herself, she is multi-talented, and had plenty of boyfriends when they were both younger. All my anorectic daughter wanted to do was to fit into her eldest sister's clothes.

Another remarked:

> My daughter is very reliant on me and always has been since she was a baby. [She] seems to want all my attention.

Mothers are likely to feel ambivalent about their anorexic daughters. They may want to nurture them, but may be worried about their lack of autonomy and feel tyrannised by their demands. Of course, an anorexic child effectively steals the limelight from her brothers and sisters for the duration of her illness. Parents repeatedly commented on this, remarking that other children had become rightfully resentful, although in certain cases brothers and sisters were exceptionally understanding of and helpful to their anorexic siblings.

## THE MYTH OF THE IDEAL BODY AND OTHER CONTRIBUTING INFLUENCES

The modern emphasis on healthy eating (low fat, low sugar) was frequently referred to as a contributing factor in the development of eating disorders.

> I have read hundreds of articles about diet and heart disease where we are made aware of the dangers of eating too much fat. I have never seen in one of those articles or leaflets a warning of what can happen to the body if it doesn't get any fats. A four-stone teenager is not a pretty sight.

An overweight mother wrote:

> I feel extremely guilty for being overweight myself. Although I've always wanted to be a little slimmer, I've dressed smartly and worn makeup and had a happy personality. I'm not nearly so outgoing now.

Parents repeatedly report teasing and name-calling of their children, who may have been somewhat overweight, as contributing causes to their development of anorexia nervosa. The mother of a Mensa member who became anorexic at the age of 10 said:

> She started puberty early and was made fun of at school. She was always trying to underachieve and tended to find it difficult to fit in with the other children, which was partly due to having an IQ of 179.

My own daughter began dieting after receiving a "Fitness-o-Gram" from her school. This was a computerised evaluation of her body done at the school, in which she was compared to an "ideal" girl of her age and height. These were routinely sent home with children at my daughter's school, and were a cause of humiliation to many children because of unfavourable comparisons with the ideal and with each other. After my daughter's anorexia nervosa developed, I asked the school principal whether the results could not be mailed home to parents in sealed envelopes. He replied that this would be too costly. When I offered to pay for the mailing myself, in order to spare other children this humiliating practice, he refused, saying that he felt this precaution was unnecessary. He seemed to resent my "interfering".

Other difficulties at school such as problems with friends and the pressure of exams were mentioned as common factors preceding the onset of anorexia nervosa. Problems at home included moves, loss of grandparents, parental divorce of marital difficulties, siblings leaving home, and changes in the mother's and father's working situations, all stress-producing life changes.

## WHAT HELPED AND WHAT DIDN'T

In the questionnaire, parents were provided with a listing of all the treatment techniques mentioned in this book. Few were familiar with even the names of all these treatments, although some had children who had been suffering from eating disorders for up to 10 years. One mother, a doctor herself, said that she was unaware of the differences between behavioural therapy, cognitive therapy, and psychotherapy.

> I am a hospital consultant who qualified [in the] early 1960s when psychiatry was a tiny part of medical curriculum. I spent a year at Great Ormond Street and knew virtually nothing about this terrible wasteful illness when it hit my family.

This woman's daughter has now had anorexia nervosa for seven years, and now, at the age of 21, weighs only five and a half stone, in spite of five long stays in hospital.

Parents were asked to rate the effectiveness of treatment techniques with which they were familiar. On a scale of "Very helpful", "Moderately helpful", and "Unhelpful", I am sorry to report that most techniques were rated as "Unhelpful". The only three that were conspicuously differently rated by parents were "Hospital Care", "Psychotherapy", and "Group Therapy". These three scored significantly more "Very helpful" and "Moderately helpful" ratings than all the others combined.

Parents whose children were helped by hospital treatment were most often those who had been referred to a specialist unit, not a general psychiatric ward. Nurses specially trained in the care of anorexics were again and again mentioned as being critically important in helping to overcome the anorexic's resistance to eating . Weight gain in hospital was frequently lost as soon as the child returned home, as parents stated there was little follow-up of their daughter's progress. One parent described her family's experience in an NHS hospital:

> At _____ the NHS professionals were secretive, and we felt patronized. Everyone seemed to feel that we were "bad parents" because our child had anorexia nervosa, and this made it all the harder for us to keep our family together during the long siege of her illness. We were not given any hopes for her recovery; on the contrary, we were told that her prospects were poor. We were never given any helpful information or advice as to how we could actively help her to recover.

This contrasts sharply with her later experience at a specialist unit:

> For the first time, we were able to really share the pain and anxiety caused by our child's illness. She lived on the unit five days a week and came home weekends. This gave us a much needed rest from coping with tantrums and constant scenes in the kitchen and at the table. Most importantly, the workers on the unit showed us, by example and encouragement, how to get our daughter to eat with us again.

Parent's responses regarding the value of psychotherapy pointed up the highly variable quality of therapists. A number mentioned psychotherapy as being helpful not only for their daughters, but for themselves. Two mothers who had been discouraged from seeking psychotherapy for their daughters at low weights, but who persisted and obtained it anyway, commented on the fact that it had, after all, been beneficial. Others felt differently:

> Certainly the psychiatry/psychology was wrong for Kate. The culmination of this treatment was her being admitted to a mental hospital adolescent's unit. She emerged after three weeks' trial like-a zombie . . . She is a super intelligent person apart from the anorexia hang-up and did not take kindly to being put away with violent, abusive and drugged-up and guarded mental cases.

The mother of the only male anorexic in our sample writes:

> Carl went to see a psychologist at _____ for seven months every week but really he was no better. I would have preferred him to see a man but it was different women every time nearly.

My daughter repeatedly requested psychotherapy, but we were told by our family therapist at first that her weight was too low for her to benefit, and later that her difficulties could be worked out within the family. Months after we finished family therapy, my husband and I again requested psychotherapy for our daughter, as we felt she was still deeply unhappy with herself. Finally, the family therapist agreed to refer her to a clinical psychologist, but by this time she then refused to go, saying it was "too late". She said that she felt that even though she had been forced to break her destructive eating habits, she still felt anxious about food, but didn't want to miss any more school or activities for doctor's visits. I am regretful about this missed opportunity to get to the bottom of what was bothering her when she might have been responsive to it, and feel that our earlier requests ought to have been respected.

It seems from our respondents as though many family therapists regard the practice as an economical form of treatment, and refuse to allow young anorexic patients private therapy apart from their families. Yet opinion on the benefits of family therapy is divided. Its usefulness no doubt depends on the family in question and the rapport they develop with the individual therapist. Many mothers dismiss it as distressing, still others swear by it and are enthusiastic about the insights gained through family therapy.

Clearly, there is family therapy that is helpful and family therapy that is destructive. Families who have been put "on camera" or watched from behind one-way mirrors without warning or permission are understandably resentful.

> Family therapy began with videotaped meetings. These were generally whodunits of family traumas and problems. Very humiliating for already highly distraught and anguished parents. The effect was to further alienate and confuse us.
>
> One day I had to bring a "picnic" for the family to eat in front of two psychiatrists, a video camera, and a one-way mirror. When my daughter violently threw food on the floor my husband and I were told we had to force it down her mouth. This was the only time actual "information" was given and it was repugnant to us all.
>
> When we told the head child psychiatrist at _____ that we could not go on any more after six harrowing months of hospital admissions and discharges as our daughter went steadily downhill, she told us that we had "failed".

Parents seem to want family therapists to consider the concept of the chicken and the egg when seeing families of anorexics. By the time the family is likely to end up in therapy, they have probably undergone months or even years of almost unbearable strain, which is reflected in their family interaction. I know I felt wooden and empty and afraid to speak for fear I would cry. I was criticised by the family therapist for this at the time. He said that I appeared to be "wearing a mask". Yet I really wanted to understand what was wrong and how to help my child. So I tried to be more vocal and express my thinking. Perhaps I overdid it and didn't give my daughter enough chance to speak, because after I talked too much at another session, he told me that by dominating the discussion I was contributing to my daughter's illness. I didn't know what I was supposed to say or do. At the end of the family therapy, the question I most wanted to ask was: "How is this supposed to help?"

I have been told that people in therapy are supposed to come to their own conclusions about what their problems are and how they can deal with them, but perhaps this rule should be bent somewhat in dealing with this particular problem. I think it would be more helpful to say, for example, "Families with anorexic children often have difficulty with . . . Here are some ways they have learned to cope with this." This way, the family would feel neither accused or confused. Concrete advice and encouragement are probably the two things parents need most in their struggle to deal with this disorder. Some explanation of therapeutic goals would also be extremely helpful.

Many mothers report experiences of having their requests for treatment ignored or swept under the carpet by health professionals. This is especially evident in their dealings with GPs.

> My doctor laughed me out of the office, told me I was an anxious mother and to leave her alone to eat the kind of food she wanted to eat. When I mentioned her periods, he said "What does she want periods for anyway? They are a nuisance."

This doctor's attitude to feminine physiology was shared by another GP consulted by one of our respondents. A mother writes:

> I would like to reiterate how woefully ignorant about anorexia our GP seemed to be. When I managed after much cajoling to get my daughter along to him and explain how she had lost a substantial amount of weight and her periods had stopped, he said she didn't look too bad to him and he was sure she didn't mind not having periods. He could always start them up for her if she wished to get pregnant. When I said she wasn't eating enough he laughed it off by saying it was probably a teenage fad and she would eat again when she felt hungry.

Not only do these responses show disrespect for mothers' judgement, but they show how deep society's repugnance towards menstruation is. If even doctors feel menstruation is distasteful, how can young girls be expected to regard it positively? Mothers have a difficult task in making the idea of having periods seem attractive to an 11- or 12-year-old child. The sight of blood is regarded as disgusting or shocking in our sanitised culture. But even in our more earthy past, menstruating women were regarded as "unclean". Today, women are encouraged by advertising to regard menstruation as a kind of secret they should keep from the world. I feel the name of a popularly sold sanitary napkin says it all: "Complice".

So, having been told by their GPs that their mothers are silly and fussy and that they are fine, the anorexic has her world view confirmed and can go back to starving until her weight is so low that she is unable to function. At that point, she may or may not be lucky enough to be hospitalised in order to save her life.

> When my daughter's sister took her to _____ for an appointment with the resident psychiatrist and she weighed six stone (down from nine stone, eleven pounds), she was sent home with anti-depressant pills and told to eat more. When admitted to hospital two weeks later (she weighed) five stone, four pounds . . .

> The waiting list for a decent hospital is so long people are becoming frantic. The waiting time for admission for a patient and the family is a time of indescribable anxiety.

The need for early detection and help was mentioned again and again, both by parents whose children have recovered and by those who are still suffering. Many parents who felt specific types of treatment would be helpful for their daughters were frustrated when asking for it.

> The answer was vague but implying "no" when I asked about group therapy and yet this hospital was supposed to be well-known for its treatment of anorexia—one of the doctors had written a book on the subject but G. was not her patient. G. was in a ward with all other psychiatric patients—horrific!

# WHAT MIGHT HAVE HELPED

All forms of alternative medicine seem to have been discouraged by the medical profession—acupuncture, hypnotism, homeopathy. Yet some parents experienced positive results with these methods.

> I tried to persuade her to take the homeopathic zinc, but she didn't want the sugar in the dose. After much cajoling, she finally relented. We went downstairs to watch TV, and she was calmer and pleasant. Half an hour later, she went into the kitchen and ate three muffins. She began to smile, and talk about how she guessed she could eat dinner without getting fat. Before she went to bed, she told me how happy she was and that she felt things were going to get better from that point on, and that she realized how difficult she had been and would never forget our efforts to help her. It was nothing short of a miraculous change.
>
> She was hungry again in the morning, and ate breakfast and lunch, and did not try to stop me from using oil in the cooking. She is becoming sociable and more outwardly-directed than we have seen her in months. Truly astonishing.

Parents find it difficult to understand why the medical profession is so reluctant to try alternative forms of treatment when traditional methods are often disappointing. Holistic forms of treatment would seem to be particularly appropriate for an illness which exhibits both physical and mental symptoms. Doctors who refuse to listen to mothers' suggestions make mothers feel their opinions are not respected, a feeling which is commonly reported to contribute to the development of anorexia nervosa itself.

It is already evident that many parents were disappointed with the information and support they received from medical professionals. Those most satisfied were families whose GPs had responded promptly to their concerns with adequate referrals. Even in such cases, there is often room for improvement.

> Although our family GP was very helpful and arranged an appointment for us for the child and family psychiatric clinic quickly, and he admitted her to hospital, we weren't informed as to what would happen next. We didn't know the purpose of family therapy and at first thought it a waste of time. The hospital didn't tell us how her stomach would react to eating more food and we found it upsetting when she would cry in pain for lengths of time without help. We would be left to worry about things like that that could have been explained to us.

Among our respondents were some whose children became or remained ill after the age of 16. These parents complained of the difficulty of obtaining adequate information about their daughters' progress.

> I have to ask for information, no one seems to think I want to know, yet I am the one who sees her 24 hours a day and has to try to see that she eats enough to stay alive.

Others expressed confusion about who has ultimate responsibility for their anorexic over-16s. They assume, probably correctly, that no-one cares about their children as much as they do, and yet feel powerless to help and are refused information because of their daughters' rights to privacy.

> The psychologist tells me the health risks have been explained and that it is up to her to make the choice. Is her mind in any fit state to make a choice?

Parents seemed to do a lot of complaining about the lack of help and support from the medical profession. Given their distress, it may be impossible to do enough for some families. But here are repeated suggestions made by parents:

> Nursing staff and doctors should *listen* to the parents.

> A more friendly and open response to enquiries would have given a feeling of working together. When ringing the hospital for information about my daughter who was attending clinics as an outpatient, I felt a nuisance, overprotective, and was treated in an unsympathetic and patronising manner.

> The psychiatrist should take the time and trouble to try and explain how and why the illness develops.

> Laxative should be sold only on prescription.

One family learned a useful technique from a psychiatrist who responded to her daughter's questions in writing:

> If [my daughter] feels desperate to have her questions answered, she now writes them down and saves them for an appropriate moment. The actual process of writing out the question seems to alleviate much of the stress. This helped the family situation a great deal, as previously, I had found myself trying to answer desperate questions at very inconvenient times.

Many praised the help obtained from the Eating Disorders Association (see address at end of chapter), for recommending appropriate medical facilities and counselling; for reviewing reading material on anorexia nervosa, self-awareness, and self-assertion; for referring parents to support groups; and for simply being there on the end of the telephone line when needed. Doctors who are too busy to take telephone calls from anxious parents should refer them to the Eating Disorders Association. Anything, even advice from a stranger who is not familiar with the details of one's particular situation, is better than a brush-off.

Literature on anorexia nervosa, particularly the work of Bruch (1974) and Palazzoli (1978), seemed to me at the time of my daughter's illness to be depressing and unhelpful. However, I found consolation in a book by Bruno Bettleheim, *The good enough parent* (1987). The loving counsel of this wise man, who speaks in this book as a parent to parents, was humane and helpful.

In discussing what most helped their children to recover from anorexia nervosa, many parents mentioned the love and support of their families. This book, particularly the early chapters, gives valuable guidance on how to convey that love and support. It might prove especially useful for parents who never received much love themselves.

## HOPE: LOST AND FOUND

Parents speak of the terrible burden of guilt that almost overwhelms them, of the necessity of having to live with constant violent and abusive behaviour for months and even years on end, and of the unspeakable grief of watching their beloved children committing long, slow suicide before their eyes. They feel like prisoners in their own homes, afraid to go out because of what might happen while they are gone, yet feeling they must take care of themselves, if only to set an example for their children. They walk a daily tightrope, trying to know when to be firm and when to be flexible, trying to do everything they can but often feeling that their efforts are worthless.

> I feel miserable and trapped in an impossible situation. I've lost a lot weight and my hair is turning white. I saw a therapist once. She told me to go off around the world, have an affair and leave Kate to herself.

> It is hard not to feel resentful especially when she uses emotional blackmail. If she feels I haven't spent long enough listening to her she will rush into the bathroom and threaten to do "something stupid" or else rush out of the house and not return for hours causing us tremendous worry. She is also violent and abusive. It is a living nightmare.

> I have been changed irrevocably by her illness. I no longer have any ambitions or hope for the future of my children . . . I feel I have let her down as a mother. I love her so much, as does her father, but on more than one occasion she has told us that she hates us both and the house also. I tried so hard to make her happy and nurse her through her illness, but I think she blames me, and maybe she is right.

> There are times when I feel I am headed for a nervous breakdown. I have nobody to turn to for support. I live in a constant state of fear.

> In the beginning I felt I hated my daughter for being so selfish, but now I think I love her more than I could ever tell her and will *never* give up on her.

> Her life is a nightmare, but I see inside the obsessive, darkened child the sunny child I remember and I know we can rescue her. Tonight she told me that she knows it is difficult to be a parent to her now. I looked at her hollow eyes and thin skull and I hugged her and told her that it was alright, and that she would be getting better soon.

The refusal to give up is a factor parents often mentioned when discussing what has helped them to survive their children's illness. Also frequently mentioned is prayer and spiritual faith. Several parents mentioned renewal of religious faith and increased sensitivity to the suffering of others as the benefits of their experience. Many referred to their good marriages, which they felt helped to give them strength and courage. One mother whose daughter was anorexic for seven years spoke proudly of her daughter's recovery:

> Sandra wrote a dissertation on the subject while she was at university. This helped us both to deal with her problem more effectively. I have been very proud of her efforts to help other sufferers. I think she has a better understanding of the illness than many members of the medical profession.

Sadly, a mother who has been anorexic herself cannot necessarily help her child avoid the same plight. She probably never received any treatment whatsoever, and came through her illness without any insight into her problems.

> I had a very unhappy and lonely childhood. There were people around but I felt isolated, particularly from my mother. I would say that I was the scapegoat of the family and became anorectic myself at the age of 18.

This mother, with the help of a counsellor, has now:

> resolved to quite a large degree the tension between myself and my own mother and have become far less anxious and guilt-ridden in general. I have changed my way of relating to other people completely. Although I feel I have still farther to go, [I] am much happier.

I suspect that I myself was somewhat anorexic for about 20 years. This is not to say that I understood this at the time. I did not think I was too thin, and I was genuinely puzzled by the fact that I seemed to have little energy, be constantly hungry, and felt consequently irritable. I explored allergies and thyroid problems as the source of these difficulties. It wasn't until my daughter became severely anorectic that I began to recognise the symptoms of the illness in myself. When I realised what I had helped bring about in my child, I felt overwhelmed with shame and guilt and could scarcely forgive myself. With the grace of God, I did, and I learned a new strength born of endurance. Without my child's breakdown, I probably would have had a hungry heart for the rest of my life. For helping to heal me, I will be grateful to her forever.

Parents of anorectics have a bad reputation. Although their daughters' responses to them are well-documented, their side of the story is seldom told.

> We were not given a chance to state our case. Our daughter told some terrible lies about us and her childhood and actively got a lot of sympathy. She has told us this since . . . Wouldn't a better picture emerge if parents and children were both interviewed?

It has been difficult for me within the space limitations of this chapter to try to represent the varying thoughts of so many different families. I very much appreciate their help and hope that I have spoken for them adequately. I also appreciate the help of my friend Katharine Haggiag and Dr Rachel Bryant-Waugh.

Women's lives are filled with much inescapable pain connected with their experiences of their bodies. As the mother of two daughters, I take comfort from the fact that each generation is standing on the shoulders of the last, and that, in consequence, our children will be able to see more clearly and perhaps live more wisely than we have been able to do.

## REFERENCES

Bettleheim, B. (1987). *The good enough parent*. London: Thames & Hudson.
Bruch, H. (1974). *Eating disorders: Obesity, anorexia nervosa and the person within*. London: Routledge.
Palazzoli, M.S. (1978). *Self starvation*. New York: Jason Aronson.

## CONTACT ADDRESS

The Eating Disorders Association
Sackville Place
44–48 Magdalen Street
Norwich
Norfolk
United Kingdom
Tel: (01603) 621414
Fax: (01603) 664915

# PART TWO

# Context and course of early onset eating disorders

CHAPTER THREE

# Overview of the eating disorders

**Rachel Bryant-Waugh**
*Great Ormond Street Hospital for Children, London, UK*

## INTRODUCTION

Eating disorders, in particular anorexia nervosa and bulimia nervosa, are commonly thought to affect adolescent girls and young adult women. Indeed, women between the ages of around 15 and 35 represent the majority of those presenting with, and receiving treatment for eating disorders. Yet eating disorders are also known to occur in men and boys (e.g. Bryant-Waugh, 1994; Fichter & Daser, 1987; Vandereycken & Van den Broucke, 1984), older women (e.g. Gowers & Crisp, 1990), and pre-pubertal children of both sexes (e.g. Jacobs & Isaacs, 1986; Fosson, Knibbs, Bryant-Waugh, & Lask, 1987; Gowers, Crisp, Joughin, & Bhat, 1991). In general there seems to be little disagreement that men and older women present with "true" eating disorders, that is, that they fulfil existing accepted diagnostic criteria for anorexia nervosa or bulimia nervosa (e.g. ICD-10—World Health Organisation, 1992; DSM-IV—American Psychiatric Association, 1994). The clinical picture in these individuals is very similar to that found in the main female population.

The situation regarding children has been less clear, and there remains some debate and confusion around the nature of the various childhood onset eating disorders. This confusion has arisen for a number of reasons. First, there is a continuum of eating and feeding difficulties that can occur from birth onwards. Infant feeding problems and subsequent weaning difficulties are relatively common. The food faddiness, or very selective eating patterns of pre-school children are also relatively common, and in the majority of cases not a particular cause for concern. Some very young children will of course present with more serious problems which may be having an adverse effect on their growth and development. Such

27

children will need to be monitored more closely, and may require some additional input to address their feeding difficulties. On the whole though, feeding problems occurring in pre-school children are commonplace, and appropriate to the child's stage of development, involving experimentation of new tastes and textures as well as of the impact their behaviour has on their carers. Such feeding difficulties tend to pass as the child matures and are correctly regarded as "phases" that in the majority of cases the child will outgrow.

One difficulty here is that when eating problems occur in older children, say from around the age of 8 years upwards, they may still be regarded as a phase to be grown out of, or as awkward or stubborn behaviour. The main difference is that feeding and eating problems are not developmentally normal in these older children. In addition, the child's cognitive development is by then much more sophisticated, and eating problems will be much more likely to be related to underlying psychological issues.

Second, there has been much confusion and inconsistency in the literature about the nature of eating difficulties in children and the terminology used to describe them. Some believe that the eating disorders commonly associated with young women simply do not occur in children. An example of this is: "[Anorexia nervosa] is really only a problem with adolescents, and there is virtually no chance at all of younger children having this condition" (Haslam, 1986, p. 95). It should be noted, however, that this particular author has since acknowledged that this statement is inaccurate (personal communication). Nevertheless, the book in which it appeared was aimed at a wide audience, dealt primarily with the commonly occurring feeding difficulties of younger children, and would have been quite widely read.

Where diagnostic criteria have been used that require the presence of amenorrhoea, pre-menarchal girls may have been excluded from consideration. In contrast to this exclusion of children is the use of the term "infantile anorexia nervosa" (e.g. Chatoor, Egan, Getson, Menvielle, & O'Donnell, 1987) to describe what appear to be infant feeding difficulties and/or failure to thrive. Infants cannot fulfil the more usually accepted diagnostic criteria for anorexia nervosa (ICD-10 and DSM-IV) as they do not have the required cognitive capacities. In our view the misapplication of existing terminology is not helpful and contributes to the confusion.

Third, there has been a lack of standardised instruments for the assessment of eating disorders in childhood (see Chapter 7). This has meant that much of the published work on the subject has been based on clinical case reports. These have described children from the age of 8 upwards (e.g. Fosson et al., 1987; Gowers et al., 1991; Higgs, Goodyer, & Birch, 1989; Jacobs & Isaacs, 1986). Whereas many of the children included in these case series have received formal diagnoses of an eating disorder, it has been difficult to demonstrate this on the basis of objective, reliable assessment because the necessary tools simply have not been available.

There has been much media interest in the occurrence of eating disorders in children over recent years. This interest has unfortunately helped to promote two myths. The first is that we are currently seeing some sort of "epidemic" and the second is that this is a new phenomenon, with eating disorder sufferers becoming ever younger. Neither are true. The first point is dealt with in more detail in Chapter 4. Although it is probably true that there is a general increase in weight sensitivity and even dieting behaviour, these do not necessarily lead on to eating disorders, which remain relatively rare in the childhood population. The second myth can be easily dispelled by looking at some of the historical literature. Two of the earliest authors who are attributed as describing cases of anorexia nervosa in children were Collins (1894) and Marshall (1895). Collins wrote a case history of a 7-year-old girl who was emaciated and refusing food. Further details of the case history suggest that this was not simply related to physical illness, but that there was a psychological component to the girl's food avoidance. Marshall wrote about what he termed "anorexia nervosa" in an 11-year-old girl, who eventually died from starvation. Since this time there have been other reports in the literature. In the earlier publications, these were mostly individual case studies, but later case series began to be described. It is evident that in the eyes of the authors of such papers, for the most part practising clinicians, the young age of the patient has never excluded a possible diagnosis of anorexia nervosa.

However, it is difficult to be certain that a similar concept of anorexia nervosa has been held throughout. After all, the diagnostic criteria we are using at the end of the 20th century remain in a constant state of revision. Criteria included under the term "anorexia nervosa" in the past may differ from current criteria. It seems likely that even more recent case series, such as Warren's (1968), include children who would not now fulfil diagnostic criteria for anorexia nervosa, but instead presented with food fads, food refusal, or other more commonly occurring childhood eating difficulties. The fact remains, however, that children have for a very long time been known to suffer from alterations in eating patterns, which are recognised to have a psychological component, and can lead to very serious physical complications. This situation is by no means new, and not a late 20th-century phenomenon.

It is only over the last two decades that children with eating disorders have come to be regarded as a subgroup of interest. The literature on all aspects of eating disorders specifically relating to this younger population remains sparse. This chapter aims to describe the different types of eating disorder and eating disturbance occurring in children aged 14 and under. In this chapter, as elsewhere in this volume, the terms "early onset" and "childhood onset" are used to refer to eating disorders occurring in children between the ages of 7 and 14 years.

## EATING DISORDERS AND EATING DISTURBANCE OCCURRING IN CHILDHOOD

Approximately half the children attending the specialist eating disorders clinic at Great Ormond Street Children's Hospital present with anorexia nervosa or symptoms characteristic of anorexia nervosa. This clinic provides at present a service for children and their families where undereating, food restriction, and avoidance of weight gain are primary features. The majority of children with anorexia nervosa are girls, although a small number of boys do present with formally diagnosable anorexia nervosa. The remainder of those who attend the clinic have a range of different types of eating disorder or eating disturbance. Many of the children we see share a strong urge to avoid food, and most have no organic cause for their eating difficulties. The types of eating problem occurring in this age range in this particular clinic population may be related to the following:

- anorexia nervosa (and atypical or subclinical forms)
- bulimia nervosa (and atypical or subclinical forms)
- food avoidance emotional disorder (FAED)
- selective eating
- restrictive eating
- food refusal
- functional dysphagia
- pervasive refusal
- appetite loss secondary to depression.

The interrelationship between these different types of eating disturbance is not always clear, and there are large areas of overlap between them. They will be described in more detail in the following sections. It should be noted that there is a further set of types of eating disorder or eating disturbance not already listed. This includes eating disturbances related to:

- binge eating disorder
- compulsive overeating
- hyperphagia
- overeating associated with organic disease.

These eating problems do not involve undereating, dietary restriction, and avoidance of weight gain, and are therefore not represented in our own clinic population.

## The diagnosis of eating disorders in children

The diagnosis of an eating disorder in children remains in many cases problematic. Diagnostic criteria are in a constant state of revision, and at the time of writing those of ICD-10 (WHO, 1992) and DSM-IV (American Psychiatric Association, 1994) are in most common use. Using the ICD-10 system the following eating disorder diagnoses are possible:

- anorexia nervosa (F50.0)
- atypical anorexia nervosa (F50.1)
- bulimia nervosa (F50.2)
- atypical bulimia nervosa (F50.3)
- overeating associated with other psychological disturbances (F50.4)
- vomiting associated with other psychological disturbances (F50.5)
- other eating disorders (F50.8)
- eating disorder, unspecified (F50.9).

However, using the DSM-IV system there are other possibilities:

- 307.1    anorexia nervosa
  - restricting type
  - binge eating/purging type
- 307.51    bulimia nervosa
  - purging type
  - non-purging type
- 307.50    eating disorder not otherwise specified (EDNOS).

If we go back to the different types of eating disorder and eating disturbance mentioned previously it can be seen that the descriptive terms used do not always neatly translate into diagnostic labels. Using DSM-IV terminology, the EDNOS group in childhood is very varied, and does appear to include a number of distinct subgroups of type of eating disturbance. For the purposes of research it is essential to strictly apply formal, accepted diagnostic criteria, and to be explicit about which diagnostic system is being used. If this is not done, the value of the results of the research may be limited as it will be difficult to make comparisons with findings from other studies. For example, comparing results of outcome studies is only possible if the selection of individuals included in the different studies has been based on similar criteria for inclusion. However, for clinical purposes, it may be less essential to apply strict diagnostic criteria as, for a large group of children with eating difficulties, this will not be a particularly meaningful exercise. The clinician works with presenting symptoms and difficulties in an attempt to alleviate the situation and it can be argued that in this respect it is in many cases relatively immaterial which diagnostic label is attached to the child's problem.

## Anorexia nervosa

Anorexia nervosa is characterised by determined attempts to lose weight or avoid weight gain. This can be achieved through food avoidance, self-induced vomiting, laxative abuse, excessive exercising, or more usually a combination of one or more of these. Weight and/or body mass index (BMI) drop to a level well below that necessary to allow the child to continue to grow and develop. Because children should be growing, failure to gain weight can be regarded as equivalent to weight loss in adults. Weight loss is a matter of considerable concern in childhood, and is particularly worrying in pre-pubertal children who have relatively low total body fat levels. Irwin (1981) has commented on the "refusal to maintain hydration" often present in children with anorexia nervosa, which can lead to a state of dangerous dehydration.

The child has abnormal cognitions about weight and/or shape, often thinking they are fat when they are underweight, or displaying a pronounced fear of becoming overweight. They have a tremendous sense of dissatisfaction regarding their bodily appearance. Children with anorexia nervosa suffer from a preoccupation with their weight, shape, food, and/or eating, to the extent that their concentration can be significantly impaired. Many children with anorexia nervosa are experts at calorie counting and are acutely aware of the calorie content of every mouthful they eat.

Children with anorexia nervosa provide a range of reasons for refusing food. The most common, in our experience, is a fear of fatness, but they may also give feelings of fullness, nausea, abdominal pain, appetite loss, and difficulty in swallowing as reasons (Fosson et al., 1987).

In terms of weight reduction/avoidance of weight gain strategies used by children, aside from restriction of food intake, the most common are excessive exercising and self-induced vomiting. Laxative abuse is less common. Excessive exercising may have developed out of an increase in activity levels that has initially been encouraged. Daily exercise workouts, excessive swimming, jogging, or other routines, can become time-consuming features of the child's life. Exercising may be done in secret, often at night. Vomiting is a strategy used by many children, to such an extent that it is often prudent to assume that a child who is not gaining weight once treatment has started must be vomiting. Laxative abuse is probably less common in younger individuals due to limitations in access. However, laxative abuse does occur and potential electrolyte imbalances and mineral deficiencies need to be monitored.

In our experience, children can develop anorexia nervosa from around the age of 8 onwards. The clinical presentation of anorexia nervosa in childhood is similar to that in adulthood. The only slight exception to this is perhaps the fact that, in boys with anorexia nervosa, shape appears to be much more of an issue than weight. These boys are more concerned to avoid becoming unfit or unhealthy, and may not be so much set on losing weight, as on preventing the development of a flabby shape. The end result is however very similar, with the avoidance of foods regarded as being fattening or unhealthy, usually excessive exercising, and subsequent significant weight loss.

There continues to be debate around which of the clinical features of anorexia nervosa should be included as prerequisites for diagnosis, and which represent commonly occurring characteristics that may or may not be present. The finer detail of the physical, behavioural, cognitive, and emotional aspects of the disorder are likely to differ between individuals, indicating that different children will require different priorities in treatment. In addition, the anorexia nervosa will be associated with an accompanying depression in a significant number of children (see also the later subsection on appetite loss secondary to depression). In some cases, it may be associated with clear obsessive-compulsive symptomatology, and may come and go in intensity in an inverse relationship with the obsessive compulsive disorder. It has been shown that, in particular, boys with anorexia nervosa present with relatively high levels of obsessive-compulsive features (Shafran, Bryant-Waugh, Lask, & Arscott, 1995).

## Bulimia nervosa

Bulimia nervosa is an eating disorder characterised by episodes of overeating in which the person experiences a sense of loss of control, with accompanying attempts to avoid weight gain by self-induced vomiting, laxative abuse, diuretic abuse, or food avoidance. Weight and shape concern are core features, as in the case of anorexia nervosa, and are manifested by attempts to control weight and minimise the weight gain that might normally result from overeating. Self-induced vomiting and laxative abuse are by far the most common methods used to avoid weight gain. Bulimia nervosa is often accompanied by other forms of self-harm such as wrist-scratching, burning the skin with lighted cigarettes, alcohol and drug abuse, overdosing, and other risk-taking behaviour. None of these additional features are essential to making the diagnosis as they are variable.

Bulimia nervosa appears to be very rare in childhood and early adolescence, at least in that not many young people of this age present for treatment. It is of interest to note, however, that many bulimic women, who typically only present for treatment after many years of having the disorder, often report that their bulimia started in early adolescence. In our own experience, we very rarely see children below the age of 13 who would receive a clinical diagnosis of bulimia nervosa. Of those whom we have seen, and one was 7 years old, none has manifested the more dramatic forms of self-harming seen in older patients. However, as they go through adolescence they do seem to develop a tendency to participate in risk-taking behaviour.

## Food avoidance emotional disorder

Food avoidance emotional disorder (FAED) is a term that was first used by Higgs and colleagues to describe a group of children who have a primary emotional disorder where food avoidance is a prominent feature (Higgs et al., 1989). They originally described a group of children who did not fully meet diagnostic criteria for anorexia nervosa, but who did present with weight loss and food avoidance. They suggested that FAED may be an intermediate condition between anorexia nervosa and childhood emotional disorder (with no eating disorder); a partial syndrome of anorexia nervosa with an overall more favourable prognosis. The characteristics of FAED were originally set out as follows (Higgs et al., 1989):

- a disorder of the emotions in which food avoidance is a prominent symptom in the presenting complaint
- a history of food avoidance or difficulty (e.g. food fads or restrictions)
- a failure to meet the criteria for anorexia nervosa
- the absence of organic brain disease, psychosis, illicit drug abuse, or prescribed drug related side-effects.

Our experience of children who fall into the FAED category is that they may be extremely unwell physically, with very low weight and growth impairment. They do not necessarily have a less serious or milder form of eating disorder than those with anorexia nervosa, although there is considerable variability within both groups in terms of prognosis and outcome. It is clear that children with FAED do not have the same preoccupation with weight and shape, nor do they have a distorted view of their own weight or shape. They do have mood disturbance, combined with weight loss and determined food avoidance. The mood disturbance may take the form of mild depression, anxiety, obsessionality, or phobias especially for specific foods.

Although organic brain disease is an exclusion criterion we have noted that many children with FAED do have other physical illnesses or disorders. They seem to develop food avoidance as part of their emotional response to physical ill-health and in such cases the food avoidance is not a direct symptom of the child's illness.

## Selective eating

This term is used to describe children who limit their food intake to a very narrow range of preferred foods. Typically they may only eat five or six different foods, sometimes being particular about brands or where the food is bought. The diet is usually high in carbohydrates, often including, bread, chips, or biscuits. A typical example might be a child who will eat only one particular brand of baked beans, white sliced bread from a certain supermarket, cheese and onion crisps, and chocolate digestive biscuits, again of a particular make. Drinks will also be selected, but many children will include milk, or a milk-based drink. Attempts to widen the repertoire of food are usually met with extreme resistance and distress.

Children with this form of extremely selective eating behaviour are often of appropriate weight and height for their age. In other words, their growth does not seem to be adversely affected by their eating habits. We see more boys than girls with this type of eating pattern. Parental requests for help and advice are usually precipitated by the impact the selective eating patterns have on social functioning, and by increasing parental concern given the advancing age of the child. In most instances, parents have been able to manage the child's extreme fussiness around food largely by making sure they have access to preferred foods. However, as the child becomes older, and engages in more social activities with peers, the eating may present more of a problem. Typical events precipitating help-seeking include an inability to take part in social events such as birthday parties or sleep-overs, impending school trips, or planned change of school. In the majority of cases, selective eaters are seen because of social rather than physical concerns, although there are strong behaviour and management issues as well.

These children are clearly distinguishable from those with anorexia nervosa and bulimia nervosa as they do not share a preoccupation with weight and/or shape or a distorted perception of their own body size, their weight is usually within normal limits, and they tend to have a relatively long-standing history of selective food intake. They do not present with a prominent fear of gagging or choking (see functional dysphagia, discussed later). In the majority of cases selective eating problems tend eventually to resolve. Peer group influence becomes stronger and the need to conform in adolescence will often result in a relaxation of the limits placed on dietary intake. Some will, however, persist in accepting only a very narrow range of foods, becoming adult selective eaters. As a rule of thumb, as long as the eating habits are not having an adverse effect on social, physical, and emotional development, they should not form a focus for concern.

## Restrictive eating

Restrictive eaters are those children who seem to have never eaten very large amounts, and who on the whole do not express a particular interest in or enjoyment of food. There is no evidence of mood disturbance, and on the whole restrictive eaters are fine as long as they are not forced to eat more than is their natural inclination. Physically, they tend to be small and light, but within the normal range of variation. Again, as long as growth proceeds steadily along a constant centile, there is usually not cause for real concern. Restrictive eaters will accept a normal range of types of food, but simply do not eat very much. They seem to have very small appetites.

These children may run into difficulties as they approach puberty with its additional energy-requirements. Height and weight centiles should be monitored, and it may be necessary to encourage the child to take some particularly energy-rich sources of food to ensure sufficient intake over this period. These children do not present with body image distortion or preoccupation with weight or shape. Their eating pattern tends to be normal and they do not actively avoid food, or attempt to lose weight. They may present with weight loss around the time of puberty, but are usually willing to accept energy supplements or dietary advice to ensure continued growth.

## Food refusal

Food refusal is a common phenomenon in younger children, and one which often causes much anxiety and distress. Pre-school children quickly learn the effects of refusing food and some will use this as a strategy to get other things. In older children, food refusal can persist, and is clearly distinguishable from the eating disorders and other types of eating disturbance. Food refusers tend to be less consistent in their avoidance of food; they will typically eat favourite foods without any problem at all, or will reserve the refusal for one or two particular people, or particular situations. Examples here include children who refuse to eat at school, but eat normally at home, or the child of separated parents, whose eating behaviour is resistant and problematic during the week when with the mother, but completely problem-free when with the father at weekends. Such children are not preoccupied with weight and shape, and tend not to have weight problems. In many cases, there is some unhappiness or worry that is underlying the child's food refusal. Once this has been identified and worked upon, hopefully the refusal will lessen. Whereas food refusal is developmentally normal in toddlers, it is not in older children, and usually represents a difficulty in the direct expression of existing concerns or uncertainties. In many cases it will not represent a serious threat to the child's general health and well-being, but it can interfere with the quality of relationships with the child.

## Functional dysphagia

Children with functional dysphagia also display a marked avoidance of food. Again this tends to be foods of a certain type or texture. The characteristic feature of this group of children is a fear of swallowing, vomiting, or choking, which makes then anxious and resistant to eating normally. There is in many cases a clear precipitant in the form of an aversive event that has resulted in the fear of swallowing, vomiting, or choking. Examples might include: traumatic gastrointestinal investigations, having had food poisoning or a bout of diarrhoea and vomiting where the child has vomited in public, a choking incident on a piece of food, or experience of abuse, which becomes associated with particular types or textures of food. Children with functional dysphagia do not have the weight and shape concerns of anorexia and bulimia nervosa.

## Pervasive refusal

"Pervasive refusal" is a term that was first used in 1991 to describe a small group of children who presented with a potentially life threatening condition manifested by a profound and pervasive refusal to eat, drink, walk, talk, or care for themselves in any way over a period of several months (Lask, Britten, Kroll, Magagna, & Tranter, 1991). The authors of this paper noted that children with this particular combination of symptoms and presenting features do not fit any existing diagnostic category, and suggested that the condition may be understood as an extreme form of post traumatic stress disorder. Since this first paper, others have been published (McGowan & Green, 1998; Nunn & Thompson, 1996; Thompson & Nunn, 1997), describing the condition, presenting case histories and offering a model for understanding the development and clinical phenomena of pervasive refusal syndrome (PRS). Thompson and Nunn (1997, p. 163) conclude that the "term PRS remains a descriptive label for a group of children who present with a constellation of clinical features which is distinct from other related disorders".

Children with PRS present as underweight and often dehydrated, adamantly refusing food and drink. In this way their presentation may be confused with that of a child with acute anorexia nervosa. However, a diagnosis of anorexia nervosa would be inappropriate because, first, the child tends not to be communicating sufficiently to ascertain whether the cognitive criteria for anorexia nervosa are fulfilled, and, second, the refusal extends across all areas of social and personal functioning, which is not the case in anorexia nervosa.

PRS is a rare, but potentially life-threatening disorder, which invariably requires hospital admission. Treatment is rarely straightforward, and often distressing for all concerned. It may be lengthy and intensive, but children can recover. It has been suggested that there may be a relationship between the length of illness prior to presentation, and the degree of improvement while in treatment and the time taken to recover (Thompson & Nunn, 1997). The differential roles of trauma, personality traits, and somatising tendencies need further investigation, and the syndrome itself requires further study before any more definite statements can be made.

## Appetite loss secondary to depression

Appetite loss secondary to depression is of course not an eating disorder in itself, but a well-recognised symptom of clinical depression. Many depressed adults suffer from poor appetite, and can lose quite substantial amounts of weight. For a number of reasons children with true "anorexia" (that is, appetite loss, not anorexia nervosa) may be referred for treatment of an eating disorder. If there is a history of poor eating and weight loss, combined with a change in mood and behaviour, an eating disorder may be suspected. It is important to distinguish between a primary depressive disorder and a primary eating disorder, as the treatment required differs considerably. It is usually not difficult to tell the difference as the central features of anorexia nervosa, such as determined food avoidance, body image distortion, and the preoccupation with body weight and shape, are absent in depressed children. Some of the other features, including social withdrawal, may however be very similar.

There is undoubtedly a common association of childhood onset anorexia nervosa with depression. Over half of our own clinical population have been found to be moderately to severely depressed (Fosson et al., 1987). There is an extensive literature relating to the relationship between affective and eating disorders, with much debate around the nature of this relationship. Most of this literature pertains to the situation in older adolescents and adults, and it may not be appropriate to extrapolate findings and conclusions in relation to a younger population. DiNicola, Roberts, and Oke (1989) have cautioned that in children the relationship between eating and mood disorder is more complex than in an older population, and suggest that the two types of disorder are even more likely to be intertwined.

## SUMMARY POINTS

This chapter gives an overview of the main types of eating disturbance occurring in children aged 8–14 years. In terms of referrals to a specialist eating disorder clinic for children in this age range, children with anorexia nervosa form the largest group. This group is predominantly female. Children who present with disorders other than anorexia nervosa represent approximately half of the clinic population. The gender balance is more even in this group as a whole, although there are some differences between the different types of eating disturbance in relation to the relative numbers of boys and girls.

Working definitions of the types of eating disorder and eating disturbance described in this chapter are as follows:

- Anorexia nervosa
  (1) determined weight loss (e.g. through food avoidance, self-induced vomiting, excessive exercising, abuse of laxatives)
  (2) abnormal cognitions regarding weight and/or shape
  (3) morbid preoccupation with weight and/or shape, food and/or eating
- Bulimia nervosa
  (1) recurrent binges and purges and/or food restriction
  (2) sense of lack of control
  (3) abnormal cognitions regarding weight and/or shape
- Food avoidance emotional disorder
  (1) food avoidance
  (2) weight loss
  (3) mood disturbance
  (4) no abnormal cognitions regarding weight and/or shape
  (5) no pre-occupations regarding weight and/or shape
  (6) no organic brain disease, psychosis, illicit drug use or prescribed drug related side-effects

- Selective eating
  (1) narrow range of foods (for at least two years)
  (2) unwillingness to try new foods
  (3) no abnormal cognitions regarding weight and/or shape
  (4) no morbid pre-occupations regarding weight and/or shape
  (5) weight may be low, normal, or high
- Restrictive eating
  (1) smaller than usual amounts for age eaten
  (2) diet is normal in terms of nutritional content, but not in amount
  (3) no abnormal cognitions regarding weight and/or shape
  (4) no morbid pre-occupations regarding weight and/or shape
  (5) weight and height tend to be low.
- Food refusal
  (1) food refusal tends to be episodic, intermittent, or situational
  (2) no abnormal cognitions regarding weight and/or shape
  (3) no morbid pre-occupations with weight and/or shape
- Functional dysphagia
  (1) food avoidance
  (2) fear of swallowing, choking, or vomiting
  (3) no abnormal cognition regarding weight and/or shape
  (4) no morbid pre-occupation with weight and/or shape
- Pervasive refusal syndrome
  (1) profound refusal to eat, drink, walk, talk, or self care
  (2) determined resistance to efforts to help.

## REFERENCES

American Psychiatric Association. (1994). *Diagnostic and statistical manual of mental disorders* (4th ed.). Washington, DC: Author.

Bryant-Waugh, R. (1994). Anorexia nervosa in boys. In B. Dolan & I. Gitzinger (Eds.), *Why women?: Gender issues and eating disorders.* London: Athlone Press.

Chatoor, I., Egan, J., Getson, P., Menvielle, E., & O'Donnell, R. (1987). Mother–infant interactions in infantile anorexia nervosa. *Journal of the American Academy of Child and Adolescent Psychiatry, 27,* 535–540.

Collins, W. (1894). Anorexia nervosa. *Lancet, I,* 202–203.

DiNicola, V., Roberts, N., & Oke, L. (1989). Eating and mood disorders in young children. *Psychiatric Clinics of North America, 12,* 873–893.

Fichter, M.M., & Daser, C. (1987). Symptomatology, psychosexual development and gender identity in 42 anorexic males. *Psychological Medicine, 17,* 409–418.

Fosson, A., Knibbs, J., Bryant-Waugh, R., & Lask, B. (1987). Early onset anorexia nervosa. *Archives of Disease in Childhood, 621,* 114–118.

Gowers, S., & Crisp, A. (1990). Anorexia nervosa in an eighty year old woman. *British Journal of Psychiatry, 157,* 754–757.

Gowers, S., Crisp, A., Joughin, N., & Bhat, N. (1991). Premenarcheal anorexia nervosa. *Journal of Child Psychology and Psychiatry*, *32*, 515–524.

Haslam, D. (1986). *Eat it up! A parent's guide to eating problems*. London: Macdonald.

Higgs, J., Goodyer, I., & Birch, J. (1989). Anorexia nervosa and food avoidance emotional disorder. *Archives of Disease in Childhood*, *64*, 346–351.

Irwin, M. (1981). Diagnosis of anorexia nervosa in children and the validity of DSM III. *American Journal of Psychiatry*, *138*, 1382–1383.

Jacobs, B., & Isaacs, S. (1986). Pre-pubertal anorexia nervosa: A retrospective controlled study. *Journal of Child Psychology and Psychiatry*, *27*, 237–250.

Lask, B., Britten, C., Kroll, L., Magagna, J., & Tranter, M. (1991). Children with pervasive refusal. *Archives of Disease in Childhood*, *66*, 866–869.

Marshall, C. (1895). Fatal case in a girl of 11 years. *Lancet*, *I*, 817.

McGowan, R., & Green, J. (1998). Pervasive refusal syndrome: A less severe variant with defined aetiology. *Clinical Child Psychology and Psychiatry*, *3*(4), 583–589.

Nunn, K.P., & Thompson, S.L. (1996). The pervasive refusal syndrome: Learned helplessness and hopelessness. *Clinical Child Psychology and Psychiatry*, *1*, 121–132.

Shafran, R., Bryant-Waugh, R., Lask, B., & Arscott, K. (1995). Obsessive-compulsive symptoms in children with eating disorders: A preliminary investigation. *Eating Disorders: The Journal of Treatment and Prevention*, *3*, 304–310.

Thompson, S.L., & Nunn, K.P. (1997). The pervasive refusal syndrome: The RAHC experience. *Clinical Child Psychology and Psychiatry*, *2*, 145–165.

Vandereycken, W., & Van den Broucke, S. (1984). Anorexia nervosa in males: A comparative study of 107 cases reported in the literature. *Acta Psychiatrica Scandinavica*, *70*, 447–454.

Warren, W. (1968). A study of anorexia nervosa in young girls. *Journal of Child Psychology and Psychiatry*, *9*, 27–40.

World Health Organisation (WHO). (1992). *The ICD-10 classification of mental and behavioural disorders: Clinical descriptions and diagnostic guidelines*. Geneva, Switzerland: Author.

CHAPTER FOUR

# Epidemiology

**Jacqueline Doyle and Rachel Bryant-Waugh**
*Great Ormond Street Hospital for Children, London, UK*

## INTRODUCTION: WHAT IS EPIDEMIOLOGY?

Epidemiology is the study of the distribution of diseases in populations. Epidemiological research tends to focus on the frequency of the disease or disorder in a population (i.e. how many people are affected), the kinds of people that tend to be afflicted, and the risk factors for the development of the disease. Children with eating disorders may receive a variety of diagnoses including anorexia nervosa, bulimia nervosa, food avoidance emotional disorder, selective eating, and pervasive refusal (see Chapter 3). Bulimia nervosa has been shown to be quite rare in children and there is very little empirical research on the epidemiology of food avoidance emotional disorder, selective eating, or pervasive refusal. This chapter will, therefore, attempt to elucidate what is known about the epidemiology of anorexia nervosa.

## WHY IS EPIDEMIOLOGICAL RESEARCH OF ANY INTEREST?

The answer to this question is quite straightforward. If we know how many people are likely to be affected by a disease or disorder it may be possible to estimate the need for treatment services within that population. Furthermore, if we can learn more about the kinds of people that develop a disorder, or the risk factors for the disorder in question, it may be possible to develop preventative strategies to eliminate the problem in the first place. For these reasons, epidemiological research has been described as the "intelligence service of public health" (Morris, 1970).

## PROBLEMS WITH EPIDEMIOLOGICAL RESEARCH

One way of reporting on the extent to which a population is affected by a disorder is to report on the "incidence" rate of that disorder. This is the number of *new* cases per 100,000 of the population. Prevalence rates, on the other hand, reflect the *actual* number of cases in a specific group of individuals at a particular point in time. There is a clear need for epidemiological studies of anorexia nervosa but there are a number of problems with the existing studies of this condition. These problems pose difficulties both in the interpretation of the results of individual studies and for building up a picture of the epidemiology of eating disorders across studies. Some of these problems are discussed next.

### Different methods of case detection

Researchers investigating the incidence or prevalence rates of eating disorders may consult a variety of sources in order to estimate the number of individuals affected by the disorder of interest. Some researchers have chosen to consult registers of cases hospitalised for the disorder. For example, both Nielsen (1990) and Moller-Madsen and Nystrup (1992) consulted the Danish Psychiatric Case Registers for their studies of anorexia nervosa. Other researchers have consulted sources documenting outpatients attending medical and psychiatric services and general practice records. When a study focuses on only one of these data sources it is unlikely that all cases of the disorder of interest will be detected. For example, Pasberg and Wang (1994) conducted a study of anorexia nervosa and bulimia nervosa in Bornholm county, Denmark. The authors searched a variety of sources in order to detect cases, including the Danish Psychiatric Case Register, outpatient records from the local psychiatric department, the records from the medical departments of the local hospital and all the physicians in primary health care. They also detected additional cases following an article in a local newspaper in which individuals were invited to participate in the research. The authors found that less than half of the cases detected were registered in the county's psychiatric case registers and 35% of the cases could only be found through a search of primary care records.

Hoek (1993) conducted a review of epidemiological studies of eating disorders. He reported that approximately 370 female cases of anorexia nervosa could be found in the community per 100,000 of the population in any one year. However, only 30 female cases of anorexia nervosa would be found per 100,000 of the population in any one year if the focus was on psychiatric inpatients. Hoek reported that a tenfold reduction of the rates of anorexia nervosa is seen when the focus is moved from the community, where many individuals with an eating disorder may not be in treatment, to psychiatric inpatients. In summary, the type of data source and the number of data sources consulted will have an effect on the overall numbers reported for a particular disorder.

## Case definition

An additional difficulty in interpreting the results of different studies is that there are a variety of ways in which to define a "case" of anorexia nervosa. Two separate systems are in common use for the classification of mental illness. One of these systems was developed by the American Psychological Association (APA). The fourth edition of the Diagnostic and Statistical Manual (DSM-IV: APA, 1994) produced by the APA is now in operation and was preceded by DSM-III (APA, 1980) and DSM-III-R (APA, 1987). The other classification system, the International Classification of Diseases (ICD) was developed by the World Health Organisation (WHO). ICD-10 (WHO, 1992) is now in operation and was preceded by ICD-9 and ICD-8.

Both the ICD and DSM systems lay out a set of diagnostic criteria which must be satisfied in order for a diagnosis to be given or for an individual to be considered a "case" of the disorder of interest. Fombonne (1995) has reviewed the epidemiological studies of the rates of anorexia nervosa. He noted that different researchers have used a wide range of diagnostic systems for the classification of anorexia nervosa, including ICD-8, ICD-9, DSM-III, DSM-III-R, and unspecified clinical diagnoses of eating disorder. The use of different diagnostic systems makes it difficult to make comparisons across studies as the two systems, ICD and DSM, do not necessarily overlap.

The fact that both diagnostic systems have been revised over time is also a potential problem. Ledoux, Choquet, and Flament (1991) conducted a study of bulimia nervosa in French boys and girls between the ages of 12 and 19 using both DSM-III (APA, 1980) and DSM-III-R (APA, 1987). Bulimia nervosa was found in 1.3% of the young people in this study when DSM-III was the classification system in use, compared to 0.7% when the more highly specific DSM-III-R diagnostic criteria were in operation. This study gives an insight of how the rates of disorders reported may be influenced by the system used to diagnose "cases" of eating disorder. Some researchers have attempted to eliminate the problem of changing diagnostic systems by retrospectively re-examining case notes of individuals with an eating disorder diagnosis and symptoms related to eating disorder, using a fixed diagnostic system (e.g. Lucas, Beard, O'Fallon, & Kurland, 1991). However, there are a number of problems in assigning diagnoses retrospectively. Pasberg and Wang (1994) pointed out that the material available on cases of eating disorder identified within medical departments tended not to include a great deal of information about psychopathology. There is, therefore, the possibility of missing cases because vital information on core symptoms is not available in the notes.

There may also be problems in the way that the various diagnostic systems are used. Diagnoses are often given by a variety of professionals working in various settings. Although these professionals may be working within the same diagnostic system, the way in which they reach a decision about the diagnosis is not standardised. It is therefore difficult to ascertain whether the diagnostic system has been used properly and reliably, i.e. whether a person given a diagnosis in one clinic by one clinician would get the same diagnosis in another clinic given by another professional.

One final but important point with regard to the use of the various diagnostic systems is that none of the systems adequately address the problems of diagnosing anorexia nervosa in children (see Chapter 3). When formal criteria are applied, many children with eating disorder symptoms may be excluded as such criteria are based on observations of older individuals. Bunnell, Shenker, Nussbaum, Jacobson, and Cooper (1990) have argued that younger individuals may not fulfil formal diagnostic criteria but may nevertheless present with considerable emotional, physical, and behavioural disturbances.

## Questionnaire measures of eating disorder

Some studies also make use of screening questionnaires such as the Eating Attitudes Test (EAT; Garner & Garfinkel, 1979; Garner, Olmsted, Bohr, & Garfinkel, 1982). This is a questionnaire that screens for the symptomatology of both anorexia nervosa and bulimia nervosa and has a cut-off score said to be indicative of "caseness". Screening questionnaires are often used in studies of non-referred samples (i.e. individuals who are not in treatment for an eating disorder) where it is not possible to interview the entire population in order to establish the presence or absence of an eating disorder diagnosis. King (1989) screened attendees at four London GP practices using the EAT and found that of 720 subjects aged 16–35 included in the study, 76 had a high EAT score. All but seven of these were interviewed to establish the presence or absence of an eating disorder. Six females and one male received a diagnosis of bulimia nervosa, whereas no cases of anorexia nervosa were found. This study highlights some of the issues for epidemiological research into eating disorders using non-referred populations. A screening instrument needs to have both high sensitivity (i.e. able to correctly identify "cases" of a disorder) and high specificity (i.e. correctly identify non-cases"). Misidentification of individuals is often inevitable when using measures such as the EAT—only 7 of the 76 high scorers turned out to have an eating disorder diagnosis. This is further complicated when one is dealing with rare disorders. Studies using these instruments must always, therefore, include some sort of interview measure as a means of verification.

King's (1989) study also highlights the fact that eating disorders, in particular anorexia nervosa, are rare—only 7 of the 720 subjects included in the research had a clinical diagnosis. This is an important obstacle to the studies aiming to estimate the numbers of people affected by eating disorders. The problem is further complicated when the focus is on children, i.e. individuals of 14 or under, where eating disorders are even more rare. In addition to this, screening instruments such as the EAT were not developed for use in this age group and in many ways are not appropriate for children (see Chapter 7).

## Subclinical cases

It has been argued that studies which focus on estimating the number of "cases" underestimate the number of individuals that may be affected by eating disorders. Studies of symptomatology in non-referred samples, for example, suggest that a substantial number of individuals may not meet full diagnostic criteria and therefore cannot be considered a "case" but none the less suffer some of the symptoms of eating disorders. Childress, Brewerton, Hodges, and Jarrell (1993) conducted a survey of eating disorder symptoms in 3129 children between the ages of 9 and 16. The authors reported that over 40% of these individuals said that they wanted to lose weight and felt that they looked fat. Hill, Oliver, and Rogers (1992) have reported that a substantial number of 9-year-olds claim to have gone on a diet as a means of weight control. Hill and Robinson (1991) conducted a study to see whether reports of dietary restraint were a reflection of actual behaviour. The children in the study were required to keep a record of everything that they ate and drank over a seven-day period. The food diaries of eight "restrained" and eight "unrestrained" children were then compared. The results showed that the "restrained" children ate 300kcal less than the "unrestrained" individuals and reported significantly higher levels of hunger than their "unrestrained" peers. The "restrained" girls also ate 11% less than the recommended daily energy intake for girls of that age.

There are a number of methodological problems with the Hill and Robinson (1991) study. For example, researchers are often dubious about the reliability of food diaries. However, Hill and Robinson have argued that their findings are worrying since dieters have been shown to be at a greater risk of developing eating disorders than non-dieters. Hsu (1990), for example, has argued that the prevalence of eating disorders is directly proportional to the prevalence of dieting behaviours within a given population. If we accept Hsu's hypothesis and believe the reports of dieting behaviour in children, we might expect to see an increase in the number of children presenting treatment for an eating disorders. However, it is important to remember that one of the cardinal features of anorexia nervosa and bulimia nervosa is that being of a low weight and a thin shape is of supreme importance to the individual. None of the studies of eating disorder symptomatology in children reported here have assessed whether being of a low weight and thin shape has any real personal significance for the respondent nor whether the symptoms reported are truly similar to those seen in eating disorders.

## Other problems with epidemiological studies of eating disorders

There are numerous other difficulties with epidemiological studies of eating disorders. Researchers focus on different regions, age groups, and time frames. Although these are not problems in themselves this does make comparison across studies a difficult task. More problematic, however, is the fact that some studies adjust the reported rates of eating disorder according to age or gender or both, whereas other report rates according to the population as a whole. As Fombonne (1995) has pointed out, crude unadjusted rates may be misleading because they relate the number of cases to the total population, whereas most studies have shown that the risk group for the development of eating disorders is females aged between approximately 15 and 24. Differences in the rates of the disorder across different time periods, for example, could reflect a change in the underlying population and the particular risk group for that disorder. The way in which extraneous variables such as changes in demography or in health service policy may influence reported rates of a disorder will be discussed later.

## HOW MANY CHILDREN ARE AFFECTED BY ANOREXIA NERVOSA AND BULIMIA NERVOSA?

The answer to the question above is largely unknown. A number of large-scale epidemiological studies have included younger individuals but have failed to differentiate between younger and older individuals when reporting the rates of people affected. For example, Nielson's (1990) study looked at the rate of anorexia nervosa in Denmark and included children from the age of 10. It is not clear what the estimated rates of the disorder were in children as distinct from the total group. It is not appropriate to use the rates reported for older individuals to assess the extent of the problem in children. The following section will focus on two studies in which incidence rates of anorexia nervosa (the number of new cases per 100,000 of the population) have been reported in children, i.e. individuals of 14 or younger. These studies demonstrate the problems encountered when doing epidemiological research into eating disorders with reference to children.

Joergensen (1992) conducted a study of the incidence of eating disorders in Fyn county in Denmark. The author consulted three sources for identification of individuals presenting with eating disorders over a period of ten years (January 1977 to December 1986) within Fyn county. The three sources were as follows:

1. The national register of patients admitted to general psychiatric and child psychiatric departments.
2. The local register of patients admitted to medical departments at the 10 hospitals serving the region.
3. The registers of outpatients at the general psychiatric and child psychiatric departments.

All patients given an eating disorder diagnosis according to ICD-8 were included in the study. The authors reported that they rediagnosed the patients listed in these sources according to criteria similar to DSM-III-R for anorexia nervosa. The incidence rate reported was 9.2 females per 100,000 of the population per year in 10- to 14-year-olds. In the 15- to 19-year-old group, 11.9 female cases of anorexia nervosa were found. Incidence rates for males were not reported.

The Joergensen (1992) study is interesting because it includes patients regis-tered within both psychiatric and non-psychiatric services. It also includes both in- and outpatients. The authors acknowledge that both the initial ICD-8 diagno-sis and the rediagnosis of patients may be potential sources of error. They have argued that this is likely to lead to an underestimation of the true rate of eating disorder in the population. It is also interesting to note that the diagnostic criteria listed by the researchers for anorexia nervosa do not coincide exactly with DSM-III-R which requires that the individual in question has a body weight that is 15% below that which is expected. The DSM-III-R criteria are somewhat less stringent than the weight criterion used by Joergensen (1992) in which patients were given a diagnosis of anorexia nervosa only if they had lost at least 25% of their body weight or were 75% below normal weight and height at admission. The weight criterion used in this study may have led to an under-estimation of the true rate of anorexia nervosa and makes it difficult to compare these results with other studies that have used the DSM-III-R diagnostic system to detect anorexia nervosa.

Lucas et al. (1991) conducted a study of the incidence rates of anorexia nervosa in Rochester, Minnesota. The authors consulted the medical records held by health care providers in the surrounding geographical region for the years 1935 to 1984. This was made possible because medical health care is delivered by a small number of providers within the community. The authors screened the medical records for cases of anorexia nervosa and other disorders that may have been missed cases of anorexia nervosa. In total they screened for 30 diagnostic terms including anorexia nervosa, amenorrhoea, and Simmonds disease. The researchers determined or confirmed a diagnosis of anorexia nervosa on the basis of DSM-III-R diagnostic criteria and reported the incidence of anorexia nervosa in nine age groups. No cases of anorexia nervosa were found in either the male or female residents of Rochester between the ages of 0 and 9 years old. However, an incidence rate of 14.6 cases of anorexia nervosa per 100,000 of the population per year was reported in the 10- to 14-year-old age group. When these figures were adjusted for gender, 25.7 females and 3.7 males per 100,000 of the popu-lation per year, between the ages of 10 and 14, were reported have anorexia nervosa. The highest incidence of anorexia nervosa was found in the 15- to 19-year-old age group. In this age group, 43.5 cases of anorexia nervosa per 100,000 of the population per year were found (69.4 females and 7.3 males per 100,000). The Lucas study appears to be one of the most thorough. The medical records of all the people living in Rochester who had ever visited a physician came under scrutiny. Furthermore, the authors reported that almost all of the residents of the community had visited a health care provider during the period of the study. The researchers argued that it would be unusual for individuals with a substantial weight loss not to be noticed by a physician, even if their symptoms were not diagnosed initially as anorexia nervosa. In addition to this, as the study takes place over a substantial period of time (50 years) it did not encounter the problem of the influence of short cycle trends.

Table 4.1 summarises the findings of the two studies of the incidence of anorexia nervosa in 10- to 14-year-olds. The studies come to very different conclusions about the incidence rate of anorexia nervosa. The rate for anorexia nervosa reported by Lucas et al. (1991) is more than twice that of Joergensen (1992), despite using the same diagnostic system. However, they used different methods of case detection and reviewed a different time frame. Lucas et al.'s study was over a 50-year period in comparison to the 9-year period of Joergensen's study.

As mentioned earlier, prevalence studies report on the *actual* number of cases in a specific group of individuals at a particular point in time. Hoek (1993) conducted a review of prevalence studies of anorexia nervosa. The more sophisticated prevalence studies employ two stages. This involves an initial screening stage of a large number of individuals using a questionnaire such as the Eating Attitudes Test. The second stage involves an interview with all the suspected cases. Interviews with a random number of individuals who are not suspected cases are also usually conducted in order to confirm absence of caseness. This is a measure of the effectiveness of the initial screening stage.

In a review of prevalence studies of anorexia nervosa, Hoek (1993) reported on nine two-stage studies of the prevalence of anorexia nervosa in young females. Szukler's (1983) study focused on females attending private and state schools

TABLE 4.1
Incidence rates of anorexia nervosa in 10–14-year-olds per 100,000
of the population per year

| Author | Population | Year | Diagnostic System Used | Case Detection | Female (10–14) | Male (10–14) |
|---|---|---|---|---|---|---|
| Lucas et al. (1991) | Rochester, USA | 1935–84 | DSM-III-R anorexia nervosa | Review of records of all the health care providers in the region for cases of AN or other disorders with AN symptoms | 25.7 | 3.7 |
| Joergensen (1992) | Fyn County, Denmark | 1977–86 | DSM-III-R anorexia nervosa | Selection of cases with an ICD-8 eating disorder from registers of psychiatric in- and outpatients and local registers of patients admitted to medical departments | 9.2 | Not reported |

aged between 14 and 19. He reported a prevalence rate of 0.2% in state schools and 0.8% in private schools using Russell's criteria for the diagnosis of anorexia nervosa (Russell, 1970). Johnson-Sabine, Wood, Patton, Mann, and Wakeling (1988) also used Russell's criteria in a study of school girls between the ages of 14 and 16 and found no cases of anorexia nervosa. Whitaker et al. (1990) and Rathner and Messner (1993) have included females below the ages of 14 in their studies. Whitaker et al. reported on anorexia nervosa in students aged between 13 and 18 using DSM-III diagnostic criteria and reported a prevalence rate of 0.3%. Rathner and Messner studied schoolgirls between the ages of 11 and 20 using DSM-III-R diagnostic criteria and reported a prevalence rates of 0.58%. In these studies, however, children and adolescents tend to be considered together and none of the researchers report prevalence rates in children specifically, i.e. individuals of 14 years or under. In conclusion, despite a considerable amount of research into the incidence and prevalence of anorexia nervosa, there remains very little information regarding children.

## IS THE INCIDENCE OF EATING DISORDERS RISING?

There remains much debate over the issue of whether the incidence of eating disorders is rising. Williams and King (1987) argued that although a number of studies have given the impression that anorexia nervosa is on the increase, many of these "are characterised by a lack of detailed statistical analysis". Nevertheless, in 1989 Russell and Treasure concluded that the literature on the epidemiology of anorexia nervosa suggested that the incidence of the disorder has increased. There are a number of factors that may account for this difference of opinion. Incidence rates may be affected by changes in the demography and underlying structure of the population being studied. For example, anorexia nervosa has been shown to be more common in females between the ages of 15 and 24. An increase in the incidence of anorexia nervosa in a population in a defined period may be nothing more than a reflection of an increase in the numbers of females aged between 15 and 24 in that population in the period of interest. Incidence rates may also be affected by changes either in terms of the availability of services, the use of services or changes in health service policy. Furthermore, it has been suggested that as more professionals learn to recognise the signs of eating disorders, incidence rates may be elevated.

As mentioned earlier, changes in population size and structure may need to be taken into account when interpreting epidemiological studies of eating disorders. For example, in an investigation of all patients aged between 10 and 64 admitted to psychiatric facilities in England with a primary diagnosis of anorexia nervosa from 1972 and 1981, Williams and King (1987) found a significant rise in the number of first admissions. Rather than taking this to be evidence of a rise in the incidence of anorexia nervosa, the authors suggested that this finding was more likely to be related to the increase in the number of young women in the general population over this nine-year period.

Willi and Grossmann (1983) conducted a study of the incidence of hospitalisations of women for anorexia nervosa in Zurich. Three time frames were considered: 1956–58, 1963–65, and 1973–75. They reported an overall significant increase from 0.38 cases per 100,000 (1956–58) to 0.55 per 100,000 (1963–65) to 1.12 per 100,000 (1973–75). The authors later extended this study to include the period 1983–85 (Willi, Giacometti, & Limacher, 1990). The researchers reported that in absolute terms the numbers of cases had increased from 1973 and 1985. In 1973–75, 38 cases of anorexia nervosa were found in contrast to the 48 cases between 1983 and 1985. However, this rise in cases between the two periods was not statistically significant. Furthermore, no difference could be found between the different time frames when the number of females between the ages of 12 and 15 in each period was taken into account.

Lucas, Beard, O'Fallon, and Kurland (1988) found no significant increase in the incidence rates of anorexia nervosa over a 45-year period (1939–75) in Minnesota after general population trends and other intervening variables had been taken into account. The authors later extended this study for a further five years (Lucas et al., 1991). They reported that the age adjusted incidence rates of anorexia nervosa in females in Rochester increased from 7.0 cases per 100,000 per year in 1950–54 to 26.3 per 100,000 in 1980–84. The authors argued that this increase was primarily due to a significant rise in incidence rates in females aged between 10 and 19. The most vulnerable group appeared to be the 15–24-year-old females who represented approximately 60% of the female cases found during the study period. Interestingly the rates for women of 20 years and older and males remained constant.

Fombonne (1995) has raised some questions about the Lucas et al. (1991) study. He has argued that the increases observed in the latter period could be partly due to differential migration in and out of Rochester and has also pointed out that the changes in local industry in Rochester may have influenced the incidence rates. Lucas et al. (1988, 1991) reported a gradual change in industry in Rochester from farming to employment based on the Mayo Clinic and computer industry. Fombonne (1995) has suggested that this change in industry may have been associated with an upward trend in social class in the region which in turn may have elevated the incidence rates, as there is some suggestion that eating disorders are more prevalent in social classes I and II (see later for a discussion of social class and eating disorders).

Changes in health service policy may affect the reported rates of eating disorders. Jones, Fox, Babigan, and Hutton's (1980) study of the number of individuals receiving treatment for anorexia nervosa in Monroe County, New York reported an incidence rate of 0.35 per 100,000 population in 1960–69 compared to 0.64 per 100,000 in 1970–76. The biggest rise occurred in females between the ages of 15 and 24, from a rate of 0.55 per 100,000 per year (1960–69) to 3.26 per 100,000 per year (1970–76). Fombonne (1995) has argued that there is evidence that this finding may be a result of an improved availability and use of local mental health services by children and adolescents for a range of disorders including eating disorders. Re-admission rates may also have contributed to the impression that there has been a rapid rise in incidence rates. Studies based on the numbers of individuals treated at any one time may not differentiate between first and subsequent admissions. For example, Williams and King (1987) have noted that there has been an increase in the rate of re-admission of patients with an eating disorder and suggest that this may have added to the impression that there has been an increase in the risk of morbidity. In such cases incidence rates may be artificially raised as some individuals may have been included more than once.

Moller-Madsen and Nystrup (1992) conducted a study of the incidence of anorexia nervosa in Denmark between 1970 and 1989. They concluded that there had been an increase in the number of first-time admissions for anorexia nervosa in the study periods, rising from 0.42 cases per 100,000 of the population in 1970 to 1.36 in 1988. The authors also reported that the increase in eating disorders was observed mostly in the age group of 15–34. The numbers of these individuals in the study period remained constant and thus changes in the base population could not account for their results. Furthermore, as the researchers were only counting first admissions the results were not elevated by re-admission rates.

The results of Moller-Madsen and Nystrup's (1992) study are particularly surprising since Nielsen's (1990) study of the incidence of anorexia nervosa in Denmark using the same data source, the Danish Psychiatric Case Register, in a similar period (1973–87) had concluded incidence rates were stable. Moller-Madsen and Nystrup used a broader case definition than Nielsen, including anorexia nervosa *and* other eating disorders. Fombonne (1995) has pointed out that most of the increases reported in this study were found after 1982 and, therefore, could be accounted for by the newly recognised "bulimic disorders". Furthermore, Fombonne has suggested that the increase reported by Moller-Madsen and Nystrup may be a reflection of changes in the use of health services by eating disorder patients. It is possible that more eating disorder patients were being admitted to psychiatric services rather than general medical services in the latter years of the Moller-Madsen and Nystrup study, which may have accounted for the apparent rise in the incidence rates of eating disorders. Both Fombonne and Munk-Jorgensen, Moller-Madsen, Nielsen, and Nystrup (1995) agree that the divergent results reported by Nielsen and Moller-Madsen and Nystrup can be accounted for by the different methodologies employed by both groups of researchers.

Improved recognition of eating disorders across a period of time and within different professions may also influence the reported rates. Szukler, McCance,

McCrone, and Hunter's (1986) study of the Aberdeen case register found an incidence of 1.6% per 100,000 population in 1966–69 compared to an incidence of 4.06 per 100,000 population in 1978–82. Fombonne (1995) has argued that this may be a reflection of better case identification methods over the study period. Pasberg and Wang (1994) conducted a study of the incidence of anorexia nervosa in Bornholm county, Denmark between 1970 and 1989. The authors reported that the incidence rate of anorexia nervosa increased from 1.6 cases per 100,000 per year in 1970–74 to 6.8 cases per 100,000 per year in 1985–89. The authors also reported that the rate of anorexia nervosa was stable during the first 15 years of the study period and then a significant increase occurred. The average annual incidence rate from 1985 to 1989 was five times higher for anorexia nervosa than in the prior period 1970–84. The researchers reported that during this time the population was numerically stable with constant number of females, approximately 20% aged between 10 and 24. However, the researchers do point out that the increase in the latter years may in part be due to an under-estimation of cases in primary care in the earlier years of the study.

Finally, the situation regarding children is less clear. Given that there have been no good estimates of incidence rates specifically in children below the age of 14, it is not possible to detect a rise in numbers. In our own experience it is true to say that we have witnessed a significant increase in the number of referrals to the Great Ormond Street Hospital for Children over the past decade. It remains debatable whether this reflects a rise in the number of children developing eating disorders, an increased awareness of the possibility that anorexia nervosa can occur in children, or the knowledge that we offer a specialist service for these children.

## WHO DEVELOPS EATING DISORDERS?

Comparing the background characteristics of children who develop anorexia nervosa, the following points emerge.

### More boys than expected

Numerous studies have shown that eating disorders, such as anorexia nervosa, are more common in females. Studies have reported a male:female ratio of between 1:29 (Pasberg & Wang, 1984) and 1:10 (Joergensen, 1992). However, these figures do not refer specifically to children, for whom the picture appears to be somewhat different. The number of boys relative to girls is higher than might be expected on the basis of comparison with older patients.

In 1985, Hawley described a follow-up study of 21 children with anorexia nervosa aged 13 or younger at onset with a relatively high percentage of boys (19%). Jacobs and Isaacs (1986) reported a gender ratio of 6:14 (male:female) in a group of pre-pubertal children with anorexia nervosa in comparison to a ratio of 1:19 in a group of post-pubertal children. The numbers in each group were small (20) and the difference in the gender between the pre- and post-pubertal group did not reach statistical significance. Nevertheless, in Fosson, Knibbs, Bryant-Waugh, and Lask's (1987) study of early onset anorexia nervosa in 48 children, 13 (27%) were boys, a figure that supported Jacobs and Isaacs' earlier finding. Two years later, Higgs, Goodyer, and Birch (1989) published a further study of anorexia nervosa and related eating disorders in children, 27 of whom met criteria for anorexia nervosa. Eight (30%) were boys again providing further support for the impression that, in children, males form a greater proportion of those presenting with eating disorders than in older individuals. In the absence of any larger scale studies, it is at present not clear whether this does represent a difference between early and later onset anorexia nervosa. Certainly it is a finding of interest that requires further investigation.

## Social class bias

Margo's (1985) report of anorexia nervosa in patients aged between 12 and 18 reported that 27 out of the 40 subjects included in the study (or 67.5%) were from social classes I and II (Office of Population Census and Surveys—Registrar General's Classification of Occupations 1970). This figure was noted to be significantly in excess of what might be expected given the population distribution of the area in which the study was carried out. There was, however, no differentiation between those below and above the age of 14, making it difficult to gain any impression of the social class bias at the younger end of the age range. Fosson et al. (1987) reported that 22 (46%) of the 48 children included in their series (all aged 13 or under at the time of onset) were from social classes I and II, again biased towards higher social classes compared with the general population. Higgs et al. (1989) found that 14 or (54%) of the 27 early onset anorexia nervosa patients included in their series had a "middle class" background but did not define this in terms of social classes. Finally, Gowers, Crisp, Joughin, and Bhat (1991) reported that 80% of 30 individuals with premenarchal onset had social classes I and II backgrounds.

It would appear that in children presenting for treatment of anorexia nervosa, higher social classes are over-represented. However, it is difficult to assess the significance of these findings. Social class structure varies between different areas and countries and different institutions may have a long history of a particular distribution of clientele. It is also often suggested that middle class families are better at making use of facilities open to them which could account for the over-representation of certain social classes in treatment. In addition to this a number of studies of non-clinical populations have failed to show that social class is a significant risk factor in the development of eating disorders. Patton, Johnson-Sabine, Wood, Mann, and Wakeling (1990) conducted a study of abnormal eating attitudes in London adolescent school girls. They reported that that there was no association between social class and either attempting weight control or "caseness" in the group studied. A later study of a group of Norwegian adolescents also showed no association between social class and eating problems (Winchstrom, 1995). It has been suggested that it is not social class *per se* but the pressure to achieve which may be associated with eating problems. Interestingly, Winchstrom also reported that a number of factors said to be indicators of the "model child", such as high grades and high occupational aspirations, were also not associated with eating problems in the group of adolescents studied.

In conclusion, the relatively small scale studies of early onset anorexia nervosa suggests some over-representation of social classes I and II. However, it is not clear whether this represents a social class bias or an important risk factor. This issue requires further investigation before firm statements can be made.

## Anorexia nervosa can occur in children from various cultural backgrounds

Until relatively recently, anorexia nervosa has been thought of as a culture-bound syndrome that occurs predominantly in Caucasians from Westernised cultures. However, there are a number of epidemiological studies and case reports that refute this view (see Dolan, 1991). Rathner et al. (1995) conducted a study of eating disorders in medical students residing in two countries in Eastern Europe (Hungary and the German Democratic Republic; GDR) and compared these with individuals in a Western democracy, Austria. The study was conducted before the political changes in 1989. The authors made use of two eating disorder questionnaires, the Anorexia Nervosa Inventory Scale (ANIS; Fichter & Keeser, 1990) and the Eating Disorder Inventory (EDI; Garner & Olmsted, 1984). They reported that there were no significant differences between the respondents from the GDR and Austria on either the ANIS or the EDI. However, the Hungarian students had significantly higher scores than those from the other two countries on both questionnaires. Rathner et al. (1995) concluded that eating disorders are a problem in Eastern European countries and are at least as common as they are in Western industrialised countries. The Hungarian students had the highest questionnaire scores indicating greater levels of eating disturbances. The researchers suggested that this may be a demonstration of over-identification with Western norms and values which may also include an identification with the Western ideal that slimness equals beauty. The result of cultural change may have brought about the high levels of eating disturbance seen in this group. The authors further speculated that the differences between the two Eastern European countries may be partly due to the fact that the political changes in Hungary began earlier than they did in the GDR.

Wlodarczyk-Bisaga and Dolan (1996) conducted a study of eating disorders in a group of Polish school girls between the ages of 14 and 16. They reported that the scores on the EAT-26 for the Polish girls were not markedly different from those reported by studies conducted in North America and Western Europe.

The researchers also demonstrated that the number of girls who scored above the EAT-26 cut off (indicative of "caseness") was similar to other studies including British adolescents. Dieting was also shown to be as common in the Polish school girls as has been reported in their Western European counterparts. The data from Rathner et al. (1995) and Wlodarczyk-Bisaga and Dolan (1996), would indicate, therefore, that it is not sufficient to say that eating disorders are problems for Western countries or societies. However, it would appear that cultural changes that bring about an identification with Western values may be associated with increased rates of eating disorders.

Over the last decade an increasing number of reports have appeared in the literature describing the development of eating disorders in non-Caucasians. Anorexia nervosa and bulimia nervosa have been identified in people of both African and Asian racial backgrounds, both in their countries of origin and elsewhere. Crago, Shisslak, and Estes (1996) conducted a review of studies of eating disorders in so called "minority groups" in America. They reported that in general eating disturbances were less frequent among black women and girls in comparison to Caucasians. They argued that black women were more weight tolerant and less likely to engage in dietary restriction and self-induced vomiting than their Caucasian peers and therefore less likely to develop eating disorders. Eating disturbances were found to be equally as common in Americans of Hispanic origin and less common in groups described as Asian American. Crago et al. reported that the risk factors for eating disturbances appeared to be greater among minority females who were younger, heavier, well-educated, and more identified with white middle class values. They also pointed to the fact that the experience of racism in "minority groups" may increase the risk for the development of eating disorders. It is important to consider Dolan's (1991) view that when researchers refer to "black" women behind this there is "an assumption that genetic/racial features are the best identifiers" and therefore the mediating effects of culture may be ignored. Consequently, research that looks at difference between white and non-white individuals must appreciate that this is a very simplistic division and may ignore a whole host of other important variables.

Bryant-Waugh and Lask (1991) have reported on the occurrence of anorexia nervosa in a group of Asian children living in Britain. Bhadrinath (1990) described three Asian children with anorexia nervosa and has argued that in view of the increasing number of reports there is now a need to attempt to understand culture specific attitudes towards food and eating and to explore their role in eating disorders in individuals from other ethnic groups. Mumford and Whitehouse (1988) also noted the occurrence of bulimia nervosa in a slightly older group of Asian girls and suggest that exposure to Western culture may be important in the aetiology of eating disorders in immigrant families. Hill and Bhatti (1995) conducted a study of dieting in 9-year-old Asian and Caucasian girls. The authors reported that both groups demonstrated that thinness was a high priority. Furthermore, the Asian children who were most concerned with dieting, had greater body dissatisfaction and lower body self-esteem were those who came from a more "traditional" family environment.

Bryant-Waugh and Lask (1991) have argued that it may be less the exposure to Western culture *per se* that precipitates the onset of the eating disorder (as there are many who do not suffer from eating disorders under similar circumstances) but more the difficulty in attempting to reconcile elements from two very different cultures. In our experience, children from different ethnic backgrounds who develop anorexia nervosa tend to be those whose families maintain their own beliefs and practices and socialise primarily with others of the same racial origins. Thus, it appears that it is not the more Westernised families who are at risk, but those whose children struggle to accommodate their experience at school and elsewhere with their home life. In conclusion, in epidemiological terms we can therefore no longer view anorexia nervosa as a culture-bound disorder.

## FINALLY: A WORD ABOUT HIGH RISK GROUPS

A number of groups of individuals have been identified as "high risk" populations. Dancers may be at a greater risk of developing eating disorders than non-dancers because of their need to maintain thin bodies. Studies of professional adult dancers asked whether they have now or have ever had anorexia nervosa have revealed that up to 23% of dancers may be affected (Hamilton, Brooks-Gunn, & Warren, 1985; Hamilton, Brooks-Gunn, Warren, & Hamilton, 1988).

One problem with such studies is that the dancers' perception of anorexia nervosa or bulimia nervosa may not have corresponded with current definitions of these disorders. Other studies have made use of a two-stage methodology to identify cases of eating disorder in dancers. As mentioned earlier, this involves an initial questionnaire screening stage and a second stage clinical interview with a clinician using a set of operational criteria for eating disorder diagnoses. A number of researchers have used this technique in studies of both adult and adolescent dancers. Garner and Garfinkel (1980) reported that 6.5% of dancers (mean age = 18.6) had anorexia nervosa. This is slightly higher than the 4% reported by Le Grange, Tibbs, and Noakes (1994). Two-stage studies of adolescent dancers with a mean age of approximately 15 have shown that between 7% (Szukler, Eisler, Gillies, & Hayward, 1985) and 25% (Garner, Garfinkel, Rockert, & Olmsted, 1987) may be affected. Comparison studies of anorexia nervosa in non-dancers in general reveal much lower rates of eating disorders.

It has been suggested that one of the reasons dancers, such as ballerinas, may be at risk for the development of eating disorder is that they have to diet in order to maintain the sylph-like bodies required for the discipline (Lowenkopf & Vincent, 1982). Patton et al. (1990) have suggested that female adolescent dieters run eight times the risk of developing an eating disorder compared to their non-dieting peers. Some forms of dance, such as ballet, are also low in energy expenditure. Cohen, Chung, May, and Ertel (1982) reported that a dancer might expend 200 calories per class whereas age-matched swimmers or skaters might expend approximately 500 calories in the same period. Brooks-Gunn, Burrow, and Warren (1988) have argued that dancers, therefore, are likely to be at a greater risk for the development of eating disorders than other athletes such as skaters. Skaters also have to be thin for their discipline but expend much more energy than ballet dancers and therefore the low weights may be easier to achieve.

Over the past few years we have had a number of referrals of very promising young dancers presenting with anorexia nervosa. These children are subject to the same pressures to be small and slim as their older colleagues, and it is our impression that this places them at greater risk of developing an eating disorder than might otherwise be the case. Very little research has focused on children who dance. A study of eating disorders in young dancers attending specialist dance schools revealed that 4% (1 of 25) of the dancers aged between 11 and 13 had anorexia nervosa (Doyle, Bryant-Waugh, Plotkin, & Lask, 1997). In this study 3% (1 of 37) of dancers aged 14–16 had anorexia nervosa. No cases of anorexia nervosa were found in a group of non-dancers similar in terms of age, gender, and residential status at school (i.e. boarder or day pupil). Although the numbers in this study were small, the data do suggest that child dancers may face the same problems as older dancers and have been inappropriately neglected.

## SUMMARY POINTS

- Epidemiology is the study of the distribution of diseases or disorders in populations. Epidemiological research focuses on the rate of disorders in populations, the types of people that are likely to be affected, and the risk factors for the development of the disorder in question.
- There are a number of problems with epidemiological studies of eating disorders. For example, differences in the diagnostic systems and case detection methods create problems for the interpretation of research across studies. Methodological differences across studies seem to account for the varying rates of eating disorder reported and it would appear that all reported rates are an underestimation of the true rate of the disorders in question.
- Very few studies have focused on children specifically.
- It is difficult to know whether the rates of eating disorders are increasing. Many researchers have argued that the apparent increases in incidence rates can be accounted for by a number of factors including changes in the structure of the base population, changes in the use of the health services and improved recognition of eating disorders over time and within

different professions. As very few studies have reported on the incidence and prevalence rates of eating disorders in children it is difficult to determine whether the rates of these disorders in individuals aged 14 or under are increasing.

• Numerous research studies have focused on the issue of who tends to develop eating disorders. Eating disorders are more common in women than men but in children boys appear to be over-represented when compared to the proportion of males seen in adults with eating disorders. It has been suggested that eating disorders are more common in social classes I and II, although this may be a reflection of a greater use of health service provision amongst these groups.

• Eating disorders are no longer considered to be culture-bound syndromes that effect only Caucasian individuals from Western countries, and eating disorders have been identified in a variety of non-Caucasians from different cultural backgrounds, living in non-Western countries.

• Finally, a number of high risk groups have been identified, including dancers. Dancers may be at a greater risk for developing eating disorders than non-dancers because of the emphasis placed on a low weight and thin shape within the discipline. Very few studies have focused on child dancers, but there is some evidence that child dancers face the same difficulties as adult dancers, and that this group have been neglected inappropriately from studies of this "high risk" population.

## REFERENCES

American Psychiatric Association. (1980). *Diagnostic and statistical manual of mental disorders* (3rd ed.). Washington, DC: Author.

American Psychiatric Association. (1987). *Diagnostic and statistical manual of mental disorders* (3rd ed., Rev.). Washington, DC: Author.

American Psychiatric Association. (1994). *Diagnostic and statistical manual of mental disorders* (4th ed.). Washington, DC: Author.

Bhadrinath, B. (1990). Anorexia nervosa in adolescents of Asian extraction. *British Journal of Psychiatry, 156,* 565–568.

Brooks-Gunn, J., Burrow, C., & Warren, M. (1988). Attitudes toward eating and body weight in different groups of female adolescents. *International Journal of Eating Disorders, 7,* 749–757.

Bryant-Waugh, R., & Lask, B. (1991). Anorexia nervosa in a group of Asian children living in Britain. *British Journal of Psychiatry, 158,* 229–233.

Bunnell, D., Shenker, I., Nussbaum, M., Jacobson, M., & Cooper, P. (1990). Sub clinical versus formal eating disorders: Differentiating psychological features. *International Journal of Eating Disorders, 9,* 357–362.

Childress, A., Brewerton, T., Hodges, E., & Jarrell, M. (1993). The kids' eating disorder survey (KEDS): A study of middle school children. *Journal of the American Academy of Child and Adolescent Psychiatry, 32,* 843–850.

Cohen, J., Chung, S., May, P., & Ertel, N. (1982). Exercise, body weight and amenorrhea in professional ballet dancers. *Physician and Sports Medicine, 10,* 92–101.

Crago, M., Shisslak, C., & Estes, L. (1996). Eating disturbances among minority groups: A review. *International Journal of Eating Disorders, 19,* 239–248.

Dolan, B. (1991). Cross cultural aspects of anorexia nervosa and bulimia: A review. *International Journal of Eating Disorders, 10,* 67–78.

Doyle, J., Bryant-Waugh, R., Plotkin, H., & Lask, B. (1997). *Emotional well-being in children and adolescents attending specialist schools for the performing arts.* Unpublished PhD thesis, University of London.

Fichter, M., & Keeser, W. (1980). Das Anorexia Nervosa-Inventarzur Selbstbeurteilung (ANIS). *Archiv Fur Psychiatrie und Nervenkrankheiten, 228,* 67–89.

Fombonne, E. (1995). Anorexia nervosa: No evidence of an increase. *British Journal of Psychiatry, 166,* 462–471.

Fosson, A., Knibbs, J., Bryant-Waugh, R., & Lask, B. (1987). Early onset anorexia nervosa. *Archives of Disease in Childhood, 62,* 114–118.

Garner, D., & Garfinkel, P. (1979). The eating attitudes test: An index of the symptoms of anorexia nervosa. *Psychological Medicine, 9,* 273–279.

Garner, D., & Garfinkel, P. (1980). Socio-cultural factors in the development of anorexia nervosa. *Psychological Medicine, 10,* 647–656.

Garner, D., Garfinkel, P., Rockert, W., & Olmsted, M. (1987). A prospective study of eating disturbances in ballet. *Psychotherapy and Psychosomatics, 48,* 170–175.

Garner, D., & Olmsted, M. (1984). *Manual for eating disorder inventory (EDI).* Odessa, TX: Psychological Assessment Resources.

Garner, D., Olmsted, M., Bohr, Y., & Garfinkel, P. (1982). The eating attitudes test: Psychometric features and clinical correlates. *Psychological Medicine, 9,* 273–279.

Gowers, S., Crisp, A., Joughin, N., & Bhat, A. (1991). Pre-menarcheal anorexia nervosa. *Journal of Child Psychology and Psychiatry, 32,* 515–524.

Hamilton, L., Brooks-Gunn, J., & Warren, M. (1985). Sociocultural influences on eating disorders in female professional dancers. *International Journal of Eating Disorders, 4,* 465–477.

Hamilton, L., Brooks-Gunn, J., Warren, M., & Hamilton, W. (1988). The role of selectivity in the pathogenesis of eating problems in ballet dancers. *Medicine and Science in Sports and Exercise, 20,* 560–565.

Hawley, R. (1985). The outcome of anorexia nervosa in younger subjects. *British Journal of Psychiatry, 146,* 657–660.

Higgs, J., Goodyer, I., & Birch, J. (1989). Anorexia nervosa and food avoidance emotional disorder. *Archives of Disease in Childhood, 64,* 346–351.

Hill, A., & Bhatti, R. (1995). Body shape perception and dieting in preadolescent British Asian girls: Links with eating disorders. *International Journal of Eating Disorders, 17,* 175–183.

Hill, A., Oliver, S., & Rogers, P. (1992). Eating in the adult world: The rise in dieting in childhood and adolescence. *British Journal of Clinical Psychology, 31,* 95–105.

Hill, A., & Robinson, A. (1991). Dieting concerns have a functional effect on the behaviour of nine year old girls. *British Journal of Clinical Psychology, 30,* 265–267.

Hoek, H. (1993). Review of the epidemiological studies of eating disorders. *International Review Psychiatry, 5,* 61–74.

Hsu, L. (1990). *Eating disorders.* New York: Guilford Press.

Jacobs, B., & Isaacs, S. (1986). Pre-pubertal anorexia nervosa: A retrospective controlled study. *Journal of Child Psychology and Psychiatry, 27,* 237–250.

Joergensen, J. (1992). The epidemiology of eating disorder in Fyn County, Denmark, 1977–1986. *Acta Psychiatrica Scandinavica, 85,* 30–34.

Johnson-Sabine, E., Wood, K., Patton, G., Mann, A., & Wakeling, A. (1988). Abnormal eating attitudes in London schoolgirls—a prospective epidemiological study: Factors associated with abnormal response on screening questionnaires. *Psychological Medicine, 18,* 615–622.

Jones, D., Fox, M., Babigan, H., & Hutton, H. (1980). Epidemiology of anorexia nervosa in Monroe County, New York, 1960–1976. *Psychosomatic Medicine, 42,* 551–558.

King, M. (1989). Eating disorder in a general practice population: Prevalence characteristics and follow-up at 12 to 18 months. *Psychological Medicine Monograph Supplement, 14.*

Ledoux, S., Choquet, M., & Flament, M. (1991). Eating disorders among adolescents in an unselected French population. *International Journal of Eating Disorders, 10,* 81–89.

Le Grange, D., Tibbs, J., & Noakes, T. (1994). Implications of a diagnosis of anorexia nervosa in a ballet school. *International Journal of Eating Disorders, 15,* 369–376.

Lowenkopf, E., & Vincent, L. (1982). The student ballet dancer and anorexia. *Hillside Journal of Clinical Psychiatry, 4,* 53–64.

Lucas, A., Beard, C., O'Fallon, W., & Kurland, L. (1988). Anorexia nervosa in Rochester, Minnesota: A 45 year study. *Proceedings of the Mayo Clinic, 63,* 433–442.

Lucas, A., Beard, C., O'Fallon, W., & Kurland, L. (1991). 50-year trends in the incidence of anorexia nervosa in Rochester, Minnesota: A population based study. *American Journal of Psychiatry, 148,* 917–922.

Margo, J. (1985). Anorexia nervosa in adolescents. *British Journal of Medical Psychology, 58,* 193–195.

Moller-Madsen, S., & Nystrup, J. (1992). Incidence of anorexia nervosa in Denmark. *Acta Psychiatrica Scandinavica, 86,* 197–200.

Morris, J. (1970). *Uses of epidemiology.* Edinburgh, UK: Churchill Livingstone.

Mumford, D., & Whitehouse, A. (1988). Increased prevalence of bulimia nervosa among Asian schoolgirls. *British Medical Journal, 297,* 718.

Munk-Jorgensen, P., Moller-Madsen, S., Nielsen, S., & Nystrup, J. (1995). Incidence of eating disorder in Danish psychiatric hospitals and wards, 1970–1993. *Acta Psychiatrica Scandinavica, 92,* 91–96.

Nielsen, S. (1990). The epidemiology of anorexia nervosa in Denmark from 1973 to 1987: A nation-wide register study of psychiatric admissions. *Acta Psychiatrica Scandinavica, 81,* 507–514.

Office of Population Censuses and Surveys. (1970). Registrar General's classification of occupations: Appendix B1. London: Her Majesty's Stationery Office.

Pasberg, A., & Wang, A. (1994). Epidemiology of anorexia nervosa and bulimia nervosa in Bornholm County, Denmark, 1970–1989. *Acta Psychiatrica Scandinavica, 90,* 259–265.

Patton, G., Johnson-Sabine, E., Wood, K., Mann, A., & Wakeling, A. (1990). Abnormal eating attitudes in London schoolgirls—a prospective epidemiological study: Outcome at twelve month follow-up. *Psychological Medicine, 20,* 383–394.

Rathner, G., & Messner, K. (1993). Detection of eating disorders in a small rural town: An epidemiological study. *Psychological Medicine, 23,* 175–184.

Rathner, G., Tury, F., Szabo, P., Geyer, M., Rumpold, G., Forgas, A., Sollner, W., & Plottner, G. (1995). Prevalence of eating disorders and minor psychiatric morbidity in Central Europe before the political changes in 1989: A cross cultural study. *Psychological Medicine, 25,* 1027–1035.

Russell, G. (1970). Anorexia nervosa: Its identity as an illness and its treatment. In J. Harding Price (Ed.), *Modern trends in psychological medicine.* London: Butterworth.

Russell, G., & Treasure, J. (1989). The modern history of anorexia nervosa: An interpretation of why the illness has changed. *Annals of the New York Academy of Sciences, 575,* 13–30.

Szukler, G. (1983). Weight and food preoccupation in a population of English schoolgirls. In G.I. Bargman (Ed.), *Understanding anorexia nervosa and bulimia.* Columbus, OH: Ross.

Szukler, G., Eisler, I., Gillies, C., & Hayward, M. (1985). The implications of anorexia nervosa in a ballet school, *Journal of Psychiatric Research, 19,* 177–181.

Szukler, G., McCance, C., McCrone, L., & Hunter, D. (1986). Anorexia nervosa: A psychiatric case register study from Aberdeen. *Psychological Medicine, 16,* 49–58.

Whitaker, A., Johnson, J., Shaffer, D., Rapoport, J., Kalikow, K., Walsh, B., Davies, M., Braiman, S., & Dolinsky, A. (1990). Uncommon troubles in young people: Prevalence estimates of selected psychiatric disorders in a non-referred psychiatric population. *Archives of General Psychiatry*, *47*, 487–496.

Willi, J., Giacometti, G., & Limacher, B. (1990). Update on the epidemiology of anorexia nervosa in a defined region of Switzerland. *American Journal of Psychiatry*, *147*, 1514–1517.

Willi, J., & Grossmann, S. (1983). Epidemiology of anorexia nervosa in a defined region of Switzerland. *American Journal of Psychiatry*, *140*, 564–567.

Williams, P., & King, M. (1987). The "epidemic" of anorexia nervosa: Another medical myth? *Lancet*, *i*, 205–208.

Winchstrom, L. (1995). Social, psychological and physical correlates of eating problems: A study of the general adolescent population in Norway. *Psychological Medicine*, *25*, 567–579.

Wlodarczyk-Bisaga, K., & Dolan, B. (1996). A two-stage epidemiological study of abnormal eating attitudes and their prospective risk factors in Polish schoolgirls. *Psychological Medicine*, *26*, 1021–1032.

World Health Organisation. (1992). *The ICD-10 classification of mental and behavioural disorders: Clinical descriptions and diagnostic guidelines*. Geneva, Switzerland: Author.

CHAPTER FIVE

# Aetiology

**Bryan Lask**
*St George's Hospital Medical School, London, UK, and
Huntercombe Manor Hospital, Taplow, UK*

## INTRODUCTION

Searching for a single cause for eating disorders is a fruitless task. If anorexia nervosa were solely due to a teenage girl being teased for being overweight, then why don't *all* teenage girls who are teased for being overweight develop the condition? And why do some boys and many adults develop it? Even combining two possible contributory factors is insufficient. For example it is widely believed that achievement-oriented adolescent girls from "conflict-avoiding" families are at risk of developing an eating disorder. However, by no means all such girls develop the disorder, and many young people with anorexia nervosa do not come from "conflict-avoiding" families. It is obvious that the eating disorders are multi-determined with a wide range of factors interacting. Genetic, biological, personality, psychological, familial, and socio-cultural factors are all likely to be relevant.

Furthermore it is important to recognise that an eating disorder does not occur at a particular moment, i.e. there can be no "big-bang theory" to explain its emergence. Rather, eating disorders develop over time with some causative factors being in place from birth, others emerging early in life, and yet others much later. Clearly we need to distinguish between (1) those factors that are necessary preconditions for the development of an eating disorder, i.e. the *predisposing* factors, without which the disorder is very unlikely to occur; (2) those that are more immediate to its emergence, i.e. *precipitating* factors, which trigger the condition; and (3) those that serve to maintain the disorder once it has arisen, i.e. the *perpetuating* factors.

The challenges are to identify the key components of all the potential contributory factors, determine which are necessary preconditions (predisposing), which are triggers (precipitating), and which are maintaining the disorder (perpetuating) and to understand how and when all these elements interact.

## GENETIC FACTORS

There is now substantial evidence that genetic factors are highly significant in the development of eating disorders. Such evidence arises from family aggregation and twin studies. Although most of the evidence is obtained from studies of populations somewhat older than that covered in this book, it is almost certainly applicable to the younger population.

A number of well-designed studies have found significant familial aggregation of eating disorders. Anorexia nervosa and bulimia nervosa appear to occur far more often in the first degree relatives of those with these disorders than in the general population (Scott, 1986; Strober, 1991, 1992; Theander, 1970). The incidence is generally up to eight times greater than even the highest reported incidence figure in population surveys (Crisp, Palmer, & Kalucy, 1976), and is matched only by figures for ballet students (Garner & Garfinkel, 1980).

Twin studies have greater significance than familial studies in that the focus is very specifically upon the genetic component, whereas familial aggregation studies cannot separate out as readily the environmental component. Twin studies focus on the difference in concordance between monozygotic and dizygotic twins. The concordance for anorexia nervosa in monozygotic twins is around 10 times greater than for dizygotic twins (Holland, Sicotte, & Treasure, 1988; Scott, 1986; Treasure & Holland, 1990). Similarly, in bulimia nervosa concordance has been shown to be significantly higher for monozygotic than dizygotic twins (Kendler, MacLean, Neale, Kessler, Keith, & Eaves, 1991).

These findings add strength to the view that genetic factors play an important part in the genesis of eating disorders (Woodside, 1993). At the time of writing there have been unpublished reports of identification of abnormalities of gene structure in anorexia nervosa. It can only be a matter of time before more specific information is available to us. Meanwhile we can be certain that genetic loading is a very important predisposing factor. A further challenge is to unravel the means by which genetic loading exerts its effect so that an eating disorder emerges. There are two likely pathways—biological abnormalities and personality traits.

## Biological abnormalities

A number of biological factors have been considered to be significant in the development of eating disorders. However it is difficult to disentangle those findings which are primary, i.e. predate the onset of the eating disorder, from those which are a consequence of (secondary to) starvation, dehydration, bingeing, or purging. Younger patients have higher energy demands and lower basal levels of body fat with consequent earlier and more severe physical sequelae. Thus, once weight loss and dehydration occur, the usual mechanisms for the release and inhibition of various regulators of eating behaviour change, and a new set of regulating mechanisms is established.

According to Russell (1992) there can be no doubt that there is an endocrine disorder affecting the hypothalamic-pituitary-gonadal axis. The exact nature of this disorder remains unclear. Possibilities include immaturity, damage, or dysfunction in the centres regulating appetite, satiety, and eating, anomalous neuronal connections in the hypothalamus, or abnormalities at the receptor sites. Weiner (1985) has proposed that hypothalamic tissue may be abnormally sensitive in some individuals, and that in times of stress dysfunction is triggered. However, the most widely accepted view suggests that most endocrine changes are a *consequence* rather than a cause of weight loss, increased exercise, and purging (Carney & Andersen, 1996).

The neuroendocrine system is but one component of an even more complex process involving interactions between chemicals known as polypeptides, various other hormones, and a number of neurotransmitters. Eating is not only controlled centrally within the hypothalamus but also peripherally in the gut. These two systems are separate but related. Food intake is regulated peripherally by the release of gastrointestinal peptides which exert a local effect in the gut. However, to some extent these peptides also work centrally by acting as neurotransmitters with receptor sites in the brain (Lucas, 1988). The system is enormously complex and rendered even more so by the changes occurring in starvation or bingeing and purging. (For more details see Silver & Morley, 1991 and Christie, Bryant-Waugh, Lask, & Gordon, 1998.)

Another area for consideration, not yet fully understood, is that of serotonin activity. This neurotransmitter enables the organism to arrange or tolerate delay before acting (Kaye, 1997). Low levels of serotonin activity are associated with *impulsivity* and may predispose to the characteristic impulsivity of bulimia nervosa. High levels may contribute to the pathogenesis of anorexia nervosa by shaping, in certain individuals, marked behavioural propensities towards *rigidity* and *constraint* (Strober, 1995).

The recent development of sophisticated neuroimaging techniques has allowed for detailed investigation of brain structure and function in the eating disorders. Abnormalities of both structure and function have been reported (Herholz, 1996; Katzman, Lambe, Mikulis, Ridgley, Goldbloom, & Zipurski, 1996; Krieg, Holhoff, Schreiber, Pirke, & Herholz, 1991) but it would seem likely that these are secondary to weight loss and dehydration in that, by and large, they reverse with weight restoration. However, the finding of unilateral reduction of blood flow in the anterior portion of the temporal lobe in children and adolescents with anorexia nervosa (Gordon, Lask, Bryant-Waugh, Christie, & Timimi, 1997) may be less likely to be a secondary phenomenon. It is difficult to explain the asymmetry in blood flow, its very specific location, and its tendency not to reverse with weight restoration, on the basis of starvation and dehydration. The authors suggest that their findings are evidence of a primary abnormality in the limbic system. (For a fuller discussion of neuroimaging findings see Christie et al., 1998.)

We are some way from being able to specify a primary (predisposing) biological basis (substrate) for any of the eating disorders. Research to date has been hampered by the difficulty in separating primary and secondary abnormalities. The consequences of starvation and dehydration have their own effects on appetite and satiety and can serve as perpetuating factors. However, there is sufficient evidence to indicate that primary biological factors do exist and the technology is now available for us eventually to identify biological substrates.

## Personality traits

Some understanding of the eating disorders has come from study of temperament and personality traits and the way in which these may render a young person vulnerable to developmental pressures. The literature is full of reference to the fact that anorexia nervosa is underpinned by unusual sensitivities and extremes of personality (e.g. Fosson, Knibbs, Bryant-Waugh, & Lask, 1987; Srinivasagan, Kaye, Plotnikov, Greeno, Weltzin, & Rao, 1995; Strober, 1995). Parents of children and adolescents with anorexia nervosa tend to describe them as previously having been "perfect children". They have always been well-behaved, conscientious, popular, and successful. The restraint of negative, but not positive, emotions is commonly reported. Silverman, an American paediatrician, has described such children as "pathologically compliant" (personal communication).

There is a considerable similarity to those children described as "high achieving" (Lask, 1985) who develop unexplained physical symptoms in times of stress. What these two groups seem to have in common is an inability to express negative feelings such as anger, sadness, or anxiety. It is as if they are not entitled to show weakness or imperfection, and, in sufficiently stressful circumstances, become unwell. The particular manifestation of this distress is determined by other factors such as their genetically determined biological substrate (see earlier). However, the perfectionist personality of those with anorexia nervosa could be an important contributing factor in the persistent restraint required to maintain a very low weight.

A commonly associated feature is that of low self-esteem (Button, Sonuga, Barke, Davies, & Thompson, 1996; Lilenfeld et al., 1998). Virtually all the children with anorexia nervosa whom we have seen appear to have a very poor self-image, seeing themselves as failures, bad, and unworthy. Such a perception may in part be reinforced by the perfectionistic traits, which impose such high standards that failure is inevitable.

Personality attributes in bulimia nervosa are quite different. Gregariousness, impulsivity, and risk-taking seem more common. Such features are incompatible with a strong and persistent need to exercise control (as in anorexia nervosa) but rather encourage the urge to binge and purge.

There is as yet insufficient information about the other eating disorders of childhood and adolescence to make any firm statements about personality attributes. Those with food avoidance emotional disorder, selective or restrictive eating patterns, and functional dysphagia all seem to have somewhat sensitive personalities but further information is required before this clinical impression can be confirmed.

Some would dispute that these factors are inherited traits, arguing rather that they are responses to environmental circumstances such as particular styles of parenting. It is more likely that both inherited traits and specific experiences combine with other factors to lead to the development of an eating disorder. Some of the psychological factors that have been considered relevant are discussed in the next section.

## PSYCHOLOGICAL FACTORS

There have been many attempted psychological explanations for the pathogenesis of anorexia nervosa. None has received any empirical support and some are particularly fanciful such as that of fear of oral impregnation (Waller, Kaufman, & Deutsch, 1940). More credible and influential has been the work of Bruch (1974). She has suggested that the refusal to eat and fear of fatness have their roots in early mother–child interactions. She has raised both a "why" and a "how" question. Why do certain individuals "misuse the eating function in their efforts to solve or camouflage problems of living that otherwise seem to them insoluble?" (p. 174). From a psychoanalytic perspective, disturbed eating can have a vast range of symbolic meanings (e.g. expressing rage and hatred, a superior sense of power, rejection of parents, etc.).

The "how" question has been neglected. How has it been possible for eating to develop in such a way that it could be misused to such an extent to deal with complex emotional and interpersonal problems? Bruch's answer is that something has gone wrong in the early experiential processes surrounding the satisfaction of nutritional and other bodily needs.

Bruch has described the way in which gratifying early experiences with feeding create for the infant a trust, both in the mother's responsiveness to cues, and in the accuracy of the infant's own internal sensations of hunger and other appetites. When appropriate confirming responses from the mother are persistently lacking (such as when the mother feeds the child to suit her own needs and rhythms) the child becomes uncertain about her ability to discriminate her inner states and her capacity to be looked after. The child neither learns to identify hunger correctly nor to distinguish it from other states of bodily need or emotional arousal. Neither the world nor herself seem trustworthy.

In Bruch's analysis this lack of emotional containment leads the child, in desperation, to be utterly compliant with what she perceives to be her mother's needs. In this way she hopes to maintain what feels like a fragile connection with her mother; hence, the typical profile of the "perfect child" (see earlier). As she grows she fails to develop a sense of herself as independent or entitled to take any initiative, but rather continues to gain maternal approval by absolute compliance. The consequence of this is a paralysing sense of ineffectiveness. Such an individual may feel helpless under the impact of her bodily urges. She may feel controlled from the outside and relies on safe and predictable routines to determine her behaviour (Bruch, 1974).

What is common to the various psychodynamic hypotheses is the notion that the angry, disappointed, and frustrated child feels unable to challenge the much-needed caretaker. She thereby adopts the idea that it is not the caretaker who is inadequate but rather that her needs are inappropriate and should be denied. The child learns to present to the world a coping and obliging self, while "the un-nurtured real self has been split off and repressed" (Orbach, 1986, p. 34).

A further challenge is to define the differences in the early psychological development of girls and boys that could account for the vastly greater number of females than males with eating disorders. Eichenbaum and Orbach (1983) have described the mother's differential response to the male and female baby. The mother will try to get to know her son's wants and needs because he is "different from her". In contrast she assumes she knows what the baby girl wants and needs because she is the "same as her". In consequence girls are more likely to have their real needs denied and in turn to deny them.

Linked to this is the notion that at the centre of female development is the pressure to make and sustain relationships, whereas boys are encouraged to be more independent and self-directed (Gilligan, 1982). For boys, failure in their relationship with their mother is less threatening. They are more able and likely to respond with greater renunciation of the maternal tie, whereas girls will seek reparation, if necessary by compliance and denial of their own needs. It follows therefore that males who develop anorexia nervosa are those who build a self based not upon a sense of difference from others, but on a close identification with the mother.

Such factors persist through childhood and may have a profound effect on the developing personality. As puberty approaches other factors become significant. Eating disorders such as anorexia nervosa and bulimia nervosa are most likely to emerge in adolescence, suggesting that the unique combination of rapid growth, pubertal development, and psychosocial challenges is a potent precipitating factor. Crisp (1980) has emphasised that anorexia nervosa reflects the individual's fear and avoidance of growth, sexuality, and independence—a phobic avoidance of puberty or growing up. This explanation does seem to fit for many adolescents who have anorexia nervosa, but fits less well for those who develop the illness before puberty or in their adult years.

Maine (1991) has introduced the concept of "father hunger". She suggests that as their daughters enter puberty fathers react in one of three ways. Most fathers manage to adjust to their daughter's emerging sexuality by gently and sensitively altering the nature of their relationship and reducing the degree of physical proximity. This represents the "ideal" response. Others, however, less sensitive to their daughter's needs, may retain the same level of involvement as previously, which will include the same degree of physical proximity. This feels uncomfortable to the daughter who is obliged to withdraw, risk alienating her father, and losing his affection. Alternatively, fathers feel uncomfortable with their daughter's emerging sexuality and react by withdrawing. The daughter feels hurt, confused, and rejected. Either of these latter scenarios is distressing to the daughter, who, suffering "father hunger", may then react by subconsciously attempting to retreat to a pre-pubertal state. The subconscious hope is that by being small and asexual, father's attention, affection, and approval will be regained.

However, not all the early onset eating disorders occur in adolescence. For example, functional dysphagia, food avoidance emotional disorder, and selective and restrictive eating patterns tend to start earlier. Indeed, the latter two patterns of eating may be almost life-long and as such cannot be considered to have a developmental component. However, they are probably unique to childhood and adolescence in that they do not seem to emerge in adult life. Food avoidance emotional disorder has not been described in adults although it may be that many people with what is diagnosed as "atypical anorexia nervosa" have an adult variant. Functional dysphagia, in contrast, is well recognised in adult life, and probably some people diagnosed as having globus hystericus may have an adult variant of this childhood condition.

No discussion of aetiological factors should neglect the role of specific stressors. Frequently the parents of children with eating disorders identify a specific trigger. In anorexia nervosa it is commonly a chance (and often relatively innocuous) remark about the girl's weight or shape. This may account for the fact that a past history of obesity or dieting have been reported to be risk factors (Patton, Johnson-Sabine, Wood, Mann, & Wakeling, 1990; Rastam, 1992). Sometimes the illness appears to be triggered by a more profound life event such as an episode of illness, a change of school, a move of home, bereavement, or other adverse life events (Gowers, North, & Byram, 1996). There is no evidence of specific triggers in anorexia nervosa (Fosson et al., 1987) and *any* stressful event may be associated with its onset.

In functional dysphagia there is not infrequently a specific episode such as witnessing someone choking on some food or vomiting. Occasionally it is actually the child who chokes or vomits. Specific stressors are harder to identify in bulimia nervosa, restrictive eating, selective eating, and food avoidance emotional disorder. This does not mean that there are none, and it is perfectly possible that hidden triggers play a significant part in some cases.

One obvious example is that of an adverse sexual experience. Evidence is growing that such experiences may well be one of the contributory factors in the aetiology of eating disorders in a significant number of individuals (Calam & Slade, 1989; Everill & Waller, 1995; Hall, Tyce, Berresford, Wooley, & Hall, 1989; Palmer, Oppenheimer, Dignon, Chaloner, & Howells, 1990; Waller, 1991;

Wonderlich, Brewton, Jocicz, Dansky, & Abbott, 1997; Wooley, 1994). Sexual trauma seems to be particularly relevant when the eating problem involves a bulimic component (Gleaves & Eberenz, 1994; Waller, 1998).

Prevalence figures for sexual trauma in those with eating disorders vary from 34% to 83%, dependent upon such factors as the definition of sexual trauma and the means of gathering information (Bryant-Waugh & Lask, 1995). However, as Wooley (1994, pp. 188–189) has said, we really have no idea how many people with eating disorders have been sexually abused: "The silencing of victims is the core phenomenon of abuse—a virtual pre-requisite for its occurrence and the source of many of the most destructive sequelae, since victims must rely on primitive and often incapacitating defences to accomplish the related psychological tasks of repression and concealment."

Furthermore, as Palmer et al. (1990), Wooley (1994), and many others have pointed out, there is commonly an extremely long delay that precedes disclosure, even among patients in intensive therapy. Our own clinical experience indicates that it is very likely that delayed or non-disclosure is particularly common in younger patients, who may be more dependent upon the perpetrator and are certainly more vulnerable to threats and silencing. Although sexual abuse can clearly be a precipitating factor, continuing abuse or the threat of recurrence, or the fear of repercussions for disclosure, can also all operate as perpetuating factors.

Clearly sexual (or other forms of) trauma is neither necessary nor sufficient for the development of an eating disorder. Indeed, it is likely that the majority of young people with eating disorders have not been sexually traumatised. Equally, there are many people who have suffered adverse sexual experiences who develop other (or no) disorders. Nor is there any evidence that childhood sexual abuse is associated with a greater severity of eating disorder symptoms (Wonderlich et al., 1997).

The mechanism by which sexual trauma leads to an eating disorder is likely to involve disgust of one's femininity and sexuality (Calam & Slade, 1989), guilt, and shame. Hall et al. (1989) noted that many people with eating disorders were clear that their wish to be skeletally thin was associated with that appearance protecting them from further sexual assault. Although this is completely understandable, Hall et al. believe that the motivation is more complex. The patients seem to want to "disgust" the individual who committed the assault, largely as a way of breaking the emotional bond between themselves and the perpetrator.

There is much that is yet to be learned about the relationship between sexual trauma and the eating disorders. Wooley (1994, p. 189) has argued persuasively that we need to adopt a far broader approach to our conceptualisation: "With so much to do, we must give careful thought to our priorities. Our first order of business is not to determine the precise rates of abuse in various populations or even the precise weighting of abuse as an etiological or maintaining factor in eating disorders; instead it is to decide how to respond as a profession to a moment thousands of years in the making."

## FAMILIAL FACTORS

Although there is no systematic evidence that birth order, family size, or structure are of any significance in aetiology (Vandereycken, 1995), familial dysfunction has been a popular area for consideration of pathogenesis of the eating disorders. Palazzoli (1974) has described families who have a child with anorexia nervosa as rigid homoeostatic systems, governed by secret rules that shun the light of day and pathologically bind the family, which are challenged by the child's emerging adolescence. Minuchin, Rosman, and Baker (1978) claimed to have identified specific family characteristics such as over involvement, rigidity, and conflict avoidance as being typical of these families.

These hypotheses have never been shown empirically to have validity and nor do they explain the emergence of anorexia nervosa specifically. Indeed, there is some empirical evidence (Kog & Vandereycken, 1988; Bryant-Waugh & Lask, 1995; Rastam & Gillberg, 1991), and considerable clinical evidence, contradicting these hypotheses. There are many families who have children with similar features who develop other disorders and other families who do have children with anorexia nervosa who show quite different features.

None the less there is empirical evidence that families of children with anorexia nervosa do manifest dysfunctional interaction and communication (Kog & Vandereycken, 1988). Our clinical experience confirms this view (see Chapters 7 and 10, on assessment and family work). It is particularly common to observe poor communication, conflict, and inconsistency between the parents, regarding management. It is by no means clear, however, whether such dysfunction predates the disorder or are a reaction to it. As Dare has noted (1985, p. 437), "the vulnerable individual may develop an eating disorder for a host of other reasons unrelated to family organisation, but find her symptoms utilised and maintained by the family for its own purposes". For the moment we can be confident that family dysfunction, possibly also including abnormal eating attitudes and behaviour, can perpetuate eating disorders, but we have little evidence that it can predispose to, or precipitate them.

## SOCIO-CULTURAL FACTORS

Any model for explaining the aetiology of anorexia nervosa and related eating disorders is incomplete if it fails to provide an adequate answer to the question of why they occur predominantly in females in "developed" Western society. It is now well recognised that the cultural pressure on women to be thin is an important predisposing factor for the development of eating disorders (e.g. Fallon, Katzman, & Willie, 1994). Being thin has become almost synonymous with being good in a society that worships the bulge-free female form. Young children are no longer exempt from this preoccupation. Hill, Oliver, and Rogers (1982) have shown that even 6–9-year-olds have concerns about their weight and shape.

Theorists from outside mainstream psychiatry have put this fact at the forefront of their analysis and have viewed eating disorders in their relation to the current cultural preoccupation with thinness and to the position of women as objects to be looked at. Cultural historian Brumberg (1988, p. 44) has noted that, prior to this interpretation, "women's dieting and weight concerns were once trivialised or interpreted as masking a strictly individual psychological problem without consideration for the ways in which culture stimulated, exacerbated and gave shape to a pattern of problematic behaviours".

The cultural approach recognises that throughout history the passive, depersonalised female form has been the object of pleasure for men and that this aspect of femininity is absorbed into each woman's experience of herself. And nor are children and teenagers invulnerable spectators of this process. There is well-documented pressure on them to conform to a fashion that stresses the achievement of shapes that are at best improbable, and even impossible, e.g. the Barbie doll (Davies & Furnham, 1986). The cultural imperative is not of course the sole explanation for the large number of people with eating disorders. Most teenage girls and most women live with a sense of body insecurity, dieting intermittently and usually unsuccessfully, but without resorting to damaging self-starvation. However, the fact that eating disorders are by and large confined to societies in which thinness is valued, and are very rare in societies where fatness is valued, adds strongly to the view that society plays an important part in their genesis. This theory is reinforced by the observation that, whereas immigrants to Western societies do not themselves develop eating disorders, their daughters seem just as vulnerable to them as do those of the indigenous population (e.g. Bryant-Waugh & Lask, 1991).

The cultural analysis, in attempting to set eating disorders in the complex inter-relationships between culture, gender, and food, acknowledges that it is still a fact that the vast majority of meals are purchased, prepared, and served by women. "Throughout history women have occupied the dual role of feeding others while denying themselves" (Orbach, 1986, p. 51). Once an economic necessity, it is now a social demand. "For women, socially identified with their bodies and stereotypically linked to food and the kitchen, the struggle for control is naturally expressed through eating disorders" (Edwards, 1987, p. 107).

The cultural model partly depends for its power, not just on the fact that eating disorders are predominantly female problems, but also on the belief that the incidence of eating disorders is steadily increasing. The hypothesis is that the dieting female is struggling to transform her body in an attempt to deal with the contradictory requirements of her role in late-20th century Western societies. She faces contradictory problems and may be confused about her authentic needs and wishes. Culturally and psychologically, she is prepared for a life in which she should continue to service the needs of others (emotional, sexual, nutritional). At the same time she is teased with the possibility of a more autonomous and self-determined life. Working with girls from rural families who have moved to the city, Palazzoli (1974) argued that sufferers from anorexia nervosa typically come from families in the midst of cultural transition. An era of changing opportunities and expectations for women may similarly be a fertile ground for the development of anorexia nervosa, conceptualised essentially as a struggle for autonomy and individuality. The struggle finds expression in the paradoxical stance of the powerful but passive anorexic (her wish to be ultra-feminine, coupled with her rejection of femininity).

Lawrence (1984) has seen this struggle played out in the field of education. She views education for women as bringing with it a whole set of difficulties which often push the educated female into a series of uneasy compromises with herself. The "middle class" bias often referred to in accounts of anorexia nervosa (e.g. Palmer, 1980) she interprets as essentially an education bias. Indeed a clear coincidence of anorexia nervosa and educational achievement is identified in the literature (Dally & Gomez, 1979). But this striving for excellence can be problematic for girls. Bruch (1973, p. 82) wrote "growing girls can experience . . . liberation as a demand and feel that they have to do something outstanding. Many of my patients have expressed the feeling that they are overwhelmed by the vast number of potential opportunities available to them . . . and [that] they have been afraid of not choosing correctly."

According to Lawrence (1984), girls may feel that they are compromising their feminine identity by achieving at school and they may strive to conform as a conventional young woman by achieving slimness. All the effort and self-denial that might have gone into schoolwork is put into the struggle to be thin. Other writers have emphasised that the scholastic excellence noted in many groups of eating disorder women is the product of a need to please others rather than of a generally high natural endowment (e.g. Bruch, 1973; Garner & Garfinkel, 1980). To this picture of identity conflict, Chermin (1986) adds the extra problem for a female of accepting advantages and opportunities denied to her mother. Girls who cross into the male spheres of self-development and social power may experience profound ambivalence and guilt.

## TOWARDS AN INTEGRATION

The essence of attempting to understand the genesis of eating disorders is to adopt a multifactorial model that emphasises also the different roles of predisposing, precipitating, and perpetuating factors. Some factors may operate at only one moment, whereas others may persist. Figure 5.1 demonstrates this model as applied to the development of anorexia nervosa in the younger population.

*Predisposing* factors include genetic vulnerability, which in itself may be expressed through both biological factors and personality traits, and sociocultural demands. The latter may also precipitate and perpetuate the disorder. *Precipitating* factors include various stressors such as pubertal development, trauma, low self-esteem in which self-evaluation is based only on weight, shape and appearance,

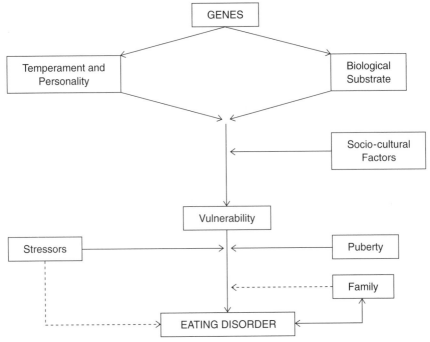

FIG. 5.1   The development of an eating disorder.

family tensions or problems, school and peer group pressures, illness, or loss. All of these can also *perpetuate* the problem, as can the way in which it is managed, the sense of achievement through gaining control of the body (or parents), and the effects of starvation.

Figure 5.2 illustrates a conceptualisation of how a child or adolescent who is predisposed to the development of anorexia nervosa responds to external stresses. These induce or exacerbate a sense of failure which in turn lowers self-esteem and contributes to a sense of loss of control. The consequent need to gain control combined with successful dieting results in a sense of achievement and further dieting, which ultimately spirals out of control.

It can be seen therefore that the challenge in understanding the aetiology of the eating disorders lies not in identifying a single cause nor even in documenting a list of all risk factors, but rather in understanding particular ways in which the various contributory factors are likely to interact in different stages in the evolution of the illness.

It is not enough, for example, to see familial overprotection and conflict avoidance as co-existing as causal factors with societal pressure for slimness. Rather it becomes important to try to elucidate how the wider culture is transmitted through the family: how, for instance, Minuchin's "anorectic families" teach their daughters the most conventional social attitudes to femininity (Edwards, 1987).

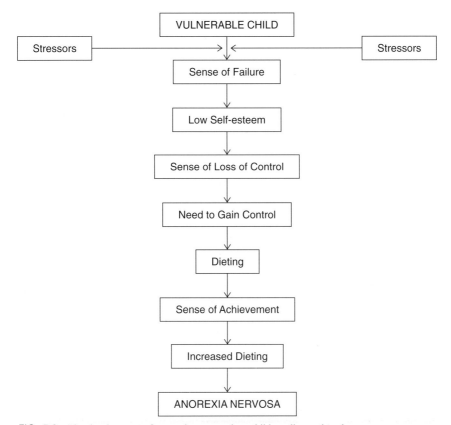

FIG. 5.2   The development of anorexia nervosa in a child predisposed to do so.

The cultural objectification of the female body can also be seen as contributing to the widespread incidence of childhood sexual abuse, which, as discussed earlier in this chapter, often has an important, if imperfectly understood, role in the development of eating disorders. The causal significance of the wish to reverse the development of normal puberty may, for some individuals, be linked to traumatic sexual experiences.

A third example of the need to understand the interactions between causal factors is the way in which the "middle class bias" in anorexia nervosa may turn out to be better understood as an education bias, which can in turn be seen as implicated in the psychological features of overcompliance and a lack of inner directiveness emphasised by some psychodynamic writers (e.g. Bruch, 1974).

We can anticipate the advent of increasingly complex models of the aetiology of eating disorders but there are two caveats. First, it is likely that the precise interaction of the many predisposing, precipitating, and perpetuating factors important in the evolution of eating disorders can never be fully delineated.

Nor may it even be entirely clear what characteristics protect some apparently vulnerable individuals. The second caveat is that the richness and complexity of the models we build should not obscure the need for a central organising idea. A number of authors from very diverse perspectives share an understanding of anorexia nervosa as essentially a syndrome of pathological self-control (Bruch, 1974; Crisp, 1983; Lawrence, 1984; Slade, 1982). Crucially, this shifts the wish to be thin from the centre of the phenomenology picture and gives clearer shape to the search for coherence in understanding the relationship between causal forces. As Bruch (1974) has lucidly stated: "The main issue is a struggle for control, or a sense of identity, competence and effectiveness. Many of these youngsters have struggled for years to be 'perfect' in the eyes of others. Concern with thinness and food refusal are late steps in this maldevelopment."

## SUMMARY POINTS

- Eating disorders have a multifactorial genesis.
- Biological, social, and psychological factors are all relevant.
- The roles of predisposing, precipitating, and perpetuating factors all require consideration.
- Different factors interact at different stages of the illness.

## ACKNOWLEDGEMENT

Some of the ideas explored in this chapter were originally presented in the first edition of this book in the chapter on aetiology, which was co-authored by Bernadette Wren and myself. I am most grateful to Bernadette for stimulating my thinking.

## REFERENCES

Bruch, H. (1973). *The golden cage: The enigma of anorexia nervosa*. London: Open Books.
Bruch, H. (1974). *Eating disorders: Obesity, anorexia nervosa and the person within*. London: Routledge & Kegan Paul.
Brumberg, J.J. (1988). *Fasting girls*. Cambridge, MA: Harvard University.
Bryant-Waugh, R., & Lask, B. (1991). Anorexia nervosa in a group of Asian children living in Britain. *British Journal of Psychiatry, 158*, 229–233.
Bryant-Waugh, R., & Lask, B. (1995). Annotation: Eating disorders in children. *Journal of Child Psychology and Psychiatry, 36*, 191–202.
Button, E., Sonuga, R., Barke, J., Davies, J., & Thompson, M. (1996). A prospective study of self-esteem in the prediction of eating problems in adolescent school girls. *British Journal of Clincal Psychology, 35*, 193–203.
Calam, R., & Slade, B. (1989). Sexual experience in eating problems in female undergraduates. *International Journal of Eating Disorders, 8*, 391–397.
Carney, C., & Andersen, A. (1996). Eating disorders: Guide to medical evaluation and complications. *Psychiatric Clinics of North America, 19*, 657–678.

Chermin, K. (1986). *The hungry self.* London: Virago.

Christie, D., Bryant-Waugh, R., Lask, B., & Gordon, I. (1998). Neurobiological aspects of early onset eating disorders. In H. Hoek, J. Treasure, & M. Katzman (Eds.), *The neurobiology of eating disorders.* Chichester, UK: John Wiley.

Crisp, A. (1980). *Anorexia nervosa—let me be.* London: Academic Press.

Crisp, A. (1983). Anorexia nervosa. *British Medical Journal, 287,* 855–858.

Crisp, A., Palmer, R., & Kalucy, R. (1976). How common is anorexia nervosa? A prevalent study. *British Journal of Psychiatry, 128,* 549–554.

Dally, P., & Gomez, J. (1979). *Anorexia nervosa.* London: Heinemann.

Dare, C. (1985). The family therapy of anorexia nervosa. *Journal of Psychiatric Research, 19,* 435–443.

Davies, E., & Furnham, A. (1986). The dieting and body shape concerns of adolescent females. *Journal of Child Psychology and Psychiatry, 27,* 417–428.

Edwards, G. (1987). Anorexia and the family. In M. Lawrence (Ed.), *Fed up and hungry: Women, oppression and food.* London: Women's Press.

Eichenbaum, L., & Orbach, S. (1983). *Understanding women: A feminist psychoanalytic approach.* London: Penguin.

Everill, J., & Waller, G. (1995). Reported sexual abuse in eating psychopathology: A review of the evidence for a causal link. *International Journal of Eating Disorders, 18,* 1–11.

Fallon, P., Katzman, M., & Willie, S. (1994). *Feminist perspectives on eating disorders.* New York: Guilford.

Fosson, A., Knibbs, J., Bryant-Waugh, R., & Lask, B. (1987). Early onset of anorexia nervosa. *Archives of Disease in Childhood, 621,* 114–118.

Garner, A., & Garfinkel, P. (1980). Sociocultural factors in the development of anorexia nervosa. *Psychological Medicine, 10,* 647–656.

Gilligan, C. (1982). *In a different voice.* Cambridge, MA: Harvard University.

Gleaves, D., & Eberenz, D. (1994). Sexual abuse histories among treatment resistant bulima nervosa patients. *International Journal of Eating Disorders, 15,* 227–232.

Gordon, I., Lask, B., Bryant-Waugh, R., Christie, D., & Timimi, S. (1997). Childhood onset anorexia nervosa—towards identifying a biological substrait. *International Journal of Eating Disorders, 22,* 159–166.

Gowers, S., North, C., & Byram, V. (1996). Life events precipitants of adolescent anorexia nervosa. *Journal of Child Psychology and Psychiatry, 37,* 469–477.

Hall, R., Tyce, M., Berresford, T., Wooley, B., & Hall, A. (1989). Sexual abuse in patients with anorexia and bulima. *Psychomsomatics, 1,* 73–79.

Herholz, K. (1996). Neuro imaging in anorexia nervosa. *Psychiatry Research, 62,* 105–110.

Hill, A., Oliver, S., & Rogers, P. (1992). Eating in the adult world: The rise of dieting in childhood and adolescence. *British Journal of Clinical Psychology, 31,* 95–105.

Holland, A., Sicotte, N., & Treasure, J. (1988). Anorexia nervosa—evidence for a genetic basis. *Journal of Psychosomatic Research, 32,* 549–554.

Katzman, D., Lambe, E., Mikulis, D., Ridgley, J., Goldbloom, D., & Zipurski, R. (1996). Cerebral gray matter and white matter volume deficits in adolescent girls with anorexia nervosa. *Journal of Paediatrics, 129,* 704–803.

Kaye, W. (1997). Persistent alterations in behaviour and sereotonic activity after recovery from anorexia and bulimia nervosa. In M. Jacobson, J. Reece, N. Golden, & C. Irwin (Eds.), *Annals of the New York Academy of Sciences: Vol. 817. Adolescent nutritional disorders, prevention and treatment* (pp. 162–178). New York: New York Academy of Sciences.

Kendler, M., MacLean, C., Neale, M., Kessler, R., Keith, A., & Eaves, L. (1991). The genetic epidemology of bulima nervosa. *American Journal of Psychiatry, 148,* 1627–1637.

Kog, E., & Vandereyecken, W. (1988). The facts: A review of research data on eating disorder families. In W. Vandereyecken, E. Kog, & J. Vanderlinden (Eds.), *The family approach to eating disorders: Assessment and treatment of anorexia nervosa and bulimia* (pp. 25–26). New York: PMA.

Kreig, J., Holhoff, V., Schreiber, W., Pirke, K., & Herholz, K. (1991). Glucose metabolism in the cordi-nuclei of patients with eating disorders measured by PET. *European Archives of Psychiatry and Clinical Neuroscience, 240*, 331–333.

Lask, B. (1985). The high achieving child. *Postgraduate Medical Journal. 62*, 143–166.

Lawrence, M. (1984). *The anorectic experience*. London: Women's Press.

Lilenfeld, L., Kaye, W., Greeno, C., Merikangas, K., Plotnicov, K., Pollice, C., Rao, R., Strober, M., Bulik, C., & Nagy, L. (1998). A controlled family study of anorexia nervosa and bulimia nervosa. *Archives of General Psychiatry, 55*, 603–610.

Lucas, A. (1988). Gut hormones and the adaptation to extra uterine nutrition. In P. Milla & D. Muller (Eds.), *Harries' paediatric gastroenterology* (2nd ed., pp. 302–317). London: Churchill Livingstone.

Maine, M. (1991). *Father hunger*. Carlsberg, CA: Gorsze Books.

Minuchin, S., Rosman, B.L., & Baker, L. (1978). *Psychosomatic families: Anorexia nervosa in context*. Cambridge, MA: Harvard University Press.

Orbach, S. (1986). *Hunger strike*. Harmondsworth, UK: Penguin.

Palazzoli, M.S. (1974). *Self-starvation*. London: Chancer.

Palmer, R.L. (1980). *Anorexia nervosa: A guide for suffers and their families*. Harmondsworth, UK: Penguin.

Palmer, R.L., Oppenheimer, R., Dignon, A.L., Chaloner, D.A., & Howells, K. (1990). Childhood sexual experiences with adults reported by women with eating disorders: An extended series. *British Journal of Psychiatry, 156*, 699–703.

Patton, G., Johnson-Sabine, E., Wood, K., Mann, A., & Wakeling, A. (1990). Abnormal eating attitudes in London schoolgirls—a prospective epidemiological study. *Psychological Medicine, 20*, 383–394.

Rastam, M. (1992). Anorexia nervosa in 51 Swedish adolescents. *Journal of the American Academy of Child and Adolescent Psychiatry, 31*, 819–829.

Rastam, M., & Gillberg, G. (1991). A family background of anorexia nervosa: A population based study. *Journal of the American Academy of Child and Adolescent Psychiatry, 30*, 283–289.

Russell, G. (1992). Anorexia nervosa of early onset and its impact on puberty. In P. Cooper & A. Stein (Eds.), *Feeding problems and eating disorders in children and adolescents* (pp. 99–111). Reading, UK: Harwood Academic Publishers.

Scott, D. (1986). Anorexia nervosa: A review of possible genetic factors. *International Journal of Eating Disorders, 5*, 1–12.

Silver, A., & Morley, J. (1991). The role of CCK in the regulation of food intake. *Progress in Neurobiology, 36*, 23–35.

Slade, P.D. (1982). Towards a functional analysis of anorexia nervosa. *British Journal of Clinical Psychology, 21*, 167–179.

Srinivasagan, N., Kaye, W., Plotnikov, K., Greeno, C., Weltzin, T., & Rao, R. (1995). Persistent perfectionism, symmetry and exactness after long-term recovery from anorexia nervosa. *American Journal of Psychiatry, 152*, 1630–1634.

Strober, M. (1991). Family-genetic studies of eating disorders. *Journal of Clinical Psychiatry, 52* (Suppl. 10), 9–12.

Strober, M. (1992). Family-genetic studies. In K. Halmi (Ed.), *Psychobiology and treatment of anorexia nervosa and bulimia nervosa* (pp. 61–78). Washington, DC: American Psychiatric Press.

Strober, M. (1995). Family-genetic perspectives on anorexia nervosa and bulimia nervosa. In K. Brownell & C. Fairburn (Eds.), *Eating disorders and obesity: A comprehensive handbook* (pp. 212–218). New York: Guilford Press.

Theander, S. (1970). Anorexia nervosa: A psychiatric investigation of 94 female patients. *Acta Psychiatrica Scandinavica* (Suppl. 214), 106–131.

Treasure, J., & Holland, A. (1990). Genetic vulnerability to eating disorders: Evidence in twin and family studies. In H. Renschmidt & M. Schmidt (Eds.), *Anorexia nervosa* (pp. 59–69.) Toronto, Canada: Hagrefe & Huber.

Vandereycken, W. (1995). The families of patients with an eating disorder. In K. Brownell & C. Fairburn (Eds.), *Eating disorders and obesity: A comprehensive handbook* (pp. 219–223). New York: Guilford Press.

Waller, G. (1991). Sexual abuse as a factor in the eating disorders. *British Journal of Psychiatry, 159,* 664–671.

Waller, G. (1998). Perceived controlling eating disorders: Relationship with reported sexual abuse. *International Journal of Eating Disorders, 23,* 213–216.

Waller, J.V., Kaufman, R.M., & Deutsch, F. (1940). Anorexia nervosa: A psychosomatic entity. *Psychosomatic Medicine, 2,* 3–16.

Weiner, H. (1985). The physiology of the eating disorders. *International Journal of Eating Disorders, 4,* 347–388.

Wonderlich, S., Brewton, T., Jocicz, V., Dansky, B., & Abbott, D. (1997). Relationship of childhood sexual abuse and eating disorders. *Journal of the American Academy of Child and Adolescent Psychiatry, 36,* 1107–1115.

Woodside, D. (1993). Genetic contributions to eating disorders. In A. Kaplan & P. Garfinkel (Eds.), *Medical issues in eating disorders: The interface* (pp. 193–211). New York: Brunner/Mazel.

Wooley, S. (1994). Sexual abuse in eating disorders: The concealed debate. In P. Fallon, M. Katzman, & S. Wooley (Eds.), *Feminist perspectives on eating disorders* (pp. 171–211). New York: Guilford.

CHAPTER SIX

# Prognosis and outcome

**Marc Neiderman**
*Huntercombe Manor Hospital, Taplow, UK*

## INTRODUCTION

The search for information that can be used to predict the course and outcome in eating disorders has had a somewhat less than distinguished history. Despite the best efforts of researchers, a comprehensive understanding of eating disorders remains elusive. Although literally hundreds of outcome studies have been published, the vast majority contain several methodological shortcomings. When combined with the multidimensional presentation of eating disordered symptomology, and human nature in general, it is no surprise that prediction has been, and remains, so very difficult. None the less, it is important to recognise that valuable knowledge has been acquired over the decades, much of it of practical use.

Although "outcome" and "prognosis" are terms that are often used synonymously, they are in fact different. Outcome is defined as "the long-term result of a pathological process", whereas prognosis is defined as the "means to make a forecast or a prediction as to the probable further course and the final outcome of the disease" (Theander, 1985, p. 493). This chapter presents current information on these concepts as they relate to eating disorders.

## OUTCOME RESEARCH

The purpose of conducting outcome research is to answer questions that may lead to more effective interventions, and to predict in a relatively reliable way what a patient can expect throughout the course of their illness. Unfortunately, reviews of outcome research point to extensive and continuing methodological shortcomings (e.g. Garner, 1987):

(1)   small sample size
(2)   absence of comparison groups
(3)   failure to specify diagnostic criteria
(4)   failure to specify if patients were "recruited" or obtained by clinical referral
(5)   failure to identify subgroups of eating disorder patients for whom treatment response may differ
(6)   failure to specify technical operations of treatment in a manner that can be replicated (i.e. use of detailed manuals)
(7)   absence of manipulation checks through tape rating to ensure that patients receive the specified treatment
(8)   use of naive therapists
(9)   inadequate reporting of screening procedures and attrition rates
(10)  assessment and outcome data gathered by therapists
(11)  failure to use standardised psychometric instruments
(12)  inadequate measurement of target symptoms
(13)  lack of convergent measures of symptom areas
(14)  inadequate follow-up.

Does the somewhat gloomy picture presented so far then mean that we are doomed to continue engaging in poorly designed research? Not necessarily, for many more recent studies have reflected this by espousing the suggested criteria for good outcome research. These include the following.

*1.   Diagnoses should be explicitly stated.*   Formal criteria such as those suggested in the DSM-IV (American Psychiatric Association, 1994) are most often used and can be useful when comparing subjects across studies, although it is important to recognise that patients may waver between diagnoses throughout the course of the follow-up period, and this should be reported. Also, patients who do not fulfil the strict criteria for either anorexia nervosa or bulimia nervosa should be accounted for, and a specific description of their symptoms detailed.

*2.   Ideally, samples should include more than 30 subjects,*   especially where parametric tests are to be used. Alternatively, where samples are small, non-parametric statistics may be useful or even preferable.

*3.   The duration of observation time should be clearly stated.*   It is common for researchers to consider as the beginning of the observation period the reported age of onset, initiation of first treatment, initiation of current treatment, or end of current treatment. Although it is beyond the scope of this chapter to discuss the advantages and disadvantages of using any one of these points in time, it is still important to emphasise that such descriptions are recorded accurately.

*4.  The duration of the follow-up period is an equally important consideration.* Ideally, a cohort should be followed over several years, taking measurements at regular intervals.

*5.  Both "dropouts" from treatment and "failure-to-trace" subjects at follow-up must be reported,*  and a description of their characteristics presented where possible. The percentage of "dropouts" in follow-up studies varies considerably, though it appears that the higher attrition rates are found in those studies composed of large numbers of cases (Steinhausen, Rauss-Mason, & Seidel, 1991). Clearly the absence of subjects at follow-up can potentially skew the results of studies, especially if it is considered that they may reflect a different course and outcome from those subjects accounted for. Van Strien, Van der Ham, and Van Engeland (1992) have argued that "drop-outs" are in fact distinctly different in composition from co-operative patients at follow-up. In an examination of the characteristics of 34 "dropouts" the authors found that they were primarily diagnosed with anorexia nervosa or atypical anorexia nervosa as opposed to the more co-operative subjects who came from the bulimia nervosa subgroup. This suggests that those suffering from anorexia nervosa may be hostile and avoidant due to the denial of their illness. Also, "dropouts" were found to be more egoistic (more concerned about themselves as opposed to others), and to come from more disadvantaged backgrounds. Unfortunately, less is known about the dropout characteristics of the younger age-onset groups.

*6.  The type and variety of outcome measures should be described in detail.* As discussed above, people with eating disorders, especially those with anorexia nervosa, represent a particularly difficult group to assess accurately due to denial and misreporting. These problems are exacerbated when postal questionnaires are used, and Hsu (1990) has challenged the accuracy of information gathered using this method. Where possible, follow-up information should be collected in person, and corroboration obtained from relatives to maximise the accuracy of results.

Additionally, as eating disorders are multi-determined and multi-faceted, multiple outcome parameters should be included in any outcome study. These would include not only physical and behavioural factors such as weight, eating, bingeing and purging frequency, etc., but also a comprehensive account of mental state, cognitions related to eating disorders, and social functioning. For a listing and description of the various measures available, see Chapter 7.

*7.  An accurate description of the population studied and treatment received is necessary.*  Subjects recruited from tertiary treatment centres typically display a more severe spectrum of eating disorders than those in primary care, though both groups may fulfil the same diagnostic criteria for anorexia nervosa or bulimia nervosa. Also, it is important to describe in as much detail as possible any treatment received during the observation period, as this may be expected to influence course and outcome.

# OUTCOME

## Weight and nutritional status

In children and adolescents, several measurements of weight and nutritional status have been used. These including medically safe weight, lean body mass, body fatness, and current weight in comparison to premorbid weight, and where applicable, menstrual onset weight. The best measures of outcome in the younger population are weight-for-height ratios and growth charts based on population norms, and the Body Mass Index (BMI; see Chapter 8). Due to the wide range of measures used to assess these parameters, differences between the various age groups are not discernable.

In the early onset age group results in terms of weight are generally more encouraging than other measures of outcome, but are none the less quite mixed. In a retrospective follow-up study of 23 children at a mean time of 7 years, Bryant-Waugh, Knibbs, Fosson, Kaminski, and Lask (1988) found that 15 (65%) had achieved a normal body weight, whereas 5 (22%) were underweight, 2 (8.5%) wasting, and 1 (4.25%) overweight; 2 had died. A prospective follow-up of 22 patients with early onset anorexia nervosa (mean age of onset 12.1 years) at a mean of 3.1 years after treatment had found that 61.1% had achieved a "good" physical outcome, 16.7% "intermediate", and 22.2% "poor" (Bryant-Waugh, Hankins, Shafran, Lask, & Fosson, 1996). Jarmon, Rickards, and Hudson (1991) reported 25% of their sample of 32 early onset cases were underweight at follow-up (mean 4.3 years), 42% were in a healthy range, and 12% were overweight. Swift's (1982) review of early onset anorexia nervosa reflects Hsu's (1990) views that, generally, outcome on these variables are encouraging.

Studies reporting on the older age groups correspond with these figures—roughly half to three-quarters of patients have achieved a reasonable weight and state of nutrition, whereas about one-third remain underweight, and a small percentage are overweight anywhere from two to twenty years after the onset of the eating disorder (Button, Marshall, Shinkwin, Black, & Palmer, 1997; Garfinkel, Moldofsky, & Garner, 1977; Hsu, 1988; Hsu, Crisp, & Callender, 1992; Ratnasuriya, Eisler, Szmukler, & Russell, 1991; Steinhausen et al., 1991).

## Eating difficulties, concerns about weight, and continuing eating disorder

Reports on these variables have increased substantially across age groups within the past decade, and the results are not promising regardless of age. In his review of early onset outcome, Swift (1982) found that three of four studies reported disappointing results in this area. Later research appears to support these earlier findings. In a sample of 32 Australian early onset subjects with anorexia nervosa followed up at a mean of 4.3 years after hospitalisation, eating behaviour was normal in 25%, mildly impaired in 16%, moderately so in 40%, and poor in 19% (Jarman et al., 1991). However, Bryant-Waugh et al. (1996) reported at a mean three-year follow-up that, in their sample of 22 early onset subjects with anorexia (mean age of onset 12.1 years), 61.1% were "good", 22.1% "intermediate", and 16.7% "poor". Strober, Freeman, and Morrell (1997) found that 29% of their sample of 95 adolescents with anorexia nervosa had developed binge eating within five years of admission. Other studies of adolescent eating disorders report similar results (Button et al., 1997; Gillberg, Rastam, & Gillberg, 1994).

Garfinkel et al. (1977) reported that, at a follow-up of at least one year (mean 58.2 months post-onset), 71% of women with anorexia nervosa still had "moderate" or "marked" food fads, 50% had bulimic episodes, 20% vomited occasionally, and 10% abused laxatives. In one 20-year follow-up of women with anorexia nervosa, one-third continued to eat irregularly and one-third re-stricted their diet—this was in those whose outcome was "good". Half continued to be preoccupied with thoughts of food and weight. Only a few developed bulimia nervosa, although patients who had died were not included in the figures, and therefore may have been under-reported (Ratnasuriya et al., 1991). Van der Ham, Van Strien, and Van Engeland (1994) have suggested that persistent pre-occupations with food and eating, and disturbed body image identify these as the core features of eating disorders, and are more resistant to change than some of the more physical manifestations of these illnesses.

## Growth and physical development

Little is known about the effects of weight loss, long-term or short, on eating disordered children and adolescents (see Chapter 8 for a more detailed dis-cussion). Results of the studies available are mixed. It is fairly well established that malnutrition in infancy and early childhood can cause growth retardation (Pfeiffer, Lucas, & Ilstrup, 1986). Dreizen, Spirakis, and Stone (1967) conducted a longitudinal study of 30 undernourished and 30 well-nourished girls from early childhood through to early adulthood and concluded that malnutrition negatively affects skeletal growth and maturation, extends the normal period of growth, and delays the onset of menstruation. Later research supports these findings, and Danzinger, Mukamel, Zeharia, Dinari, and Mimouni (1994) have suggested that in pre-pubertal children with anorexia nervosa with a duration of illness of six months or more, stunted growth is commonly observed. They also urge a recognition of this variable in future diagnostic criteria, and that restoration of ideal height be included as a goal of treatment.

Many of these studies have also reported results which question the notion that growth and development is seriously affected by low weight or poor nutri-tion. Dreizen and colleagues (1967) concluded that undernutrition delayed the growth spurt, but had an insignificant effect on final adult height. Pfieffer et al. (1986) found that, despite significant weight loss prior to 16 years of age, growth continued within acceptable norms, and in the study conducted by Danzinger et al. (1994), results were similar—growth is arrested during an active phase of anorexia nervosa, but catch-up growth is commonly observed upon rehabilitation. Despite these more optimistic findings, many participants were involved in intensive restoration of weight, thus statistics for those maintaining a chronic low weight are less understood. In the opinion of Golden et al. (1994, p. 659), "The ability to reverse these findings with nutritional rehabilitation emphasises the need for aggressive treatment to prevent potentially irreversible growth retardation and to maximise height potential."

## Menstrual functioning

In young females, menstrual status is obviously more difficult to measure reliably, especially in those underweight girls on the cusp of menarche. Compounding this problem is the fact that menstrual functioning is very closely associated with weight, although the weight at which an individual's menses return varies, sometimes markedly, between individuals (see Chapter 8). To overcome these difficulties, pelvic ultrasound scans have been used to good effect as changes in the ovaries and uterus in response to fluctuations in weight may be observed, and a "snapshot" of menstrual status taken to help gauge appropriate weight-related interventions (Lai, deBruyn, Lask, Bryant-Waugh, & Hankins, 1994).

Although there remains a great deal of variation in terms of populations and characteristics studied, the results in studies reporting on the outcome of menstrual functioning is quite consistent, perhaps because body weight is the prime target for treatment intervention in anorexia nervosa, regardless of treatment setting. Improvements are often quite considerable (Van der Ham et al., 1994). In his review of outcome studies of early onset anorexia nervosa, Swift (1982) found that, in the three that reported it, menstrual functioning was regular in 56–92% of cases, irregular in 4–24%, and absent in 4–28%. One follow-up study of early onset anorexia nervosa found menstrual functioning regular in 56%, irregular in 25%, and amenorrhoeic in the remaining 19% of early onset participants at a mean 4.3-year follow-up (Jarman et al., 1991). Bryant-Waugh et al.'s (1996) outcome study into early onset anorexia nervosa (mean age 12.1 years) found 53.3% with regular periods, 20% were irregular, and 26% had amenorrhoea. Others report similar results for adolescents (Gillberg et al., 1994; Hsu et al., 1992; Steinhausen et al., 1991).

Most post-menarcheal females could expect menstruation to return at around 90% average body weight (Garfinkel et al., 1977), although in one study, all but one of 41 women at 20-year follow-up reported menstruating providing they were above only 75% average body weight (Ratnasuriya et al., 1991). In the older age groups, Button and colleagues (1997) reported that in their cohort of 64 patients (mean age of onset 20.5 years, range 11–65, mean duration of illness

4.8 years) 36% of those with anorexia nervosa, 43% of those with bulimia nervosa, and 50% of those with a mixed diagnosis were menstruating regularly at two- to four-year follow-up.

## Mental state

Despite continuing criticism of a lack of standardised measures used in follow-up studies of eating disorders, reported prevalence of co-morbid psychiatric disorders remains fairly consistent across studies. Also, results seem to be similar for early onset, adolescent, and older populations (Bryant-Waugh et al., 1988; Steinhausen et al., 1991). The most commonly observed psychiatric problems in patients with eating disorders, even those who have recovered from their eating disorder, include depression, anxiety disorders, obsessive-compulsive disorder, and drug and alcohol abuse, or less severe symptoms of these illnesses (Steinhausen et al., 1991; Theander, 1985). Schizophrenic and other psychotic symptoms are rare, and seem to occur no more frequently than they do in the general population. Earlier studies which reported a high incidence of schizophrenic/psychotic diagnoses (29% in one sample) must be looked upon with a critical eye as they are in such marked contrast to more recent research, and based on populations observed between the 1930s and 1960s—a time when diagnoses were more liberally assigned (Swift, 1982).

In one follow-up study of 23 patients with adolescent onset anorexia nervosa, 30% qualified for a diagnosis of affective disorder, and 43% for anxiety disorder at six years post-presentation (Smith, Feldman, Nasserbakht, & Steiner, 1993). Halmi, Eckert, Marchi, Sampugnaro, Applea, and Cohen (1991) in a 10-year follow-up study found that their sample of adolescent and adult patients with anorexia nervosa also had anxiety disorders (34%), and affective disorders (29%). Other studies focusing on adolescent onset eating disorders have described similar results (Hsu, 1988; Toner, Garfinkel, & Garner, 1986). Among adults the results are similar, and in their own follow-up study of 47 women who were diagnosed with anorexia nervosa five to fourteen years earlier, Toner et al. (1988) concluded that:

(1)   affective and anxiety disorders developed frequently, regardless of the outcome of anorexia nervosa

(2)   major depression and anxiety disorders developed before the eating disorder in half and three-quarters of these cases, respectively

(3)   the symptomatic group (at follow-up) had a higher incidence of anxiety disorders prior to their eating disorder compared with the asymptomatic group.

These results continue to fuel the interest in the relationship between eating disorders and the other psychiatric conditions. Unfortunately, few studies are methodologically sound enough to determine the extent to which these relationships exist, let alone make reasonable guesses about them. Future researchers studying mental state must take into account long-standing recommendations to conduct prospective studies, use control groups, standardised interviews and rating scales, and explicitly defined criteria (Smith et al., 1993).

## Psychosexual adjustment

Psychosexual adjustment remains one of the most difficult aspects of outcome to measure. It is hard to define adequately, and even more difficult to quantify given that society's norms and attitudes in this area are subject to change. Also, some questions which attempt to measure psychosexual status can be particularly difficult for researchers to ask, and their participants to answer (Swift, 1982). Predictably, these problems are even more pronounced in the younger population and results for this age group are in very short supply.

With regard to early onset and adolescent eating disorders, Steinhausen and colleagues (1991) have noted that attitude toward sexuality, as well as sexual behaviour, varies considerably between studies. In one early onset study (mean age 12 years) 88% had a "poor" outcome in this area (Swift, 1982), although this may not necessarily the case due to the difficulties in determining "abnormal" sexual adjustment. Contrary to earlier findings, Bryant-Waugh and colleagues (1996), using a modified subscale of the Morgan-Russell outcome scales, found that 73.3% of their sample (mean age 12.1 years) were functioning well in this area. Gillberg et al. (1994) found that, generally, attitudes toward sexual matters were positive in their 51 cases with anorexia nervosa at follow-up, but significantly less so than a comparison group of sex-, age-, and school-matched subjects. Another study following 49 adolescents found no significant differences in sexual behaviours over time (Van der Ham et al., 1994). Ratnasuriya et al. (1991) found that, although their results were mixed, attitude toward sex was clearly related to a more global outcome, with those in the well-adjusted groups generally faring better in this area. None the less, it is clear that many practical and methodological shortcomings need to be addressed before meaningful observations can be made.

## Psychosocial functioning

Typically, three different areas of psychosocial functioning are measured in outcome studies: educational (level attained and attendance) and/or occupational (working/not working) achievement, relations with the family, and social relationships. Overall, functioning at follow-up is generally reported as good across age groups (Bryant-Waugh et al., 1988, 1996; Swift, 1982). In a recent follow-up study of 22 children with anorexia nervosa (mean age at onset 12.1 years) psychosocial functioning was found to be good in a particularly high number of cases (72.2%), whereas none were described as "poor" at three-year follow-up (Bryant-Waugh et al., 1996). Jarman et al. (1991) reported results in this area to be similar to the general population for the children and young adolescents in their study. Those who remain ill or have a poor outcome, however, may fare worse in each of the three areas (Gillberg et al., 1994). Also, there appears to be a distinction between educational/occupational achievement, and social/family relationships, with most subjects scoring slightly better on the former construct than on the latter (Swift, 1982), although this is not always the case.

In terms of employment, Ratnasuriya and colleagues (1991) reported that, at 20-year follow-up (mean age of onset 18 years), less than half of their former patients were employed, and that of the 13 single women only 4 were working. Garfinkel et al. (1977) reported that less than half of their follow-up sample were engaged in education or work on a regular and satisfying basis. Others report more optimistic results (Button et al., 1997). Perhaps because most eating disordered patients tend to be driven to succeed, many studies confirm that, on the whole, they are able to work and/or study acceptably, even when they are physically compromised to a significant degree (Yates, 1990; Smith et al., 1993; Swift, 1982).

Social relationships within and outside the family are more mixed. In a four-year follow-up of 49 eating disordered adolescents, Van der Ham et al. (1994) found significant improvements in family relations, increased independence, and friendships. The six-year follow-up of Smith and colleagues (1993) found good relationships with family and friends (73% and 66% respectively), and that there were no significant differences on psychosocial factors between those with or without psychiatric disorders. Others reporting on adolescents and adults, however, have noted particular difficulties when relating to the opposite sex, peers, and especially the family, with emancipation being of significant concern (Garfinkel et al., 1977; Gillberg et al., 1994; Ratnasuriya et al., 1991; Yates, 1990). Because of these results, it is perhaps no surprise that some consider psychosocial functioning to be "the most diverse and elusive outcome parameter to study" (Steinhausen et al., 1991).

## Mortality

Though results across outcome studies are highly variable with few discernible patterns, it is clearly evident that anorexia nervosa remains among the most damaging, and potentially fatal, of the psychiatric disorders. Reported mortality rates over the past few decades have ranged from 0% (Bryant-Waugh et al., 1996; Moller-Madsen, Nystrup, & Nielsen, 1996), to as high as 22% (Lucas, Duncan, & Piens, 1976) across age ranges. The primary causes of death related to anorexia nervosa are primarily reported as suicide and physical complications of the illness, especially malnutrition and electrolyte imbalance (Crisp, Callender, Halek, & Hsu, 1992; Swift, 1982). Unfortunately, there remain discrepancies in the reports of death among people with eating disorders, especially in regard to cause of death. Neumarker (1997) has called for more thorough investigation and reporting, particularly in those deaths with somatic causes.

Comparisons across differing populations provide a mixed picture. The few studies focusing on early onset eating disorders do not necessarily provide an optimistic account (Theander, 1988). In one seven-year follow-up study of 30 children with eating disorders (mean age 11.7 years, mean age at follow-up 20.8 years), Bryant-Waugh et al. (1988) reported two deaths, although one was not attributed to an eating disorder. In their prospective three-year follow-up study, Bryant-Waugh and colleagues (1996) reported no deaths in their sample of 22 children with anorexia nervosa. Van der Ham et al. (1994) suggest that the low mortality rate (0%) among their adolescent sample may have been due to their young age and less severe disturbance. However, others report mortality among their own adolescent cohorts to be above that expected (Steinhausen, 1995).

Reports of mortality rates among males do not appear to differ significantly from those of females (Burns & Crisp, 1984; Powers & Spratt, 1994), although samples of males with eating disorders are usually small. Of important note is the lack of follow-up data on mortality in those people with a primary diagnosis of bulimia nervosa. In their review of outcome in this disorder, Keel and Mitchell (1997) have cautiously suggested that deaths may be less common in bulimia nervosa than with anorexia nervosa, though they emphasise that short follow-up periods and incomplete accounting of subjects at follow-up may lead to the underestimation of mortality rates.

Perhaps equally disturbing are reports that a better short-term outcome in the course of the disorder does not necessarily lead to a lowered risk of death (Ratnasuriya et al., 1991), and that mortality increases with longer follow-up periods (Steinhausen et al., 1991; Theander, 1983). The highest mortality rates are reported in studies with long observation periods (Schwartz & Thompson, 1981). Hsu (1988) has suggested that those who continue to suffer from the illness at five years post-onset may be more likely to die, though not all support this premise. Tolstrup and colleagues (1985) found mortality rates to be fairly evenly distributed and cumulative over time.

Unfortunately, most studies continue to contain crude mortality rates (percentage of deaths in the sample studied) without comparisons to mortality rates in the general population matched for age, gender, and length of the follow-up period. Nielsen et al. (1998) have reviewed mortality in terms of a standardised mortality ratio, and found a statistically significant increase in deaths up to 15 years after presentation.

Despite the alarming results of many studies, it appears that, generally, crude mortality rates have decreased over the past decade to less than 5% (Steinhausen, 1995), which may be due to earlier and more comprehensive medical and therapeutic interventions (Crisp et al., 1992). None the less, definitive conclusions cannot be made, and optimism should be guarded for the time being; eating disorders remain serious and potentially lethal illnesses.

# PROGNOSIS

The ability of clinicians and researchers to make reasonable predictions of the course and outcome of illnesses given a set of patient attributes or symptoms is based on prognostic research. The search for prognostic indicators in eating disorders is most often rooted in outcome research, thus the same methodological problems found in outcome studies affect the quality of prognostic indicators as well. Despite a long and fierce search for predictive variables over the past several decades, the results are far from promising of good predictability or of good outcome (Theander, 1985), and no factors have been found to be consistently predictive of patient outcome (Herzog et al., 1993). Sohlberg, Norring, and Rosmark (1992, p. 121) go so far as to suggest that "perhaps prediction is inherently impossible". Hopefully this is not the case, and researchers will continue to present more methodologically sound data. Although results across studies are inconclusive, the most commonly studied prognostic variables, with a brief review, are now presented.

## Age

Age of onset is the most frequently examined prognostic factor. Some authors have claimed a younger age of onset to be predictive of better outcome (Frazier, 1965; Garfinkel et al., 1977; Halmi, Broadland, & Loney, 1973; Herzog, Keller, & Lavori, 1988; Lesser, Ashenden, Delruskey, & Eisenberg, 1960; Pierloot, Wellens, & Houben, 1975; Rowland, 1970; Seidensticker & Tzagournis, 1968; Theander, 1970; Thoma, 1967). In their 20-year follow-up of patients with anorexia nervosa, Ratnasuriya and colleagues (1991) found that of those with an onset of between 11 and 15 years of age, only two had a poor outcome. Eating disorders of late onset have been associated with poor outcome (Hsu & Crisp, 1979; Morgan & Russell, 1975; Steinhausen & Glanville, 1983; Theander, 1970).

Another host of studies have found no significant correlation between age of onset and outcome (Askevold, 1983; Browning & Miller, 1968; Bryant-Waugh et al., 1996; Hawley, 1985; Nussbaum, Shenkar, Baird, & Saravay, 1985; Steinhausen & Glanville, 1983; Tolstrup et al., 1985; Warren, 1968). Burns and Crisp (1984) also failed to find statistically significant results in their male patients. Dally (1969) found early onset of illness to be indicative of a poorer prognosis, and Bryant-Waugh and colleagues (1988) found less favourable results in those who were very young at the time of referral. Clearly there is a need for further study in this area.

## Gender

No studies have focused exclusively on the differences in outcome between males and females, and as yet this cannot be regarded as a reliable prognostic indicator. The lack of predictibility in this area is understandable. It is difficult enough to constitute large samples of females with eating disorders, and this problem is compounded in males, where they represent only about 10% of the eating disordered population. In the one study that did evaluate outcome in males, no significant differences were highlighted (Burns & Crisp, 1984).

## Family functioning

Another area of considerable interest is the level of family functioning as a prognostic indicator. It seems logical to speculate that poor family relationships may significantly affect any one of its members' psychological health. Though no causal links have been confirmed, there seems to be a fair degree of association between morbid family functioning and poor prognosis among those with anorexia nervosa regardless of age, as reported in many studies (Burns & Crisp, 1984; Ratnasuriya et al., 1991; Steinhausen, 1995), although not all researchers have been unanimous regarding these findings (Askevold, 1983).

In early onset anorexia nervosa, Bryant Waugh and colleagues (1988) found that an anomalous family structure is predictive of a poorer outcome. In another study of 35 children and young adolescents with anorexia nervosa, North, Gowers, and Byram (1997) found that good outcome was associated with better family functioning at assessment, in the judgements of the adolescent and clinician; however, the mothers' subjective impressions were not predictive of outcome. In a follow-up study of 100 adolescent and adult patients (mean 20.8 years) with eating disorders, Hsu and Crisp (1979) found that both a disturbed relationship with parents, and a poor relationship between parents, was associated with a poor outcome. In another sample, participants perceived poor mutual understanding, failure to comprehend empathically with others' feelings, and generally poor functioning among their families (Hoberman & Kroll-Mensing, 1992). In a large survey of over 600 American high school students, those who diet excessively, vomit, or use other extreme methods to control weight experienced lower perceived emotional bonding and greater psychological distress in their families. Among females, overprotection, lower maternal care, and a generally less cohesive family were predictive of binge eating (Wertheim, Paxton, Mavde, Szmukler, Gibbons, & Hiller, 1992). Although more research is required to make more meaningful statements regarding these relationships, it is evident that a conflictual family environment negatively affects prognosis in those with eating disordered symptomology.

## Continuing eating disorder symptoms and effect on outcome

The symptoms of dieting, binge eating, and purging behaviours have been found to be predictive of outcome in many (Garfinkel et al., 1977) but not all studies (Sohlberg et al., 1992). In two reviews of outcome studies, Theander (1983) and Steinhausen et al. (1991) have reported extreme weight loss, bulimia, and purging behaviours, and a chronic eating disorder to be associated with a poorer long-term outcome, and many other authors have reported similar finding in these areas to varying degrees (Ratnasuriya et al., 1991). In a related topic, Baran, Weltzin, and Kaye (1995) have suggested that patients with anorexia nervosa, who are discharged from treatment while still severely underweight, are more likely to exhibit poor mood and morbid eating behaviours, leading to an increased likelihood of rehospitalisation. Although these findings may seem outwardly obvious, continued observations of this kind are important in an age when there is increased pressure to reduce lengths of treatment. In the long run, premature termination of treatment may prove more detrimental and costly than currently thought.

## TREATMENT FACTORS ASSOCIATED WITH OUTCOME

There are a wide variety of approaches to the treatment of eating disorders. This is no surprise given the massive variety and variability of factors at play. Numerous decisions must be made with regard to point of intervention, treatment settings, lengths of stay, and types of treatment intervention such as pharmacological, psychotherapeutic, and general management. Unfortunately, evidence is still lacking in most areas which might guide these decisions, especially for anorexia nervosa (Pike, Loeb, & Vitousek, 1996). This is particularly the case in the childhood onset age group. Many have assumed that eating disorders in children constitute a less severe variant than that experienced in the older population, thus perhaps making them more amenable to treatment and predisposing them to a generally better outcome. Whatever the truth may be, it is important to note that no randomised, controlled treatment trials have been aimed specifically at the childhood onset age group; therefore caution should continue to be exercised when generalising about this population.

With regard to time of intervention, most believe that the sooner treatment is received the better, and many authors have called for screening of at-risk populations in order that cases may be identified earlier. However, in an extensive review of both the early and later onset outcome literature, Schoemaker (1997) concluded that, due to the extensive methodological shortcomings in outcome research, there exists no solid evidence to support the idea that early intervention significantly affects the course of eating disorders.

Treatment settings most appropriate for eating disorder patients have also been the focus of research. For the most part, patients are assigned to inpatient, daypatient, or outpatient status according to severity and complexity of symptoms, wishes of the patient and/or the family, and availability of resources. However, the need for inpatient treatment has been questioned altogether, even in those patients who are severely underweight. Freeman and Newton (1992) have argued that intervention at such a level is unnecessary, and that there are no significant differences in outcome when inpatients are compared to daypatients. They also claim that daypatient treatment has the added benefit of instilling a greater sense of control over eating behaviour in patients. Whatever setting is chosen for a particular patient, it is not known which is most effective for whom under any given set of conditions, and research comparing various settings is still lacking (Gowers, Norton, Halek, & Crisp, 1994).

Management factors related to outcome are inconclusive. Most of these are aimed at weight gain and normalisation of eating behaviours, and though often successful in the short term, long-term gains are not in evidence, and it seems that weight gain alone is not an effective intervention when specifically evaluated, in this case, in the older onset age groups (Gowers et al., 1994; Russell, 1977).

Psychopharmacological interventions, although effective in dealing with some bulimic symptoms, have not been found effective in anorexia nervosa, with most results either mixed or poor (Herzog, Keller, Strober, Yeh, & Pai, 1992).

Psychological interventions are the most commonly used of all treatment for eating disorders, and the most intensively evaluated. The picture of therapeutically effective treatments for bulimia nervosa is relatively less blurred than that of anorexia nervosa, but even so it is far from clear.

Most studies evaluating treatment efficacy contain poor if any detailed descriptions of how therapy was conducted, making it notoriously difficult to replicate conditions. Even where results do suggest a specific form of therapy, there continues to be little consensus of how best to treat eating disorders (Herzog et al., 1992). Often, the therapeutic approach taken is determined more by opinion and the therapist's theoretical alliance than by research findings. Until the research and practice issues are more consistently and comprehensively addressed, it seems that for many eating disorder patients recovery will be determined largely by the patients themselves.

## Treatment effects associated with positive outcome

Despite the somewhat gloomy picture, there are some treatment factors which seem to have a positive impact on both general and specific aspects of eating disordered psychopathology. In anorexia nervosa, where the few randomised, controlled studies have been conducted, results are still far from conclusive, although worthy of note. In one study, family therapy was compared to "supportive" individual therapy in a group of former inpatients with anorexia nervosa. At a follow-up of one year, family therapy was found superior for those patients whose onset of illness was 18 years of age or earlier, with a duration of three years or less (Russell, Szmukler, Dare, & Eisler, 1987). Another study compared conjoint family therapy, where the entire family was seen together, and family counselling, where only the parents were seen and given advice on how best to manage their child. The authors found no significant differences between the two interventions, suggesting that further research should focus on the elements of these approaches necessary for change (Le Grange, Eisler, Dare, & Russell, 1992).

Others have found a multidisciplinary approach effective. Hall and Crisp (1987) combined individual and family therapy with dietary advice and found significant improvements in their patients at one-year follow-up. Another combined approach including cognitive, behavioural, and psychodynamic elements produced significant improvement in weight gain, menstrual functioning, and psychosocial functioning at one-year follow-up. At two years many improvements were maintained (Gowers et al., 1994). Strober et al. (1997), however, have pointed out that full recovery after two years post-hospitalisation is rare, but that among their sample of 95 adolescents three-quarters were free of eating disorder symptoms at 10–15 years after initial presentation. Crisp and colleagues (1991), in a controlled treatment study of 90 patients with anorexia nervosa also found a behavioural approach to diet and weight gain combined with family and individual therapy to be significantly effective. It seems that the most prudent approach to a multifaceted, multidetermined disorder such as anorexia nervosa, is a multidimensional one.

With regard to bulimia nervosa practically all studies have focused on adolescent or adult onset. It is widely acknowledged that the disorder is extremely rare among the pre-pubertal population (Kent, Lacey, & McCluskey, 1992). The treatment effects are much more clearly understood, despite it being defined as a distinct clinical entity as late as 1979.

Cognitive behavioural therapy (CBT) has been rigorously evaluated and found to be the treatment of choice for bulimia nervosa, and results are consistently replicated across studies (Pike et al., 1996). Controlled studies have shown significant reductions in binge eating (mean range of 73–93%), purging (77–94%), and remission rates are similar; attitudes toward weight and shape are also found to improve (Pike et al., 1996). This equals or outperforms control conditions and most other therapies with regard to improving bingeing and purging frequency, attitudes to shape and eating, and general psychological functioning. Antidepressants are also effective in dealing with bulimic and depressive symptoms and, when combined with CBT, incremental effects may be achieved (Fairburn, 1993; Pike et al., 1996). Interpersonal therapy (IPT) has also been recommended for the treatment of bulimia nervosa, the benefits of which take place over time and in many areas, and may be a particularly attractive approach for those who do not respond to CBT (Fairburn, 1993). Positive treatment effects have also been found using group therapy, and self-help groups (Herzog et al., 1992; Rathner, Bonsch, Maurer, Walter, & Sollner, 1993).

In a more general sense, counselling/psychotherapy can be useful for anorectic, bulimic, and co-morbid symptoms such as depression, anxiety, and obsessions and compulsions, and effects can be realised in a relatively short period of time. Several patient characteristics have been identified that seem to be associated with better outcomes, though whether these differ significantly between age groups is not known. These include lesser severity of the illness and shorter duration, lesser complexity of the presenting symptoms or comorbidity, motivation for change, lack of active defence operations, and the acceptance of personal responsibility for change (Lamert & Cattani-Thompson, 1996). Beside patient variables, which are of prime importance, the therapist factors that are related to better outcomes in all age groups are primarily relational in nature, and include empathy, respect for the patient, and collaboration (Lamert & Cattani-Thompson, 1996). Finally, but perhaps most importantly, are the factors which are perceived as most helpful by the patients (Hsu, Crisp, & Callender, 1992). These included will-power or personality strength, leaving a destructive environment, being "fed up" with the illness, and faith. These concepts eloquently highlight the very human side of eating disorders, and emphasise what is of most importance in relation to research and treatment—the person.

## CONCLUSIONS

It is clear that there is a relative shortage of information about the outcome and prognosis of early onset eating disorders. Consequently, significant differences between age groups are no more apparent than within groups. At present, for the most part no definitive conclusions may be drawn concerning their course or outcome, and results between studies are often contradictory. In anorexia nervosa especially, little is known about what treatment elements are most effective. Unfortunately, what remains quite clear about eating disorders in all age groups is that they represent the severe end of psychiatric morbidity, having an adverse impact in virtually all areas of life, and not infrequently leading to a premature death.

Amidst this pessimistic account, however, there exists some hope. On the whole, more recent researchers have attempted to heed the advice of those who have gone before. Diagnostic criteria, although by no means perfect and under continual criticism and revision, have been formalised to the point where comparisons between studies are more practical. More randomised, controlled studies have emerged, as have prospective approaches to data collection. Treatment for bulimia nervosa is better understood in terms of efficacy and type, despite its more recent identification as a distinct eating disorder. Finally, it is important to note that research into eating disorders is in its relative infancy when compared to other psychiatric conditions. With continued interest, dedication, and effort, the boundaries of our current knowledge will undoubtedly be breached, hopefully with the end result of a more robust and optimistic account of the course, treatment, and outcome.

## SUMMARY POINTS

- Outcome is defined as the long-term result of a pathological process. Prognosis is defined as the means to make a forecast or a prediction as to the probable further course and the final outcome of the disease. Despite concerted efforts over several decades, a comprehensive understanding of the outcome and prognosis of eating disorders remains elusive.
- Most studies that have focused on the outcome and prognosis of eating disorders suffer from methodological shortcomings. More recent studies, however, have more closely followed the available guidelines for conducting such research.
- Not enough data has been collected to make differential conclusions regarding the various age groups presenting with eating disorders.
- Outcome in terms of weight and nutritional status is generally positive in all age groups, including those with an early onset of anorexia nervosa.
- Measures of the outcome of eating difficulties, concerns about weight and shape, and continuing eating disorder have produced disappointing results.
- Results of outcome measures focusing on growth and development, menstrual functioning, mental state, and psychosexual functioning are largely mixed, primarily due to the difficulties in assessing such variables.
- Psychosocial functioning is generally reported as good at follow-up across age groups.
- Anorexia nervosa remains among the most fatal of psychiatric illnesses, with mortality rates as high as 22% in some samples, although reports are highly variable. Mortality rates in the younger age onset group is similar to that of other age groups.
- Variables predictive of the outcome of early onset eating disorders have been sought, although results are mixed.
- Age and gender have not been found to be predictive of outcome, thought due to methodological difficulties the results are not conclusive.
- There seems to be a fair degree of association between morbid family functioning and poor prognosis among those with anorexia nervosa, regardless of age.
- No specific treatment factors have been demonstrated to be consistently effective for anorexia nervosa, including the younger age onset groups.
- Some positive treatment effects have been observed using family therapy, family counselling where parents are given advice regarding the management of their child, and multidisciplinary approaches, although results are far from conclusive.

- Both cognitive-behavioural therapy and interpersonal therapy are useful in the treatment of bulimia nervosa, and results are generally consistent across studies.
- Though on the surface pessimistic, more recent advances in research methodology and adherence to this, operationally defined diagnostic criteria, and therapeutic approaches have given cause for more hope in the understanding and treatment of early onset eating disorders.

# REFERENCES

American Psychiatric Association. (1994). *Diagnostic and statistical manual of mental disorders* (4th ed. Rev.). Washington, DC: Author.

Askevold, F. (1983). What are the helpful factors in psychotherapy for anorexia nervosa? *International Journal of Eating Disorders*, *2*(4), 193–197.

Baran, S.A., Weltzin, T.E., & Kaye, W.H. (1995). Low discharge weight and outcome in anorexia nervosa. *American Journal of Psychiatry*, *152*, 1070–1072.

Browning, C.H., & Miller, S.I. (1968). Anorexia nervosa: A study in prognosis and management. *American Journal of Psychiatry*, *124*, 1128–1132.

Bryant-Waugh, R., Hankins, M., Shafran, R., Lask, B., & Fosson, A. (1996). A prospective follow-up of children with anorexia nervosa. *Journal of Youth and Adolescence*, *25*(4), 431–437.

Bryant-Waugh, R., Knibbs, J., Fosson, A., Kaminski, Z., & Lask, B. (1988). Long-term follow-up of patients with early onset anorexia nervosa. *Archives of Disease in Childhood*, *63*, 5–9.

Burns, T., & Crisp, A.H. (1984). Outcome of anorexia nervosa in males. *British Journal of Psychiatry*, *145*, 319–325.

Button, E.J., Marshall, P., Shinkwin, R., Black, S.H., & Palmer, R.L. (1997). One hundred referrals to an eating disorders service: Progress and service consumption over a 2–4 year period. *European Eating Disorders Review*, *5*(1), 47–63.

Crisp, A.H., Callender, J.S., Halek, C., & Hsu, L.K.G. (1992). Long-term mortality in anorexia nervosa. *British Journal of Psychiatry*, *161*, 104–107.

Crisp, A.H., Norton, K., Gowers, S., Halek, C., Bowyer, C., Yelham, D., Levett, D., & Bhat, A. (1991). A controlled study of the effect of therapies aimed at adolescent and family psychopathology in anorexia nervosa. *British Journal of Psychiatry*, *159*, 325–333.

Dally, P. (1969). *Anorexia nervosa*. New York: Grune & Stratton.

Danziger, Y., Mukamel, M., Zeharia, A., Dinari, G., & Mimouni, M. (1994). Stunting of growth in anorexia nervosa during the prepubertal and pubertal period. *Israeli Journal of Medical Science*, *30*, 581–584.

Dreizen, S., Spirakis, C.N., & Stone, R.E. (1967). A comparison of skeletal growth and maturation in undernourished and well-nourished girls before and after menarche. *Journal of Paediatrics*, *70*(2), 256–263.

Fairburn, C.G. (1993). Interpersonal psychotherapy for bulimia nervosa. In G.L. Klerman & M.M. Weissman (Eds.), *New applications of interpersonal psychotherapy* (pp. 353–378). Washington, DC: American Psychiatric Press.

Frazier, S.H. (1965). Anorexia. *Diseases of the Nervous System*, *26*, 155–159.

Freeman, C.P., & Newton, J.R. (1992). Anorexia nervosa: What treatments are most effective? In K. Hawton & P. Cowen, *Practical problems in clinical psychiatry* (pp. 77–92). Oxford, UK: Oxford University Press.

Garfinkel, P.E., Moldofsky, H., & Garner, D.M. (1977). The outcome of anorexia nervosa: Significance of clinical features, body image, and behavior modification. In R.A. Vigersky (Ed.), *Anorexia nervosa* (pp. 315–329). New York: Raven Press.

Garner, D.M. (1987). Psychotherapy outcome research with bulimia nervosa. *Psychotherapy and Psychometrics*, *48*, 129–140.

Gillberg, I.C., Rastam, M., & Gillberg, C. (1994). Anorexia nervosa outcome: Six-year controlled longitudinal study of 51 cases including a population cohort. *Journal of the American Academy of Child and Adolescent Psychiatry*, *33*(5), 729–739.

Golden, N.H., Kreitzer, P., Jacobson, M.S., Chasalow, F.I., Schebendach, J., Freedman, S.M., & Shenker, I.R. (1994). *Journal of Pediatrics*, *125*, 655–660.

Gowers, S., Norton, K., Halek, C., & Crisp, A.H. (1994). Outcome of outpatient psychotherapy in a random allocation treatment study of anorexia nervosa. *International Journal of Eating Disorders*, *15*(2), 165–177.

Hall, A., & Crisp, A. (1987). Brief psychotherapy in the treatment of anorexia nervosa: Outcome at one year. *British Journal of Psychiatry*, *151*, 185–191.

Halmi, K., Broadland, G., & Loney, J. (1973). Prognosis in anorexia nervosa. *International Medicine*, *78*, 907–909.

Halmi, K., Eckert, E., Marchi, P., Sampugnaro, V., Applea, R., & Cohen, J. (1991). Comorbidity of psychiatric diagnoses in anorexia nervosa. *Archives of General Psychiatry*, *48*, 712–718.

Hawley, R.M. (1985). The outcome of anorexia nervosa in younger subjects. *British Journal of Psychiatry*, *146*, 657–660.

Herzog, D.B., Keller, M.B., & Lavori, P. (1988). Outcome in anorexia and bulimia nervosa: A review of the literature. *Journal of Nervous Mental Disorders*, *176*, 131–143.

Herzog, D.B., Keller, M.B., Strober, M., Yeh, C., & Pai, S.Y. (1992). The current status of treatment for anorexia nervosa and bulimia nervosa. *International Journal of Eating Disorders*, *12*(2), 215–220.

Herzog, D.B., Sacks, N.R., Keller, M.B., Lavori, P.W., VonRanson, K.B., & Gray, H.M. (1993). Patterns and predictors of recovery in anorexia nervosa and bulimia nervosa. *Journal of the Academy of Child and Adolescent Psychiatry*, *32*, 835–842.

Hoberman, H.M., & Kroll-Mensing, D. (1992). Adolescent eating disorders. *Current Opinion in Psychiatry*, *5*, 523–534.

Hsu, L.K.G. (1988). The outcome of anorexia nervosa: A reappraisal. *Psychological Medicine*, *18*, 807–812.

Hsu, L.K.G. (1990). *Eating disorders*. New York: Guilford Press.

Hsu, L.K.G., & Crisp, A.H. (1979). Outcome of anorexia nervosa. *The Lancet*.

Hsu, L.K.G., Crisp, A.H., & Callender, J.S. (1992). Recovery in anorexia nervosa—the patient's perspective. *International Journal of Eating Disorders*, *11*(4), 341–350.

Jarman, F.C., Rickards, W.S., & Hudson, I.L. (1991). Late adolescent outcome of early onset anorexia nervosa. *Journal of Paediatric Child Health*, *27*, 221–227.

Keel, P.K., & Mitchell, J.E. (1997). Outcome in bulimia nervosa. *American Journal of Psychiatry*, *154*, 313–321.

Kent, A., Lacey, H., & McCluskey, J.E. (1992). Pre-menarchal bulimia nervosa. *Journal of Psychosomatic Research*, *36*(3), 205–210.

Lai, K.Y., deBruyn, R., Lask, B., Bryant-Waugh, R., & Hankins, M. (1994). Use of pelvic ultrasound to monitor ovarian and uterine maturity in childhood onset anorexia nervosa. *Archives of Disease in Childhood*, *71*, 228–231.

Lamert, M.J., & Cattani-Thompson, K. (1996). Current findings regarding the effectiveness of counseling: Implications for practice. *Journal of Counseling and Development*, *74*, 601–608.

Le Grange, D., Eisler, I., Dare, C., & Russell, G.F.M. (1992). Evaluation of family treatments in adolescent anorexia nervosa: A pilot study. *International Journal of Eating Disorders*, *12*(4), 347–357.

Lesser, L.I., Ashenden, B.J., Delruskey, M., & Eisenberg, L. (1960). Anorexia nervosa in children. *American Journal of Diseases in Children*, *143*, 1322–1327.

Lucas, A., Duncan, J.W., & Piens, V. (1976). The treatment of anorexia nervosa. *American Journal of Psychiatry*, *133*, 1034–1038.

Moller-Madsen, S., Nystrup, J., & Nielsen, S. (1996). Mortality in anorexia nervosa in Denmark during the period 1970–1987. *Acta Psychiatrica Scandinavica*, *94*, 454–459.

Morgan, H.G., & Russell, G.F.M. (1975). Value of family background and clinical features as predictors of long-term outcome in anorexia nervosa: Four year follow-up of 41 patients. *Psychological Medicine*, *5*, 355–371.

Nussbaum, M., Shenker, I.R., Baird, D., & Saravay, S. (1985). Follow-up investigation in patients with anorexia nervosa. *Journal of Pediatrics*, *106*, 835–840.

Neumarker, K. (1997). Mortality and sudden death in anorexia nervosa. *International Journal of Eating Disorders*, *21*, 205–212.

Nielsen, S., Moller-Madsen, S., Isager, T., Jorgensen, J., Pagsberg, K., & Theander, S. (1998). Standardised mortality ratios in eating disorders. *Journal of Psychosomatic Research*, *44*, 413–434.

North, C., Gowers, S., & Byram, V. (1997). Family functioning and life events in the outcome of adolescent anorexia nervosa. *British Journal of Psychiatry*, *171*, 545–549.

Patton, G. (1988). Mortality in eating disorders. *Psychological Medicine*, *18*, 947–951.

Pfeiffer, R.J., Lucas, A.R., & Ilstrup, D.M. (1986). Effect of anorexia nervosa on linear growth. *Clinical Pediatrics*, *25*(1), 7–12.

Pierloot, R.A., Wellens, W., & Houben, M.B. (1975). Elements of resistance to a combined medical and psychotherapeutic program in anorexia nervosa. *Psychotherapy and Psychosomatics*, *26*, 101–117.

Pike, K.M., Loeb, K., & Vitousek, K. (1996). Cognitive-behavioural therapy for anorexia nervosa and bulimia nervosa. In K. Thompson (Ed.), *Body image, eating disorders, and obesity* (pp. 253–302). Washington, DC: American Psychological Association Press.

Powers, P.S., & Spratt, E.G. (1994). Males and females with eating disorders. *Eating Disorders*, *2*(3), 197–214.

Rathner, G., Bonsch, C., Maurer, G., Walter, M.H., & Sollner, W. (1993). The impact of a "guided self-help group" on bulimic women: A prospective 15 months study of attenders and non-attenders. *Journal of Psychosomatic Research*, *37*(4), 389–396.

Ratnasuriya, R.H., Eisler, I., Szmukler, G.I., & Russell, G.F.M. (1991). Anorexia nervosa: Outcome and prognostic factors after 20 years. *British Journal of Psychiatry*, *158*, 495–502.

Rowland, C.F. (1970). Anorexia nervosa—a survey of the literature and review of thirty cases. *International Journal of Psychiatry Clinics*, *7*, 37–137.

Russell, G.F.M. (1977). General management of anorexia nervosa and difficulties in assessing the efficacy of treatment. In R.A. Vigersky (Ed.), *Anorexia nervosa* (pp. 277–289). New York: Raven Press.

Russell, G.F.M., Szmukler, G.I., Dare, C., & Eisler, I. (1987). An evaluation of family therapy in anorexia nervosa and bulimia nervosa. *Archives of General Psychiatry*, *44*, 1047–1056.

Schoemaker, C. (1997). Does early intervention improve the prognosis in anorexia nervosa? A systematic review of the treatment-outcome literature. *International Journal of Eating Disorders*, *21*(1), 1–15.

Schwartz, D.M., & Thompson, M.G. (1981). Do anorectics get well? Current research and future needs. *American Journal of Psychiatry*, *138*(3), 319–323.

Seidensticker, J.R.F., & Tzagournis, M. (1968). Anorexia nervosa—clinical features and long term follow-up. *Journal of Chronic Disorders*, *21*, 361–367.

Smith, C., Feldman, S.S., Nasserbakht, A., & Steiner, H. (1993). Psychological characteristics and DSM-III-R diagnoses at 6-year follow-up of adolescent anorexia nervosa. *Journal of the American Academy of Child and Adolescent Psychiatry*, *32*, 1237–1245.

Sohlberg, S.S., Norring, C.E.A., & Rosmark, B.E. (1992). Prediction of the course of anorexia nervosa/bulimia nervosa over three years. *International Journal of Eating Disorders, 12*(2), 121–131.

Steinhausen, H.C. (1995). Treatment and outcome of adolescent anorexia nervosa. *HORMRES, 43*, 168–170.

Steinhausen, H.C., & Glanville, K. (1983). Follow-up studies of anorexia nervosa: A review of research findings. *Psychological Medicine, 13*, 239–249.

Steinhausen, H.C., Rauss-Mason, C., & Seidel, R. (1991). Follow-up studies of anorexia nervosa: A review of four decades of outcome research. *Psychological Medicine, 21*, 447–454.

Strober, M., Freeman, R., & Morrell, W. (1997). The long-term course of severe anorexia nervosa in adolescents: Survival analysis of recovery, relapse, and outcome predictors over 10–15 years in a prospective study. *International Journal of Eating Disorders, 22*, 339–360.

Swift, W.J. (1982). The long-term outcome of early onset anorexia nervosa: A critical review. *Journal of the American Academy of Child Psychiatry, 21*, 38–46.

Theander, S. (1970). Anorexia nervosa: A psychiatric investigation of 94 female patients. *Acta Psychiatrica Scandinavica* (Suppl. 214).

Theander, S. (1983). Research on outcome and prognosis of anorexia nervosa and some results from a Swedish long-term study. *International Journal of Eating Disorders, 2*(4), 168–174.

Theander, S. (1985). Outcome and prognosis in anorexia nervosa and bulimia: Some results of previous investigations, compared with those of a Swedish long-term study. *Journal of Psychiatric Research, 19*(2/3), 493–508.

Theander, S. (1988). Outcome and prognosis in anorexia nervosa with an early age of onset. In D. Hardof & E. Chigier (Eds.), *Eating disorders in adolescents and young adults: An international perspective.* London: Freund Publishing House.

Thoma, H. (1967). *Anorexia nervosa.* New York: International Universities Press.

Tolstrup, K., Brinch, M., Isager, T., Nielsen, S., Nystrup, J., Severin, B., & Olesen, N.S. (1985). Long-term outcome of 151 cases of anorexia nervosa. *Acta Psychiatrica Scandinavica, 71*, 380–387.

Toner, B.B., Garfinkel, P.E., & Garner, D.M. (1986). Long-term follow-up of anorexia nervosa. *Psychosomatic Medicine, 48*, 520–529.

Toner, B.B., Garfinkel, P.E., & Garner, D.M. (1988). Affective and anxiety disorders in the long-term follow-up of anorexia nervosa. *International Journal of Psychiatry in Medicine, 18*(4), 357–364.

Van der Ham, T., Van Strien, D.C., & Van Engeland, H. (1994). A four-year prospective follow-up study of 49 eating-disordered adolescents: Differences in course of illness. *Acta Psychiatrica Scandinavica, 90*, 229–235.

Van Strien, D.C., Van der Ham, T., & Van Engeland, H. (1992). Dropout characteristics in a follow-up study of 90 eating-disordered patients. *International Journal of Eating Disorders, 12*(4), 341–343.

Warren, W. (1968). A study of anorexia nervosa in young girls. *Journal of Child Psychology and Psychiatry, 9*, 27–40.

Wertheim, E.H., Paxton, S.J., Mavde, S.J., Szmukler, G.I., Gibbons, K., & Hiller, L. (1992). Psychosocial predictors of weight loss behaviours and binge eating in adolescent girls and boys. *International Journal of Eating Disorders, 12*(2), 151–160.

Yates, A. (1990). Current perspectives on the eating disorders: II. Treatment, outcome, and research directions. *Journal of the American Academy of Child and Adolescent Psychiatry, 29*(6), 1–9.

# PART THREE

# Assessment and treatment

# CHAPTER SEVEN

# Assessment

**Deborah Christie**
*Middlesex Hospital, London, UK*

**Beth Watkins and Bryan Lask**
*St George's Hospital Medical School, London, UK, and*
*Huntercombe Manor Hospital, Taplow, UK*

> *No breakfast had she many a morn,*
> *No dinner many a noon,*
> *And 'stead of supper she would stare*
> *Full hard against the moon.*
>
> —Keats, *Meg Merrilies*

## INTRODUCTION

An eating disorder sentences its victim to a slow, relentless decline in health and well-being. Restricted or chaotic eating are justified and weight loss is disguised until the deceit is discovered. The shock of finally seeing their perhaps skeletal child or finding evidence of vomiting jolts confused and distressed parents to seek help from professionals. Although it is the child who appears to be the central figure, the parents have a critical role in helping the treatment team understand the development of the problem. In this chapter we describe the assessment of the family and the child and provide, as an Appendix, details of existing standardised measures and interviews that can be used for children and adolescents with eating disorders.

## FAMILY ASSESSMENT

This is a crucial component of a complete assessment. The aim is to evaluate not only whether there may have been contributory factors to the child's illness, but much more importantly whether any aspects of family functioning are perpetuating the problem. Usually there are, and these will be far more accessible to change than anything that has happened in the past. It is useful to obtain a family history and details of family eating and dieting behaviour as these may have contributed or be contributing to the current problem. Family assessment aims to explore both past and present issues, but of course with subtlety. It is achieved partly through observing the relationships between all family members, particularly focusing on the quality of interaction between each person. Although the focus invariably drifts toward the child with the eating disorder, a proper assessment takes into account not only the quality of the parental and marital subsystem and the integrity of the generational boundaries but also the general atmosphere of the family, the family's affective responses, the communication processes, and the degree of autonomy afforded each person. It is important to consider the family strengths as well as weaknesses. Areas for consideration include cohesion, adaptability and flexibility, hardiness and resilience, and problem-solving.

We find it to be most helpful to meet with the whole family. We try to meet with the family in a comfortable room, suitably furnished and equipped with drawing materials and age-appropriate toys. Family members are invited to take whichever seats they wish and how they do this often provides useful information. Commonly the child with the eating disorder is seated between her parents, sometimes particularly close to one parent. Sitting between the parents might indicate that she is acting as a buffer between them, a detour of conflict, or that she has a significant amount of control, or that she is the centre of concerned attention. Unusually, she may sit on the edge of the family, hunched up and withdrawn, and clearly peripheral.

## The quality of the parental relationship

This is of particular significance. It is important to distinguish here between the parental and the marital relationship. The former has the task of working together to care for the children, whereas the latter has the task of caring for each other. It is quite possible for parents to work well together as parents even if they do not get on so well in their own marital relationship. The therapist's priority must be to help the parents look after their daughter, not to attempt to repair a problematic marriage.

Ideally, parents have a close relationship characterised by mutual respect and affection. They are able to work together in the best interests of their children, being consistent both between each other and over a period of time. There are clearly defined generational boundaries and the parents are able to identify problems and conflicts, and discuss and resolve them. They make decisions in agreement with each other and take charge of family rules. They communicate openly and directly, and acknowledge and accept each other's feelings.

Such features represent an ideal and of course rarely all occur. More commonly parents of children with eating disorders will be in conflict about the management of the problem. Even if previously they did have a good relationship, the anxieties induced by the illness tend to create conflict. Sometimes there has been pre-existing conflict and the child acts as a buffer between them, or gives them a common focus, a cause for shared concern. Most commonly one parent will want to take one particular approach to managing the illness whereas the other parent wants to do something quite different. Even if they can agree what to do at any particular moment, rarely are they able to remain consistent between each other and over a period of time. One parent may assume responsibility for helping the child recover and the other then feels undermined. For example, a father may adopt a quite coercive approach, from which the mother may wish to protect her daughter. He becomes irritated and frustrated by his wife's lack of support. Alternatively, the mother may herself have some difficulties with body image and not want her daughter to put on too much weight. Her husband's anxieties about his daughter are ignored and he withdraws. Both mother and daughter then perceive him as uninterested.

## Boundaries

An integral part of the family assessment relates to the boundaries or space between individuals. Individual space is an essential part of being and we all need space around us. All relationships vary along a continuum from over-involved to distant. Extreme closeness between a parent and very young child is quite appropriate. However, this should change as the child matures, with increasing autonomy to the point that by the late teenage years the young person is relatively independent. In some families who have a child with an eating disorder this does not always occur, and the child and one parent remain "over" close. These examples of dysfunctional parental relationships commonly lead to abnormalities of generational boundaries, with the child being caught between the parents or over-involvement of one parent and distancing of the other.

> Lucy, 13, had always been closer to her mother than her father. This was exacerbated by the recent onset of anorexia nervosa. Mother complained bitterly that father was not sufficiently supportive, whereas father replied that his wife took unilateral decisions, never consulted him, and he felt undermined. This split was highlighted when mother asked for an emergency consultation and father failed to attend as he was playing golf.

## The family atmosphere

This refers to the feelings experienced by the therapist when with the family. These can vary from warmth to hostility, calmness to tension, caring and empathy to indifference and even dislike. The therapist's reaction to the family is often a reflection of what family members are experiencing themselves. Attention is paid to such features as whether or not it appears safe for family members to express their views and have their views respected; whether or not differences of opinion can be expressed and resolved, problems solved, and decisions made.

## Affective status and responsiveness

Closely linked to the family atmosphere is the affective status and responsiveness of each family member. The therapist notes the general mood of each person, e.g. sad, anxious, angry, resentful, the ability to express those feelings, and the responses of other family members. Thus, a parent may appear to be angry but unable to show this overtly. Alternatively, the anger may be overt but ignored by the other parent, or attempts made to divert or dilute the anger. This would be in contrast to a clear expression, acknowledgement, and acceptance of the anger. The same applies to any such feelings. All too often in such families, feelings are denied, ignored, denigrated, or dismissed.

## Communication processes

The aim of communication is to convey and receive information. We communicate in many different ways, most of which are effective. However, as with emotional expression and responsiveness, much can go wrong. In some families there is rather inhibited communication with little being said, prolonged periods of silence, and failure to respond to what is said. At the other extreme are families in which there is excessive communication, where there is little silence and much noise, frequent interruptions, a failure to listen to each other, and long statements, the full meaning of which are difficult to grasp. Communications are sometimes non-congruent, i.e. there is a discrepancy between what is said and how it is conveyed. For example, a family member may make an angry statement but deny the anger, or conceal it with a smile. Alternatively, something may be said that is later denied or contradicted. Sometimes thought and feelings are expressed by behaviour or physical symptoms rather than through words. This is particularly so in young people with eating disorders. Their ability to convey negative feelings and thoughts seems to be quite restricted and these are often concealed by the eating difficulties. Occasionally families have quite a distorted communication pattern. For example, all communications are channelled through one person rather like a switchboard operator; or one person assumes (or is convinced) that they know exactly what others are thinking or feeling (as if they are mind readers) and speak for them; or communications are so vague or nebulous that the intended message is never understood.

## Siblings

Siblings often play an important but unacknowledged part in the family struggle with the eating disorder. It is always worth meeting the siblings and ascertaining their views of the family and the eating disorder. Their contribution can be both positive and negative.

John, 10, mercilessly mocked the attempts of his sister, Emma, 13, to lose weight, frequently calling her "fatty".

Evelyn, 14, bitterly resented the apparent ease with which her sister Julie, 15, made friends and attributed this to her (Evelyn) being overweight.

Brian, 18, was much taller and stronger than William, 14, who was a short and thin selective eater. They had frequent arguments, which usually ended with Brian hitting William, who in turn would complain to his parents. However, Brian being far more mature was also more credible, and his parents tended to believe his account and blame William. He seemed to accept the role of scapegoat.

An important component of the anorexia nervosa from which Nassrin, 14, suffered was her fear of her father's anger and violence. She had been unable to mention this previously. In the family assessment, when the therapist asked her sister, Leila, 18, what she thought were Nassrin's concerns, Leila responded by describing her father's stress and anger. From this point on Nassrin was able to say how frightened she was and how hard she tried to please and placate her father.

Family assessment pays attention to each of these aspects of the family. Talking with the family about the eating disorder, their concerns about and management of it, and about other aspects of family life allows for sufficient observation and information to begin to understand in what ways family functioning may have contributed to, and be maintaining, the eating disorder. Attention can then turn to how the family may use its strengths and resilience to overcome the eating disorder. (More details of family function is provided in Chapter 10.)

## INDIVIDUAL ASSESSMENT

Many children with eating disorders are silent during the family assessment. They may be withdrawn, detached, or distressed by what their parents are saying. Others appear defiant and unconcerned. Children may be unwilling or unable to voice an opinion in front of their parents if they believe it will produce an angry or distressed response. The individual assessment is an opportunity to try to understand the child's perceptions and to give the child a voice.

The child is given a voice by making it clear that talking about things in front of parents can sometimes be difficult. It is important to emphasise that the individual assessment is a chance for the child to talk in private about things that might be worrying her. The child is reassured that what she talks about will not be directly repeated to her parents unless she says something that makes the therapist feel she is not safe. Examples of this would be active suicidal thoughts or being hit by her parents. Although the session is confidential, the team is presented as working collaboratively to help her get better.

this seems to be a big enough problem for you and your parents to have had to come to this hospital to try and sort things out. I may need to talk to my colleagues about your worries so that we can all think together about how best to help you and your family sort things out

## Talking to the child

The first part of the assessment aims to help the child articulate how big she thinks the problem is and how large a problem she thinks her parents see it. It is also possible to discuss the impact it is having on her and her family. Some useful questions that can be asked include the following.

*"Why do you think you are here today?"*   This shows the child we are willing to listen to her point of view. The way this question is answered provides information about her understanding and insight into her difficulties. Most children will say "because of my eating". The range and quantity of food eaten can then be discussed as well as whether she feels hungry or not. In our experience children with different eating disorders will respond differently to these questions.

*Selective eaters* describe a small list of preferred foods. They see the problem as being their inability to go to their friend's houses for parties or go out to restaurants because they are anxious about appearing different. Selective eaters may have expressed concern about their eating difficulties in front of their parents in the family assessment. However, this concern can change to ambivalence in the individual assessment. They may have been content with a limited range of preferred food for a long time, be physically well, and not *really* see why their parents are so upset.

Children with *food avoidance emotional disorder* complain of getting full up very quickly and are often very sad about never being hungry enough to eat the same amount as their friends or siblings. They can't understand why they can't eat more and usually share their parents' concern about it being a problem.

In contrast, the child with *anorexia nervosa* may be able to describe the limited amount of food she eats but will maintain categorically that there is no need for her to eat more. Mealtimes are stressful for her because of her parents failing to understand that there *isn't* a problem.

*"Tell me about mealtimes?"*   The aim here is to observe the emotional tone attached to the process of eating. When, where, and how does the family eat together? How do different people in the family react when the child won't/can't eat. Do her parents react differently? What do her parents say or do? Perhaps one of the parents has given up trying to get the child to eat, which results in arguments between the parents? Perhaps both parents have given up and nobody bothers to say anything anymore.

*"If this is average where are you?"*   The next part of the assessment helps the child to communicate non-verbally what she believes and thinks about her

body. The easiest way to do this is to draw a horizontal line on a piece of paper and explain that the middle of the line represents the average size, shape, or weight for children of her age. The extreme left is as thin as possible and the extreme right is as big as possible. The child is asked to mark where she is on this line right now. Siblings and friends can also be placed on the line. "Where were you when the problem began?", and "Where would you like to be?" are other simple and concrete ways of determining the degree of misperception about body size and shape. How would she feel if she were further to the right than she is now? Other questions about how she feels about her clothes, does she look in the mirror or weigh herself, can contribute to a better understanding of the value placed on physical appearance.

*"How do you feel?"*   The next area to be explored is usually the possibility of co-morbid affective disorders. Although failing to eat may be the presenting symptom this may be masking an overwhelming anxiety disorder.

Jackie's, 10, parents believed she was unable to eat because she had a phobia about being sick. During the assessment it became clear that her anxiety was much more widespread and related to a fear of separation from her parents. This manifested itself as a fear of vomiting and school phobia.

School phobia alone is a well-documented behavioural manifestation of underlying separation anxiety disorder (Last, Francis, Hersen, Kazdin, & Strauss, 1987). Fear of choking or retching underpins functional dysphagia. However, for some children with selective eating disorder this anxiety is also present albeit not explicitly recognised.

It is well recognised that depression plays an integral part in eating disorders and clarifying whether the child is also depressed is essential in order to guide the therapeutic process. Probes for co-morbid depression should investigate both biological symptoms (e.g. sleep and appetite disturbances), "When you're not worrying about food how do you sleep at night", and cognitive symptoms (e.g. dysthymia, anhedonia), "Does this worry ever stop you doing things that you would like to do?" The pervasiveness of the low mood should also be explored. "Do you think about it all the time or just at mealtimes?" The child may have cried during the family interview or will begin to cry when she is asked to think about how big a worry the eating problem is.

Kate, 9, was only able to eat apples and cheese and tomato pizza. She began to cry when she said that she wasn't going to be able to go on her school trip because she was scared that there was nothing that she would be able to eat, and all her friends would laugh at her.

Felicity, 13, had been cheerful all through the assessment. She began to cry when asked how she felt when she found herself unable to finish her dinner every day.

As part of the process exploring the child's underlying mood and the effect the eating disorder is having on her it is important to see that we can understand her terror and fear.

It is essential to ask about possible suicidal thoughts, e.g. "I can see that thinking about this is very hard, I wonder if it makes you so sad that there are times when you just want to go to sleep and not wake up?", "I wonder if it has ever got so bad that you have thought about ways of trying to kill yourself?" A child who acknowledges feelings of overwhelming hopelessness may not yet have actively thought about suicide. However, children who are helped to acknowledge the intensity of their distress often appear to have a sense of relief that someone has been able to listen to them and help them articulate their sense of overwhelming despair.

Asking children to "speak of the unspeakable" includes considering in every case the *possibility* of abuse. Eating disorders may be a response to having been abused (see Chapter 5). Although it is important not to lead children, nor put words in their mouths, it is critical that they are given permission "to tell" and to be heard. However difficult it is to hear, it is essential to explore any possible role trauma may have played in the onset or maintenance of the eating disorder. One way of introducing this difficult topic is to think out loud how difficult it is to understand why people find it difficult to eat.

> sometimes people in the family are always arguing with each other; or school work is hard and people can worry about not being top of the class. Another reason can be trying to keep difficult secrets about things that may have happened to you, things that you don't understand or are afraid to talk about; someone may have touched you in a way that didn't feel right or made you feel confused. Sometimes people just have to keep secrets about . . . friends or classmates being unkind, bullying or teasing.

This is spoken out loud, slowly as if talking to oneself, watching the child's body language to see if there is any physical reaction to the statements, like turning away, dropping her head, or wringing her hands. At the end of this musing we may ask if any of the things that were mentioned made sense or had she ever worried about any of these things? The language and events described are non-specific to avoid leading the child in any way. It is not expected, and is certainly very rare, that a child would make any disclosure of physical, emotional, or sexual abuse at this point. The aim is to begin the dialogue, to give the child a signal that we can ask about and listen to distressing revelations.

Children usually listen intently to this and most respond immediately by nodding wisely and saying they know just what you mean and nobody has ever done anything like that to them! For a few children, however, there is a silence while they look down at their hands, confused and anxious.

Mia, 14, had had anorexia nervosa for over two years. She had been an inpatient and was in regular therapy with another team who requested a second opinion. As the clinician mused, Mia became silent. When asked directly if anyone had ever done something to her that she hadn't been able to talk about she looked at the clinician and nodded before disclosing the details of an incident of sexual abuse by a stranger. She had kept this secret for two years from her parents and her therapist. When asked why she had chosen to speak about it now she said because no-one had ever asked her if it had happened.

Given the very short time available to the adult asking these initial questions, the child must be helped to feel safe and confident that the therapist can hear her and empathise with her distress. The child is being given the important message that when she feels safe enough to tell, we will be strong enough to listen and act.

Carla, 14, had been seen with her parents for family therapy over a nine-month period. When she began individual sessions she disclosed intense suicidal thoughts and longstanding physical abuse by her father towards herself and her mother. The team was able to discuss the abuse with the parents and organise a place of safety. No-one had ever asked her if things felt unsafe at home or if she felt like killing herself.

It is only possible to ask these painful questions in the context of a multi-disciplinary team that can provide immediate back up if the individual assessor believes the child is in danger.

The immediate acknowledgement of the possibility of abuse can also be applied to the school setting, by taking it for granted that most schools have bullies. Here again this signals to children that this is an issue they can talk about—when they are ready.

## School and peer group

At this point in the assessment there is also an opportunity to ask more about school "What is your favourite (or most hated) lessons; what are your teachers like?" Such questions allow the child to discuss where she sees herself in the classroom hierarchy and her attitude to achievement. This is often a critical area for children with low self-esteem. If needed a simple diagram can help the child show where she sees her self now and how far away she is from her "ideal self" (see Fig. 7.1).

Peer relationships are also an area that should be considered. How many friends does she have and how do her friends react to the "eating problem". Friends of a child with selective eating disorder may never be aware of the obsessive predilection for peanut butter sandwiches, whereas those who are may

FIG. 7.1    The child is given a line on a piece of blank paper. The therapist says "if you were the most stupid person in the class this is where you would be" pointing to the left-hand edge of the line. "If you were the cleverest person in the class this is where you would be", pointing to the extreme right side edge of the line. The child is invited to mark on the line where they think they are in the class and where they would like to be. Children can also be asked to indicate where best friends/enemies are to determine how they see themselves in relation to favoured and non-favoured peers.

be bemused but unconcerned. In marked contrast, the child who is consistently disposing of and refusing to eat lunch may generate acute concern in her friends. This results in them being whistle blowers, telling parents and teachers about missed lunches and trips to the toilet to vomit. This may be an important issue for the child in treatment as she may be struggling with considerable anger at the perceived betrayal.

## Defensiveness

The child's description of the problem and her reaction to our questions are critical in helping to develop a formulation that will be discussed with the team and understood in the context of the family assessment. Is everything perfect? Does she have lots of friends, no worries, no arguments with her parents, siblings, or friends? Apart from not being able to eat very much, is she emphatic that she has no problems?

Excessive and emphatic denials of any problems, in any area, may not feel in need of as urgent a response as the desperate, depressed, and emaciated child who can think of no reason to continue with her life. However, the high level of defensiveness that generates the "unreal" picture of perfection marred only by the "eating problem" may often offer an even greater challenge therapeutically.

## Motivation

The final part of the assessment is a consideration of the child's response to a therapeutic programme. The importance of motivation as a predictor of outcome has been well documented in adults (Ward, Troop, Todd, & Treasure, 1996). How motivated is the child to change? How much does she believe that change could, or might, come from within herself, given the right kind of support? One way to explore this is to offer a choice of medicine, magic, or talking as a "cure" and see which is chosen. The child with anorexia nervosa may choose none of the three, although her physical condition will clearly determine if she requires treatment. The individual assessment should aim to establish if the child is ready to think about many, often painful, issues. If not, then helping the parents to feed their child, and rediscover their ability to be parents, may be what is needed for the immediate future.

*"Three wishes".* A useful technique for assessing a child's fantasy world is to ask what she would ask for if she had three wishes or a magic wand. Few children are dismissive of such questions. Answers can be categorised into areas associated with personal, family, or social desires. They may pertain to the problem itself (e.g. "I want the eating problem to go away"), personal appearance ("I want to be thinner, taller, stronger, prettier, cleverer"), family ("I want all my family to be happy and well"), or grandiose/philanthropic ("I want all the wars in the world to stop"). The pattern of the three wishes can be looked at in the context of the other information that has been obtained from the interview. Even older children can be encouraged to believe in magic for a few seconds, given that things are pretty bad already, so it won't hurt them to pretend!

## Thinking about the future

The individual assessment should determine the child's ability to engage in a therapeutic relationship and consider the level and quality of that engagement. This brief time provides an often silent and desperate child with a voice in the decision-making process. It offers her a chance to articulate her distress in an alternative way to her current response.

## CONCLUSION

The assessment of a child with an eating disorder and her family marks the beginning of a process. It offers glimpses of a complex and dynamic system that may shift and turn in its attempt to defeat those who attempt to identify, name, and ultimately destroy it. The assessment of the family and the child is, therefore, the beginning of the journey. The questions we ask and the way we ask them must be searching and detailed and sensitive to what is not said as well as what is.

Demonstrating that we have listened and heard everyone who is affected by the eating disorder allows the team to enter into a partnership with the parents. This allows us to help parents understand that neither they nor their child is to blame, but that they do have a responsibility to take charge of recovery. Children are helped to see that their parents and the team are not overawed by, or held ransom by, the eating disorder, and that these first meetings are part of a process that will help them escape from the eating disorder that is holding them captive. The team and parents together can then discuss how best to proceed. (see Chapter 9)

## SUMMARY POINTS

The child is part of a family unit therefore the team must work with both the family and the child to achieve an understanding of the illness in order to make clear and appropriate decisions about treatment.

The family assessment focuses on the past and the present by examining:

* the quality of the parental relationship
* physical, psychological, and generational family boundaries
* the family atmosphere
* affective status and responsiveness
* communication processes.

The individual assessment offers children a voice independent of their parents and should:

* *understand* the child's perception of the problem
* *determine* the feelings associated with the process of eating
* *measure* the degree of body image distortion and the impact weight gain would have
* *describe* and document co-existing affective disorders
* *assess* hopelessness and suicidal thoughts
* *open* channels of communication about possible abuse
* *acknowledge* possible problems at school
* *ascertain* the readiness of the child to participate in a programme of change
* *offer* hope for the future.

## APPENDIX

Standardised methods are in common use to help describe and diagnose eating disorders. Within the adult population there is a wide choice of standardised methods for specifically assessing eating disorders. These fall broadly into two categories—self-report question-naires and structured or semi-structured interviews. Most general psychopathology measures also have an eating disorders section. In contrast, there are very few similar measures for the child and adolescent populations. The general psychopathology measures may have eating disorder sections, e.g. the Diagnostic Interview for Children and Adolescents (DICA: Reich, Herjanic, Welner, & Gandhy, 1982), but it is often preferable to use a more detailed specific eating disorder psychopathology measure. This applies particu-larly when a more detailed profile of the child's eating pathology is required. Many of the specific eating disorder adult measures have been used with adolescents, but may lack data for adolescent norms. Only two measures have been formally adapted for use with children, with one self-report measure specifically designed for children.

This Appendix includes some of the eating disorder instruments and interviews that have been used within the younger population and those instruments and interviews specifically designed for the younger population. Reliability and validity data are provided, for it is particularly important to ensure that adult-oriented assessment techniques are appropriate for use with younger patients. In general, they should be used only with considerable caution.

## Adult questionnaires used within the child and adolescent populations, general eating disorder pathology

*The Eating Attitudes Test.* The Eating Attitudes Test (EAT: Garner & Garfinkel, 1979) is a self-report 40-item measure that employs a 6-point Likert rating scale. It was designed to measure attitudes and behaviours associated with anorexia nervosa, and, although not diagnostic, can be used to measure symptoms. Following factor analysis, a shorter 26-item version (EAT-26: Garner, Olmsted, Bohr, & Garfinkel, 1982) was developed and found to be highly correlated with the original version ($r = 0.98$). The EAT is easy to administer and takes less than 10 minutes to complete. This measure has seven factors: food preoccupation, body image for thinness, vomiting, and laxative abuse, dieting, slow eating, clandestine eating, and perceived social pressure to gain weight. The measure proved to have high internal consistency for both an anorexia nervosa group (coefficient alpha = 0.79), and for a mixed group of anorexia nervosa and normal controls (coefficient alpha = 0.94) (Garner et al., 1982). The EAT also proved to have high test–retest reliability ($n = 56$, $r = 0.84$) (Carter & Moss, 1984).

The EAT has been found to differentiate between binge eaters, and those with anorexia nervosa or bulimia nervosa (Prather & Williamson, 1988), and between normal controls and eating disorder groups (Garner & Garfinkel, 1979). However, the measure does not discriminate between those with anorexia nervosa and those with bulimia nervosa (Williamson, Cubic, & Gleaves, 1993). The EAT has also been found to be sensitive to therapeutic changes (Williamson, Prather, Bennett, Davis, Watkins, & Grenier, 1989) and has been shown to be moderately correlated with the Bulimia Test (BULIT: $r = 0.67$; Smith & Thelen, 1984) and the Bulimic Investigatory Test (BITE: $r = 0.70$; Henderson & Freeman, 1987). This is the only questionnaire that has been specifically adapted for use with children (ChEAT: Maloney, McGuire, & Daniels, 1988; see later).

*The Eating Disorder Inventory.* The Eating Disorder Inventory (EDI: Garner, Olmsted, & Polivy, 1983) is a 64-item measure, consisting of eight subscales: three to assess attitudes and behaviours towards weight, body shape, and eating (Drive for Thinness, Bulimia, and Body Dissatisfaction) and five to assess psychological characteristics common to anorexia and bulimia nervosa (Ineffectiveness, Perfection, Interpersonal Distrust, Interoceptive Awareness, and Maturity Fears). The measure has been revised, to create the Eating Disorder Inventory-2 (EDI-2: Garner, 1991), with the addition of 27 additional items, forming three extra subscales—Asceticism, Impulse Regulation, and Social Insecurity. Adolescent norms are available for this measure (Rosen, Silberg, & Gross, 1988; Shore & Porter, 1990), and the measure has been used in groups with an age range of 11–18 years. The EDI and EDI-2 are widely used as screening measures, and as measures of treatment outcome. It is also possible to detect subtypes of anorexia nervosa or bulimia nervosa, as well as symptom severity, using this measure. Garner et al. (1983) found that 88–93% of subjects were correctly classified using the EDI, and also found that 85% of subjects were correctly classified into bulimic and restricter subtypes of anorexia nervosa, using discriminant analysis, and comparing the self-report EDI with clinicians ratings of the subscales. The concurrent validity between the EDI and the EAT is good, as scores on all of the EDI subscales have been found to be positively correlated with scores on the Eating Attitudes Test (EAT: Garner et al., 1982). Norring (1990) found that the Bulimia scale of the EDI is a stable predictor of binge eating at both one-year and two-year follow-ups, thus having high predictor validity. In a sample of 11–18-year-olds good reliability was found for both the EDI and EDI-2 (Garner, 1991).

*The Questionnaire for Eating Disorder Diagnoses.* The Questionnaire for Eating Disorder Diagnoses (Q-EDD: Mintz, O'Halloran, Mulholland, & Schneider, 1997) is a self-report questionnaire that takes approximately 10 minutes to complete, and comprises 50 questions, which are answered either yes or no, or using a Lickert-type rating scale. Each question is linked directly to a DSM-IV criterion for eating disorders diagnoses, and each question has a decision rule to facilitate the scoring of the questionnaire. The Q-EDD was designed to operationalise the DSM-IV criteria for eating disorders. It is a revision of the Weight Management Questionnaire (WMQ: Mintz & Betz, 1988), based on DSM-III-R criteria for eating disorders, which was revised from Ousley's (1986) DSM-III questionnaire.

The measure differentiates between those who meet diagnostic criteria for an eating disorder, and those that do not. Within the group who meet diagnostic criteria for eating disorders, it differentiates between individuals who meet the diagnostic criteria for anorexia nervosa and those who meet the diagnostic criteria for bulimia nervosa; and within the group that does not meet the diagnostic criteria for eating disorders, the measure differentiates between those who have some eating disorder symptomatology, and those who are asymptomatic.

In a clinical sample that included some adolescents ($n$ = 37, age range 15–44 years old, mean age 24.68 years, SD 7.59), in which clinicians had independently diagnosed all participants as eating disordered, the Q-EDD and clinicians' independent diagnoses of anorexia nervosa and bulimia nervosa were 100% in agreement. Calculations of false-negative rates were used to examine criterion validity, and it was found that there was 78% accuracy between clinicians and the Q-EDD when differentiating eating disordered and non-eating disordered individuals. Of the 22% of cases that were not deemed to reach diagnostic levels by the Q-EDD, 75% were rated as non-eating disorder but symptomatic, with only 25% (two cases) being rated as non-eating disordered and asymptomatic, using the Q-EDD. It is interesting that neither of the cases deemed to be non-eating disordered and asymptomatic by the Q-EDD were near normal weight (one severely underweight and one severely overweight), which may suggest a clinical diagnosis based predominantly around body weight (Mintz et al., 1997).

The measure has been used with a non-clinical sample of older adolescents. It has high test–retest reliability between eating disordered and non-eating disordered groups, and between eating disordered, non-eating disordered (symptomatic), and non-eating disordered (asymptomatic) groups, respectively.

Inter-rater reliability on 50 randomly selected Q-EDDs produced 100% agreement (Mintz et al., 1997).

*The Setting Conditions for Anorexia Nervosa Scale.* The Setting Conditions for Anorexia Nervosa Scale (SCANS: Slade & Dewey, 1986) is a 40-item questionnaire that employs a five-point, Likert-type rating scale, and comprises five scales—dissatisfaction and loss of control (D), social and personal anxiety (S), perfectionism (P), adolescent problems (A), and need for weight control (WC). It was designed to identify those at risk of developing anorexia nervosa and bulimia nervosa (Slade, 1982), and has been used for this purpose in a large sample of adolescents (219 boys and 174 girls aged 14–18 years old) in a study examining the relationship of gender and family environment to eating disorder risk (Felker & Stivers, 1994). The SCANS exists both as a pencil and paper questionnaire, and also in a computerised version (Butler, Newton, & Slade, 1988). The measure is quick and easy to use, and can be used with younger adolescents, as the reading level of the questionnaire is aimed at this age group. The measure takes between 10 and 20 minutes to complete, and 10 minutes to score. The SCANS has been used in a large sample of children and adolescents aged 11–16 years to assess two specific risk factors thought to be associated with eating disorder, namely perfectionism and general dissatisfaction.

Slade and Dewey (1986), found that the scales of the SCANS have a high internal consistency, with similar alpha co-efficients being found on all scales in two separate non-clinical samples (co-efficient alphas for sample 1 and sample 2, respectively, for each scale: D = 0.84, 0.89; S = 0.76, 0.81; P = 0.66, 0.66; A = 0.81, 0.83; WC = 0.81, 0.90). The SCANS adequately differentiates between non-clinical controls and eating disordered subjects, but does not discriminate between anorexia nervosa subjects and those with bulimia nervosa.

*The Stirling Eating Disorder Scales.* The Stirling Eating Disorders Scales (SEDS: Williams et al., 1994) is an 80-item eight-scale measure designed to be used with eating disordered patients. The eight scales can be broadly split into two groups—four dietary scales: anorexic dietary behaviour, anorexic dietary cognitions, bulimic dietary behaviour, bulimic dietary cognitions; and four non-dietary scales: high perceived external control, low assertiveness, low self-esteem, and self-directed hostility. The measure was devised to produce a comprehensive assessment schedule that addressed, not only the cognitive and behavioural aspects of both anorexia nervosa and bulimia nervosa, but also the cognitive/emotional features that have been shown to be important characteristics of both of the disorders, with the use of the four non-dietary scales. The reading age of the SEDS items have been calculated to be 9 years and 3 months; however, no studies were found that had used this instrument in such a young age group.

For a sample group consisting of three comparison groups—anorexia nervosa (mean age 24.7 years, SD 5.3), bulimia nervosa (mean age 25.0 years, SD 4.9), and normal controls (mean age 23.8, SD 4.9)—the three-week test–retest correlations for all eight of the Stirling Eating Disorders Scales produced highly significant correlations, $P < .001$, and the scale consistency for each of the eight scales is also high, Cronbach's alpha > 0.8 (Williams et al., 1994).

All eight scales discriminate between eating disordered subjects and normal controls, whereas the four dietary scales discriminate between the anorexia nervosa group and the bulimia nervosa group. On the four non-dietary scales, there is no differentiation between the two eating disordered groups (Williams et al., 1994). The concurrent validity between the SEDS and the Eating Attitudes Test-40 (EAT: Garner & Garfinkel, 1979) and the

Bulimia Investigatory Test—Edinburgh (BITE: Henderson & Freeman, 1987), produced highly significant correlations, $P < .001$ (Williams et al., 1994).

*The Body Shape Questionnaire.* The Body Shape Questionnaire (BSQ: Cooper, Taylor, Cooper, & Fairburn, 1987) is a 34-item questionnaire with a six-point Likert-style rating scale, and was developed to measure boyd weight and shape concern in those with eating disorders or other body image related problems. The measure takes appproximately 10 minutes to complete, and may be useful for screening those at risk of developing eating disorders. However, as body weight and shape concern are only one of the criterion items in the diagnosis of eating disorders, this measure may be better suited for assessment of body weight and shape concern in community samples, or to assess any changes in body image disturbance of eating disordered patients in treatment over time.

The BSQ has proved to be a significantly reliable measure overall, $P < .001$, with significantly high reliability for each of the 34 items, $P < .01$, for test–retest reliability (Rosen, Jones, Ramirez, & Waxman, 1996).

The BSQ correlates with other body image measures, such as the Body Dysmorphic Disorder Examination (BDDE: Rosen, Reiter, & Orosan, 1995) and has good concurrent validity, for both clinical and non-clinical samples, in that negative body image attitudes reported on the BSQ are correlated with other negative body image symptoms, such as concerns about appearance features that are non-weight related.

The BSQ has been widely used to examine body weight and shape dissatisfaction in adolescents from 12 years old upwards; usually in large school samples (e.g. Le Grange, Tibbs, & Selibowitz, 1995; Mumford, Whitehouse, & Choudry, 1992), and has also been used to examine sociocultural differences in body weight and shape dissatisfaction in adolescents (e.g. Mumford, Whitehouse, & Platts, 1991).

*The Body Satisfaction Scale.* The Body Satisfaction Scale (BSS: Slade, Dewey, Newton, Brodie, & Kiemle, 1990), is a 16-item self-report questionnaire that measures body dissatisfaction. Each of 16 body parts is rated on a seven-point Likert-type scale, ranging from "very satisfied" to "very dissatisfied". This questionnaire has two subscales, assessing dissatisfaction with the head and dissatisfaction with the body. It is useful in making a quick assessment of body satisfaction, and has reasonably high internal consistency (co-efficient alpha range 0.79–0.89). The measure is well validated against other body satisfaction scales, and is highly correlated with the BSQ. The BSS only takes about 5 minutes to complete and 5 minutes to score, but does not measure the nature of the dissatisfaction.

Cok (1990) used the BSS in a large sample of children and adolescents aged 11–18 years old, with no reported difficulties in the administration of this measure with the younger participants in the study.

## Measures for children and young adolescents

Only two self-report questionnaires have been adapted for use with children aged 12 and under—the Children's Eating Attitudes Test (ChEAT: Maloney et al., 1988), and the Kids' Eating Disorder Survey (KEDS: Childress, Jarrell, & Brewerton, 1992). Both the ChEAT and the KEDS were designed as screening tools for the general population, and therefore have limited utility in a clinical setting.

*The Children's Eating Attitudes Test.*   The ChEAT (Maloney et al., 1988) is a modified version of the Eating Attitudes Test (EAT: Garner et al., 1982; see earlier). It asks about perceived body image, obsessions/preoccupation with food, and dieting practices. There are 26 questions, and the rating of each question is via a six-point Likert-type scale. The wording of items on the EAT was modified in order to make the questions more comprehensible to children as young as 8 years old. The norms for this questionnaire were gathered from a sample of 318 children aged 8–13 years (mean age 9.7yrs), 92% of whom were white, and all of whom came from middle to upper socio-economic backgrounds. Instructions on how to complete the questionnaire are delivered orally to the child; and, in the case of children at the younger end of the spectrum, each item is also read to them. The measure is easy to administer and takes approximately 30 minutes to complete, including time taken to read the instructions to the child.

The questionnaire is especially easy to administer to children who have reached the reading level required to complete the questionnaire without help from the administrator, and thus can be administered to a large group. However, if administering orally to a younger child, this negates the benefits of it being a questionnaire measure, as staff resources are needed to read the questions to the child. Another problem with it is that it does not assess eating disorders *per se*, but rather attitudes toward eating and dietary behaviour. The ChEAT is not therefore diagnostic, but can be useful as a screening tool to assess children potentially at risk of developing an eating disorder. Both internal consistency and test–retest reliability are reasonably high, co-efficient alpha of 0.76 and 0.81 respectively (Maloney et al., 1988). Smolak and Levine (1994) also found the ChEAT to have high internal consistency, co-efficient alpha = 0.87. Concurrent validity test showed the ChEAT to be significantly correlated with weight management behaviour, $r = 0.36$, $P < .001$, and with body dissatisfaction, $r = 0.39$, $P < .001$ (Smolak & Levine, 1994).

*The Kids' Eating Disorders Survey.*   The KEDS (Childress et al., 1992) was developed from the Eating Symptoms Inventory (ESI: Whitaker et al., 1989), which is based on DSM-III criteria, and was used in a high school survey of eating disorders in adolescents. Childress, Brewerton, Hodges, and Jarrell (1993) developed the KEDS to address the marked differences in cognitive development between children and adolescents, by producing a simpler and shorter questionnaire, in which "yes", "no", and "don't know" responses are all that are required. There are 14 items on the questionnaire, which include a set of eight drawings of boys and eight drawings of girls, which range from very underweight to very overweight. The child is asked to circle the drawing that looks most like them, in order to assess weight and body dissatisfaction. The measure was designed to be used within the general population as a screening device. The KEDS has been found to have highly significant test–retest reliability (0.83, $P < .01$) when re-administered to 230 children within four months of the original survey (Childress et al., 1993). However, the results of extensive external validity studies are not yet available.

## Interview measures

There are at least four stand alone interview measures in existence for the assessment of eating disorders in adults. Three of these are structured interviews—the Clinical Eating Disorder Rating Instrument (CEDRI: Palmer, Christie, Cordle, Davis, & Kendrick, 1987), the Interview for the Diagnosis of Eating Disorders (IDED: Williamson, 1990), and the Structured Interview for Anorexia and Bulimia Nervosa (SIAB: Fichter, Elton, Engel, Meyer, Mall, & Poustka, 1991). The fourth interview is a semi-structured interview developed by Cooper and Fairburn (1987)—the Eating Disorder Examination (EDE). This interview is now in its 12th edition (Fairburn & Cooper, 1993), and is the only instrument that has been adapted for use with children (Bryant-Waugh, Cooper, Taylor, & Lask, 1996). Here is a brief overview of the EDE, and a detailed description of the child version of the EDE.

*The Eating Disorder Examination.*    The EDE (Fairburn & Cooper, 1993) is an instrument designed to assess specific eating disorder psychopathology, and is currently viewed as the "gold standard" in eating disorders assessment (Wilson, 1993). It is a semi-structured, investigator-based interview, which means that the interviewer asks key questions but can then ask additional questions in order to clarify the concept that is being investigated. It is very important that all interviewers are trained to administer this instrument, to ensure that the key concepts being assessed by the EDE are clearly understood.

The EDE provides either frequency or severity ratings for key behavioural and attitudinal aspects of eating disorders, and comprises four subscales: Restraint, Eating Concern, Shape Concern, and Weight Concern. The instrument also produces operationally defined eating disorder diagnoses for both anorexia nervosa and bulimia nervosa, based on DSM-IV criteria. The EDE is a present state interview, which produces information pertaining to the four weeks preceding the interview. However, on some key diagnostic questions, the instrument is designed to enable the interviewer to question the subject about the previous three months, thus allowing sufficient information to be gathered to satisfy DSM-IV criteria for certain aspects of eating disorder diagnoses. The EDE has been used both as an assessment/diagnostic tool and as a means of monitoring progress within therapy (Beaumont, Kopec-Schrader, Talbot, & Touyz, 1993). There are adult female norms available for both of these disorders as well as for other groups, namely restrained eaters, overweight individuals, dieters, and normal controls.

The EDE has good reliability data, with co-efficient alpha of the subscales ranging from 0.67 to 0.90 for internal consistency of the measure (Cooper, Cooper, & Fairburn, 1989). This reliability data was gathered using a previous version of the EDE, when it included a bulimia subscale, which was subsequently dropped for the 12th edition of the interview. There are no reported test–retest reliability studies for the EDE. Cooper et al. (1989) also demonstrated good discriminant validity for this measure, using a sample of 100 eating disordered patients and 42 normal controls, and Rosen, Vara, Wendt, and Leitenberg (1990) found that the weight concern and shape concern subscales discriminated between patients with bulimia nervosa and a group of restrained eaters. The EDE has also been adapted for use in questionnaire format.

*The Child EDE.*    The children's version of the EDE (Bryant-Waugh et al., 1996) includes four main modifications. First, the language of the measure has been changed slightly to make the interview more comprehensible for children. Second, the introduction to the interview has been altered; the parents are asked to complete a diary, which is given to the child at the beginning of the interview and used as a memory cue.

A further difference between the main EDE and the child version relates to the issue of intention. As some children's eating behaviours are controlled by parents or carers, it was felt necessary to get a sense of what behaviours the child might engage in when unsupervised or not controlled by their parents or carers. Thus, a number of the questions on the child version of the EDE ask about both actual behaviour and intended behaviour. However, only ratings on actual behaviour are used to calculate scores, whereas intended ratings are used for clinically descriptive purposes.

Finally, two key items, namely importance of weight and importance of shape, are administered as a card sort task on the child version of the instrument. Rather than being asked direct questions about the extent to which weight and shape are important in terms of self-evaluation, children are asked a more general, "what things are important to you in your judgement of yourself". The child is given examples to help clarify the concept of self-evaluation, such as performance at school, popularity, looks, family harmony, talents, etc. The child is then asked what things are personally important, and these are written on separate cards. The child is then asked to arrange them in order of importance (Bryant-Waugh et al., 1996).

Bryant-Waugh et al. (1996) piloted the children's version of the EDE with a group of 16 children aged between 7 and 14 in a child Eating Disorders Clinic, and found that the interview was well-tolerated, and, on the whole, the children co-operated well throughout. Most of the responses to individual items were found to be consistent with clinical observation, thus suggesting the potential validity of this measure. A further study was undertaken by Frampton (1996), who interviewed 30 clinical subjects and 30 normal controls between the ages of 8 and 14 years. He found that children given a clinical diagnosis of anorexia nervosa virtually mirrored the subscale scores of the adult anorexia nervosa standardised sample (Cooper & Fairburn, 1987). He also found that children given a clinical diagnosis of either selective eating (Chapter 3) or Food Avoidance Emotional Disorder (Chapter 3) scored similarly on the EDE subscales to the normal controls. This would suggest that this measure has a degree of discriminant validity, in that it can discriminate between those children with and without a clinical diagnosis of anorexia nervosa. Bryant-Waugh et al. are currently undertaking a study to generate norms and reliability data for the child version of the EDE.

# REFERENCES

Beaumont, P., Kopec-Schrader, E., Talbot, P., & Touyz, S. (1993). Measuring the specific psychopathology of eating disorder patients. *Australian and New Zealand Journal of Psychiatry, 27*(3), 506–511.

Bryant-Waugh, R., Cooper, P., Taylor, C., & Lask, B. (1996). The use of the eating disorder examination with children: A pilot study. *International Journal of Eating Disorders, 19*, 391–398.

Butler, N., Newton, T., & Slade, P. (1988). Validation of a computerized version of the SCANS questionnaire. *International Journal of Eating Disorders, 8*, 239–241.

Carter, P., & Moss, R. (1984). Screening for anorexia and bulimia nervosa in a college population: Problems and limitations. *Addictive Behaviors, 9*, 417–419.

Childress, A., Brewerton, T., Hodges, E., & Jarrell, M. (1993). The kids' eating disorders survey (KEDS): A study of middle school students. *Journal of the American Academy of Child and Adolescent Psychiatry, 32*, 843–850.

Childress, A., Jarrell, M., & Brewerton, T. (1992). *The kids' eating disorders survey (KEDS): Internal consistency, component analysis, and test–retest reliability.* Paper presented at the 5th International Conference on Eating Disorders, New York.

Cok, F. (1990). Body image dissatisfaction in Turkish adolescents. *Adolescence*, *25*, 409–413.

Cooper, P., Taylor, M., Cooper, Z., & Fairburn, C. (1987). The development and validation of the body shape questionnaire. *International Journal of Eating Disorders*, *6*, 485–494.

Cooper, Z., Cooper, P., & Fairburn, C. (1989). The validity of the eating disorder examination and its subscales. *British Journal of Psychiatry*, *154*, 807–812.

Cooper, Z., & Fairburn, C. (1987). The eating disorder examination: A semi-structured interview for the assessment of the specific psychopathology of eating disorders. *International Journal of Eating Disorders*, *6*, 1–8.

Fairburn, C., & Cooper, Z. (1993). The eating disorder examination (12th ed.). In C.G. Fairburn & G.T. Wilson (Eds.), *Binge eating: Nature, assessment and treatment* (pp. 317–360). New York: Guilford Press.

Felker, K., & Stivers, C. (1994). The relationship of gender and family environment to eating disorder risk in adolescents. *Adolescence*, *29*, 821–834.

Fichter, M., Elton, M., Engel, K., Meyer, A., Mall, H., & Poustka, F. (1991). Structured interview for anorexia and bulimia nervosa (SIAB): Development of a new instrument for the assessment of eating disorders. *International Journal of Eating Disorders*, *10*, 571–592.

Frampton, I. (1996). *Are overvalued ideas about weight and shape overvalued ideas in the diagnosis of eating disorders? Evidence from early onset anorexia nervosa.* Unpublished research dissertation, University of Exeter, UK.

Garner, D. (1991). *Eating disorders inventory 2: Professional manual.* Odessa, FL: Psychological Assessment Resources.

Garner, D., & Garfinkel, P. (1979). The eating attitudes test: An index of the symptoms of anorexia nervosa. *Psychological Medicine*, *9*, 273–279.

Garner, D., Olmsted, M., Bohr, Y., & Garfinkel, P. (1982). The eating attitudes test: Psychometric features and clinical correlates. *Psychological Medicine*, *12*, 871–878.

Garner, D., Olmsted, M., & Polivy, J. (1983). Development and validation of a multi-dimensional eating disorder inventory for anorexia nervosa and bulimia. *International Journal of Eating Disorders*, *2*, 15–34.

Henderson, M., & Freeman, C. (1987). A self-rating scale for bulimia: The "BITE". *British Journal of Psychiatry*, *150*, 18–24.

Last, C.G., Francis, G., Hersen, M., Kazdin, A.E., & Strauss, C.C. (1987). Seperation anxiety and school phobia: A comparison using DSM-III criteria. *American Journal of Psychiatry*, *144*, 653–657.

Le Grange, D., Tibbs, J., & Selibowitz, J. (1995). Eating attitudes, body shape, and self-disclosure in a community sample of adolescent girls and boys. *Eating Disorders: The Journal of Treatment and Prevention*, *3*, 253–264.

Maloney, M., McGuire, J., & Daniels, S. (1988). Reliability testing of a children's version of the eating attitude test. *Journal of the American Academy of Child and Adolescent Psychiatry*, *28*, 541–543.

Mintz, L., & Betz, N. (1988). Prevalence and correlates of eating disordered behaviour among undergraduate women. *Journal of Counselling Psychology*, *35*, 463–471.

Mintz, L., O' Halloran, M., Mulholland, A., & Schneider, P. (1997). Questionnaire for eating disorder diagnoses: Reliability and validity of operationalizing DSM-IV criteria into a self-report format. *Journal of Counselling Psychology*, *44*, 63–71.

Mumford, D., Whitehouse, A., & Choudry, I. (1992). Survey of eating disorders in English-medium schools in Lahore, Pakistan. *International Journal of Eating Disorders*, *11*, 173–184.

Mumford, D., Whitehouse, A., & Platts, M. (1991). Sociocultural correlates of eating disorders among Asian schoolgirls in Bradford. *British Journal of Psychiatry*, *158*, 222–228.

Norring, C. (1990). The eating disorder inventory: Its relation to diagnostic dimensions and follow-up status. *International Journal of Eating Disorders*, *9*, 685–694.

Ousley, L. (1986). *Differences among bulimic subgroups, binge-eaters, and normal dieters in a female college population.* Unpublished doctoral dissertation, University of Florida, Gainsville.

Palmer, R., Christie, M., Cordle, C., Davis, D., & Kendrick, J. (1987). The clinical eating disorder rating instrument (CEDRI): A preliminary description. *International Journal of Eating Disorders*, *6*, 9–16.

Prather, R., & Williamson, D. (1988). Psychopathology associated with bulimia, binge eating and obesity. *International Journal of Eating Disorders*, *7*, 177–184.

Reich, W., Herjanic, B., Welner, Z., & Gandhy, P.R. (1982). Development of a structured psychiatric interview for children: Agreement on diagnosis comparing child and parent interviews. *Journal of Abnormal Child Psychology*, *10*, 325–336.

Rosen, J., Jones, A., Ramirez, E., & Waxman, S. (1996). Body shape questionnaire: Studies of validity and reliability. *International Journal of Eating Disorders*, *20*, 315–319.

Rosen, J., Reiter, J., & Orosan, P. (1995). Assessment of body image in eating disorders with the body dysmorphic disorder examination. *Behaviour Research and Therapy*, *33*, 77–84.

Rosen, J., Silberg, N., & Gross, J. (1988). Eating attitudes test and eating disorder inventory: Norms for adolescent girls and boys. *Journal of Consulting and Clinical Psychology*, *56*, 305–308.

Rosen, J., Vara, L., Wendt, B., & Leitenberg, H. (1990). Validity studies of the eating disorder examination. *International Journal of Eating Disorders*, *9*, 519–528.

Shore, R., & Porter, J. (1990). Normative and reliability data for 11–18 year olds in the eating disorder inventory. *International Journal of Eating Disorders*, *9*, 201–207.

Slade, P. (1982). Towards a functional analysis of anorexia nervosa and bulimia nervosa. *British Journal of Clinical Psychology*, *21*, 67–79.

Slade, P., & Dewey, M. (1986). Development and preliminary validation of SCANS: A screening instrument for identifying individuals at risk of developing anorexia and bulimia nervosa. *International Journal of Eating Disorders*, *5*, 517–538.

Slade, P., Dewey, M., Newton, T., Brodie, D., & Kiemle, G. (1990). Development and preliminary validation of the body satisfaction scale (BSS). *Psychology and Health*, *4*, 213–220.

Smith, M., & Thelen, M. (1984). Development and validation for a test for bulimia. *Journal of Consulting and Clinical Psychology*, *52*, 863–872.

Smolak, L., & Levine, M. (1994). Psychometric properties of the children's eating attitudes test. *International Journal of Eating Disorders*, *16*, 275–282.

Ward, A., Troop, N., Todd, G., & Treasure, J. (1996). To change or not to change—"how" is the question? *British Journal of Medical Psychology*, *69*, 139–146.

Whittaker, A., Davies, M., Shaffer, D., Johnson, J., Abrams, S., Walsh, B., & Kalikow, K. (1989). The struggle to be thin: A survey of anorexic and bulimic symptoms in a non-referred adolescent population. *Psychological Medicine*, *19*, 143–163.

Williams, G., Power, K., Miller, H., Freeman, C., Yellowlees, A., Dowds, T., Walker, M., & Parry-Jones, W. (1994). Development and validation of the Stirling Eating Disorder Scales. *International Journal of Eating Disorders*, *16*, 35–43.

Williamson, D. (1990). *Assessment of eating disorders: Obesity, anorexia and bulimia nervosa*. Elmsford, NY: Pergamon.

Williamson, D., Cubic, B., & Gleaves, D. (1993). Equivalent body image disturbances in anorexia and bulimia nervosa. *Journal of Abnormal Psychology*, *102*, 1–4.

Williamson, D., Prather, R., Bennett, S., Davis, C., Watkins, P., & Grenier, C. (1989). An uncontrolled evaluation of inpatient and outpatient cognitive behaviour therapy for bulimia nervosa. *Behaviour Modification*, *13*, 340–360.

Wilson, G. (1993). Assessment of binge eating. In C.G. Fairburn & G.T. Wilson (Eds.), *Binge eating: Nature, assessment and treatment* (pp. 227–249). New York: Guilford Press.

CHAPTER EIGHT

# Physical assessment and complications

**Dasha Nicholls**
*Institute of Child Health, and Great Ormond Street Hospital for Children, London, UK*

**Rose de Bruyn and Isky Gordon**
*Great Ormond Street Hospital for Children, London, UK*

## INTRODUCTION

Physical monitoring is integral to the assessment and treatment of eating disorders, perhaps more than for any other mental health problem. This chapter is about how to differentiate a thin but normal, healthy body from a body that is starving; a physically unwell child from a chronically malnourished but stable one; and about the long-term effects of malnourishment during childhood and early adolescence. These issues are of importance to all clinicians who are likely to encounter patients with eating disorders. Initial presentation will often not be to an eating disorder specialist. In one series of 48 children presenting with determined food avoidance, 52% spent some time on a general paediatric ward (Fosson, Knibbs, Bryant-Waugh, & Lask, 1987) before referral to a child psychiatry team. Atypical presentations and a particular lack of awareness that these conditions can arise in boys may lead to delay in referral, diagnosis, and treatment (Fosson et al., 1987; Jacobs & Isaacs, 1986). Once recognised, the severity of the problem may be missed because of failure to recognise the physical signs of starvation. Physical assessment involves far more than measuring the child's weight, weight/height, or BMI, although these are of course essential starting points.

Physical well-being in eating disorders lie on a spectrum from normal to seriously ill. Normal eating patterns, weight, growth, and development are at one end of the spectrum; anorexia nervosa, which affects all of these, lies at

127

the other. In between is a spectrum of disorders affecting one or more of these parameters, but not necessarily all. They include: (1) bulimia nervosa, in which weight may be low, normal, or high, but eating patterns are grossly disturbed and physical effects are seen in metabolic and hormonal functioning; (2) select-ive eating in which, despite an extremely limited diet, weight, growth, and development are usually unaffected; and (3) food avoidance emotional disorder (FAED), in which weight may be extremely low and have a serious impact on growth and development (Nicholls, Casey, Stanhope, & Lask, in preparation). The eating disorders need also to be distinguished from emotional disorders resulting in stunted growth (psychosocial dwarfism) (Albanese, Hamill, Jones, Skuse, Matthews, & Stanhope, 1994; Skuse, Albanese, Stanhope, Gilmour, & Voss, 1996), and from adjustment difficulties associated with constitutional delay of growth and puberty.

## Children differ from adults

There is a wealth of literature about the physical aspects of eating disorders in adults. For a number of reasons these findings are only in part generalisable to children. First, since children are still growing and developing, effects in adults that are known to be reversible with weight gain may be irreversible in children. Second, illness during development may influence the course as well as the timing and completeness of those changes. Third, the potential for intervening in children may be greater, if recognition and treatment are rapid. For example, despite severe illness, catch-up growth may be possible following successful inter-vention. However, there is little available information on the physical aspects of pre-pubertal children with eating disorders and many of the studies quoted in this chapter represent work carried out on young women. Occasionally they may be studies of adolescents, but the majority of these will have secondary amenorrhoea.

The clinical picture at presentation in children with anorexia nervosa may differ from that of adults. Children tend to dehydrate more quickly than adults; amenorrhoea may be primary and therefore not a useful marker; chronic mal-nutrition may be manifest as poor longitudinal growth and pubertal delay rather than low body weight *per se*. Pre-pubertal children have also been said to become emaciated more quickly because of the relative deficiency of body fat (Irwin, 1981).

## PHYSICAL EFFECTS OF CHILDHOOD EATING DISORDERS

The acute effects of starvation are dependent on fat stores. The proportion of body composition that is due to fat varies throughout childhood, and is usually at a peak during puberty, but may be relatively low earlier in childhood. Thus, very early onset eating disorders (age 6 or 7) occur at a time when energy reserves in the body are in short supply.

When the body is deprived of food a process of conservation of energy occurs, such that those functions most essential to the functioning of the person are affected last. Non-essential organs receive as limited an energy supply as possible, and blood flow to these areas is reduced. This includes the limb peripheries, the stomach and gut, and to the skin, resulting in the characteristic cold hands and feet, pale skin, weak pulses, and slowed gut motility. Many organs seem to be able to function on very little blood flow, but if any additional strain is placed on that organ, for example the heart, there may be insufficient reserve to sustain it. The brain is always the last organ to be affected by a fall in blood flow.

The process of body tissue breakdown, catabolism, supplies the energy necessary to sustain organ function. Fat is the richest source of energy, which is supplied in the form of ketones. All organs can use ketones except for the brain, which requires glucose. Glucose is supplied at first from glycogen stores in the liver. These only last for a few days, however, and thereafter protein from muscle is broken down to supply glucose. Over several weeks the brain slowly adapts to using ketones as its energy source. Ketone bodies are small volatile compounds, which, when excreted through the lungs, give breath a sweet smell. Ultimately the body's energy reserves are exhausted and death ensues.

## Clinical features

Physical examination is a *sine qua non* of assessment of a child or adolescent with a suspected eating disorder. Not only will the physical findings help in confirming the diagnosis, but the child's behaviour during the examination and attitude to being weighed may also give important clues. However, any practitioner undertaking such an examination should keep in mind that, for the patient, exposure of her body to a stranger is to expose to others the most disliked aspect of herself. At best this may be embarrassing; at worst traumatic. It is self-evident that an examination should be carried out with sensitivity to these issues.

Adolescent patients typically present with their body covered, partly from a wish to hide their body and partly from feeling cold. They may wear many layers of clothes in all seasons. Younger children, however, may not be self-conscious about their low weight, and even seem to wish to display it at times. This is particularly true of children with food avoidance emotional disorder, but also applies in early onset anorexia nervosa. The child may be weak and gaunt looking, with sallow skin, and, if vomiting regularly, swollen parotid glands give a pouch-like appearance to the cheeks. Dehydration may be evident from sunken eyes, dry lip mucosae, poor skin turgor, and crying without tears. The patient's breath may have an aromatous, sweet smell due to ketones.

On examination, the pulse may be weak and slowed. Significant bradycardia and hypotension may be associated with a history of fainting and dizziness. Hands and feet will be cold with bluish discolouration, and peripheral pulses in the feet may be absent. In extreme cases ulceration and gangrene can result.

(The patient may have been diagnosed as suffering from Raynaud's disease.) In addition to dry, flaky skin, the patient typically has lanugo hair—a soft downy hair similar to that covering a newborn baby—particularly over the back and arms. The skin may have an orange discolouration, seen best on the soles of the feet. This is carotenaemia, a sign of vitamin A overload, and evidence that the liver is not functioning fully in its metabolic role.

## Laboratory findings

*Serum electrolytes.* The electrolyte abnormalities commonly seen in anorexia nervosa and bulimia nervosa are described here. The majority of studies have been performed in adults, except where indicated. There are no studies published in relation to FAED or selective eating. Since patients with FAED can be just as malnourished as those with anorexia nervosa, it is likely that those findings due to low body weight would apply equally to these children.

Electrolyte abnormalities have been identified in up to 50% of adult patients with bulimia nervosa (Mitchell, Pyle, Eckert, Hatsukami, & Lentz, 1983) and are well described in association with dehydration and compensatory behaviours in anorexia nervosa and bulimia nervosa (Mira, Stewart, Vizzard, & Abraham, 1987). No specific studies of biochemical abnormalities in children have been described.

Dehydration results in raised serum urea and sodium, and urine will be dark and concentrated. If dehydration is extreme and renal compromise has occurred, raised serum creatinine and potassium may be found. More commonly, electrolyte disturbances are associated with compensatory behaviours. Vomiting, laxative and diuretic misuse all result in relative potassium depletion (hypokalaemia). Hypokalaemia may result in cardiac arrhythmias and sudden death. Of the 10–18% of all deaths from anorexia nervosa, about half are due to cardiac events (Sharp & Freeman, 1993).

However, serum potassium is a poor measure since only 5–6% of potassium is found in extracellular fluid and the rest is intracellular. Powers, Tyson, Stevens, and Heal (1995) found significant deficits in total body potassium, despite normal serum potassium levels. Russell, Prendergast, Darby, Garfinkel, Whitwell, and Jeejeebhoy (1983) found that total body potassium was low in adult patients with anorexia nervosa on admission, and increased on refeeding. Random serum potassium measurements can fluctuate widely in the presence of a low total body potassium, suggesting that serum potassium is a poor predictor of risk of cardiac arrhythmias. Serum potassium measurements are of value and clinical importance, however, as abnormal potassium is a sensitive, but not a specific, marker of frequent vomiting in bulimia nervosa (Crow, Salisbury, Crosby, & Mitchell, 1997). Studies of this effect have not been replicated in children.

Raised serum amylase may indicate "refeeding pancreatitis" in anorexia nervosa, or be a measure of salivary amylase in association with vomiting. Most assays do not differentiate the two types of amylase. Raised serum bicarbonate levels indicate metabolic alkalosis, usually in association with vomiting, although this is an inconsistent finding.

*Metabolism.* Glucose metabolism in patients with anorexia nervosa tends to be erratic during starvation, and low blood glucose levels may be found on random sampling. Rebound hypoglycaemia may be a repercussion of refeeding following a hyperinsulinaemic response. Patients with bulimia nervosa will have more wildly fluctuating glucose levels associated with bingeing and vomiting. This is a particular risk in patients with co-morbid diabetes mellitus (Carney & Andersen, 1996). Serum protein levels are usually normal, unless many years of chronic malnutrition have passed.

Raised serum cholesterol, possibly related to low cholesterol turnover, and elevated carotene have been described (Mira et al., 1987). Low zinc levels are reversed on refeeding, and may result in impaired taste especially for bitter and sour tastes (Lask, Fosson, Rolfe, & Thomas, 1993). Low phosphate levels have been reported in adults with anorexia nervosa, and this can contribute to feelings of weakness and fatigue (Waldholtz & Andersen, 1988). There are relatively few mineral or vitamin deficiencies that are not readily corrected with treatment.

Other metabolic changes seen are usually a result of acid-base balance in association with purging. Metabolic alkalosis is said to occur in 27% of adult patients, and metabolic acidosis in 8% (Carney & Andersen, 1996). Again, the information in children is limited.

*Blood system.* In the majority of acutely ill, underweight patients no abnormality is found on full blood count. Anaemia when it occurs is usually mild, and is associated with iron deficiency, although low levels of serum folate have also been reported and may result in a megaloblastic blood picture (Sharp & Freeman, 1993). In bulimia nervosa or other causes of protracted vomiting, anaemia may indicate oesophageal tears, or bleeding due to colonic damage secondary to laxative abuse. These features would be unusual in an early onset population. Leucopenia has been found, and more rarely, pancytopenia and hypoplastic anaemia (Sharp & Freeman, 1993). The erythrocyte sedimentation rate (ESR) has not been reported as abnormal in anorexia nervosa, but may be raised in bulimia nervosa if associated with oesophageal inflammation. Despite no reports in the literature, we find a raised ESR is not infrequent as an isolated finding. The ESR tends to return to normal on recovery from anorexia nervosa, and co-morbid physical disorder is rarely found.

*Liver function tests.* Liver enzymes such as alanine transaminase (ALT), aspartate transaminase (AST), and alkaline phosphatase (ALP) are usually raised (Halmi & Falk, 1981) and less frequently gamma-glutamyl transpeptidase (GGT).

Total bilirubin is usually normal, and albumin levels may be low or normal. These changes probably reflect fatty degeneration of the liver associated with malnutrition. The studies have been performed in adult patients, although clinical experience suggests that they hold true for children too.

*Endocrine abnormalities.*   The impact of eating disorders on endocrine function is extensive, and important, both for the acute and long-term consequences. The abnormalities of the growth and sex hormone are discussed later, together with their long-term effects. Here we mention the abnormalities of endocrine functioning that may be found on initial presentation.

In anorexia nervosa, as in other starvation states, there is an increase in plasma cortisol level, a reduction in cortisol metabolism, and an impairment of responses to dexamethasone (Newman & Halmi, 1988). Hypercortisolism is a common finding in anorexia nervosa, and at times cortisol levels can be found that are comparable to those found in Cushing's disease (Heinz, Martinez, & Haenggeli, 1977). Interestingly, Marcus, Blanz, Lehmkuhl, Rothenberger, and Eisert (1989), in a study of 94 young adolescents (mean age 15.4 years) found lower cortisol levels in those admitted for treatment with extremely low weight.

Thyroid function is variable in anorexia nervosa. Thyroxine levels ($T_4$) have consistently been in the normal range and unrelated to body weight. Triiodothyronine ($T_3$), on the other hand, is found to be low (dubbed the "low $T_3$ syndrome") and related to body weight. Unlike growth hormone, this low $T_3$ does not normalise until substantial weight gain has occurred, suggesting a metabolic adaptation to starvation (Newman & Halmi, 1988). Despite low $T_3$, thyroid stimulating hormone (TSH) levels are not usually elevated.

In the past decade many new hormones have been implicated in the control of weight and appetite. Those of particular interest are the gastrointestinal hormones and those related to fat and body composition. Many of these hormones are known to be peripherally secreted but to be present in high concentrations in the brain, suggesting a neurotransmitter role (Wakeling, 1985). Vasoactive peptide, somatostatin, neurotensin, and cholecystokinin, amongst others, have all been implicated in aspects of eating disorder pathology, including regulation of satiety, control of vomiting, altered activity, and sexual arousal (Katz, Boyar, Weiner, Gorzynski, Roffwarg, & Hellman, 1976; Kaye, 1996; Wakeling, 1985). Alderice, Dinsmore, Buchanan, and Adams (1985) showed a delayed rise in blood sugar levels and a slow release of insulin, and a flattening of the gut peptide "gastric inhibitory peptide" responses to a meal.

More recently, interest has focused on leptin, a hormone secreted by adipose tissue, and implicated in the regulation of pituitary-gonadal function. Leptin, which shows a relationship with body fat mass, results in weight loss, increased activity, and the normalisation of glucose metabolism in previously hyperphagic, obese, and infertile mice (Barash et al., 1996). Together with neuropeptide Y, which has a more direct effect on the hypothalamic control of appetite, this new avenue of research may further our understanding of the link between appetite, body fat, and gonadal functioning.

All these endocrine abnormalities normalise with treatment, although weight loss alone cannot account for all the endocrine findings. Patients with cystic fibrosis, with low weights comparable to patients with anorexia nervosa and no significant eating disorder or other psychopathology, have been shown to menstruate normally (Weltman, Stern, Doershuk, Moir, Palmer, & Jaffe, 1990). In addition, amenorrhoea can precede weight loss in up to one-third of patients (Theander, 1970). It is also true that there is often a delay in recommencing menses despite weight gain. Return of menstruation has been shown to be associated with psychological improvement (Van Binsbergen, Bennink, Odink, Haspels, & Koppeschaar, 1990). In children with primary amenorrhoea, resumption of age appropriate growth and pubertal development, with progression in ultrasound scan maturation (in girls) herald the onset of menarche and indicate a return of normal endocrine function. These events also appear not to be wholly dependent on weight restoration.

The endocrine abnormalities of bulimia nervosa are less well characterised, in part because of the wide variation in weight and menstrual functioning. What studies there are have been in adult women, and their relevance and applicability to children and adolescents is uncertain.

## EFFECTS ON SEXUAL DEVELOPMENT

Low weight pre-pubertal children may be appropriately pre-pubertal for their age and therefore apparently normal. In these children therefore, suppression of the hypothalamic/pituitary gonadal axis may have no apparent impact. However, at a physiological level nocturnal pulsatile gonadotrophin secretion from the pituitary, the primary event in the initiation of puberty, will be suppressed and hence delay onset of puberty. Children may therefore be pre-pubertal as a result of pubertal delay consequent on an eating disorder. Pubertal delay may also be due to constitutional delay, chronic disease, hypothalamic/pituitary disorders, or gonadal failure (Salardi et al., 1988).

More commonly, the eating disorder occurs after puberty has started, and the patient presents with arrested development and/or regression in some aspects of puberty. Depending on the stage at which has occurred, a girl may have primary amenorrhoea (i.e. periods have never started) or secondary amenorrhoea (periods started then stopped). Amenorrhoea or failure of onset of menarche are integral to the diagnosis of anorexia nervosa. Amenorrhoea in girls is a cardinal sign of endocrine dysfunction and the loss of adequate sex steroid production during pubertal development has lasting consequences.

Many features of anorexia nervosa have been shown to normalise on weight gain. Increasingly factors associated with persistent deficit are being identified (Russell, 1985; Ward, Brown, & Treasure, 1997), and many of these are a consequence of continued endocrine dysfunction, particularly the sex steroids. In adult patients, persistence of amenorrhoea for six months or more is associated with lowered bone density (Biller, Saxe, Herzog, Rosenthal, Holzman, & Klibanski, 1989). Russell (1985) described girls with early onset anorexia nervosa in whom pubertal development was incomplete, in whom adult breast development was limited and poorly oestrogenised. The impact of lack of oestrogen or testosterone during childhood and adolescence is wide reaching. Sex steroids and gonadotrophins are important not only for the development of healthy bones, but are necessary for growth, and for the development of secondary sexual characteristics and reproductive function.

## Ovarian development

The ovaries are active throughout childhood with continual follicular growth and follicular atresia (regression). Ovarian maturation continues throughout childhood, with an increase in ovarian volume and in the number and size of the developing follicles, as puberty approaches. After 14 years of age the ovary is essentially mature in the majority of females (Peters, Himelstein Braw, & Faber, 1976).

Ultrasound studies have shown the ovarian volume to be $0.8cm^3$ in the first 3 months of life increasing in volume from a mean of $1cm^3$ at 2 years of age to $2cm^3$ at 12 years of age. Normal standards for ovarian volume in childhood and puberty are available (Bridges, Cooke, Healy, Hindmarsh, & Brook, 1993; Griffin, Cole, Duncan, Hollman, & Donaldson, 1995). The mean ovarian volume at age 11 years is 1.58ml, and at age 14 the mean volume is 2.52ml, with 8ml at about the 97th centile.

The volume of the ovary is affected by the presence of large cysts, either primordial or ovulatory follicles, or a corpus luteal cyst (see later). These cysts are all normal, and represent various states of maturation, or stages of the menstrual cycle, but ovarian volume cannot be reliably calculated when these structures are present.

There appear to be two particular periods of increased growth rate of the ovary. The first occurs at approximately 8 years of age, coinciding with the rise in androgen secretion from the adrenal cortex at adrenarche. Adrenal androgen secretion also frequently results in pubic hair development and a minor growth acceleration. The second growth spurt occurs immediately before and during puberty, and may be influenced by a number of factors, including a rise in gonadotrophin secretion and increasing concentrations of growth hormone, and growth hormone mediators.

In the neonate the size of the ovary and the number of visible follicles is variable although follicles are often surprisingly numerous. This follicular activity in the infant is related to the maternal hormone influence. Occasionally a follicle may grow large so as to precipitate torsion of the ovary. Throughout childhood the ovarian follicles increase in size and number. Their size varies, and they may become atretic at any stage of their development.

*Polycystic ovaries.*   Polycystic ovaries (PCO) are a distinct morphological entity, and are a variation of normal ovarian appearance, occurring in 22–25% of the normal adult population (Bridges et al., 1993; Clayton et al., 1992; Polson, Adams, Wadsworth, & Franks, 1988). They should not be confused with the polycystic ovarian syndrome (PCOS)—the association of PCO, hirsutism, obesity, oligo-amenorrhoea, and infertility as originally described by Stein and Leventhal (1935). PCO and its variable associated endocrine abnormalities clearly represent a spectrum (Franks, 1995). Although PCO is associated with infertility, this is not always so (Conway, Honour, & Jacobs, 1989). Women with PCO tend to be obese, and as a group there is an increased tendency to hirsutism and menstrual irregularities than those who are lean. Polycystic ovaries (PCO) may be found with the clinical and biochemical features of the polycystic ovarian syndrome (PCOS). Typical biochemical abnormalities include raised serum LH, raised LH to FSH ratio (above 3), and raised serum testosterone (or androstenedione).

It is thought that PCO is primarily an ovarian disorder, although debate continues about the aetiology (Rosenfield, 1997). That PCO is linked to puberty is well recognised (Brook, Jacobs, & Stanhope, 1988; Stanhope, Adams, & Brook, 1988). Wedge resection of a part of the polycystic ovary is highly effective in restoring ovulation, although the mechanism is ill understood. Many hypotheses exist and much research is still to be done in the field. Women with PCOS have a family history of relatives with PCO and there appears to be a strong hereditary component. Conditions associated with high levels of androgen that originate from an external source, such as congenital adrenal hyperplasia, are known to be associated with PCO (Nestler, 1997; Salardi et al., 1988). PCO is also associated with high insulin levels (e.g. in diabetes) and insulin resistance (Poretsky & Piper, 1994; Prelevic, 1997).

Interestingly, PCO has been reported in 75% of adult women with bulimia nervosa (McCluskey, Lacey, & Pearce, 1992). Even women with normal weight bulimia nervosa have a high incidence of menstrual irregularity. The reason for the higher incidence of PCO in this eating disorder is unknown, but is thought to be related to the swings in insulin levels due to the associated bingeing and vomiting. These changes, when they occur during ovarian development, may have a lasting impact on ovarian morphology. Our group have noted PCO occurring in a high proportion of our patients with pubertal onset eating disorders, although few of them have frank bulimia nervosa. The relationship between disordered eating and PCO, as either precipitating or maintaining factors, needs further exploration.

## Menarche

The principal regulators of ovarian function are luteinising (LH) and follicle-stimulating hormone (FSH). In response to rising levels of FSH, between five and twelve primordial follicles begin to enlarge and are then called primary follicles. The ovarian follicles gradually enlarge until a follicle of at least

16mm is attained. There is follicular secretion of oestrogen, which results in the development of an endometrium. Without ovulating (an anovulatory cycle) the follicle regresses and the subsequent fall in oestrogen results in a withdrawal bleed. Withdrawal bleeds are usually shorter and less regular than ovulatory bleeds, and account for much of the apparent irregularity of the first periods of adolescence.

Eventually, when a follicle diameter of over 20mm is achieved, that follicle gains primacy, while the remainder of the other follicles, recruited during the cycle, degenerate. The remaining follicle is now known as a mature or dominant Graafian follicle. After ovulation the granulosa cells of the ruptured follicle wall begins to proliferate and give rise to the corpus luteum. The corpus luteum is an endocrine structure that secretes steroid hormones that maintain the uterine endometrium in readiness to receive an embryo. If no embryo implants in the uterus the corpus luteum degenerates after about 14 days.

Amenorrhoea, the result of widespread suppression of the hypothalamo-pituitary-gonadal axis, is hypothalamic in origin. Weight loss is a significant contributor to this effect. Additional factors leading to amenorrhoea may be hypothalamus-mediated "stress", or exercise-induced amenorrhoea, which some authors have argued is a discrete entity (Schwartz, Cumming, Riordan, Selye, Yen, & Rebar, 1981). In the 1970s it was hypothesised that there was a "critical weight" at which menstruation occurred (Frisch & McArthur, 1974; Frisch & Revelle, 1971). It now seems clear that it is not simply weight, but body composition that is important. A certain amount of body fat is needed to maintain a critical level of circulating sex steroids. The exact mechanism for this remains to be elucidated, but a number of mediators have been postulated, including a recently described hormone leptin (Barash et al., 1996; Rosenbaum et al., 1996).

Recovery of normal menstrual function in patients with early onset anorexia nervosa is highly variable. In a series of young patients (Lai, de Bruyn, Lask, Bryant-Waugh, & Hankins, 1994), 50% with primary and 50% with secondary amenorrhoea, the average weight/height ratio of those who resumed or commenced menstruation, half of each group, was 96.5% weight/height (range 90–108%). In those with continuing amenorrhoea the average was 87.5% weight/height (range 76–96%). At follow-up (mean 7.2 years) of a cohort of younger patients, 55% of patients were having regular periods, 14% were having irregular periods, and 31% had continuing amenorrhoea (Bryant-Waugh, Knibbs, Fosson, Kaminski, & Lask, 1988). These findings are comparable to those in adults, in whom Treasure, Gordon, King, Wheeler, and Russell (1985) found that the presence of a dominant follicle on ultrasound (heralding onset of menses) was associated with weight restoration to a mean of 97% of premorbid weight.

In children premorbid weight is of no relevance, unless reliable weight centiles can be obtained. In an individual child therefore, prediction of onset of menses relies heavily on progress through puberty and pelvic ultrasound scan findings. When polycystic ovary (PCO) appearances are present menstruation may be harder to predict, and this can cause problems in determining a healthy weight for the patient.

The relationship between atypical eating disorders of childhood and menstrual disturbance has not been reported. Children with FAED are of equivalent low weight to patients with anorexia nervosa, but are younger and therefore more likely to have primary amenorrheoa and pubertal delay (Nicholls et al., in preparation). Whether the other endocrine findings are identical to those of anorexia nervosa is not yet clear.

## Uterine development

In the neonate the uterus is still under the influence of maternal hormone stimulation. There is often a prominent endometrium and enlargement is predominantly in the uterine body or corpus. After about one month, the size of the uterus starts to regress and it assumes a normal pre-pubertal configuration with prominence of the cervix. During this period the cervix to corpus ratio is approximately 2:1 and this configuration remains until about 9 years of age (Orsini, Salardi, Pilu, Bovicelli, & Cacciari, 1984). At this time, and to coincide with the rise of androgen release from the adrenal glands, uterine growth begins. First, there is a lengthening of the body, and later a growth in both the cervix and body lead to a tubular shape, until finally an adult size and shape uterus are reached.

## Endocrine aspects of sexual development

A widespread endocrine dysfunction of the hypothalamic-pituitary-gonadal axis is integral to the definition of anorexia nervosa. Garfinkel et al. (1996) have argued that, in eating disorders where there is no endocrine dysfunction, psychosocial characteristics are similar to those with the full anorexia nervosa syndrome, and that the distinction is therefore arbitrary. For the purposes of long-term risk to physical health, however, the endocrine dysfunction is a crucial aspect. A further aspect of these biological characteristics is that most, but not all, are reversible with weight gain. Far more is known about endocrine aspects of anorexia nervosa than bulimia nervosa (see Newman & Halmi, 1988 for review). Studies specific to premenarchal or pubertal children, or to atypical eating disorders are rare.

In 1974, Boyar et al. demonstrated that, in adult patients with anorexia nervosa, the pattern of secretion of gonadotrophic hormones regressed to a pre-pubertal state with weight loss, and restored to the mature pattern with weight gain. The same is true of pubertal children, although the degree of restoration will depend on the stage of puberty at which the illness onset. Sherman, Halmi, and Zamudio (1975) demonstrated that LH and FSH levels, suppressed during the low weight period, could be stimulated by exogenous gonadotrophic releasing hormone but that the pattern of secretion resembled the pre-pubertal pattern, with a significantly greater FSH response, and a blunted LH response. This persisted even with weight restoration to 90–94% of ideal body weight.

## Assessment of sexual development

### Assessing pubertal delay

The assessment of pubertal status in children with eating disorders is important in determining the impact of the disorder on growth and development. Pubertal delay is determined by assessment of Tanner stage compared to population norms (Tanner & Whitehouse, 1966), pre-pubertal pelvic ultrasound appearances, a discrepancy between the bone age and the chronological age of the patient, and suppression of the gonadotrophins—luteinising hormone (LH) and follicular simulating hormone (FSH).

Pubertal delay is defined arbitrarily as when the absence of any signs of puberty when the chronological age is two standard deviations above the mean age for the onset of puberty. In the UK this is at age 13.4 for girls and 13.8 for boys. Menses are deemed to be delayed if there is failure of onset within 4.5 years of the start of puberty, or by a chronological or bone age of 14 years.

Pre-pubertal levels of gonadotrophins on serum sampling in boys and girls of low weight will confirm that pituitary-gonadal functioning is suppressed. In boys there is no sign as obvious as periods, and no investigation as useful as pelvic ultrasound, in assessing the impact of the eating disorder on sexual development.

### Pelvic ultrasound

*Technique.*   Successful sonographic examination and evaluation of disorders of sexual development in young girls requires an accurate knowledge and assessment of both uterine and ovarian size and morphology as they grow and develop throughout childhood. Recent advances in ultrasound equipment have resulted in equipment that can produce images of superb resolution and have the advantage of variable focus for deeper structures in the older child. This equipment is essential for scanning a child's pelvis in order to be able to measure small 1–2mm follicles and for careful measurement and recognition of the endometrium. Generally, small footprint transducers of 5–7MHz are best for this purpose. Endovaginal scanning (using a vaginal probe), although important in adult gynaecology, can only be used in those older girls who are sexually active, and is not widely employed in routine paediatric practice.

A full bladder is needed as an acoustic window in all children. Older children and adolescents should be well hydrated and given 300–500ml of still fluid, preferably water, some 45 minutes before the examination is due. Timing is critical, as an overfull bladder will distort the appearance of the uterus and displace or obscure the ovaries, whereas a partially empty bladder will result in inadequate visualisation of these structures.

The ovaries are identified by scanning obliquely through the full bladder in the angle between the iliac vessels and bladder and then transversely, usually at the level of the uterine fundus. The ovaries are measured in three planes, and the ovarian volume is calculated according to the formula for a prolate ellipse. The number, size, and distribution of the follicles are noted, the uterine length measured in the longitudinal axis, and the anteroposterior measurements taken at the cervix and fundus. If the endometrium is seen, the thickness is measured at the maximum depth of the body away from the cervix.

*The ovaries.*    Pre-pubertally, the ovaries may appear quite active, with follicles of up to 9mm in size. With onset of the high LH pulses at night, at about 8–9 years of age, the ovaries become multifollicular, defined on ultrasound appearances as more than six follicles of 4mm in diameter. This is a normal phase of development and heralds the onset of puberty. The follicles continue to increase in size with the progression through puberty. With the constant maturation and regression of the follicles there is a wide range of diameters seen at different pubertal stages. Also, with lower levels of gonadotrophin in pre-pubertal girls, this can result in larger follicles of up to 12mm. This limits the value of follicular diameter in assessing pubertal status.

*Polycystic ovaries.*    Prior to recent developments in pelvic ultrasound the morphological diagnosis of PCO was based on findings on surgical examination and histology. Typical appearances of the ovary on ultrasound are an important criterion for the diagnosis of PCO in women with suggestive clinical features, although these may not be present in all such women. PCO is defined on ultrasound as ovaries with an increased ovarian volume, a necklace of follicles with at least 10 follicles around the periphery of the ovary measuring between 2 and 8mm, and an increase in the dense central stroma (Adams, Polson, & Franks, 1986). In the adult PCO population studied by Polson et al. (1988), the mean ovarian volume was more than 10ml, which is at the maximum size of normal ovaries; however, some were diagnosed as PCO morphology at a volume of 4ml. Bridges et al. (1993) have reported the morphological appearance of PCO as early as 6 years in their study of normal girls, with a peak incidence at puberty corresponding to the rise in IGF-I and insulin at this time. It is thought that, once present, PCO morphology in the ovary does not disappear, although preliminary evidence suggests that this may not always be so (Morgan et al., in preparation). There is no way currently of predicting which individuals with the PCO appearance will become symptomatic.

*The uterus.*    Pre-pubertally the uterine length is 26–38mm with an antero-posterior diameter at the cervix of between 5 and 10mm. As puberty approaches and follicle development matures, the increasing levels of oestrogen result in both an increase in uterine size and endometrial thickness. The uterus attains its adult "pear"-shaped configuration with fundal (corpus) dominance. The endometrium is seen as an echogenic mid-line echo.

*Pubertal delay and ultrasound.* Ultrasound will demonstrate the presence of normal (usually multifollicular) ovaries and uterus in a girl whose puberty is constitutionally delayed. Amenorrhoea, either primary or secondary, is an integral part of the diagnosis of anorexia nervosa. Patients with primary amenorrhoea show the pre-pubertal appearance of the uterus and ovaries (Figs. 8.1 and 8.2), whereas those who become ill and lose weight after menses have commenced show a marked regression in the size of the uterus and ovaries (Figs. 8.3 and 8.4). In particular, the ovaries become quiescent and show no follicular activity. Ultrasound now plays a major clinical role in determining when an "ideal" (i.e. healthy) target weight has been achieved (Adams, 1993; Lai et al., 1994).

### Bone age

This parameter, used in the measurement of growth and pubertal development, is the radiological assessment of skeletal maturity. Several methods have been devised. The most widely used method of determining bone age is the Greulich and Pyle (1959) atlas. This was based on the radiographs of the left hands of white children from Cleveland, USA. Social, racial, and economic factors are known to influence the rate of skeletal maturation, and the atlas when applied to non-USA children may result in an under- or over-estimation of skeletal maturity. For this reason, Tanner, Whitehouse, Cameron, Marshall, Healy, and Goldstein (1983) developed a technique that requires evaluation of each bone individually. From these a score can be obtained which is then compared to a reference centile chart. The 50th centile values represent the average bone age of an individual.

## EFFECTS ON GROWTH

Arrested development may be seen as a premature slowing in growth velocity, occasionally amounting to near growth arrest, and a failure to maintain the tempo of pubertal progression. Rate of growth for age is one of the most sensitive markers of illness in childhood, but currently there is little information about the expected growth patterns in childhood onset eating disorders, particularly for boys.

The effect of anorexia nervosa on linear growth is an issue of continued debate. Although cases have been described in which growth retardation has clearly occurred (Brinch & Manthorpe, 1987; Pugliese, Lifshitz, Grad, Fort, & Marks-Katz, 1983), retrospective studies in adults found no difference in height between those patients who had had anorexia nervosa in adolescence and those who developed anorexia nervosa later (Joughin, Varsou, Gowers, & Crisp, 1992;

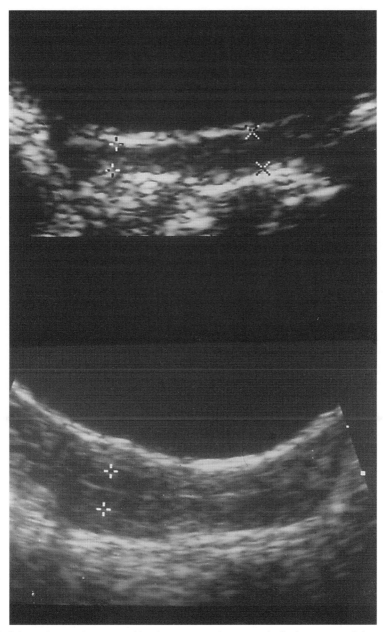

FIG. 8.1 Patient aged 13 years with primary amenorrhoea. Longitudinal sonogram of the uterus. Top: Pre-pubertal uterus with the cervix thicker than the fundus (marked ×). Bottom: One year later, after successful treatment, the uterus has grown and now has an adult configuration with a measurable endometrium.

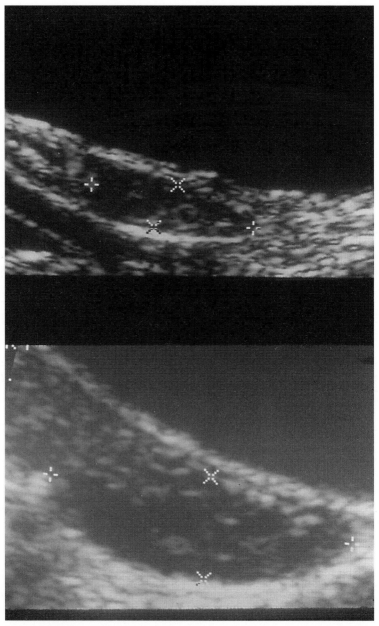

FIG. 8.2 Patient aged 13 years with primary amenorrhoea. Sonogram of the right ovary. Top: Small ovary with virtually no follicular activity. Bottom: After one year, and weight gain, a much larger ovary with much more follicular activity seen.

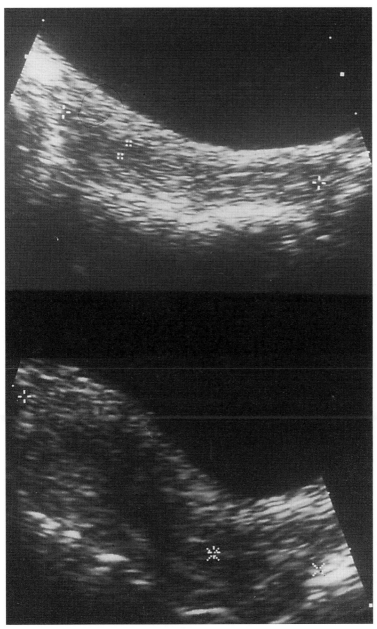

FIG. 8.3  Patient aged 13 years with secondary amenorrhoea. Longitudinal sonogram of the uterus. Top: Small uterus with adult configuration. In patients with secondary amenorrhoea the uterus never regresses to the pre-pubertal appearance. Bottom: After one year with weight gain. The uterus has grown to a more pronounced adult configuration.

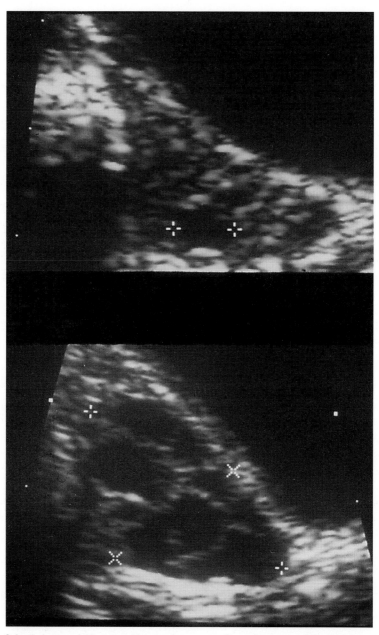

FIG. 8.4  Patient aged 13 years with secondary amenorrhoea. Sonogram of the right ovary. Top: Only a single follicle is evident on the ovary (between +), which is also small in volume. Bottom: After one year and weight gain, the ovary now shows a multifollicular appearance, containing more than six follicles of 4mm in diameter.

Pfeiffer, Lucas, & Ilstrup, 1986). In one of the few studies of early onset anorexia nervosa, Danzinger, Mukamel, Zeharia, Dinari, and Mimouni (1994) studied the growth patterns of 15 patients (13 female, 2 male) with early onset anorexia nervosa, all of whom had been suffering from anorexia nervosa for at least six months. Mean age at referral was 13.3 ± 1.3 years. All had growth arrest for 13 ± 8.5 months prior to admission. Catch-up growth occurred in 9 out of the 13 patients, all at Tanner stage 1–3. Catch-up did not occur in two patients at Tanner stage 3 and 5, despite weight gain, and in two patients who did not complete treatment. The authors suggest that growth arrest is a common, if not universal, sign of anorexia nervosa during the pubertal and peripubertal period of six months duration or more, and that projected height should be included in the calculation of target outcomes.

The vast majority of studies have been on patients with secondary amenorrhoea. The clinical significance of this is that menarche is a relatively late pubertal event (just before stage 4 breast development). In terms of the impact on linear growth and bone density, onset earlier in puberty may have the most serious consequences. The fastest period of growth (peak height velocity) in girls occurs on average at the age of 11.3 years (during stage 2 and 3 of breast development). The patient with secondary amenorrhoea will have completed much of her pubertal growth spurt, and therefore would be expected to have a less compromised final height.

The picture in boys is slightly different, since the pubertal growth spurt in boys occurs late in puberty and the endocrine events of puberty occur roughly two years later than in girls. In boys peak growth velocity occurs on average at age 15, during stage 4 of genital development, or when testicular volume reaches 10ml. The potential for compromise of final height with onset before or during puberty could therefore be greater in boys than in girls, although catch-up growth could occur. There are no studies as yet confirming these issues. Studies of growth in the atypical eating disorders such as selective eating and food avoidance emotional disorder are in progress (Nicholls et al., in preparation).

There is little information available about bone age in early onset anorexia nervosa, although the effects of malnutrition in childhood on bone age have been studied. Dreizen, Spirakis, and Stone (1967) compared 30 undernourished and 30 well-nourished girls from early childhood to early adulthood. Using bone age and height measurements they found that chronic malnutrition slowed the rate of skeletal maturation, delayed menarche, and prolonged the growth period. The longer the malnutrition the greater the bone age delay. Age of menarche was more closely related to skeletal than to chronological age. No appreciable difference was found between the two groups in their final adult height, as the prolonged growth period seemed to have compensated for the slower skeletal growth. In our own sample of 14 children with anorexia nervosa between the ages of 9 and 15, bone age delay has varied between none and 54 months.

## Assessment of growth

*Anthropometric measurements.*   Weighing should be carried out consistently on the same scales if possible, with the patient wearing minimal clothing and the weight corrected for likely or suspected water loading, i.e. when the young person drinks an excessive amount of water before being weighed in order to apparently increase their weight (1 litre of water weighs 1kg). This is most likely to occur in anorexia nervosa and should be considered when sudden weight changes occur. Water loading is difficult to detect clinically.

Height should ideally be measured using a stadiometer, and measurement of sitting height and subischial leg lengths should be performed if linear growth is affected, as these measures reflect the relative contributions of gonadotrophin or growth hormone insufficiency to growth delay. Segmental disproportion, with a relatively short spine at final height, is a feature of pubertal delay (Albanese & Stanhope, 1993). These figures, when plotted on standard growth charts, will allow comparison to population norms (Freeman, Cole, Chinn, Jones, White, & Preece).

Children who develop eating disorders after their pubertal growth spurt may show no deficit of linear growth (and are often tall for their age; Joughin et al., 1992) and their weight may be within the normal range for the population. For example, height may be on the 90th centile, and weight just above the third. The weight/height discrepancy may not therefore be immediately apparent, and calculation of the weight to height ratio is a better indicator of weight deficits. This weight-for-(height-for-age) is obtained by taking the child's height and finding the age where the child's height is equal to the median reference height (the child's height-age). Using the reference weight at this age as the denominator, the ratio of observed to reference weight can be calculated. This can be done using a Cole's slide rule (Cole, 1979; Cole, Donnet, & Stanfield, 1981); software is also available to perform the computation (Frampton & Austin, 1997).

As an alternative to weight for height ratios there are now body mass index (BMI) normal data in children allowing comparison to the normal population (Cole, Freeman, & Preece, 1995) (Fig. 8.5). Current diagnostic criteria, both DSM-IV and ICD-10, require a weight of 15% below that expected for age or a BMI of 17.5 or below for the diagnosis of anorexia nervosa. BMI is not useful in children and adolescents, since normal BMI varies with age, particularly through puberty. Clinically, rate of weight loss may be more significant than absolute weight/height or BMI. Previous growth data will help in ascertaining whether there has a been a fall off in weight and growth over time (see Fig. 8.6).

*Growth hormone.*   Growth hormone (GH) levels are elevated in about half of emaciated patients with associated decreased levels of somatomedin-C (Argente et al., 1997; Cabranes, Almoguera, Santos, Hidalgo, Borque, & del Olmo, 1988).

Refer a girl whose BMI falls above the 98th centile as obese. Consider referral, as overweight, a girl whose BMI falls above the 91st centile even on the basis of a single measurement. Consider for referral a girl whose BMI falls below the 2nd centile as being significantly underweight even on the basis of a single measurement. During infancy large but transient changes in centile may occur due to the shape of the charts, and these changes are normal. It should be remembered that the earlier the age of the second rise, the greater the risk of future obesity. Remember also that while BMI has a high correlation with relative fatness or leanness it is actually assessing the weight-to-height relationship: **this may give misleading results in girls who are very stocky and muscular who might appear obese on the BMI alone.**

# GIRLS
## BMI CHART
**(BIRTH - 20 YEARS)**
United Kingdom cross-sectional reference data : 1997/1

Name.......................................................

NHS No.

### How to calculate BMI

Divide weight (kg) by square of length/height (m²)
e.g. when weight = 25kg and length/height = 1.2m (120cm),
BMI = 25 ÷ (1.2 x 1.2) = 17.4

| Date | Age | Length/Height | Weight | BMI | Initials |
|------|-----|---------------|--------|-----|----------|
| : : | : | : | : | : | : |
| : : | : | : | : | : | : |
| : : | : | : | : | : | : |
| : : | : | : | : | : | : |
| : : | : | : | : | : | : |
| : : | : | : | : | : | : |
| : : | : | : | : | : | : |

**Body Mass Index (kg/m²)**

years

99.6th
98th
91st
75th
50th
25th
9th
2nd
0.4th

Data: 1990

Manufacture 2 October '97

**Reference**
Body Mass Index reference curves for the UK, 1990 (TJ Cole, JV Freeman, MA Preece) *Arch Dis Child* 1995; **73**: 25-29
Sex differences in weight in infancy (MA Preece, JV Freeman, TJ Cole) *BMJ* 1996; **313**: 1486

*Designed and Published by*
© CHILD GROWTH FOUNDATION 1997/1
(Charity Reg. No 274325)
2 Mayfield Avenue,
London W4 1PW

*Printed and Supplied by*
HARLOW PRINTING LIMITED
Maxwell Street ◊ South Shields
Tyne & Wear ◊ NE33 4PU

FIG. 8.5   BMI centile chart for girls (reproduced with permission of the Child Growth Foundation, London, UK).

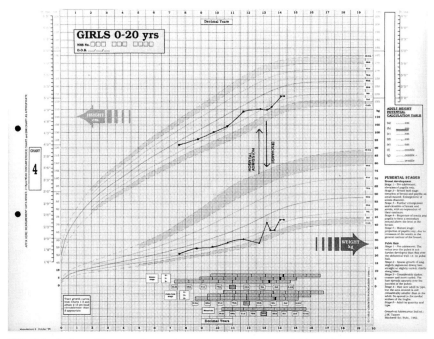

FIG. 8.6    Patient with onset of anorexia nervosa at age 11 years. With weight loss (bottom half of chart), her growth rate slows (top of chart), and puberty is delayed (bars below charts). Weight gain occurs during inpatient treatment. Some months later growth is restored and catch-up growth occurs. Puberty onsets and progresses normally provided weight is maintained.

Thus, feedback control of growth hormone production is impaired. This effect is likely to be hypothalamus mediated, since GH production in response to stimulation tests are normal or attenuated (Muller, Cavagnini, Panerai, Massironi, Ferrari, & Brambilla, 1987; Nussbaum, Blethen, Chasalow, Jacobson, Shenker, & Feldman, 1990). The relationship between growth hormone levels and rates of growth has not been characterised.

## EFFECTS ON BONE DENSITY

Osteoporosis is defined as a bone mineral density (BMD) of more than 2.5 standard deviations (SDs) below peak bone mass (T score) for gender. It is characterised by low bone mass and an increase in bone fragility, leading to an increase in fracture risk. Osteopenia, less marked thinning, is defined as a BMD of 1 to 2.5 SDs below T score (World Health Organisation, 1994). Osteoporosis as a complication of anorexia nervosa was first described by Rigotti, Nussbaum, Herzog, and Neer (1984) and is now one of the principle concerns in long-term morbidity associated with eating disorders, particularly in children, in whom bone strength is developing.

The principal factors that affect bone density are familial, race, nutrition and body weight, sex steroids and growth hormone, and exercise (Dhuper, Warren, Brooks Gunn, & Fox, 1990; Lloyd et al., 1992; Ott, 1991). Anorexia nervosa has an impact on all those factors over which it is possible to have influence (i.e. all but genetic and racial influences). Research findings suggest that in anorexia nervosa severity of osteoporosis is related to the duration of amenorrhoea, and that only partial protection is provided by taking the contraceptive pill or other oestrogen supplements (Klibanski, Biller, Schoenfeld, Herzog, & Saxe, 1995; Seeman, Szmukler, Formica, Tsalamandris, & Mestrovic, 1992). The issue of pre-scribed oestrogen remains controversial (Scholte & Van de Aast, 1995). Current recommendations are that in children and young persons the goal of treatment should be to maximise peak bone mass by weight restoration, and oestrogen should be reserved for cases where prevention of bone loss is the priority and weight restoration is not seen as a realistic goal, i.e. severe and chronic cases in adults. In children, oestrogen fuses the epiphyses and prevents further growth.

Osteoporosis is one of the principal reasons why restoration of menses is such a priority in the treatment of anorexia nervosa. Not only is osteoporosis correlated to amenorrhoea, but it is clear from studies in other populations, e.g. Turner's syndrome, that oestrogen is crucial in the accretion and maintenance of bone mass (Davies, Gulenki, & Jacobs, 1995). Although bone accretion may continue into early adulthood, the time for maximal bone accretion is during the pubertal growth period, and that peak bone mass is attained in girls and boys at shortly after reaching stage 5 in puberty (15–16 in girls; 17–18 in boys) (Bachrach, 1993; Bonjour, Theintz, Buchs, Slosman, & Rizzoli, 1991). Finkelstein, Neer, Beverley, Biller, Crawford, and Klibanski (1992) has demonstrated that in boys who had significant delay in puberty, bone density was reduced relative to normal men in later life. Therefore, it seems that a relative lack of sex steroids during adolescence may prevent attainment of adequate peak bone mass, and that there is a limited window of opportunity for bone accretion. Bone density in males with anorexia nervosa has not specifically been studied.

Weight-bearing exercise is known to influence bone density. In ballet dancers who have low body weight and amenorrhoea, bone density at the femoral neck is higher than in population norms, but at the lumbar spine is significantly lower (Young, Formica, Szmukler, & Seeman, 1994). Trabecular bone, particularly in the lumbar spine, seems particularly susceptible to osteopenia. In anorexia nervosa, where patients are often keen to exercise, there is a need to balance the benefits of limited weight-bearing exercise with the increase in calorie requirement needed to do that.

Calcium and calcium supplementation is an area requiring further consid-eration. Some practitioners include calcium supplements routinely in refeeding programmes, whereas others focus on normalisation of eating habits and weight restoration with less attention to the dietary content. That sufficient calcium is necessary for healthy bone development is clear (Boot, de Ridder, Pols, Krenning,

& de Muinck Keizer Schrama, 1997; Johnston et al., 1992; Lloyd et al., 1996). Of all the factors in anorexia contributing to low bone density, calcium deficit is likely to play only a part. It is estimated that one-third of normal adolescents have less than half the recommended daily intake of calcium a day (Bachrach, 1993). Calcium only affects the bone mineral content (BMC) and may not influence the rate of fractures, which depends in part on bone elasticity. To date there are no controlled trials of calcium supplementation.

In summary, adolescence is a crucial time for the accretion of bone mass, necessary to last a lifetime. It is also the time for peak incidence of onset of anorexia nervosa, which affects almost all parameters influencing bone mass. The earlier in puberty the illness develops, the greater may be its impact on bone density. The targets for treatment are weight restoration, resumption of menses, and maintenance of the tempo of pubertal development. The use of oestrogen replacement is not advocated except in extreme circumstances, and the role of calcium supplementation has not yet been fully evaluated.

## Assessment of bone density in children

Using dual energy X-ray absorptiometry (DEXA) methods both bone and soft tissue composition can be measured *in vivo*. Comparison to normal data for children allows a z-score to be calculated. This takes into account the standard deviation for age and sex. The total body radiation dose to the adult patient is <70μSV which is equivalent to the amount of radiation exposure on a flight from London to New York, or 1/15th of a chest X-ray. Alternative methods of measuring bone mineral density include single and dual photon absorptiometry (SPA and DPA), single X-ray absorptiometry, and quantitative computed tomography. Newer techniques being applied include bone ultrasound and magnetic resonance.

Normal values for BMC and BMD using DEXA have been established for children from the age of 3 years onwards (Faulkner, Bailey, Drinkwater, McKay, Arnold, & Wilkinson, 1996; Hannan, Cowen, Wrate, & Barton, 1995; Kroger, Kotaniemi, Kroger, & Alhava, 1993). The measured BMD reflects not only the true bone volumetric density but also bone size. Therefore, the assessment of bone density in the growing skeleton should take growth into account (Lu, Cowell, Lloyd Jones, Briody, & Howman Giles, 1996; Molgaard, Thomsen Lykke, Prentice, Cole, & Michaelsen, 1997).

Quantitative ultrasound is a non-invasive, rapid, relatively inexpensive procedure which is well tolerated by both children and adults (Jaworski, Lebiedowski, Lorenc, & Trempe, 1995; Langton, 1994). Normative data for children using bone ultrasound have recently been published (Mughal, Ward, Qayyum, & Langton, 1997), but as yet there are few studies of broadband ultrasound attenuation (BUA) in eating disorders. The BUA technique provides valuable information on the structure of bone, and hence its fragility and fracture risk, as well as an indirect measure of its density. This assessment of bone integrity is calculated by measuring the reduction of intensity of a pulse of ultrasound as it traverses a sample of bone. For a number of reasons the commonest site for ultrasound measurement is the calcaneum. Of particular importance is the high content of trabecular bone in the calcaneum, which makes it highly comparable to the weight-bearing fracture sites of the femoral neck and vertebrae.

## EFFECTS ON THE DIGESTIVE TRACT

Despite gastrointestinal symptoms being the most frequent reported by patients with eating disorders (Carney & Andersen, 1996), there may be very little abnormal to find on examination. Symptoms also generally resolve with refeeding (Rigaud, Bedig, Merrouche, Vulpillat, Bonfils, & Apfelbaum, 1988; Waldholtz & Andersen, 1990). Patients with anorexia nervosa may demonstrate significantly slower gastric emptying rates for both solids and liquids (McCallum, Grill, Lange, Planky, Glass, & Greenfeld, 1985). It has been suggested that foregut motility disorders may contribute to or perpetuate eating disorders by inducing nausea and other aversive food related sensations. Studies in adults have consistently shown that abnormalities of the motor activity of the gastric antrum (outlet) are impaired during fasting and after feeding, and that this correlates with symptoms of satiety, bloating, nausea, and vomiting.

In one of the few studies of the gastrointestinal tract that has been performed in children with eating disorders, Ravelli, Helps, Devane, Lask, and Milla (1993) demonstrated that gastric antral electrical dysrhythmias were not a feature of children with anorexia nervosa (age range 11.6 to 15.5). In this study, 8 of 14 patients complained of upper gastrointestinal symptoms. The authors suggest that the gastric antrum abnormalities found in adults are a secondary phenomenon, and that treatment with prokinetic drugs (promoting gastric emptying) was not appropriate in children and young adolescents.

The superior mesenteric artery syndrome (SMA) is a result of compression of the third part of the duodenum between the aorta and the vertebral column behind and the nerves and vessels of the superior mesenteric bundle in front. This is thought to occur when the cushion of fat protecting the bundle is lost (Adson, Mitchell, & Trenkner, 1997). The classic presentation is characterised by chronic abdominal pain, feeling full after a meal, and vomiting. The symptoms tend to be episodic. SMA syndrome alone is associated with a number of physical disorders. In eating disorders the syndrome occurs most commonly together with acute gastric dilatation, usually after a binge, in both anorexia nervosa and normal-weight bulimia nervosa. Of the two cases reported in 14-year-old girls, one occurred on the second day of nasogastric refeeding (Jennings & Klidjian, 1974).

Although children often complain of constipation, the use or misuse of laxatives in younger patients is not a common phenomenon.

## Assessment of the gastrointestinal tract

Physical examination will identify extreme constipation. A raised ESR (see blood tests, mentioned earlier) may indicate inflammatory disease of the gut, including oesophagitis, Crohn's disease, or colitis. Barium studies or a white cell scan may be indicated according to blood indices and clinical judgement. Anti-gliadin antibodies may indicate further investigation for coeliac disease. Gastro-oesophageal reflux can be identified on barium studies, or milk scans, and severity of acid reflux quantifiable by pH studies. The SMA syndrome is best diagnosed by barium study of the upper gastrointestinal tract. However, since a large number of patients with eating disorders complain of gastrointestinal symptoms with no evident pathology, investigation should be considered in the context of a comprehensive approach to treatment. For example, although gastro-oesophageal reflux may contribute to a child's wish not to eat, it should not be concentrated on as the main factor. In addition, investigations such as endoscopy are invasive and should be considered with care, particularly in children with functional dysphagia when it may exacerbate the symptoms.

## EFFECTS ON THE HEART

Significant bradycardia (pulse <60 per minute) has been considered a cardinal sign of cardiovascular compromise, and a medical indication for admission to hospital. This compensatory slowing and conservation of circulation is however, at least at first, adaptive. The effect of prolonged starvation and strain on the heart can result in reduced cardiac muscle mass, increasing the likelihood of hypotension and peripheral oedema. The more alarming sign is that of arrhythmias, sudden alterations in cardiac rhythm, which are unpredictable. The risk is far greater in the presence of associated hypokalaemia (most commonly due to vomiting or purgative abuse).

## ECG

ECG usually shows bradycardia, although tachycardia may occur if cardiac collapse is imminent (Siegel, Hardoff, Golden, & Shenker, 1995), or if dehydration is marked. There is prolongation of the QT interval. The severity of both bradycardia and QT interval are an indication of the degree of cardiac compromise. In a study of adult women with anorexia nervosa there was a tendency for the QT interval to revert to normal after refeeding (Cooke et al., 1994). Two patients who died during the study had QT intervals at or above the 95th confidence interval. Of interest, Marcus et al. (1989) found no connection between ECG changes and either body weight or potassium levels in adolescents with anorexia nervosa, and that pulse and blood pressure showed more marked fluctuations than in adults.

# EFFECTS ON THE LIVER AND KIDNEYS

Dehydration, renal stones, and metabolic alkalosis may be the result of low fluid intake, vomiting, diuretic or purgative abuse. Increased levels of serum creatinine, and low creatinine clearance may reflect both reduced muscle mass and renal micro-vascular changes (Abdel Rahman & Moorthy, 1997; Brotman, Stern, & Brotman, 1986). Renal failure has been reported in one 16-year-old girl as result of rhabdomyolysis (muscle breakdown) (Wada, Nagase, Koike, Kugai, & Nagata, 1992). Breakdown of muscle increases nitrogenous by-products, overloading the kidneys' excretion capacity. Renal failure is also a rare but serious complication of laxative abuse (Copeland, 1994).

Hepatic steatosis or fatty infiltration of the liver is well recognised in kwashiorkor and other states of severe malnutrition and its presence has been confirmed histologically. More recently, hepatic steatosis has been assessed non-invasively by using hepatic sonography.

## Assessment of liver and kidneys

Liver and kidney function is assessed through blood tests in the first instance (see earlier). If these tests are abnormal, further investigation is generally only indicated if the abnormalities do not correct with refeeding and fluid balance. Ultrasound is the least invasive method of investigating thereafter.

Ultrasonically the liver develops an increased echogenicity as compared to the kidney with loss of the normally visible portal tracts. Less commonly, one may see a focal area of fatty infiltration. The extent of steatosis is not related to the size of the liver (Doherty, Adam, Griffin, & Golden, 1992). We have used hepatic sonography to assess the presence of hepatic steatosis in 23 girls with anorexia nervosa. Hepatic steatosis was found in all subjects and its severity correlated positively to the degree of weight loss. These findings were reversed on weight restoration. Hepatic sonography appears to be a useful technique and may be of importance in those severe patients with impaired liver function.

# EFFECTS ON THE BRAIN

Structural abnormalities have been noted on the brain scans of patients with anorexia nervosa, in particular enlargement of the cerebral ventricles (see neuro-imaging later). These abnormalities may be partially reversible on weight gain, and in younger patients may be entirely so (Golden et al., 1996). Autopsy results on a girl aged 13.5 years suggested that, alongside degenerative changes, there was some evidence of repair mechanisms and neuronal plasticity (Neumarker, Dudeck, Meyer, Neumarker, Schulz, & Schonheit, 1997). Hypercortisolism may play an important part in the development of brain abnormalities in anorexia nervosa.

The impact of anorexia nervosa, or the other eating disorders of childhood, on the developing brain are largely unknown, both in terms of physical sequelae and cognitive functioning.

## Assessment of brain function

*Neuroimaging.* Neuroimaging in anorexia nervosa has revealed both morphological and functional alterations. Although most changes are currently interpreted as consequences of starvation and are reversible, at least partially, after weight gain, one functional study has shown changes that can persist even after weight gain (Gordon, Lask, Bryant Waugh, Christie, & Timimi, 1997).

Anatomical studies have used computerised tomography (CT) and more recently magnetic resonance imaging (MRI), and show similar features. There is enlargement of cerebro-spinal fluid spaces, mainly of cortical sulci, evident on CT and MRI. This reversible shrinkage of brain tissue ("pseudoatrophy") also affects the pituitary gland (Herholz, 1996). MRI has shown that adolescent girls (age $15.2 \pm 1.2$ years) with anorexia nervosa had larger total CSF volumes in association with deficits in both total grey matter and total white matter volumes (Katzman, Lambe, Mikulis, Ridgley, Goldbloom, & Zepursky, 1996). Total CSF volume and total grey matter volume were correlated with body mass index (BMI) and cortisol. Lowest reported body mass index was inversely correlated with CSF volume, and positively correlated with total grey matter, whereas the reverse was true for urinary free cortisol levels.

Functional imaging of the brain in patients with eating disorders has used glucose metabolism. Regional cerebral glucose metabolism measured with 18F-2-fluoro-2-deoxyglucose (18 FDG) and positron emission tomography (PET) in nine adult patients with bulimia nervosa and in seven patients with anorexia nervosa showed an increase in glucose metabolism in the caudate (Krieg, Holthoff, Schreiber, Pirke, & Herholz, 1991). Caudate hyperactivity appeared to be characteristic of anorexia nervosa. Whether increased caudate function is a consequence of starvation or whether it is directly involved in the pathogenesis of anorexia nervosa was not clear to these authors.

However, other researchers have reported different findings with 18 FDG PET studies of anorexia nervosa. Underweight anorectic patients showed a global hypometabolism and an absolute, as well as relative, hypometabolism of glucose in cortical regions, with the most significant differences found in the frontal and the parietal cortices, when compared with controls (Delvenne et al., 1995). No correlations were found between absolute or relative metabolic rate of glucose (rCMRGlu), and anxiety scores, or Hamilton scores of depression in either the anorexia nervosa or the control group. The same has recently been demonstrated for women with bulimia nervosa (Delvenne, Goldman, Simon, De Maertelaer, & Lotstra, 1997).

Another report of 18 FDG PET from the same group showed that under-weight patients with anorexia nervosa, when compared to control subjects, showed a global and regional hypometabolism that normalised with weight gain (Delvenne, Goldman, De Maertelaer, Simon, Luxen, & Lotstra, 1996). No global difference could be found between patients with anorexia nervosa and controls. However, a trend was observed toward parietal and superior frontal cortex hypometabolism, associated with a relative hypermetabolism in the caudate nuclei and the inferior frontal cortex. After weight gain, all regions normalised, although again a trend was noted toward relative parietal hypometabolism and inferior frontal cortex hypermetabolism in weight-restored patients. The authors suggest that absolute brain glucose hypometabolism might result from neuroendocrinological or morphological aspects of anorexia nervosa, or might be the expression of altered neurotransmission following deficient nutritional state. As some differences exists in relative values in underweight patients and tend to persist in weight-gain states, this could support a potential abnormal cerebral functioning, a different reaction to starvation within several regions of the brain, or different restoration rates according to the region.

Functional imaging of the brain using regional cerebral blood flow (rCBF) with single photon emission computerised tomography (SPECT) has been reported in children (Gordon, Lask, Bryant-Waugh, Christie, & Timimi, 1997). This is the only study to date of functional imaging in children with anorexia nervosa. The initial rCBF SPECT scans in 13 out of 15 children showed hypoperfusion in the temporal lobe (Fig. 8.7). In eight this was on the left side and in five on the right, even though all children were reported to be right handed. Follow-up scans undertaken in three children when they had regained normal weight, i.e. weight/height ratio of more than 97%, all showed reduced rCBF in the temporal lobe on the same side as the initial scan. In one child there was also reduced rCBF in the basal ganglia on the same side. This child underwent magnetic resonance imaging which showed no abnormality. Fourteen more children have had SPECT scans since the original study, and the same, specific, unilateral abnormality has been found in 80% of all children studied.

Changes in rCBF that are purely secondary to starvation would be expected to produce global and symmetrical decreases in blood flow. The unilateral decreased rCBF described, together with the persistence of an abnormality in the small percentage of patients re-scanned after weight restoration, suggests that the findings cannot be explained as secondary to starvation. The authors believe that the asymmetry may reflect an underlying primary neurological abnormality that is contributing to the development of anorexia nervosa in these young patients.

In another study of rCBF by Nozoe et al. (1995), adult patients with anorexia nervosa failed to show asymmetry, but there was a change between the before and after eating rCBF studies in all areas except the left temporal region. This lends further support to a temporal lobe abnormality in anorexia nervosa.

# Front

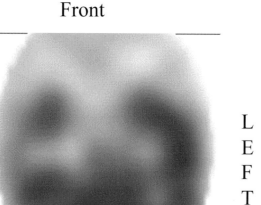

L
E
F
T

# Back

FIG. 8.7    A 13 year old girl with anorexia nervosa. Weight for height 78%. This is the transaxial slice along the long axis of the temporal lobe of the Tc99m ECD regional cerebral blood flow study. There is marked asymmetry in the anterior portion of the temporal lobes with the right showing significantly less blood flow than the left.

*Neuroendocrine findings.*    There are very few studies specific to children, when considering neuroendocrine aspects of eating disorders (Waldholtz & Andersen, 1990). This is for a number of reasons, including ethical considerations and a low number of subjects, particularly with bulimia nervosa. This section is a brief overview of the findings from adult populations. We can at present only speculate on their relevance to children.

The regulation of sexual development and growth and other endocrine function through the hypothalamo-pituitary pathway has been discussed earlier. Here, influences on the hypothalamus are considered, including neurotransmitter function.

Endogenous opiates are elevated in the CSF of patients with anorexia nervosa and, with beta endorphins, are implicated in the regulation of pain, temperature, eating and energy expenditure, and pituitary hormone secretion. Endorphins intensify the appetite in normal conditions, and naloxone, an opioid antagonist, decreases the appetite. However, there may be a critical state of starvation beyond which the opioids act to decrease, rather than increase, appetite and it has been hypothesised that this may occur in anorexia nervosa and serve to perpetuate the illness once established (Baranowska, Rozbicka, Jeske, & Abdel Fattah, 1994; Kaye, 1996).

Beta endorphins are elevated in patients with bulimia nervosa compared to those who do not vomit, and it has been suggested that the feeling of lightness or euphoria experienced by patients after they vomit may be due to this effect. Bulimic patients also have a relative deficit of serotonin compared to anorexia patients, and may account for the absence of satiety experienced by bulimic patients. In part this may also be attributed to the lack of cholecystokinin, normally secreted slowly into the blood stream following a meal. In bulimic patients this effect may be deficient, either because the patient has vomited or because gastric emptying has been delayed (Phillipp, Pirke, Kellner, & Krieg, 1991). This is unlikely to cause the lack of satiety experienced in bulimic patients, but again may perpetuate it.

Patients with anorexia nervosa also have low levels of serotonin and noradrenaline, both of which are deficits in neurotransmitter functioning associated with depressive illness, and may also have a bearing on appetite (Fava, Copeland, Schweiger, & Herzog, 1989; Leibowitz, 1990; Pirke, 1996; Pirke, Pahl, Schweiger, & Warnhoff, 1985). Although levels of noradrenaline return to normal on weight gain, they have also been found to be significantly decreased at long-term follow-up in those who have recovered from anorexia nervosa. Similar studies have not been performed in children.

About 40–50% of adult patients with bulimia nervosa have a positive dexamethasone suppression test, similar to the rates found in depression. A positive result was found to be unrelated to severity of bulimia (Levy, 1989). In anorexia nervosa, the findings of dexamethasone non-suppression in two-thirds of patients show greater correlation with weight loss than with mood disturbance (Abou Saleh, Oleesky, & Crisp, 1985).

## DIFFERENTIAL DIAGNOSIS AND CO-MORBIDITIES

Disorders in childhood affecting growth, development, and weight gain have a number of names and guises (see Chapter 3). A thorough medical history and examination are essential, as is access to appropriate paediatric expertise.

The commonest co-morbid diagnosis that merits attention in its own right is gastro-oesophageal reflux (GOR), particularly in association with functional dysphagia. The child may have developed a phobic response to eating, and may benefit from the dual therapy of treatment for GOR and systematic desensitisation.

Finally, it is of course important that all clinicians maintain an open mind; if the treatment of choice for a diagnosed eating disorder is not working, it may be the diagnosis that is wrong. For example, we have identified four intracranial tumours masquerading as early onset anorexia nervosa (De Vile, Sufraz, Lask, & Stanhope, 1995).

## CONCLUSIONS AND FUTURE DIRECTIONS

It is increasingly clear that the morbidity and mortality associated with eating disorders constitutes a major health issue for our teenage population. Already anorexia nervosa is the third commonest chronic disorder of adolescence in the USA, with obesity the first (Lucas, Beard, O'Fallon, & Kurland, 1991). The recognition and appropriate management of the medical aspects of these illnesses must be seen as central to any treatment programme.

In younger children the issues may be more acute. The potentially reversible effects in older, physically mature adolescents may be irreversible in the growing and developing child. The relationship between disordered eating and abnormal ovarian morphology is far from clear, and has important implications for fertility. Bone density may be more easily affected during early puberty but the potential for "catch-up", as for stature, needs clarification. The development of more sophisticated functional imaging allows the possibility of linking cognitive function, behaviour, and physiological functioning in ways not previously possible.

Exciting though these developments are, the goal of treatment for all of the eating disorders of childhood remains essentially the same: for the child to be able to eat sufficient to grow and develop normally, and to find a way of addressing emotional issues that does not involve food. The treatment of choice for most physical complications remains a normal, healthy, and adequate diet.

## SUMMARY POINTS

- Change in weight must take into account age, gender, and height.
- In children, pelvic ultrasound, growth rate, and progress in pubertal development are the best methods for assessing physical recovery.
- Complications that are reversible in adults may be irreversible in developing children, particularly in relation to growth, ovarian development, bone density, and the brain.
- A "normal diet, eaten normally" is the best treatment for most physical problems.

## ACKNOWLEDGEMENT

The work of Dasha Nicholls is funded by the Child Growth Foundation.

## REFERENCES

Abdel Rahman, E.M., & Moorthy, A.V. (1997). End-stage renal disease (ESRD) in patients with eating disorders. *Clinical Nephrology, 47*, 106–111.

Abou Saleh, M.T., Oleesky, D.A., & Crisp, A.H. (1985). Dexamethasone suppression and energy balance: A study of anorexic patients. *Journal of Psychiatric Research, 19*, 203–206.

Adams, J. (1993). The role of pelvic ultrasound in the management of paediatric endocrine disorders. In C.G.D. Brook (Ed.), *Clinical paediatric endocrinology* (pp. 675–691). Oxford, UK: Blackwell Scientific Publications.

Adams, J., Polson, D.W., & Franks, S. (1986). Prevalence of polycystic ovaries in women with anovulation and idiopathic hirsutism. *British Journal of Hospital Medicine, 293*, 355–359.

Adson, D.E., Mitchell, J.E., & Trenkner, S.W. (1997). The superior mesenteric artery syndrome and acute gastric dilatation in eating disorders: A report of two cases and review of the literature. *International Journal of Eating Disorders, 21*, 103–114.

Albanese, A., Hamill, G., Jones, J., Skuse, D., Matthews, D.R., & Stanhope, R. (1994). Reversibility of physiological growth hormone secretion in children with psychosocial dwarfism. *Clinical Endocrinology, 40*, 687–692.

Albanese, A., & Stanhope, R. (1993). Does constitutional delayed puberty cause segmental disproportion and short stature? *European Journal of Paediatrics, 152*, 293–296.

Alderdice, J.T., Dinsmore, W.W., Buchanan, K.D., & Adams, C. (1985). Gastrointestinal hormones in anorexia nervosa. *Journal of Psychiatric Research, 19*, 207–213.

Argente, J., Caballo, N., Barrios, V., Munoz, M.T., Pozo, J., Chowen, J.A., Morande, G., & Hernandez, M. (1997). Multiple endocrine abnormalities of the growth hormone and insulin-like growth factor axis in patients with anorexia nervosa: Effect of short- and long-term weight recuperation. *Journal of Clinical Endocrinology Metabolism, 82*, 2084–2092.

Bachrach, L.K. (1993). Bone mineralization in childhood and adolescence. *Current Opinion Pediatrics, 5*, 467–473.

Baranowska, B., Rozbicka, G., Jeske, W., & Abdel Fattah, M.H. (1984). The role of endogenous opiates in the mechanism of inhibited luteinizing hormone (LH) secretion in women with anorexia nervosa: The effect of naloxone on LH, follicle-stimulating hormone, prolactin, and beta-endorphin secretion. *Journal of Clinical Endocrinology Metabolism, 59*, 412–416.

Barash, I.A., Cheung, C.C., Weigle, D.S., Ren, H., Kabigting, E.B., Kuijper, J.L., Clifton, D.K., & Steiner, R.A. (1996). Leptin is a metabolic signal to the reproductive system. *Endocrinology, 137*, 3144–3147.

Biller, B.M., Saxe, V., Herzog, D.B., Rosenthal, D.I., Holzman, S., & Klibanski, A. (1989). Mechanisms of osteoporosis in adult and adolescent women with anorexia nervosa. *Journal of Clinical Endocrinology Metabolism, 68*, 548–554.

Bonjour, J.P., Theintz, G., Buchs, B., Slosman, D., & Rizzoli, R. (1991). Critical years and stages of puberty for spinal and femoral bone mass accumulation during adolescence. *Journal of Clinical Endocrinology Metabolism, 73*, 555–563.

Boot, A.M., de Ridder, M.A., Pols, H.A., Krenning, E.P., & de Muinck Keizer Schrama, S.M. (1997). Bone mineral density in children and adolescents: Relation to puberty, calcium intake, and physical activity. *Journal of Clinical Endocrinology Metabolism, 82*, 57–62.

Boyar, R.M., Katz, J., Finkelstein, J.W., Kapen, S., Weiner, H., Weitzman, E.D., & Hellman, L. (1974). Anorexia nervosa: Immaturity of the 24-hr luteinizing hormone secretory pattern. *New England Journal of Medicine, 291*, 861–865.

Bridges, N.A., Cooke, A., Healy, M.J., Hindmarsh, P.C., & Brook, C.G. (1993). Standards for ovarian volume in childhood and puberty. *Fertility and Sterility, 60*, 456–460.

Brinch, M., & Manthorpe, T. (1987). Short stature as a possible etiological factor in anorexia nervosa. *Acta Psychiatrica Scandinavica, 76*, 328–332.

Brook, C.G.D., Jacobs, H.S., & Stanhope, R. (1988). Polycystic ovaries in childhood. *British Medical Journal, 296*, 878.

Brotman, A.W., Stern, T.A., & Brotman, D.L. (1986). Renal disease and dysfunction in two patients with anorexia nervosa. *Journal of Clinical Psychiatry, 47*, 433–434.

Bryant-Waugh, R., Knibbs, J., Fosson, A., Kaminski, Z., & Lask, B. (1988). Long term follow-up of patients with early onset anorexia nervosa. *Archives of Disease in Childhood, 63*, 5–9.

Cabranes, J.A., Almoguera, I., Santos, J.L., Hidalgo, I., Borque, M.M., & del Olmo, J. (1988). Somatomedin-C and growth hormone levels in anorexia nervosa in relation to the puberal or post puberal stages. *Progress in Neuropsychopharmacological and Biological Psychiatry, 12*, 865–871.

Carney, C.P., & Andersen, A.E. (1996). Eating disorders: Guide to medical evaluation and complications. *Psychiatric Clinics of North America, 19*, 657.

Clayton, R.N., Ogden, V., Hodgkinson, J., Worswick, L., Rodin, D.A., Dyer, S., & Meade, T.W. (1992). How common are polycystic ovaries in normal women and what is their significance for the fertility of the population? *Clinical Endocrinology, 37*, 127–134.

Cole, T.J. (1979). A method for assessing age-standardized weight-for-height in children seen cross-sectionally. *Annals of Human Biology, 6*, 249–268.

Cole, T.J., Donnet, M.L., & Stanfield, J.P. (1981). Weight-for-height indices to assess nutritional status—a new index on a slide-rule. *American Journal of Clinical Nutrition, 34*, 1935–1943.

Cole, T.J., Freeman, J.V., & Preece, M.A. (1995). Body mass index reference curves for the UK, 1990. *Archives of Disease in Childhood, 73*, 25–29.

Conway, G.S., Honour, J.W., & Jacobs, H.S. (1989). Heterogeneity of the polycystic ovary syndrome: Clinical, endocrine and ultrasound features in 556 patients. *Clinical Endocrinology, Oxford, 30*, 459–470.

Cooke, R.A., Chambers, J.B., Singh, R., Todd, G.J., Smeeton, N.C., Treasure, J., & Treasure, T. (1994). QT interval in anorexia nervosa. *British Heart Journal, 72*, 69–73.

Copeland, P.M. (1994). Renal failure associated with laxative abuse. *Psychotherapy and Psychosomatics, 62*, 200–202.

Crow, S.J., Salisbury, J.J., Crosby, R.D., & Mitchell, J.E. (1997). Serum electrolytes as markers of vomiting in bulimia nervosa. *International Journal of Eating Disorders, 21*, 95–98.

Danziger, Y., Mukamel, M., Zeharia, A., Dinari, G., & Mimouni, M. (1994). Stunting of growth in anorexia nervosa during the prepubertal and pubertal period. *Israeli Journal of Medical Science, 30*, 581–584.

Davies, M., Gulenki, B., & Jacobs, H.S. (1995). Osteoporosis in Turner's syndrome and other forms of primary amenorrhoea. *Clinical Endocrinology, 43*, 741–746.

De Vile, C.J., Sufraz, R., Lask, B., & Stanhope, R. (1995). Occult intracranial tumours masquerading as early onset anorexia nervosa. *British Medical Journal, 311*, 1359–1360.

Delvenne, V., Goldman, S., De Maertelaer, V., Simon, Y., Luxen, A., & Lotstra, F. (1996). Brain hypometabolism of glucose in anorexia nervosa: Normalization after weight gain. *Biological Psychiatry, 40*, 761–768.

Delvenne, V., Goldman, S., Simon, Y., De Maertelaer, V., & Lotstra, F. (1997). Brain hypometabolism of glucose in bulimia nervosa. *International Journal of Eating Disorders, 21*, 313–320.

Delvenne, V., Lotstra, F., Goldman, S., Biver, F., De Maertelaer, V., Appelboom Fondu, J., Schoutens, A., Bidaut, L.M., Luxen, A., & Mendelwicz, J. (1995). Brain hypometabolism of glucose in anorexia nervosa: A PET scan study. *Biological Psychiatry, 37*, 161–169.

Dhuper, S., Warren, M.P., Brooks Gunn, J., & Fox, R. (1990). Effects of hormonal status on bone density in adolescent girls. *Journal of Clinical Endocrinology Metabolism, 71*, 1083–1088.

Doherty, J.F., Adam, E.J., Griffin, G.E., & Golden, M.H. (1992). Ultrasonographic assessment of the extent of hepatic steatosis in severe malnutrition. *Archives of Disease in Childhood, 67*, 1348–1352.

Dreizen, S., Spirakis, C., & Stone, R. (1967). A comparison of skeletal growth and maturation in undernourished and well nourished girls before and after menarche. *Journal of Paediatrics, 70*, 256–263.

Faulkner, R.A., Bailey, D.A., Drinkwater, D.T., McKay, H.A., Arnold, C., & Wilkinson, A.A. (1996). Bone densitometry in Canadian children 8–17 years of age. *Calcified Tissue International, 59*, 344–351.

Fava, M., Copeland, P.M., Schweiger, U., & Herzog, D.B. (1989). Neurochemical abnormalities of anorexia nervosa and bulimia nervosa. *American Journal of Psychiatry, 146*, 963–971.

Finkelstein, J.S., Neer, R.M., Beverley, M.D., Biller, M.K., Crawford, J.D., & Klibanski, A. (1992). Ostoepenia in men with a history of delayed puberty. *New England Journal of Medicine, 326*, 600–604.

Fosson, A., Knibbs, J., Bryant-Waugh, R., & Lask, B. (1987). Early onset anorexia nervosa. *Archives of Disease in Childhood, 62*, 114–118.

Frampton, I., & Austin, I. (1997). *W4H* (computer program). (Details available from the editors.)

Franks, S. (1995). Polycystic ovary syndrome—review article. *New England Journal of Medicine, 333*, 853–861.

Freeman, J.V., Cole, T.J., Chinn, S., Jones, P.R., White, E.M., & Preece, M.A. (1995). Cross sectional stature and weight reference curves for the UK, 1990. *Archives of Disease in Childhood, 73*, 17–24.

Frisch, R.E., & McArthur, J.W. (1974). Menstrual cycles: Fatness as a determinant of minimum weight for height necessary for their maintenance or onset. *Science, 185*, 949–951.

Frisch, R.E., & Revelle, R. (1971). Height and weight at menarche and a hypothesis of menarche. *Archives of Disease in Childhood, 46*, 695–701.

Garfinkel, P.E., Lin, E., Goering, P., Spegg, D., Goldbloom, D., Kennedy, S., Kaplan, A.S., & Blake Woodside, B. (1996). Should amenorrhoea be necessary for the diagnosis of anorexia nervosa? *British Journal of Psychiatry, 168*, 500–506.

Golden, N.H., Ashtari, M., Kohn, M.R., Patel, M., Jacobson, M.S., Fletcher, A., & Shenker, I.R. (1996). Reversibility of cerebral ventricular enlargement in anorexia nervosa, demonstrated by quantitative magnetic resonance imaging. *Journal of Pediatrics, 128*, 296–301.

Gordon, I., Lask, B., Bryant-Waugh, R., Christie, D., & Timimi, S. (1997). Childhood-onset anorexia nervosa: Towards identifying a biological substrate. *International Journal of Eating Disorders, 22*, 159–165.

Greulich, W.W., & Pyle, S.I. (1959). *Radiographic atlas of skeletal development of the hand and wrist.* Stanford, CA: Stanford University Press.

Griffin, I.J., Cole, T.J., Duncan, K.A., Hollman, A.S., & Donaldson, M.D. (1995). Pelvic ultrasound measurements in normal girls. *Acta Paediatrica, 84*, 536–543.

Halmi, K.A., & Falk, J.R. (1981). Common physiological changes in anorexia nervosa. *International Journal of Eating Disorders, 1*, 16–27.

Hannan, W.J., Cowen, S.J., Wrate, R.M., & Barton, J. (1995). Improved prediction of bone mineral content and density. *Archives of Disease in Childhood, 72*, 147–149.

Heinz, E.R., Martinez, J., & Haenggeli, A. (1977). Reversibility of cerebral atrophy in anorexia and Cushing's syndrome. *Journal of Computer Assisted Tomography, 1*, 415–418.

Herholz, K. (1996). Neuroimaging in anorexia nervosa. *Psychiatry Research, 16*, 105–110.

Irwin, M. (1981). Diagnosis of anorexia nervosa in children and the validity of DSM-III. *American Journal of Psychiatry, 138*, 1382–1383.

Jacobs, B.W., & Isaacs, S. (1986). Pre-pubertal anorexia nervosa: A retrospective controlled study. *Journal of Child Psychology and Psychiatry, 27*, 237–250.

Jaworski, M., Lebiedowski, M., Lorenc, R.S., & Trempe, J. (1995). Ultrasound bone measurement in pediatric subjects. *Calcified Tissue International, 56*, 368–371.

Jennings, K.P., & Klidjian, A.M. (1974). Acute gastric dilatation in anorexia nervosa. *British Medical Journal, 2*, 477–478.

Johnston, C.C., Jr., Miller, J.Z., Slemenda, C.W., Reister, T.K., Hui, S., Christian, J.C., & Peacock, M. (1992). Calcium supplementation and increases in bone mineral density in children. *New England Journal of Medicine, 327*, 82–87.

Joughin, N., Varsou, E., Gowers, S., & Crisp, A.H. (1992). Relative tallness in anorexia nervosa. *International Journal of Eating Disorders, 12*, 195–207.

Katz, J.L., Boyar, R.M., Weiner, H., Gorzynski, G., Roffwarg, H., & Hellman, L. (1976). Toward an elucidation of the psychoendocrinology of anorexia nervosa. In E.J. Sachar (Ed.), *Hormones, behavior, and psychopathology* (pp. 263–283). New York: Raven Press.

Katzman, D.K., Lambe, E.K., Mikulis, D.J., Ridgley, J.N., Goldbloom, D.S., & Zepursky, R.B. (1996). Cerebral gray matter and white matter volume deficits in adolescent girls with anorexia nervosa. *Journal of Pediatrics, 129,* 794–803.

Kaye, W.H. (1996). Neuropeptide abnormalities in anorexia nervosa. *Psychiatry Research, 62,* 65–74.

Klibanski, A., Biller, B.M., Schoenfeld, D.A., Herzog, D.B., & Saxe, V.C. (1995). The effects of estrogen administration on trabecular bone loss in young women with anorexia nervosa. *Journal of Clinical Endocrinology Metabolism, 80,* 898–904.

Krieg, J.C., Holthoff, V., Schreiber, W., Pirke, K.M., & Herholz, K. (1991). Glucose metabolism in the caudate nuclei of patients with eating disorders, measured by PET. *European Archives of Psychiatry and Clinical Neuroscience, 240,* 331–333.

Kroger, H., Kotaniemi, A., Kroger, L., & Alhava, E. (1993). Development of bone mass and bone density of the spine and femoral neck—a prospective study of 65 children and adolescents. *Bone Mineralogy, 23,* 171–182.

Lai, K.Y., de Bruyn, R., Lask, B., Bryant-Waugh, R., & Hankins, M. (1994). Use of pelvic ultrasound to monitor ovarian and uterine maturity in childhood onset anorexia nervosa. *Archives of Disease in Childhood, 71,* 228–231.

Langton, C.M. (1994). The role of ultrasound in the assessment of osteoporosis. *Clinical Rheumatology, 13*(Suppl. 1), 13–17.

Lask, B., Fosson, A., Rolfe, U., & Thomas, S. (1993). Zinc deficiency and childhood-onset anorexia nervosa. *Journal of Clinical Psychiatry, 54,* 63–66.

Leibowitz, S.F. (1990). The role of serotonin in eating disorders. *Drugs, 39*(Suppl. 3), 33–48.

Levy, A.B. (1989). Neuroendocrine profile in bulimia nervosa. *International Journal of Eating Disorders. 25*(1), 98–109.

Lloyd, T., Martel, J.K., Rollings, N., Andon, M.B., Kulin, H., Demers, L.M., Eggli, D.F., Kieselhorst, K., & Chinchilli, V.M. (1996). The effect of calcium supplementation and Tanner stage on bone density, content and area in teenage women. *Osteoporosis International, 6,* 276–283.

Lloyd, T., Rollings, N., Andon, M.B., Demers, L.M., Eggli, D.F., Kieselhorst, K., Kulin, H., Landis, J.R., Martel, J.K., Orr, G., et al. (1992). Determinants of bone density in young women: I. Relationships among pubertal development, total body bone mass, and total body bone density in premenarchal females. *Journal of Clinical Endocrinology Metabolism, 75,* 383–387.

Lu, P.W., Cowell, C.T., Lloyd Jones, S.A., Briody, J.N., & Howman Giles, R. (1996). Volumetric bone mineral density in normal subjects, aged 5–27 years. *Journal of Clinical Endocrinology Metabolism, 81,* 1586–1590.

Lucas, A.R., Beard, C.M., O'Fallon, W.M., & Kurland, L.T. (1991). Fifty year trends in the incidence of anorexia nervosa in Rochester, Minnesota: A population-based study. *American Journal of Psychiatry, 148,* 917–922.

Marcus, A., Blanz, B., Lehmkuhl, G., Rothenberger, A., & Eisert, H.G. (1989). Somatic findings in children and adolescents with anorexia nervosa. *Acta Paedopsychiatrica, 52,* 1–11.

McCallum, R.W., Grill, B.B., Lange, R., Planky, M., Glass, E.E., & Greenfeld, D.G. (1985). Definition of a gastric emptying abnormality in patients with anorexia nervosa. *Digestive Disease Science, 30,* 713–722.

McCluskey, S., Lacey, J.H., & Pearce, J.M. (1992). Binge-eating and polycystic ovaries. *Lancet, 340,* 723.

Mira, M., Stewart, P.M., Vizzard, J., & Abraham, S. (1987). Biochemical abnormalities in anorexia nervosa and bulimia. *Annals of Clinical Biochemistry, 24,* 29–35.

Mitchell, J.E., Pyle, R.L., Eckert, E.D., Hatsukami, D., & Lentz, R. (1983). Electrolyte and other physiological abnormalities in patients with bulimia. *Psychological Medicine, 13,* 273–278.

Molgaard, C., Thomsen Lykke, B., Prentice, A., Cole, T.J., & Michaelsen, K.F. (1997). Whole body bone mineral content in healthy children and adolescents. *Archives of Disease in Childhood, 76,* 9–15.

Mughal, M.Z., Ward, K., Qayyum, N., & Langton, C.M. (1997). Assessment of bone status using the contact ultrasound bone analyser. *Archives of Disease in Childhood, 76,* 535–536.

Muller, E.E., Cavagnini, F., Panerai, A.E., Massironi, R., Ferrari, E., & Brambilla, F. (1987). Neuroendocrine measures in anorexia nervosa: Comparisons with primary affective disorders. *Advances in Biochemical Psychopharmacology, 43,* 261–271.

Nestler, J.E. (1997). Role of hyperinsulinemia in the pathogenesis of the polycystic ovary syndrome, and its clinical implications. *Seminars in Reproductive Endocrinology, 15,* 111–122.

Neumarker, K.J., Dudeck, U., Meyer, U., Neumarker, U., Schulz, E., & Schonheit, B. (1997). Anorexia nervosa and sudden death in childhood: Clinical data and results obtained from quantitative neurohistological investigations of cortical neurons. *European Archives of Psychiatry and Clinical Neuroscience, 247,* 16–22.

Newman, M.M., & Halmi, K.A. (1988). The endocrinology of anorexia nervosa and bulimia nervosa. *Neurological Clinics, 6,* 195–212.

Nicholls, D., Casey, C., Stanhope, R., & Lask, B. (in preparation). *Atypical childhood onset anorexia nervosa or food avoidance emotional disorder: Physical and psychological characteristics.*

Nozoe, S., Naruo, T., Nakabeppu, Y., Soejima, Y., Nagai, N., Nakajo, M., & Tanaka, H. (1995). Comparison of regional cerebral blood flow in patients with eating disorders. *Brain Research Bulletin, 36,* 251–255.

Nussbaum, M.P., Blethen, S.L., Chasalow, F.I., Jacobson, M.S., Shenker, I.R., & Feldman, J. (1990). Blunted growth hormone responses to clonidine in adolescent girls with early anorexia nervosa: Evidence for an early hypothalamic defect. *Journal of Adolescent Health Care, 11,* 145–148.

Orsini, L.F., Salardi, S., Pilu, G., Bovicelli, L., & Cacciari, E. (1984). Pelvic organs in premenarcheal girls: Real-time ultrasonography. *Radiology, 153,* 113–116.

Ott, S.M. (1991). Bone density in adolescents. *New England Journal of Medicine, 325,* 1646–1647.

Peters, H., Himelstein Braw, R., & Faber, M. (1976). The normal development of the ovary in childhood. *Acta Endocrinologica Copenhagen, 82,* 617–630.

Pfeiffer, R.J., Lucas, A.R., & Ilstrup, D.M. (1986). Effect of anorexia nervosa on linear growth. *Clinical Pediatrics, 25,* 7–12.

Phillipp, E., Pirke, K.M., Kellner, M.B., & Krieg, J.C. (1991). Disturbed cholecystokinin secretion in patients with eating disorders. *Life Science, 48,* 2443–2450.

Pirke, K.M. (1996). Central and peripheral noradrenalin regulation in eating disorders. *Psychiatry Research, 62,* 43–49.

Pirke, K.M., Pahl, J., Schweiger, U., & Warnhoff, M. (1985). Metabolic and endocrine indices of starvation in bulimia: A comparison with anorexia nervosa. *Psychiatry Research, 15,* 33–39.

Polson, D.W., Adams, J., Wadsworth, J., & Franks, S. (1988). Polycystic ovaries—a common finding in normal women. *Lancet, 1,* 870–872.

Poretsky, L., & Piper, B. (1994). Insulin resistance, hypersecretion of LH, and a dual-defect hypothesis for the pathogenesis of polycystic ovary syndrome. *Obstetrics and Gynecology, 84,* 613–621.

Powers, P.S., Tyson, I.B., Stevens, B.A., & Heal, A.V. (1995). Total body potassium and serum potassium among eating disorder patients. *International Journal of Eating Disorders, 18,* 269–276.

Prelevic, G.M. (1997). Insulin resistance in polycystic ovary syndrome. *Current Opinion in Obstetrics and Gynecology, 9,* 193–201.

Pugliese, M.T., Lifshitz, F., Grad, G., Fort, P., & Marks-Katz, M. (1983). Fear of obesity: A cause of short stature and delayed puberty. *New England Journal of Medicine, 309,* 513–518.

Ravelli, A.M., Helps, B.A., Devane, S.P., Lask, B.D., & Milla, P.J. (1993). Normal gastric antral myoelectrical activity in early onset anorexia nervosa. *Archives of Disease in Childhood, 69,* 342–346.

Rigaud, D., Bedig, G., Merrouche, M., Vulpillat, M., Bonfils, S., & Apfelbaum, M. (1988). Delayed gastric emptying in anorexia nervosa is improved by completion of a renutrition program. *Digestive Disease Science, 33,* 919–925.

Rigotti, N.A., Nussbaum, S.R., Herzog, D.B., & Neer, R.M. (1984). Osteoporosis in women with anorexia nervosa. *New England Journal of Medicine, 311*, 1601–1606.

Rosenbaum, M., Nicolson, M., Hirsch, J., Heymsfield, S.B., Gallagher, D., Chu, F., & Leibel, R.L. (1996). Effects of gender, body composition, and menopause on plasma concentrations of leptin. *Journal of Clinical Endocrinology Metabolism, 81*, 3424–3427.

Rosenfield, R.L. (1997). Is polycystic ovary syndrome a neuroendocrine or an ovarian disorder? *Clinical Endocrinology, 47*, 423–424.

Russell, D.M., Prendergast, P.J., Darby, P.L., Garfinkel, P.E., Whitwell, J., & Jeejeebhoy, K.N. (1983). A comparison between muscle function and body composition in anorexia nervosa: The effect of refeeding. *American Journal of Clinical Nutrition, 38*, 229–237.

Russell, G.F.M. (1985). Pre-menarchal anorexia nervosa and its sequelae. *Journal of Psychiatric Research, 19*, 363–369.

Salardi, S., Orsini, L.F., Cacciari, E., Partesotti, S., Brondelli, L., Cicognani, A., Frejaville, E., Pluchinotta, V., Tonioli, S., & Bovicelli, L. (1988). Pelvic ultrasonography in girls with precocious puberty, congenital adrenal hyperplasia, obesity, or hirsutism. *Journal of Pediatrics, 112*, 880–887.

Scholte, R., & Van de Aast, M. (1995). Estrogen substitution in osteoporotic anorexia nervosa patients. *Eating Disorders: The Journal of Treatment and Prevention, 3*, 237–242.

Schwartz, B., Cumming, D.C., Riordan, E., Selye, M., Yen, S.S.C., & Rebar, R.W. (1981). Exercise-induced amenorrhoea: A distinct entity? *American Journal of Obstetrics and Gynecology, 15*, 662–670.

Seeman, E., Szmukler, G.I., Formica, C., Tsalamandris, C., & Mestrovic, R. (1992). Osteoporosis in anorexia nervosa: The influence of peak bone density, bone loss, oral contraceptive use and exercise. *Journal of Bone and Mineral Research, 7*, 1467–1474.

Sharp, C.W., & Freeman, C.P. (1993). Medical complications of anorexia nervsoa. *British Journal of Psychiatry, 162*, 452.

Sherman, B.M., Halmi, K.A., & Zamudio, R. (1975). LH and FSH response to gonadotropin-releasing hormone in anorexia nervosa: Effect of nutritional rehabilitation. *Journal of Clinical Endocrinology Metabolism, 41*, 135–142.

Siegel, J.H., Hardoff, D., Golden, N.H., & Shenker, I.R. (1995). Medical complications in male adolescents with anorexia nervosa. *Journal of Adolescent Health, 16*, 448–453.

Skuse, D., Albanese, A., Stanhope, R., Gilmour, J., & Voss, L. (1996). A new stress-related syndrome of growth failure and hyperphagia in children, associated with reversibility of growth-hormone deficiency. *Lancet, 348*, 353–358.

Stanhope, R., Adams, J., & Brook, C.G.D. (1988). Evolution of polycystic ovaries in a girl with delayed menarche. *Journal of Reproductive Medicine, 33*, 482–484.

Stein, I.F., & Leventhal, M.L. (1935). Amenorrheoa associated with bilateral polycystic ovaries. *Annals of Obstetrics and Gynaecology, 29*, 181–185.

Tanner, J.M., & Whitehouse, R.H. (1966). Standards from birth to maturity for height, weight, height velocity and weight velocity: British children 1965, Pts. 1 and 2. *Archives of Disease in Childhood, 41*, 454–471, 613–635.

Tanner, J.M., Whitehouse, R.H., Cameron, N., Marshall, W.A., Healy, M.J., & Goldstein, H. (1983). *Assessment of skeletal maturity and prediction of adult height (TW2 method).* London: Academic Press.

Theander, S. (1970). Anorexia nervosa: A psychiatric investigation of 94 female patients. *Acta Psychiatrica Scandanavica* (Suppl. 214), 1–194.

Treasure, J.L., Gordon, P.A.L., King, E.A., Wheeler, M.J., & Russell, G.F.M. (1985). Cystic ovaries: A phase of anorexia nervosa. *Lancet, iii*, 1379–1382.

Van Binsbergen, C.J.M., Bennink, H.J.T.C., Odink, J., Haspels, A.A., & Koppeschaar, H.P.F. (1990). A comparitive and longitudinal study on endocrine changes related to ovarian function in patients with anorexia nervosa. *Journal of Clinical Endocrinology Metabolism, 71*, 705–711.

Wada, S., Nagase, T., Koike, Y., Kugai, N., & Nagata, N. (1992). A case of anorexia nervosa with acute renal failure induced by rhabdomyolysis: Possible involvement of hypophosphatemia or phosphate depletion. *Internal Medicine, 31,* 478–482.

Wakeling, A. (1985). Neurobiological aspects of feeding disorders. *Journal of Psychiatric Research, 19,* 191–201.

Waldholtz, B.D., & Andersen, A.E. (1988). Hypophosphataemia during starvation in anorexia nervosa. *International Journal of Eating Disorders, 7,* 551–555.

Waldholtz, B.D., & Andersen, A.E. (1990). Gastrointestinal symptoms in anorexia nervosa: A prospective study. *Gastroenterology, 98,* 1415–1419.

Ward, A., Brown, N., & Treasure, J. (1997). Persistent osteopenia after recovery from anorexia nervosa. *International Journal of Eating Disorders, 22,* 71–75.

Weltman, E.A., Stern, R.C., Doershuk, C.F., Moir, R.N., Palmer, K., & Jaffe, A.C. (1990). Weight and menstrual function in patients with eating disorders and cystic fibrosis. *Pediatrics, 85,* 287.

World Health Organisation. (1994). Assessment of fracture risk and its application to screening for postmenopausal osteoporosis. *World Health Organisation Technical Report Service, 843,* 1–129.

Young, N., Formica, C., Szmukler, G.I., & Seeman, E. (1994). Bone density at weight bearing and non-weight bearing sites in ballet dancers: The effects of exercise, hypogonadism and body weight. *Journal of Clinical Endocrinology Metabolism, 78,* 449–454.

CHAPTER NINE

# Overview of management

**Bryan Lask**
*St George's Hospital Medical School, London, UK, and*
*Huntercombe Manor Hospital, Taplow, UK*

## INTRODUCTION

Eating disorders in childhood and adolescence have a complex pathogenesis and the potential for severe complications and a poor outcome. Clearly, therefore, a rapidly initiated treatment programme is indicated. In all but the mildest cases this will need to be both intensive and comprehensive. This chapter offers an overview of such a programme as provided in our own work contexts, and in succeeding chapters some of the more specific treatments are described in depth. It is acknowledged that many services will not be as well-resourced, but it should be possible to provide the key components of the programme with relatively few staff. The ingredients of an integrated and comprehensive treatment programme might include:

(1) Creating a therapeutic alliance
(2) The provision of information and education for the parents and other family members
(3) Involving the parents and ensuring that the adults take responsibility
(4) Consideration and implementation of any need for hospitalisation
(5) Calculation of a healthy weight range
(6) Family work and/or parental counselling
(7) Schooling considerations
(8) Restoration of healthy eating patterns
(9) Cognitive-behavioural therapy
(10) Psychodynamic psychotherapy
(11) Group work
(12) Physiotherapy and exercise
(13) Medication.

There is no one treatment of choice, although the first six components would usually be considered in all cases. One or more of the remainder is very likely to be necessary. The choice of specific therapies is in practice determined more by availability than need. However, ideally, parental counselling and/or family therapy should always be available, cognitive behavioural therapy used for most children with eating disorders when the family approach alone is unlikely to be sufficient, especially for the much younger ones, and psychodynamic psychotherapy when psychopathology is so deeply entrenched that a more in-depth approach is required.

## CREATING A THERAPEUTIC ALLIANCE

Successful treatment is dependent upon the creation of a therapeutic alliance, initially with at least the parents, and eventually also the child or adolescent. The key components to this process are through the provision of information and education about eating disorders, and discussion of who takes responsibility for ensuring the child's health and safety. These themes are discussed later. It is unusual to effect a therapeutic alliance with younger patients with anorexia nervosa early in the treatment process; their fear and denial are too strong. However, by ensuring a good working relationship with and between the parents and the implementation of appropriate treatment for the child, an alliance is usually gradually formed. Those young patients with other eating disorders such as bulimia nervosa, food avoidance emotional disorder, and selective eating are more likely to want treatment and therefore easier to engage in a therapeutic alliance.

## PROVISION OF INFORMATION AND EDUCATION

Explanation and education form an essential part of the management of the eating disorders. Parents and child need a clear statement about the diagnosis, the course and complications of the condition, possible perpetuating factors, and proposed treatment. Parents are understandably eager to understand the cause of their child's illness, but this rarely proves fruitful. Given the multifactorial aetiology of the eating disorders (see Chapter 5), we are extremely unlikely to understand the detailed pathogenesis of one particular person's eating disorder. It generally proves more useful to focus on those factors that may be maintaining the problem, and to find ways of overcoming them.

Parental understanding of the seriousness or otherwise of their child's problem is very variable. For example, in anorexia nervosa some parents are stunned to discover how ill their child has become. In other instances they have had considerable difficulty convincing clinicians to take their child's eating difficulties seriously. In contrast, parents of selective eaters are often convinced that their child has suffered, or will suffer, irreversible damage because of their limited range of foods. These worries may occur despite the fact that their child is obviously in very good health.

We find it helpful to adopt a clear method of conveying our understanding of the situation. This varies depending upon the diagnosis and its implications. In anorexia nervosa, having completed the initial assessment, we make a statement such as:

As you are probably aware your daughter has anorexia nervosa. You probably have read and heard quite a bit about this illness but we think it might be helpful to explain it to you in some detail. It is hard to take everything in at once so we will provide you with information in writing and we will be happy to answer any questions at any time.

Anorexia nervosa is a mean and mysterious disorder which plays a lot of tricks and can be difficult to overcome. It makes you think you are fat when actually you are very thin, it makes you feel guilty when you eat, and it supports your view that you are generally a bad and useless person. It can even make you feel like it's your friend. It really can take you over completely.

No-one fully understands how it occurs but certainly there is no single cause and many different factors come together to create it. Parents sometimes wonder if it is something they have done wrong but there is no evidence that parents cause anorexia nervosa. It is actually more useful to try and identify what keeps it going for this is usually something that we can tackle together. As parents you are in a strong position to help your daughter overcome it and that is why we will work closely with you to help you.

Meanwhile, it is important to acknowledge that it is a serious illness and at least one-third of young people with anorexia nervosa don't make a full recovery. It can delay growth, impair development and fertility, and lead to osteoporosis and many other complications. Some people become desperately ill and a few die. That is why we take it so seriously.

Fortunately we do know some of the factors that contribute to recovery. The children who do well are those whose parents are able to work well *together*, and are able to work *with us* to ensure their child's health. It is often a long hard struggle because the anorexia nervosa makes people so desperate to avoid gaining weight that they often resort to a wide range of methods to stay dangerously thin. These include not only avoiding food, but also inducing vomiting, taking laxatives, and excessive exercising. You may think your daughter hasn't or wouldn't do these things but most people with anorexia nervosa from time to time use other methods beside food avoidance. So it will be necessary for a while for you to take responsibility for your daughter's health care, including what she eats. You will need to ensure that she doesn't vomit after meals, or use laxatives, or take excessive exercise. However, if you as parents can resolve to work together, and with us, to ensure her health, then we will be doing everything we can to ensure a full recovery.

When you leave here today it is very likely that she will tell you that we have got it all wrong and that we don't understand. She may promise to eat properly and beg you to give her a chance. It is important for you to understand that this is the "anorexia" speaking. It really is like "the enemy within" and it will fight all your efforts to overcome it. You will need to be strong and determined; as strong and as determined as the "anorexia". We will all have to fight together if we are to win.

This sort of statement can be adjusted to suit the circumstances, and may be addressed predominantly to the parents or shared equally between child and parents. Using the child's name, rather than "your daughter" probably has a greater impact. The analogy of a battle against a vicious and deceitful enemy is deliberately chosen for two reasons. First, this is so often just how it feels to all concerned. Second, it is useful to "externalise" the problem so that the child does not feel even more persecuted. So often the parents believe that she has deliberately chosen to behave this way, and respond accordingly by getting into fights with her. This is hardly helpful to a young person who is already in distress. It feels better to all concerned "if we can all work together to fight the anorexia".

The message we communicate to parents of children with selective eating is obviously quite different. It would usually sound something like:

> We are pleased to be able to tell you that your son's condition is nothing more serious than what we call selective eating. This is a condition with which we are very familiar and is far more common than realised and fortunately far less serious than you have probably feared. Basically it is an extension of that normal phase you see in toddlers known as food faddiness. Most toddlers go through such a phase but usually grow out of it. Selective eaters seem to take much longer to grow out of it but fortunately almost all of them do so in their teenage years.
>
> It rarely does any harm and as you can see your son is thriving. He is normal weight and height for his age and shows no evidence of ill-health. It is amazing how children can thrive on such a *narrow* range of foods, but obviously they are having perfectly adequate *amounts* of food and usually getting all the necessary nutrients.
>
> The important thing to do here is just let him get on and eat what he likes rather than trying to make him eat foods he doesn't like. If you do try to make him eat foods he insists he does not like, this is likely to make the situation worse rather than better. I expect you have already discovered that for yourselves. He won't come to any harm and when he is ready he will gradually start trying other foods. No treatment is necessary at present but when he says he would like some help, we would be happy to offer it.

Again the message can be adjusted to fit the circumstances. In those rare instances when selective eating does impair growth we might offer a treatment programme including parental counselling (Chapter 10) and cognitive-behaviour therapy (Chapter 11).

Most parents seem to find this approach very helpful, and appear grateful to us for being so clear and direct. Often they state that they have not previously been given any clear explanation of what is wrong. Understandably they also seem to value the opportunity to share the responsibility for their child's care.

We give all parents written information about eating disorders and recommend other reading. The handouts have proved so useful that we have now published a parent's guide to eating disorders (Bryant-Waugh & Lask, 1999). At the next meeting we ensure sufficient time to answer further questions and discuss areas of concern or uncertainty. In our experience it has proved invaluable to provide this information and to allow considerable time for questions and concerns to be raised early in our contact with families, for otherwise unresolved anxieties can interfere with the process of treatment. Once the parents feel fully informed we can then move on to ensure that the adults take responsibility for tackling the eating disorder.

## INVOLVING THE PARENTS

Three important aspects of some of the eating disorders are (1) their potential for severe damage to health; (2) the patient's lack of insight; and (3) battles around control. It is possible, therefore (as is commonly the case in anorexia nervosa), that the child or teenager may be seriously ill, have little insight into her condition, and yet she fights vigorously to retain control over what she eats. People with anorexia nervosa often feel they have little control over their lives, and that two areas in which they can have control are their food intake and their weight. An understandable reaction is to over-control food intake, with a resultant sense of achievement. This ability to control food intake and body shape and size is so satisfying that it can develop an addictive quality. However, its health- and life-threatening nature demands intervention.

For this reason it is vital that the adults responsible for the young person's welfare take charge. In the case of anorexia nervosa this will almost always appear to be against the child's expressed wishes. Giving a clear message that parents/adults should be take charge can be even harder for the child as this is so commonly a change of approach. Previously the parents may have colluded with their daughter's weight loss, either by not having noticed just how much weight she had lost, or by not intervening firmly enough once the weight loss had become obvious. Understandably parents may have considered that the weight loss was due to physical ill-health and seek alternative explanations to self-starvation. Also, even when the weight loss becomes apparent, parents are often loath to take a firm approach for fear of upsetting their daughter. Commonly young people with anorexia nervosa become very angry when any attempt is made to discuss their eating habits and their weight.

It is clear then that a key feature of management is that the adults responsible for the child's welfare take firm control. A clear statement to this effect should be made to the parents at an early stage. For example:

You can see that Alison is very ill, having lost nearly a third of her body weight. You can also see that that she does not accept that she is ill. If this is allowed to continue unchecked, she will get worse and may even die. Therefore, as from this moment it is NOT appropriate for Alison to continue taking responsibility for her health and diet. She has shown you that she cannot do that safely. You must make a decision as to how you want to proceed from here, but it would be unwise to be influenced by Alison's protests. These protests are coming from the anorexia nervosa.

At this stage it is likely that Alison will indeed be protesting, but if not she will almost certainly start to once discussion turns to her required food intake, for this is likely to be substantially greater than current intake. The child may challenge the right of clinicians to dictate such terms or the right of her parents to take control, or she may start crying or screaming. Whatever the topic of discussion at the time the protest commences, it is important to demonstrate the battle for control to the parents, and to help them recognise the need for them to win.

This does not mean that the parents should take control over *all* aspects of their daughter's life, but specifically those concerning her health. It is important that she retains control in other areas of less immediate importance, such as the choice of clothing, hobbies, or friends.

This is a useful time to reiterate the importance of the parents working together, offering mutual support, and agreeing a consistent plan of management. It is not at all unusual for parents to be in conflict over various issues, but particularly in relation to how to handle the eating disorder. One parent may feel unsupported or that the other is too strict or too lax. Frequently, the child is sided with one parent against the other. Clearly, the parents cannot be in charge as long as they are in disagreement.

Issues over which the parents may disagree, and therefore need help to resolve, include how to help their daughter to eat, whether or not they wish to accept treatment, and whether or not their child should be admitted to hospital. The clinician's role here is not to take sides but rather to offer advice, and to help the parents to reach agreement, preferably without being influenced by their daughter's protests.

It is sometimes difficult to feel sympathetic towards a child who has what initially appears to be a self-inflicted problem, who denies that she is ill, and angrily rejects all attempts to help. None the less, it is obviously important to acknowledge her distress, and a statement along the following lines may be helpful:

> Alison, I know that just now you are feeling very angry with me because of what I have said to your parents, and angry with them for listening to me. You may not believe me but I do understand not only how angry you are, but also that you are worried about what has happened to you, and whether everything will get completely out of control. If your parents want me to, I will help them to get you well again. We are not going to let you die and nor will we let you get overweight. Now if you have any questions I will do my best to answer them.

Often at this point the child renews her protests or turns to her parents for support. It is helpful to note whether the parents are able to adopt a firmer and more united stance when this happens. If necessary the clinician can demonstrate how their daughter continues to control the situation by her protests or distress, and reiterate the need for her parents to take responsibility and not give way on life-threatening matters. It is always helpful to frame this as parents joining with their daughter in the fight against the illness rather than against her.

As treatment proceeds successfully there should be a gradual return of responsibility to the child so that ultimately she is taking full responsibility for her eating and health. The timing is crucial in that giving too much responsibility too soon almost always delays recovery. The emphais is on "gradual", with a degree of trial and error in the process.

It is important to emphasise that not all children with eating disorders will need such a vigorous approach. Indeed, selective eaters for example (see Chapter 3) are rarely physically ill and the parents may need help to allay their anxieties and to accept that their child is not ill (see earlier). Some children with food avoidance emotional disorder (FAED) lose as much weight as those with anorexia nervosa and their parents will need to adopt a similar approach. Others, however, are less ill and may benefit more from their parents adopting a less coercive approach that focuses on their sadness or anxieties.

Similarly children with functional dysphagia need an approach that tackles their dread of vomiting, choking, or suffocating. Coercion to eat will have the most dramatic adverse effects. Parental responsibility here is to ensure their child receives the appropriate help needed to overcome the fears and is encouraged to progress at the right pace.

Bulimia nervosa requires yet another approach, in that most young people with this disorder accept that they have a problem and want help. Often, however, their parents have taken to monitoring all their activities in an attempt to stop them from bingeing or vomiting. Although it is perfectly reasonable for parents to try to help, it is usually more helpful if they do so by agreeing a plan not only between each other but also with their daughter. People with bulimia nervosa are usually far more able to accept help than those with anorexia nervosa, and are able to explore with their parents strategies to help them resist the urge to binge and then purge.

## CONSIDERATION OF HOSPITALISATION

An early and important decision that needs to be made involves whether or not the child or teenager needs hospitalisation. A range of factors need to be considered in making this decision, including the child's physical and mental state, the parents' anxieties, and the availability of appropriate resources. In general, we give serious consideration to the possibility of hospitalisation under any of the following circumstances:

- the weight-height ratio (see Chapter 8) is less than 75% or below the 3rd BMI centile
- dehydration
- circulatory failure, as manifested by low blood pressure, slow or irregular pulse rate, or poor peripheral circulation (see Chapter 8)
- electrolyte deficiency (see Chapter 8)

- persistent vomiting or vomiting blood
- marked depression, suicidal ideation or intent, or other major psychiatric disturbance
- failed outpatient treatment.

In practice, this means that those young people most likely to need hospital admission are those with anorexia nervosa and pervasive refusal syndrome (which cannot be treated on an outpatient basis). Less commonly, admission may be necessary for those with bulimia nervosa, FAED, and functional dysphagia. Selective eaters very rarely require admission.

The clinician's task is to advise the parents so that they can make an informed decision. It is perfectly reasonable to attempt a brief trial of outpatient treatment even for those who are seriously ill, but this should be very closely monitored. For those whose physical health is seriously compromised, progress should be reviewed on a day-by-day basis. If there is no immediate improvement the trial should be terminated and hospitalisation arranged.

It is also necessary to consider what resources are available. For urgent medical treatment such as rehydration or electrolyte replacement, admission to a paediatric unit is clearly appropriate. However, for the more long-term treatment of underlying emotional problems the emphasis in such a unit on immediate physical care makes admission less appropriate. In these circumstances if out-patient care has proved insufficient, admission to a unit that has some experience and expertise in the management of eating disorders in this age group should be considered. Ideally, there should be specialist units for young people with eating disorders, which can offer all aspects of the treatment required. However, there are very few such units. A possible compromise involves a short admission to a paediatric unit for medical emergencies as required, linked with intensive outpatient treatment for the psychological issues. Day-care programmes have been shown to be of value for adults (Freeman, 1991) and their use for the younger population warrants consideration if the practicalities can be overcome. Whatever programme is being considered, it must be remembered that such patients need highly skilled psychiatric treatment allied with close medical supervision.

## TARGET WEIGHT RANGES

In most of the early onset eating disorders, achieving and maintaining a healthy weight is invariably a matter of concern to parents, but it is important to acknowledge that it is only those young people with anorexia nervosa and bulimia nervosa who are unduly preoccupied with their weight. The others have unusual eating patterns for other reasons and they are rarely concerned about their weight.

Thus, when considering what constitutes a healthy weight range the reactions are likely to differ depending upon the type of eating disorder. In anorexia nervosa there is such a preoccupation with, and dread of, weight gain that the clinician's reaction may reflect this. The temptation is either to distract the child from this theme, or to fix a very specific target weight, or to become embroiled in endless discussions and negotiations about the target. Clinicians are in danger of becoming as preoccupied with a correct weight as are their patients.

We do not find any of these approaches in the least bit helpful. Trying to ignore the pleas to be set a target weight simply increases the anxiety and the demands. Attempting to determine a specific target is at best arbitrary as the ideal for any individual is determined by a number of factors including age, gender, height, and genetic make-up. It is impossible to know prospectively what is right for any one individual. Even if a target is set on the basis of age, gender, and height population norms, this will then lead to considerable challenging by the young person concerned who will not only disagree with the target set, but will also ensure that she stays below that point.

We prefer to avoid completely the concept of a target weight for those reasons. It is certainly possible to give the young person an idea of what constitutes a healthy weight range for someone of her age and height, but it is important to emphasise that we do not know if this will be right for her. Furthermore, we avoid getting into debates about this.

Instead, we use pelvic ultrasound scanning (see Chapter 8) to help determine a healthy weight. Once the ovaries and uterus have reached the appropriate size, shape, and appearance for age we know that they are mature and that the weight is satisfactory. In consequence we carry out regular pelvic ultrasound scans and advise the girl concerned of the findings. Most girls reach ovarian and uterine maturity at between 95 and 100% weight-height ratios. However, some achieve maturity at much lower weights, whereas a few need to be higher. For example, twins Diana and Sally, aged 13, both had a weight-height ratio of 130% at the start of their illness. Menstruation ceased when the ratio dropped to 115% and by the time they had reached 105% both were very ill. With refeeding, menstruation resumed at 115%.

We find it helpful to plot out on a graph the anticipated weights on a monthly basis. This is illustrated in Fig. 9.1, which shows that the current weight is 27kg (weight-height ratio 75%) and the estimated healthy weight range is between 34 and 36kg (weight for height ratio 95–100%). As weight recovery takes time (approximately 2–3kg per month), and during the childhood and teenage years weight and height should be increasing as time goes by, the estimated weight range should take these factors into account. Therefore, in the case example in Fig. 9.1, the projected weight after one month is 29.5kg, after two months 32.3kg, and after three months 35kg. Thereafter, the projected weight will be between the two lines representing 95 and 100% weight-height ratio. This can be quite confusing for a young person who is already very frightened by the prospect of weight gain and it is helpful to let her have a copy of the graph. This is obviously particularly important for boys, for whom pelvic ultrasound is inapplicable.

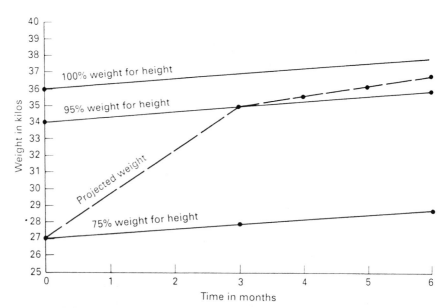

FIG. 9.1    A sample growth chart. (Lask, 1993) Reprinted with permission.

Pelvic ultrasound examination can be repeated at approximately three-monthly intervals, and once maturity is shown on ultrasound no further weight gain is required. Menstruation usually commences or returns within three months of maturity being attained.

## FAMILY WORK

Involving the parents in the treatment programme for early onset eating disorders is a *sine qua non* of management. No young person with an eating disorder, or for that matter any other problem, should be treated without there being parental involvement at some level. Family and parental counselling are considered in depth in Chapter 10. There is sound evidence for the effectiveness of family-oriented treatments in early onset anorexia nervosa (e.g. Eisler, Dare, Russell, Szmukler, le Grange, & Dodge, 1997).

## SCHOOLING CONSIDERATIONS

Whatever the eating disorder and its severity, there will be a need to consider the child's schooling. It is always helpful to have information available from the school about the child's abilities, performance, peer relationships, and eating behaviour. Schools may find it useful to know how to handle mealtimes, and of course schooling must be provided within the context of a hospital admission. Schooling is discussed in detail in Chapter 16.

# RESTORATION OF HEALTHY EATING

The implementation or restoration of healthy eating patterns is one of the main goals of treatment for nearly all the eating disorders. However, this should be distinguished from refeeding, i.e. ensuring adequate nutrition and hydration. This is only indicated when there is evidence of nutritional deficiency such as electrolyte deficiency, dehydration, circulatory failure, or growth delay as might be found in anorexia nervosa, functional dysphagia, FAED, and pervasive refusal syndrome. Young people with bulimia nervosa are generally at normal weight and the main risks are of electrolyte imbalance and complications of recurrent vomiting. Selective eaters rarely show evidence of physical complications and early restoration of healthy eating patterns is not necessary; indeed, it tends to occur spontaneously during the teenage years and there is usually no need for treatment unless the child specifically requests it.

This distinction between refeeding and regularising eating patterns is of considerable importance. Refeeding must take priority when physical well-being is at risk. How, when or what a young person eats and drinks is far less important than that they eat and drink sufficiently to restore physical health. Selective eaters are a good example of the fact that a seemingly inadequate and unhealthy diet can actually be perfectly adequate and healthy.

When indicated, refeeding may be achieved by oral, naso-gastric, or, rarely, intravenous feeds. The decision on how to proceed is made on the urgency of the situation. When a child is severely dehydrated or has electrolyte deficiency, a delay of more than a few hours can be dangerous. In consequence, it is reasonable to spend some time encouraging and helping the child to eat and drink, but if there is no immediate success, further delay in instituting artificial feeding is not advisable. Fortunately, the majority of children do not require artificial feeds and respond over time to encouragement to resume sufficient nutritional intake.

Whether this is best achieved by a graded refeeding programme (see later and Chapter 13) or trying to impose a normal diet immediately is debatable. In fact, it really does not matter at this stage how, when, or where calories are consumed, so long as the intake is adequate. In general, however, children whose weight loss is not too severe, whose illness is of recent onset, and who are being treated on an outpatient basis should be encouraged to resume a normal eating pattern and diet as soon as possible. For children whose weight loss is substantial or long lasting, it may be easier and safer for them to resume eating if offered a graded refeeding programme.

## Graded refeeding

The full details of such a programme are described in Chapter 13. When dietary intake has been very low it is best to start with a slight increase on the current calorie total. This may mean initially only 1000Cal daily for a few days. Once the child is used to having slightly more there can be a further increment to say 1200Cal and so on, with 200Cal increments every few days. How the diet is constituted can be determined by discussion between child, parents, and a dietician. Although it is important to try to include foods that the child likes and are appealingly presented, it is also important that the adults take ultimate responsibility for determining the diet. (A useful tip is that a small portion served on a large plate is more likely to be consumed than the same portion served on a small plate!)

The dietician is an invaluable member of the clinical team. Her role is to act as a consultant to the parents and other members of the clinical team. She can be particularly helpful in a number of ways including:

- planning an intake acceptable to the child
- increasing the intake gradually as food becomes less "scary"
- recommending substitutions as necessary
- emphasising the essential nutrients
- advising regarding supplements such as high-calorie drinks.

We do not believe that the dietician should offer individual support and counselling to this younger age group. The potential for splitting is far too high and we have seen time and again children who mislead the dietician with regard to what they are actually eating and then mislead their parents or the clinicians with regard to what the dietician has said. It is far better for the dietician to be a consultant to the parents and team advising on the meal plan (see Chapter 13).

## Naso-gastric feeding

When the child's physical state demands immediate refeeding, and if this cannot be achieved orally, a naso-gastric feeding programme should be implemented. Such a programme is carefully co-ordinated with liaison between medical and nursing staff and the dietician. The aim should be to ensure the child is receiving an adequate diet and preferably in the region of 2–3000Cal daily. It is usually helpful to tell the child exactly what the planned intake will be, and to say that any amount taken by mouth will be deducted from the 24-hour total naso-gastric feed (see Chapter 13).

Naso-gastric feeding of young people with eating disorders does cause some concern with regard to the infringement of rights and the mistaken view that this is force-feeding. If a child has a life-threatening illness and is unable to consume sufficient nutrition there is general agreement within paediatric practice that artificial feeding by naso-gastric tube is perfectly acceptable, and no-one would consider such action as infringing the child's rights. However, because anorexia nervosa and some of the other eating disorders present with the child *refusing* to eat sufficiently, anxieties then arise about over-ruling the child's wishes. Such views are based on an underlying misunderstanding of the psychopathology, which renders the child just as unable to eat adequate amounts as a child with any illness that impairs the appetite. If the child's life or long-term health is put at risk by the diminished intake, then whatever the underlying illness, remedial action has to be taken (see Chapter 17 for a fuller discussion of the ethical issues).

The intended course of action should always be discussed with the child and her parents, and their agreement sought. Surprisingly, it is very rare for a child to refuse. It seems that most children in these circumstances are relieved that the responsibility for eating is taken away from them, at least temporarily. As much as possible they should always be given choices about who passes the tube, where, and with whom present. If a child does strongly object to naso-gastric feeding, she can be offered the alternative of intravenous feeds (see later).

There is some debate as to whether or not naso-gastric feeds should be administered at night. The advantage of night feeding is purported to be that the child can lead as normal a life as possible during the day without being perceived as being different from others. This potential advantage is often outweighed by the possibility of her interfering with the feeds during the night. Further, whether or not repeated passing of the tube each evening is useful is unclear. Some children find it aversive, and quickly opt to eat adequate amounts by mouth, whereas others very quickly adapt to it and pass their own tubes! Other disadvantages of overnight feeds include the discomfort associated with being fed while lying in bed and the fact that it is physiologically unnatural to be fed overnight. On balance, it is likely that daytime feeding is more likely to hasten a normal eating pattern than is overnight feeding.

Occasionally, children can seem to become dependent on the tube and make no effort to eat normally.

> Hannah, 12, was admitted to hospital having lost 52% of her weight over a 12-month period. Her physical state was such that artificial feeding was essential. She refused to eat or drink anything by mouth for a further 18 months. All efforts to withdraw naso-gastric feeding failed. Eventually, Hannah started eating normally after living with a foster family for six months.

Such circumstances are unusual and possibly in her case related more to her fear of returning to her family than to dependency on the tube. There is no evidence that long-term dependency on tube feeding does occur. In general, however, naso-gastric tube feeding should be seen as a life-saving measure, preferably to be used for time-limited periods.

Finally, an audit of child and parent responses to naso-gastric tube feeding has shown that in retrospect the vast majority of children who had been tube-fed and their parents were grateful that such action had been taken and had few regrets (Niederman, Richardson, Farley, & Lask, submitted). The fact that the treatment was perceived as life-saving far out-ruled any concerns about its intrusiveness.

## Intravenous feeding

Intravenous feeding may be used as an alternative to naso-gastric feeds. All necessary nutrients are fed directly into a vein via an in-dwelling needle or catheter. The advantages are rapid rehydration and electrolyte replacement. The disadvantages are that it can only be implemented on a medical or paediatric ward and for short periods. Intravenous feeding is best reserved for the rare times when immediate fluid or electrolyte replacement is required and the child can tolerate neither oral nor naso-gastric feeds.

## COGNITIVE AND BEHAVIOURAL THERAPY (CBT)

The cognitive and behavioural approaches to therapy are of considerable value in the treatment of early onset eating disorders. They seem to be particularly helpful in bulimia nervosa, selective eating, and functional dysphagia but may also be used in the other eating disorders. A full account of these techniques is provided in Chapter 11.

## PSYCHODYNAMIC PSYCHOTHERAPY

Psychodynamically oriented psychotherapy seems to have particular value in the treatment of anorexia nervosa and FAED, but may be applied to other conditions including bulimia nervosa and pervasive refusal syndrome. A full account is provided in Chapter 12.

## GROUP WORK

Group work is commonly used in the management of eating disorders. These include groups for children, teenagers, and parents and can take the form of discussions, psycho-education, art, drama, dance, body-awareness, and social skills training. A full account of group work is provided in Chapter 15.

## PHYSIOTHERAPY AND EXERCISE

These physical therapies have an important part to play in the management of eating disorders in terms of providing controlled exercise programmes, muscle strengthening, relaxation, massage, and body-awareness exercises. A full account of such techniques is provided in Chapter 14.

## MEDICATION

Medication has but a small part to play in the management of eating disorders. Those preparations that have been considered include appetite stimulants, vitamins, zinc, magnesium, and other forms of mineral supplementation, anxiolytics, anti-depressants, calcium, iron, and oestrogens.

It is debatable whether there are any true appetite stimulants, but in any event they would have little part to play, for there is rarely a true loss of appetite, with the possible exception of FAED. Nor is there is any evidence that vitamin or mineral supplements enhance appetite. Deficiencies of these substances are usually rapidly remedied by the implementation of a normal diet. What little evidence that exists suggests that supplementation is no more effective than a refeeding programme in overcoming the deficiencies (e.g. Lask, Fosson, Thomas, & Rolfe, 1993).

Anxiolytics have a very limited role. There is no evidence for their value in bulimia nervosa or anorexia nervosa, despite the fact that anxiety, phobias, and obsessionality often accompany eating disorders. Anxiolytics, particularly alprazolam, may be of some help in functional dysphagia. They may also be helpful when used for short periods for those children suffering from extreme anxiety.

Antidepressants do have a slightly more useful role in early onset eating disorders than any other form of medication. When a young person is depressed with psychomotor retardation, feelings of guilt and worthlessness, and biological changes such as poor sleep and diurnal mood variation, tricyclics such as amitryptilline, and the selective serotonin re-uptake inhibitors (SSRIs), such as fluoxetine, do seem to have value. This may particularly apply to anorexia nervosa and FAED. In addition the SSRIs have been shown to reduce the urge to binge in adults with bulimia nervosa (American Psychological Association, 1993).

Caution should always be taken when using psychotropic medication in the younger population. It is wise to check for normal cardiovascular, hepatic, and renal functioning, and to start with low doses building up slowly through weekly increments.

The value of calcium supplementation has yet to be established (see Chapter 8). In long-standing eating disorders with markedly delayed growth and/or puberty, growth hormone or oestrogens may be indicated (testosterone for boys!) but generally hormonal treatment should be avoided in the younger population.

Finally, it is worth cautioning against the use of laxatives when constipation is troublesome. This is best overcome by dietary means.

## INTEGRATED TREATMENT

It is beyond dispute that the management of all but the mildest cases of early onset eating disorders requires a comprehensive approach. This includes focusing on biological, social, and psychological factors, and requires a multidisciplinary team. The team might include nurses, psychologists, psychiatrists, family therapists, psychotherapists, social workers, dieticians, and physiotherapists or occupational therapists. Between them they can provide a comprehensive (physical, social, and psychological) assessment, and an integrated treatment, which might include parental counselling and/or family therapy, cognitive, behaviour, and psychodynamic psychotherapy, medication, meal plans, meal support, exercise activities, and body-awareness programmes. Teachers should be consulted and advised with regard to school-related issues and they are essential for an inpatient programme. A social work input is necessary when neglect or abuse is suspected, or on the rare occasions when parents decline or sabotage treatment for their sick child. On such occasions the social worker can advise on the need for, and if necessary organise, a network meeting or case conference. It is important to share information and exchange views in such worrying circumstances before making decisions about management.

Such comprehensive teams are more likely to be available within an inpatient service, and the majority of children and adolescents with eating disorders are likely to be treated as outpatients. However, every effort should be made to ensure that the essential ingredients of the treatment programme are available, whatever the context. Generally it should be possible to provide the essential ingredients with even a relatively small team. It is our experience that early onset eating disorders become even more problematic as a result of the failure to acknowledge the need for, and/or to implement, appropriate treatment.

## STAGES OF RECOVERY

In young people with anorexia nervosa particularly, but also those with FAED, pervasive refusal syndrome, and indeed most emotional disorders, we have noticed specific patterns of behaviour which predominate at certain times. These are illustrated in Fig. 9.2 and are usefully categorised as three stages. The first is that of the presenting problem, when the eating disorder is the predominant feature. The young person with anorexia nervosa tends to be preoccupied with weight and food intake almost to the exclusion of other considerations. With the possible exception of schoolwork, she shows no interest in anything else. She is unable to recognise that she has any problem other than that "stupid adults are trying to make me fat". A similar picture can be painted for other eating disorders.

Once treatment is initiated, and usually within a few weeks, a slow improvement in the presenting problem occurs, and on average after about six months it has almost resolved, providing the next stage is allowed to occur. This stage 2 is one of increasing assertiveness and expression of very powerful, negative feelings, with an apparent absence of concern for those to whom the feelings are directed—most commonly the parents, but also clinicians. The young person behaves in a manner that is totally uncharacteristic, and causes great distress to her parents. Indeed they often blame us for turning their child "into a monster". This stage has now become so familiar to us as a necessary step to recovery that we not only predict it but also positively welcome it. We advise the parents in advance along the following lines:

> If your child is to make a full recovery she will go through a phase that you will probably find extremely difficult; this is a stage of complete obnoxiousness; she will be horrible to you and probably to us as well. You will be very angry with us,

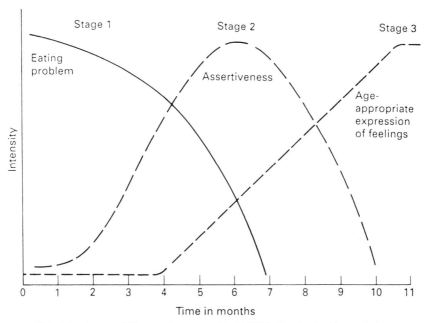

FIG. 9.2  Stages of illness and recovery. (Lask, 1993). Reprinted with permission.

and feel that we have made her worse. However, we will be pleased because this will mean that she is getting better. It is as if she has been unable to express these feelings and they have built up inside her almost to the point when she cannot eat. Once treatment starts, however, these feelings will come pouring out, almost like a volcano exploding. We will of course do our best to support you during this stage and it will come to an end. However, if you block her feelings, if you don't let her express them, or you punish her, she will withdraw and lock them up inside. You may then feel better but her eating problems won't resolve. Of course, you will need to set limits such as no breaking things or physical violence, but if you can tolerate the rest you will be helping her to recover.

As stage 2 behaviour diminishes it is gradually replaced by a more age-appropriate expression of feelings. For example, the young person may express her anger directly at the person concerned, but within a few minutes is able to discuss it all in a relatively calm and rational manner. Once this behaviour predominates over eating problems and excessive negativism, stage 3 has been achieved and the child is well on the way to complete recovery.

As can be seen from Fig. 9.2, there is considerable overlap between these stages, leading to some confusion and much distress, especially when stages 1 and 2 overlap in the first few months. However, it can be seen that this overlap is part of a process and so long as it can be tolerated there will be movement forward to recovery.

Some children, especially those who have been severely traumatised either by neglect or abuse, are likely to go through a stage of regression, before they enter stage 2. They may behave like a child much younger than their years, and even adopt quite infantile behaviour, such as drinking from a baby's bottle or wetting the bed. Again, tolerance of this and sympathetic understanding and support aids recovery.

## SUMMARY POINTS

The ingredients of successful management are:

- comprehensive (physical, social and psychological) assessment
- provision of information and education to parents and child
- involvement of the parents and ensuring that adults take responsibility for the young person's health
- consideration of the need for hospitalisation
- determination of a healthy weight range
- parental counselling and/or family therapy
- liaison with the school (usually via the parents)
- implementation of other treatments such as refeeding, individual therapy (cognitive or psychodynamic), physiotherapy, and group work, as required.

These are discussed in the relevant sections in this chapter or the relevant chapters elsewhere in the book.

There is increasing interest developing in the use of motivational approaches, e.g. motivational enhancement therapy. However, most of the work done in this area has been applied in adult eating disorders and, as yet, there is very little information on its relevance to the younger age group.

## REFERENCES

American Psychological Association. (1993). Practice guidelines for eating disorders. *American Journal of Psychiatry*, *150*, 208–228.

Bryant-Waugh, R., & Lask, B. (1999). *Eating disorders in childhood and adolescence: A parent's guide*. London: Penguin.

Eisler, I., Dare, C., Russell, G., Szmukler, G., le Grange, D., & Dodge, E. (1997). Family and individual therapy in anorexia nervosa—a five-year follow-up. *Archives of General Psychiatry*, *54*, 1025–1030.

Freeman, C. (1991). Day treatment for anorexia nervosa. *British Review of Bulimia and Anorexia Nervosa*, *6*, 3–8.

Lask, B. (1993). Management Overview. In B. Lask & R., Bryant-Waugh (Eds.), *Childhood onset anorexia nervosa and related eating disorders* (1st Ed.). (pp. 127–136). Hove, UK: Lawrence Erlbaum Associates Ltd.

Lask, B., Fosson, A., Thomas, S., & Rolfe, U. (1993). Zinc deficiency and childhood onset anorexia nervosa. *Journal of Clinical Psychiatry*, *54*, 63–66.

Niederman, M., Richardson, J., Farley, A., & Lask, B. (submitted). *Naso-gastric tube feeding in early onset eating disorders—an audit of 50 cases.*

CHAPTER TEN

# Family work

**Peter Honig**
*Phoenix Centre, Cambridge, UK*

## MOVING BEYOND BLAME

Some research suggests that the most effective treatment for early onset anorexia nervosa is family therapy (Eisler et al., 1997; Russell, Szmukler, Dare, & Eisler, 1987), but to be told this can confirm for many parents that their family is dysfunctional and has somehow caused the illness to occur in their child. Seminal texts in the family therapy literature such as Palazzoli (1989, p. 177), describe "the anorectic process in the family" where the onset of anorexia is seen as an inevitable consequence of certain toxic family interactions. Minuchin (1978) describes psychosomatic families as typically being over-involved or enmeshed. These views can strongly influence clinicians in the same negative direction as parents. There is therefore a potentially malignant context where professional and non-professional belief systems coincide, feeding off each other in a spiral, which can all too easily result in blame, guilt, and frustration.

The task of those working with children and adolescents who have eating disorders is to recognise the importance of helping families move beyond this sense of blame. For this reason it is crucial to recognise a distinction between family factors, which precipitate an onset of an eating disorder, and current family functioning, which may perpetuate it (see Chapter 5). This therapeutic dilemma is perfectly described by Speed (1995, p. 7):

> Whilst we may never know if family members' behaviour was causal in a child's eating distress and related difficulties, we may nevertheless be of the opinion, after careful observation in any one case, that such behaviour at least partly maintains it. We then still have the difficult task of inviting family members to consider any

187

inter-connectedness in their behaviour without them leaving therapy because they feel criticized and blamed.

This dilemma applies equally to working with families where the young person is not diagnosed with anorexia nervosa. All childhood eating disorders seem to have the capacity to create an overwhelming sense of failure and guilt in the parents, resulting in lowered self-esteem. In essence, therefore, the task of the clinician working with parents is to help the family see themselves as a resource for recovery, rather than as a breeding ground for pathology.

## INVOLVING PARENTS AS PARTNERS

Achieving such a major shift in perception requires an approach to treatment, which is inclusive of parental involvement at many different levels. Accordingly, in this chapter I describe a variety of interventions and not just the formal arena of family therapy.

Partnership, if it is to be meaningful, needs to permeate all contacts with parents, not just because it is a fashionable slogan, but primarily because research suggests that the most successful way to treat young people with eating disorders is to empower their parents and to focus attention on the familial context rather than at the intrapsychic level alone (Russell et al., 1987). The process of achieving partnership is continuous, and requires a commitment to sharing information, in particular making available research findings—providing, in other words, a psycho-educational approach. In so doing we are more likely to achieve the goal of moving beyond blame, as much of the recent research concerning aetiology and treatment points profoundly away from any one-dimensional view of causality.

In order to plot the development of a family approach I will begin by describing parental counselling and then move onto a variety of different family therapy techniques that I have found to be useful.

## PARENTAL COUNSELLING

Parental counselling is an approach that offers parents an opportunity to regain eroded parenting skills. This may include encouraging parents to work together whether or not they have differences in other areas of their relationship. Lask (1997) describes the approach in some detail. Parental counselling should not be seen as a discrete intervention that is conducted for a number of sessions and then abandoned in favour of something more sophisticated. It is more helpful to perceive its value as a continuous process throughout the course of a young person's treatment. Where there is a lone parent, attention should be paid to ways in which such persons can ensure support for themselves throughout the course of the illness. An overt recognition of the stress the illness is likely to cause to any one parent should be made, so that such a suggestion is not received as criticism of the lone parent's status. Where parents have separated, attention will need to be given to who should be involved in the parental counselling. I will return to this in more detail later.

There are a number of different purposes to parental counselling in addition to the overarching therapeutic goal of empowerment (as previously described).

## Enabling informed decision making

For some of the treatment, particularly in connection with food intake, parents are in a position where they will need to override their child's expressed wishes, usually connected to eating sufficient amounts to remain healthy. Overriding a child's strongly held views requires confidence that the parents' view can be more in the child's long-term interests than is the child's. It is well-recognised that one of the effects of starvation is to alter cognitions so that perceptions become distorted. Time and again we see that the power of these distortions is such that they can be influential on others close to the patient. For example, it is likely that a young person with anorexia nervosa will negotiate endlessly about calorie intake. Although the parents may see that their daughter is unwell, they may also consider that an increase in conflict between them can be avoided if sufficient time is given to engage their child in an agreement. Parental counselling clarifies the symptomatic nature of these patterns of behaviour, and emphasises the reasons why urgency is stressed in the treatment of early onset eating disorders. In such circumstances, avoiding conflict may be a factor that maintains the illness rather than relieving it.

Many parents report subsequently that advice about the likely course of recovery, with the expectation that different stages will need to be negotiated, was particularly helpful in containing their anxiety that the relationship with their child would be irrevocably damaged if they refused to accede to her demands. Knowing about and recognising a familiar process can help us to master otherwise unmanageable situations. In particular, it is helpful to inform parents that their child's intense anger with them, which is initially restricted to disagreements about food but develops into more generalised conflict, is in itself a positive sign. Although parents might long for a return to the previously compliant child they knew before the onset of the illness, the treatment team will be encouraged by the child's increasing capacity to voice negative feelings. This "reframing" of behaviour can for most parents be a welcome sign of a return to health. It should be a matter of some concern to the treatment team if parents remain unable to confront the anorexic "voice" emanating from their child. With this in mind, and however the parents chose to challenge the symptoms of the eating disorder, progress will need to be measured in terms of weight gain as well as other psychological factors.

Certainly anorexia nervosa has the capacity to confuse and one of the hardest tasks can be to see the wood for the trees. Parents may report significant improvements in the mood of the child and a lessening of the restrictive food intake (e.g. their child may start to broaden the variety of foods that they are prepared to eat). However, if there is no evidence of a parallel consistent weight gain the task of parental counselling is to help the parents to recognise this and to continue to educate them in the ways of anorexia nervosa. We have found that at these times the influence of other parents can be most effective—the views of peers can be accepted more readily than those of clinicians. (See Chapter 15 on group work, and Magagna & Nicholls, 1997).

In our experience most parents respond positively when encouraged to take back responsibility, provided they are supported in the process. Occasionally, we are not successful in persuading them to take this course and if their child's health improves it does not matter that our advice is not followed. If, however, there is no improvement within a reasonable period of time it remains the clinicians' responsibility to explore all avenues available. This may include the option of discussing concerns with statutory child protection agencies for alternative options of care if it is apparent that non-cooperation with treatment is jeopardising the patient's long-term physical and psychological health.

## Providing parents with a space apart

There needs to be a recognition that being the parent of a child with an eating disorder is a frustrating experience. Feeling manipulated and undermined by the child's denial will inevitably cause intense feelings of anger in even the most tolerant of parents. We know that an openly hostile environment with a high level of expressed emotion is not one that is likely to promote recovery (Le Grange, Eisler, Dare, & Hodes, 1992). For this reason we like to offer some meetings for parents that do not include their children; we can then encourage these negative feelings to be expressed without fear of the damage they might be causing to the young person's self-esteem.

## Maintaining the therapeutic link between parents and the treatment team

This can be as important as the task of helping parents to work together more effectively. Eating disorders affect a variety of relationships—and, although these relationships may not have caused the illness, they are undoubtedly essential to the successful treatment of it. Consequently time and space need to be devoted to the nurturing of these relationships in order that differences can be openly acknowledged and overcome. The special dynamic of persuading and supporting parents in their task of apparently working against their child's wishes is likely to impose an unusual strain upon the relationship between staff and parents.

Susan, 10, had been an inpatient for approximately three months. Her parents complained that the feedback they received from staff was inconsistent and insufficient. Staff on the eating disorders unit felt criticised and harassed, as though they could never do anything right. A number of meetings between parents and staff were held to address the difficulties in the relationship between them, as it was increasingly apparent that Susan was aware of the hostility and caught in divided loyalties. Following these meetings a restructured regimen focusing on communication between staff and parents was created. The regimen was different to the usual programme but seemed to meet the needs of this particular circumstance better. There were immediate signs of improvement in the relationship and Susan's health began steadily to recover. Whether or not there was a link between these two events is impossible to prove, but it can certainly be claimed that there were no ill-effects from the focus on the parent/staff interactions. Before this focus there was a danger of a breakdown in the relationship with potentially disastrous consequences for Susan.

In conclusion, parental counselling should emphasise the multidetermined nature of anorexia nervosa and other related eating disorders. By stressing all the factors that can affect the child and create a context in which the illness develops, a culture of blame will hopefully be avoided. Instead, we aim to promote an environment in which parents can be helped to find their own solutions, given a framework of advice based on the experience of those who work daily with these problems.

## FROM PARENTAL COUNSELLING TO FAMILY THERAPY

We can now say that we would never embark upon the treatment of childhood onset eating disorders unless parents could attend for parental counselling sessions. Family therapy, on the other hand, may occasionally be considered unnecessary although it is unusual for this to be the case. There are many indicators for family therapy:

- enhancing the child's voice in the family
- considering how a future without an eating disorder might differ from a future where the eating disorder remains
- clarifying marital difficulties and how these might affect the children
- providing a space for other family members to discuss how they are suffering from the stress of living with an eating disorder in their household.

Helen, 9, with a six-month history of anorexia nervosa, was the youngest of three sisters. Her 12-year-old sister was increasingly distressed; she began missing school, finding it difficult to get up in the mornings. She developed behavioural problems, becoming verbally aggressive, and even violent on occasions. She repeatedly threatened to leave home.

Inviting siblings to attend in such situations can be helpful, not necessarily because it allows for an airing of negative feelings, for more often than not an "airing" is a regular occurrence at home, but primarily because it permits discussion concerning a "recovery plan". In other words, we discuss how each family member can offer a unique contribution to overcoming the illness, and how the family can work out ways to minimise the impact of the illness on their everyday lives.

> Flora, 13, was furious with her brother's insensitivity to her difficulties around food. He would constantly tease her and comment on her "obsession" with diet products. In a family therapy session, Flora and her parents were able to help him understand the inappropriateness of his remarks and he agreed to make no further comments on the subject.

Family therapy also offers an opportunity to consider the future and how relationships in the family might develop. Families can understandably lose sight of anything beyond the next meal, but the therapist can introduce family life cycle issues, which have been temporarily obscured by the illness. This can be particularly important when considering the impact of the illness on sibling relationships.

> Anna, 13, had been an inpatient for approximately six months when she decided that she no longer wanted to live with her mother and siblings, preferring instead to move to her father's house. From this point she refused to have anything to do with her brother and sister, avoiding their company when they visited their father at weekends. Despite considerable discussion focusing on what her father could do to enable her to communicate with her siblings, no change was achieved. The therapist then wrote a letter to Anna and her father documenting what could be the gains and losses of this situation continuing into her adult life. The dilemma was described and four months later Anna, at her own request, resumed contact with her sister and became eager to spend time with her at every opportunity. Some months later she felt ready to write to her mother and subsequently began seeing her again regularly.

Family therapy can offer a context in which marital conflict can be acknowledged and the impact of any disharmony on the patient can be explored. As Dare and Lindsay (1979) point out, this should not imply that family therapy turns into marital therapy with the children as on lookers, but it can be recognised as a problem that needs tackling and for which the patient no longer needs to feel responsible.

Another focus for family therapy can be to facilitate a helpful response from parents to any disclosures of abuse. We know that abuse can be present in a variety of different ways. We also know that approximately 30% of adult women diagnosed with anorexia nervosa report adverse sexual experiences as children (Palmer, Oppenheimer, Dignon, Chaloner, & Howells, 1990). We must, therefore, find ways within our treatment programmes of screening for abuse and keeping alive the possibility of discussing this issue throughout the course of treatment with a family. For this reason, working in close liaison with the child's individual therapist/key worker is crucial, as initial disclosure is far more likely to come in this setting than in the context of family work. Alternatively, where family therapy is the only treatment, the therapist must not shirk from meeting the patient alone where the level of suspicion is high. Should disclosure of intrafamilial abuse come to light the first consideration must be to consider matters of safety, both of the patient and of any siblings in the household. Information about the disclosure should only be shared with parents once there is certainty about the safety of the child. Often this will require a preliminary discussion or meeting with child protection agencies. There are exceptions to this, for instance where the perpetrator is known to be dead or living in another country, but always a clear plan for protecting the child must be considered as a matter of urgency. Following any disclosure a change in who attends family therapy is indicated until a child protection plan is in place. This may be a good time to undertake work with dyads or triads within the family, e.g. sessions between mother and daughter when the father is implicated as the perpetrator.

If disclosure is connected to somebody outside the family the task of the therapist would be to facilitate the child sharing this information with her parents. Sensitive management of this most confidential of areas will be required if the child is to feel supported and not betrayed. Working closely with the child's individual therapist, when there is one, can be most fruitful and may result in joint work for a period, with the individual therapist possibly attending family sessions. Clearly, the child's view on this needs to be sought.

> Jessica, 13, disclosed to her key worker that she had been sexually abused by a stranger three years prior to the onset of her illness. After ascertaining that she felt in no danger within her own family, she was gradually persuaded that her parents should be given this information. Considerable discussion took place, with Jessica being encouraged to describe what would be the most helpful way for her parents to be informed. She decided that she wanted the family therapist and her key worker to discuss the matter with her parents, initially without her present. She was also able to say how she wanted her parents to respond to her once the information had been shared. This was discussed with her parents who were encouraged to respect their daughter's wishes, which included a request for her father not to talk to her about the matter. The parents achieved this and Jessica was then able to raise the subject with her mother some weeks later, when she was feeling more confident about discussing it.

Particular attention should be paid to helping the child speak during family therapy. We have found that working closely with the child's individual therapist can be of assistance. Clearly, this raises issues of confidentiality but these do generally seem to be manageable. It is much easier to achieve this model of integrating the therapies on an inpatient programme, but any efforts made in this direction, even in outpatient treatment, are likely to bear fruit. If only family therapy is available it can be useful for the family therapist to make a link with the child outside of the family meetings (possibly meeting before the session) in order to help the child feel supported, and to ascertain if there are areas for discussion in the meeting to follow that they would like raised.

> Donna, 12, was seen by the family therapist prior to a family meeting. She was clear that there were two main things she wanted to discuss with her parents in the session: (1) her desire to have her nose pierced, and (2) wanting to have her way regarding a colour scheme for her bedroom. The therapist clarified that he was not in a position to support her requests, but he was prepared to help her raise them for discussion, and to focus on what would usually make it so difficult for her to bring up such issues.

It is also helpful to meet the parents alone early in treatment in order to explain how crucial it will be for their child to begin the process of communicating openly in these sessions, and how their responses to their child's communication will influence how much the child is willing to contribute.

## WORKING WITH SINGLE-PARENT AND SEPARATED FAMILIES

As briefly mentioned previously, any work with a single-parent family should recognise the additional strain that exists for the parent. Although the single parent will not face the potential strain of working consistently with an antagonistic partner, she usually will have the task of being responsible for every mealtime. This can place an enormous burden on any one person and it is therefore useful to help the parent seek support for this task. The idea of occasional respite should be considered as an essential part of treatment, rather than as an indicator that the parent is not coping.

> Alice, 15, had a two-year history of anorexia nervosa and was close to discharge from her second admission to a psychiatric unit. The family therapist, recognising the strain that Alice's mother would soon be facing, suggested to her that a network meeting be convened to which the mother would invite all those adults who she anticipated being involved with her daughter following her discharge home. Alice's mother chose to invite six other adults: her daughter and her daughter's partner, her sister and brother-in-law, and her next-door neighbours, who were best friends. The meeting focused on a discussion concerning the nature of anorexia nervosa and how each one of them could be helpful by supporting Alice's mother in her task of helping Alice to eat. In addition, it was possible to look at

the needs of Alice's younger brother who, all were agreed, had lost out because so much of his mother's attention had necessarily been focused on his sister.

In working with separated and step-families it is crucial to establish the different roles of the adults involved in the child's life. As a rule of thumb, when both birth parents are in regular contact with the child, undertaking some joint sessions with them both is strongly indicated. Meetings can focus on the shared task of parenting, which requires good communication between them. Given the well-documented capacity of anorexia nervosa to divide, any residual splits between the parents are likely to be rapidly exposed and exploited. Acknowledging these divisions and the history of disagreements between the couple, while stressing the need for joint decision making, can be a helpful intervention.

Karen's parents had divorced shortly before the onset of her illness, when she was 8 years old. Five years later, following extensive treatment as both an in- and outpatient, very few meetings with both parents present had been held. The family therapist chose to engage in a series of meetings with the parents together, the stated aims being: (1) a reduction in the level of blame still being attributed between the parents, and (2) clarifying the roles of the parents/step-parents. Despite a scepticism that these meetings would be of any benefit, there was a lowering of the hostility and criticism between the two. Although there was some improvement in Karen's condition during this phase of the work with her family, she remained chronically ill. However, her parents were better able to support each other and to accept the long-term nature of her eating disorder without any longer blaming each other.

## FAMILY THERAPY TECHNIQUES

The premise of family therapy is that individuals and behaviour always exist within a context; a context either of other people (e.g. a family) or of ideas. For instance, there is the belief in Western societies that tall and thin women are considered beautiful. It is the interrelationship between various parts of the context that is the focus of family therapy.

Most theories of family functioning in anorexia nervosa have emphasised the dysfunctional organisation of families where an eating disorder exists (Minuchin et al., 1978; Palazzoli, 1974). These authors have seen the task of the family therapist as finding ways to change the patterns of interaction which bring about this dysfunction. Different models of therapy have utilised different techniques and strategies, which are largely dependent upon each model's theory of change. This preoccupation with uncovering dysfunction has been one of the main criticisms of family therapy. In particular, some of the earlier models have been accused of imposing a rigid view of eating disorders aetiology invariably linking it to family factors. What is apparent is that abiding by the "rules" of any one model is unlikely to be helpful as the therapist can all too easily fall into the trap of fitting the family into the template for treatment, rather than struggling to understand what may or may not work with each particular situation. Most models do have techniques and perspectives that are enriching and next I will outline a number of these which seem to be particularly useful when working with families in this field.

## Enhancing the parental subsystem

This way of working, as described by Minuchin et al. (1978), emphasises the need for clear structure in families. In particular, there is concern for inter-generational boundaries being maintained, in order that individuation of each family member is ensured. This is seen as of central importance to the adolescent, whose developmental task, at least in Western cultures, is to separate and move towards independence. Families in which one member develops a "psychosomatic disorder" are perceived as too close or "enmeshed". This closeness is manifested in an inability to express hostility (openly) and thus the task for the therapist is to provide an environment in which such feelings can be safely experienced. A focus on communication is therefore very strongly promoted in this way of working.

The reader will note that parental counselling fits very closely with this structural notion of clear subsystems in which roles are delineated and hierarchical boundaries are respected. There is little doubt that such an approach is helpful in the early stages of treatment when the primary focus is on weight restoration and physical health.

Jessica, 13, was severely emaciated on referral, despite a two-week admission to a paediatric ward. Her weight/height ratio was 63% and her potassium levels had dropped dangerously low. She had been an inpatient on two previous occasions. On admission to an eating disorders unit there was discussion with Jessica and her parents outlining proposed treatment, including the possibility of naso-gastric tube feeding if weight gain did not occur. From the outset, Jessica's father was concerned that this course of action should be avoided at all costs, only granting permission should her life be in immediate danger.

Jessica's weight increased consistently for six weeks and then stopped when her physical state had slightly improved. Jessica refused to increase her weight further. Her parents withdrew permission for naso-gastric feeding and a 10-week period of negotiation between Jessica and her parents ensued regarding the rate of weight gain. Treatment focused on helping her parents reach joint decisions, but throughout this period there was division between them, and often also between them and the treatment team. Psychological interventions with Jessica were ineffective as her thinking remained distorted as a result of persisting malnourishment.

At this stage of treatment parental counselling was emphasised. Jessica's parents were encouraged to talk with other parents who had come through these early stages of the illness. There was considerable exploration of the parents' dilemma: weighing up the long-term physical risks for their daughter's health against the short-term gain of doing what she demanded and thus avoiding conflict.

After 16 weeks of admission a decision by the treatment team was reached that naso-gastric feeding should again be implemented and that legal proceedings would be instituted if the parents were unable to agree to this action. (These proceedings are designed to hear the details of a case and to reach a decision on a specific issue of treatment—they are not designed to prove a case against parents, and do not result in a restriction of parental rights.) This course of action, however, proved to be unnecessary as Jessica's parents found the strength to overcome the pleas of their daughter by agreeing to naso-gastric feeding. From this point, Jessica resumed eating sufficient amounts, and did not require artificial feeding (Fig. 10.1). In the six-week period that followed, her weight increased by the same amount as during the previous 16 weeks. Her physical condition improved significantly and, perhaps most crucially, she was able to use the psychological treatments that were available to the full. She gradually learnt to trust staff, who were able to help her rebuild bridges with her parents. It seemed that having her parents show they were capable of resisting the most destructive forces in her life propelled her into a different way of thinking. Clearly, this is an important message for any adolescent to receive, but was particularly pertinent in this situation, as it was a precursor to Jessica feeling safe enough to disclose to her mother that she had been sexually abused by a stranger when she was 10 years old. Issues of guilt, anger, and sorrow could be explored, and finding ways to open communication between Jessica and her parents came to the fore.

## Focusing on communication

From the early days of family therapy, observing and identifying patterns of communication has been seen as the bread and butter of interventions for those working with families. In a seminal text Watzlawick, Beavin, and Jackson (1967) explained how communication between individuals has meaning beyond the words they use. There are different levels of communication that contribute to meaning and it is when these levels are not congruent that difficulties in relationship may arise. See Lask and Bryant-Waugh (1997) for a more detailed discussion of this. It is the therapist's task to point out these incongruences either by commenting on them directly, or by asking the recipient of the message what they thought was meant by the sender of it.

There are many other patterns of communication that are often encountered, all of which can be problematic as they can mitigate against problem resolution, for instance, communication in which individuals talk across each other, allowing

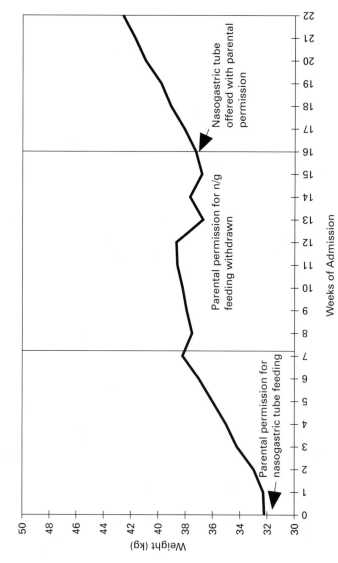

FIG. 10.1   Jessica's weight chart.

no silences and no space for opinions to be heard and considered. Humour is often a good way to draw attention to these patterns, as often it is simply a matter of bringing to light what is already well known by the family.

> Sandra, 16, her mother, and father were having their first meeting with a family therapist. The therapist became aware after some 10 minutes that there had been no pause in communication and that he had said very little. Sandra interrupted her mother and was in turn interrupted by her father until she shouted over him, saying that she did not agree with anything he was saying. After observing this pattern for much of the session, and establishing that the family shared a sense of humour, the therapist said that he had just seen that in the last four sentences the person who started the sentence had not finished it. Were they talking in this way because they were nervous or was this typical? All three family members broke into laughter and confirmed that this was the way they always talked to each other. Sandra commented that this was the reason why nothing was ever sorted out—because nobody listened to what anyone else was saying!

Another example of communication difficulties is when people talk *for* others without consulting them first. This produces a mind-reading style which is most clearly visible when one family member begins a sentence with the phrase "he thinks . . ." or "she feels . . .". It may be helpful in such circumstances for the therapist to state positively that they value everyone's opinion highly and that for this reason a rule of talking only for oneself should be observed. If this rule is "broken" the therapist can check with the individual who is being mind-read, whether the person talking has conveyed their thoughts/feelings accurately.

## Separating the marital from the parental relationship

It can be useful to recognise that alongside the symptom may lurk some other relationship difficulties but this is a far step from suggesting that these difficulties are the *cause* of the illness. We would advise an approach that acknowledges these issues, e.g. marital difficulties, but which separates them from the primary task of parenting. In the acknowledging, the therapist can offer to discuss such difficulties at another time if the couple consent.

By approaching other relationship issues in this way therapists are more likely to maintain congruence between themselves and the family. It also reflects a stance that implicitly communicates respect—respect that parents are experts on their situation just as much as the therapist.

> Flora, 12, had a six-month history of anorexia nervosa. Parental counselling revealed a repeated inability on the part of her parents to agree on meal-time management. Flora's father thought that his wife was far too lenient

and inconsistent, whereas her mother accused her husband of being old-fashioned and out-of-touch with girls (and women) in the 1990s.

It soon became clear that the criticism each partner was making of the other, in relation to how they treated their daughter, was a coded criticism of how they viewed their partner in relation to themselves. Once this was explicitly acknowledged, with Flora present, there was a recognition that neither partner was satisfied with their marital relationship and agreement to discuss this was reached. Flora was relieved that her perception of her parent's relationship had been in tune with her parents, although until this time there had been a denial that any such tensions existed. She was informed that her parents would have some discussions with the therapist without her present in order for these difficulties to be tackled. This freed Flora to focus more of her attention on her own discomfort in relation to food and how this connected to her poor self-esteem.

This approach differs from the "trickery" of some strategic family therapy models, for example Palazzoli's (1989, p. 17) "invariant prescription", which never overtly addresses the marital discord. The task that she prescribed, however, where the marital couple are advised to keep a secret from their children, is an attempt to strengthen the marital relationship by removing the patient from the inappropriately close position they occupy to one of their parents. It is a task that undoubtedly perturbs the system, but is not one that fits comfortably with notions of partnership and respect.

## Incorporating the cultural context in therapy

The feminist model of family therapy pays detailed attention to how issues of gender are perpetuated through the crucible of family life, but it probably pays less attention to aetiology as a result of family dysfunction than some other models. Instead, much greater emphasis is put on the part played by cultural factors in the formation of eating disorders. In the classic text on feminist approaches to eating disorders edited by Fallon, Katzman, and Wooley (1994), 18 out of 22 chapters refer to the cultural dimension and how this defines family relationships. When intra-familial relationships are described there is an attempt to reframe them. "Honouring the mother–daughter relationship", the title of one such chapter (Rabinor, 1994), is a good example in which this relationship is reframed as a source of nourishment and not as the cause of eating disorders.

In addition, a feminist perspective attends to the therapist's role more than most other models. A clear recognition of the impact of certain styles (e.g. directive versus non-directive), which are often prescribed by gendered behaviour, has been of considerable importance to the family therapy field. The feminist perspective (Walters, Carter, Papp, & Silverstein, 1988) has determinedly brought the issue of power, so often neglected in the clinical setting and yet so pervasively influential in women's everyday lives, into the consulting room. In so doing, the sharing of alternative perspectives has become a much utilised intervention, ridding therapists of their expert status, as expertise often produces a sense of helplessness on the part of the client/recipient of the expert knowledge. The reflecting team approach, as described by Andersen (1987), is one version of this and has had an important impact on the family therapy field even if not many teams follow the format rigidly. It is an approach that stresses transparency of process and thus divests therapists of their power.

> Julie, 16, had exhibited features of anorexia nervosa for over two years. As well as severely restricting her food intake she had become a compulsive over-exerciser. Her weight was of serious concern, but she was at additional risk of long-term harm as a result of the stress she incessantly put on her body by carrying out, on average, 2500 sit-ups per day. Julie recognised that she required very close supervision in order to break the cycle of exercising.
>
> Family therapy, conducted by a male therapist, had focused primarily on the function of her behaviour as a means of maintaining "inappropriate" closeness with her mother and an inability to move towards independence. The therapist, recognising that he was perceived as persecutory in focusing on this line of investigation, requested a live consultation with two female colleagues. The consultation consisted of the two colleagues viewing from behind a one-way screen, followed by a discussion between them and the therapist in front of the family. In the discussion, an alternative perspective was offered, one in which the closeness between mother and daughter was reframed as a protective link, with Julie's mother willing to supervise and support her daughter in the struggle against anorexia nervosa. A marked difference in mother's affect was immediately evident and therapy proceeded on a far more positive footing.

## Externalising the problem

As with all the previously discussed techniques, externalising has not developed as a specific treatment for eating disorders. However, the idea is very useful to the treatment of this disorder. The technique has been refined by the narrative therapy model, which is closely allied to the feminist perspective and which has at its core a particular focus on the issue of gender. Narrative approaches emphasise the "dominant ideology" (White & Epston, 1990, p. 18) of a culture and how this comes to influence people's personalities and contributes profoundly to the formation of problems. With regards to anorexia nervosa, the dominant discourse would involve a recognition of the influence on women of the value which our culture places on thinness.

The model highlights how pervasively a problem can take over the identity of an individual. This is particularly true for those problems which are given the additional power of a psychiatric diagnosis. Externalisation is an attempt to detach the problem from the person, and in so doing the problem establishes an identity of its own. Once this has been achieved, those affected by the problem can join together in an attempt to find exceptions to it, rather than confirming this as the identity of the person "within" whom the problem resides. This, as the reader will appreciate, is an ideal approach for the treatment of anorexia nervosa and for any treatment that is concerned with moving away from explanations that emphasise pathology and blame. It is particularly appealing to children who can be captivated by the opportunity to fight against "anorexia" which is personified as a character who befriends and influences the patient, persuading them to adopt an anorexic lifestyle. Parents, who are often overwhelmed with guilt, and siblings, who can be frustrated to the point of extreme anger, invariably appear relieved by the description of an intruder coming into, and taking over, their family's life. Once the problem has been perceived in this way, strategies for countering the influence of "anorexia" can be created.

> Diana and Sally were 13-year-old twins who had developed anorexia nervosa within six months of each other. They had two brothers aged 5 and 15. In the first family session the influence of "anorexia" was discussed and it was established that, for approximately 90% of the family's life, "anorexia" bossed them around and succeeded in getting them to behave in ways which were not familiar to them. Particular attention was paid to the way in which the older brother, Tony, had become increasingly like a partner to his mother, to support her at mealtimes when his father was often absent because of work commitments. Tony was encouraged to extricate himself from this position so that he could reconnect with his peers and begin to pursue a more age-appropriate lifestyle.
>
> In addition, the mother's enslavement to "anorexia" was recognised and attempts were made to help her regain some control over her existence. As this remained problematic for the mother an exploration of the premise of motherhood was embarked upon, in order to understand how this had come into being in her family-of-origin and how these ideas were supported in the wider society. The negative impact of these ideas on her day-to-day life then became clearer and lifestyle adjustments, in order to overcome them, were made.

Narrative therapy offers some powerful techniques, which grow out of a view of the world that is concerned, possibly more than any other model, with context, particularly the context of ideas, which are reflected in society's structures and which have the power to shape the lives of individuals. This view of personality development is particularly pertinent to an understanding of the dynamics of eating disorders.

## A pragmatic approach

This brief presentation of family therapy models relevant to the treatment of eating disorders highlights the wealth of ideas which are available to the clinician when undertaking family sessions. My view is that the approach taken in a particular case should be dependent upon the specifics of *that* family's situation and the interaction between the family and the therapist. An adherence to only one way of working irrespective of these factors is to deny the complexity and severity of the disorder and the richness of different patterns of family inter-action. A pragmatic approach is surely more acceptable than an approach that claims certainty and implies that the family is at fault if treatment does not appear to be working. Having said this, it would be equally unacceptable to ignore evidence from research findings (Russell et al., 1987) and from the con-sistent feedback of parents. From both these sources it seems clear that the involvement of parents in treatment is absolutely crucial. As stated earlier, this involvement means not only attendance at regular family therapy sessions. There are many other ways to ensure a sense of empowerment, which is such a crucial factor in the parents' capacity to find a way of helping their child overcome life-threatening problems. By recognising that they can have some influence over the course of their child's illness, parents are likely to feel less helpless and less to blame. Furthermore, they are more likely to reach solutions that fit with their context than could be prescribed by an outsider. In so doing, it is probable that they will also become more open to an exploration of family factors without feeling over-criticised.

We have learnt a great deal from the views of many parents, communicated to us in conversations and in the writing of McDonald (Chapter 2). Perhaps the most crucial is that to be "bewildered, blamed, and broken-hearted" is unlikely to be a vantage point from which sensitive parenting can occur. It is our task, as clinicians working with families, to create a different type of context; one in which it is possible to share information, to encourage the taking of responsibility where this seems appropriate, and to travel the journey alongside parents from powerlessness to empowerment always looking out for successes along the way.

## SUMMARY POINTS

- Research evidence suggests family therapy and parental counselling are effective methods of treating children and adolescents with eating disorders.
- Family therapy can imply a causative link between family functioning and eating disorders. This chapter focuses on an approach to working with families that aims to lower blame and enhance family problem solving. Any intervention directed to parents and families should be based on this premise.
- Family therapy provides a wealth of ideas and techniques for achiev-ing these aims. These are described in detail through the use of clinical examples.

## ACKNOWLEDGEMENT

I would like to thank Sue McNab for her helpful thoughts on the planning of this chapter.

## REFERENCES

Andersen, T. (1987). The reflecting team. *Family Process*, *26*, 415–428.

Dare, C., & Lindsay, C. (1979). Children in family therapy. *Journal of Family Therapy*, *1*, 253–269.

Eisler, I., Dare, C., Russell, G., Szmukler, G., le Grange, D., & Dodge, E. (1997). Family and individual therapy in anorexia nervosa: A five year follow-up. *Archives of General Psychiatry*, *54*, 1025–1030.

Fallon, P., Katzman, M., & Wooley, S. (Eds.). (1994). *Feminist perspectives on eating disorders.* New York: Guilford Press.

Lask, B. (1997). Chapter title. In D. Garner & P. Garfinkel (Eds.), Handbook of treatment for eating disorders (2nd ed., pp. 479–481). New York: Guildford Press.

Lask, B., & Bryant-Waugh, R. (1997). In D. Garner & P. Garfinkel (Eds.), *Handbook of treatment for eating disorders* (2nd ed., p. 480). New York: Guilford Press.

Le Grange, D., Eisler, I., Dare, C., & Hodes, M. (1992). Family criticism and self-starvation: A study of expressed emotion. *Journal of Family Therapy*, *14*(2), 177–192.

Magagna, J., & Nicholls, D. (1997). A group for the parents of children with eating disorders. *Clinical Child Psychology and Psychiatry*, *2*(4), 565–578.

Minuchin, S., Rosman, R., & Baker, L. (1978). *Psychosomatic families.* Cambridge, MA: Harvard University Press.

Palazzoli, M. (1989). *Family games: General models of psychotic processes in the family.* London: Karnac.

Palmer, R., Oppenheimer, R., Dignon, A., Chaloner, D., & Howells, K. (1990). Childhood sexual experiences with adults reported by women with eating disorders: An extended series. *British Journal of Psychiatry*, *156*, 699–703.

Rabinor, J. (1994). Honouring the mother–daughter relationship. In P. Fallon, M. Katzman, & S. Wooley (Eds.), *Feminist perspectives on eating disorders* (pp. 272–287). New York: Guilford Press.

Russell, G., Szmukler, G., Dare, C., & Eisler, I. (1987). An evaluation of family therapy in anorexia nervosa and bulimia nervosa. *Archives of General Psychiatry*, *44*, 1047–1056.

Speed, B. (1995). Editorial—perspectives on eating disorders. *Journal of Family Therapy*, *17*(1), 1–12.

Walters, M., Carter, B., Papp, P., & Silverstein, O. (1988). *The invisible web—gender patterns in family relationships.* New York: Guilford Press.

Watzlawick, P., Beavin, J., & Jackson, D. (1967). *Pragmatics of human communication.* New York: Norton.

White, M., & Epston, D. (1990). *Narrative means to therapeutic ends.* London: Norton.

# CHAPTER ELEVEN

# Cognitive-behavioural therapeutic techniques for children with eating disorders

**Deborah Christie**
*Consultant Clinical Psychologist, Adolescent Services,*
*Middlesex Hospital, London, UK*

## INTRODUCTION

The old adage "it's not what you do it's the way that you do it" is an often repeated mantra with therapeutic principles of warmth, genuineness, and empathy being as critical to successful outcome as much as slavish devotion to theoretically driven therapeutic techniques (Fonagy & Target, 1996). The accuracy of this statement has been increasingly questioned particularly by Roth and Fonagy (1996), who noted in a review of psychotherapy research outcome that Cognitive Behavioural Therapy (CBT) was the most effective in producing long-lasting change for adults with eating disorders. This was especially so for patients with bulimia nervosa (Fairburn, 1997). In contrast, very few well-controlled, methodologically sound treatment trials in children have been described (Target & Fonagy, 1997).

This lack of information is clearly reflected by the content of peer-reviewed research reports. A recent special issue of a professional journal for clinical psychologists, dedicated to eating disorders, contained no articles about working with children (Bell & Vetere, 1996), and a volume entitled *Cognitive Behavioural Therapy for Children* has no reference in the index to eating disorders (Meyers & Craighead, 1984). This lack of information extends to both describing symptoms and associated treatment techniques for the childhood eating disorders other than anorexia nervosa.

It is not unusual for professionals to disagree about the best therapy for a child with an eating disorder. Differences between (or even within) teams may ironically mirror the difficulty the child's parents have in working together in a consistent and predictable way to help "make the child better". Working together requires people to listen to each other and develop a range of ideas that may contribute towards helping the child begin, and hopefully finish, a journey into health, that previously has not been possible. The kind of therapy offered will depend on what the therapist believes works best for the presenting problem. As a general principle, individual therapy, regardless of style, should give the child a private and personal space (see Chapter 12). It is critical that the parents support the treatment and respect the privacy of the therapeutic session. This is more likely to occur if the therapist is open and willing to share successes with the parents via colleagues from a team who are offering direct support to the parents in a parents' group, parental counselling, or family therapy sessions (see Chapters 10 and 15). Therapy—whatever its label—ultimately has to help the child make sense of her world and how to cope with it. The style of therapy offered by individual therapists will be determined by their preference and expertise, but it is critical to ensure that the therapy addresses the child's needs.

The first part of this chapter briefly describes learning, cognitive, and behavioural theories that have contributed to the development of techniques that can be used with children who have a range of eating disorders. Obviously any "how-to chapter" runs the risk of presenting a series of techniques driven by dogma rather than practice. It may also be so theoretically driven that the reader may be suspicious that the author has ever seen a patient.

The ideas presented *here* are not part of a research-driven treatment manual, although they *are* primarily driven by the unifying theoretical framework of cognitive behavioural theory. Perhaps heretically, they also borrow freely from psychodynamic and systemic theory and practice. For those who are still reading at this point, the techniques have been developed from a belief that "therapy" is a set of tools and techniques that can be used by innovative and skilled therapists (of any persuasion) to help children unlock their worries and unhappiness. These techniques should also help the child, and their families, rebuild the way they behave, feel, and think about their lives. It offers a selection of ideas that have helped silent children to talk and given silenced children an opportunity to articulate their needs to those adults charged with their care.

## LEARNING THEORY

The most important principle of learning theory is the way in which animals (including humans) learn about the relationship between an experience (or stimulus) and their reaction to that experience (the response). Classical conditioning was formalised by Pavlov (1927). He observed that laboratory dogs anticipated the arrival of food, by salivating, when they heard a bell signalling the arrival of the food. This suggested that the dogs had linked the two events (bell and food) together. The biological response (salivation) to a stimulus (food) was designated the unconditioned response (UR). The food was the unconditioned stimulus

(US). If any US (e.g. food) consistently occurs after a different event or stimulus (e.g. a bell), the animal becomes conditioned to respond to the preceding event. The salivation is now a conditioned response (CR), which will occur following presentation of the new event (the bell) that is the conditioning stimulus (CS).

This simple and elegant representation of a chain of events was applied to other stimulus–response pairings. Emotional responses (like an increase in heart rate), which occurred following an aversive stimulus like an electric shock (US), could be triggered by a non-aversive conditioning stimulus (CS), like a red light. The conditions under which this stimulus–response pairing could occur were limited. In order for the response to become conditioned, both stimulus events must occur in the same order and be reasonably close together (contingency rule). After the response has become conditioned, if the second stimulus does not appear the conditioned response will eventually stop (extinguish).

The way a behaviour could influence (or operate on) the environment was described by Thorndike (1898). Operant conditioning described how behaviour that was followed closely by a reward would be reinforced and would be likely to occur more frequently. In contrast, behaviours that were closely followed by an unpleasant or aversive experience (negative reinforcement) would be less likely to occur. If the behaviour resulted in the *avoidance* of a punishment this would cause an increase in the behaviour's frequency, just as did gaining a reward. Interestingly, if the behaviour was performed to avoid a punishment, it was very unlikely to become reduced in frequency. In contrast, it may only take a few occasions where a reward is not given for an animal to learn that the relationship between the two events (behaviour–reward) is no longer present. If, however, the reward is offered unpredictably, the likelihood of the behaviour continuing is increased. Because the reward is unpredictable, the animal will keep on producing the behaviour in "the hope" of ultimately getting a reward.

## BEHAVIOUR MANAGEMENT

The theoretical relationship between stimulus and response and behaviours and outcome were used by Mowrer (1960) to explain fear and avoidance behaviour in humans. If an unpleasant experience (e.g. vomiting) is associated with a behaviour (eating or swallowing), the child will reduce that behaviour, therefore avoiding the negative reinforcement. The physiological symptoms associated with fear are unpleasant, therefore behaviour occurs that avoids the stimulus, and therefore avoids the fear. The principles of stimulus association, and the contingent reinforcement of behaviour, provide a theoretical framework which helps to both explain and modify behaviours. Most parents will have been trained by their babies to pick them up to avoid the negative reinforcement of the baby crying!

In children, it is important to recognise that the nature of the reinforcement (i.e. positive or negative) is defined by the receiver, not by the giver. Getting angry and telling children off may be seen as punishment (negative reinforcement) by an adult, whereas in contrast the child may see the adult's behaviour as attention and therefore positive, regardless of the negative content (shouting and yelling). This will therefore result in an increase in behaviours that obtain the attention. Concrete or abstract rewards (money, sweets, praise, or star charts), if provided every time a particular behaviour occurs, will increase the frequency of the behaviour.

Consistency at the beginning of a management programme is critical. Every time a desired behaviour (completing homework, finishing dinner, eating a new food), occurs, it should be rewarded. As the desired behaviour becomes well established, the frequency of the rewards can be altered. For example, instead of giving an older child a concrete reward *every* night, acknowledging the behaviour with a small tick on a chart and then giving pocket money based on the number of ticks obtained at the end of the week can be just as effective.

To reduce an undesirable behaviour, ignoring (non-attending) and helping the child to find an alternative behaviour can be effective. The unwanted behaviour will decrease if it is not being reinforced through attention. However, if a previously learned (but unwanted) behaviour continues to receive sporadic reinforcement (e.g. child gets attention one night out of seven, or the parent gives in to a demand) the behaviour will continue, with the child "hoping" that it will be eventually reinforced at some point in time.

## Principles in practice

A systematic evaluation of the behaviours, events, and outcomes (functional analysis) can be used to help clearly describe factors that are involved in precipitating and maintaining behaviours. This analysis does not focus on what has first caused the behaviour to develop (predisposing factors). Carefully kept diaries allow the events that occur before a behaviour (antecedent stimuli or precipitating factors) to be clearly defined; the behaviours are described in detail and the consequences (reinforcement) of all components of the behaviour are described. This allows the behaviour therapist to formulate what events are triggering the behaviour, what events and behaviour of others are maintaining the behaviour, and what activities performed by the individual and those in their environment are providing positive and/or negative reinforcement.

## BEHAVIOUR THERAPY AND EATING DISORDERS

The principles of learning theory underpin techniques used by a behavioural therapist in the treatment of an eating disorder. As part of this model, measures of the severity of the condition for children with eating disorders (e.g. weight-height ratio, behaviour ratings, the child's rating of body image, shape, and weight on linear scales) can be used to define clear and specific outcome measures incorporated into a treatment programme. Desired behavioural change associated with different aspects of the disorder (target weight, mood changes on rating scales) can also be considered as treatment goals.

A behavioural formulation must comprise clearly stated goals that incorpor-ate measurable behavioural change. This could include:

- when the child eats
- who is present at mealtimes
- what happens at mealtimes
- types of food the child will eat
- quantity of food eaten
- stimulus–response situations associated with eating that need altering.

This model works best with younger children with selective eating disorder and/or functional dysphagia. For many of these children there is a history of an unpleasant experience when very young. This is often vomiting or choking associated with feeding at the time of a stomach bug or viral infection or in the presence of gastro-oesophageal reflux. Food and associated environmental stimuli therefore become the conditioning stimuli. The behaviour of avoiding food (or limiting intake to a few "safe" stimuli) therefore acts to avoid the con-ditioned fear.

These children have a marked avoidance of a large number of food types and exposure to non-preferred foods is often associated with retching or vomiting (negative reinforcement). A critical first step towards the development of treat-ment for this group of children is identifying these early precipitants and the current factors maintaining the avoidance behaviour.

James, 14, had been a faddy eater after weaning and had only eaten chips, bread and butter, and crisps since the age of 3. He became anxious and thought he might be sick if he tried a different food. A programme of gradual introduction (desensitisation) was used to help him gradually increase the range and quantity of new foods he was able to eat.

The use of behaviour therapy in an eating disorder treatment programme means that the child is being asked to stop "not eating" and stop "losing weight". The abnormal eating behaviour must be replaced with the alternative behaviour of normal eating and weight gain. A behavioural approach would therefore reward (positively reinforce) eating/weight gain with treats or exercise and punish (negat-ively reinforce) not-eating/weight loss, usually with bed rest—anathema to those with anorexia nervosa, or loss of "privileges". This was the mainstay of treatment for many years and still persists in some units.

Comparisons of behavioural programmes focusing on reward vs. punishment suggest limited success. Short-term success of strict punitive programmes is no greater compared to more humane approaches, whereas there is some evidence to suggest a greater risk of relapse (see Chapter 6). Management programmes that focus entirely on behavioural weight gain are punitive and inappropriate on both ethical and moral grounds when working with a deeply distressed child.

Behavioural techniques have a role to play in changing concrete, measurable aspects of behaviour but will result in very little change in the thoughts, beliefs, or feelings that form the basis of anorexia nervosa and related eating disorders.

## COGNITIVE BEHAVIOUR THERAPY AND EATING DISORDERS

Beck (1967) has postulated that emotional responses are a result of how individuals structure their experience. Depression is a set of symptoms that arise from a pervasive triad of negative attitudes about the self (being unworthy and inadequate), the world (filled with insurmountable obstacles), and the future (unchangeable and pervasive hopelessness).

The combination of Cognitive Therapy with methods for behavioural change resulted in the formal development of Cognitive Behaviour Therapy (Hawton, Salkoviskis, Kirk, & Clark, 1989). The primary goal of cognitive behaviour therapy (CBT) is to understand how an individual's thoughts and feelings are associated with the environment. It is important to make clear how these thoughts influence feelings during certain events (e.g. eating—"I am a bad, weak person") and what thoughts and feelings are associated with the consequences of the behaviour (e.g. vomiting—"I feel empty and happy"). Cognitive behaviour therapy is therefore explicit. In the initial stages of assessment and treatment it is focused on the here and now. Its success in the treatment of adult eating disorders has been extensively documented, particularly for bulimia nervosa and increasingly for anorexia nervosa (Fairburn, 1997; Vitousek & Orimoto, 1993).

## COGNITIVE BEHAVIOUR THERAPY AND CHILDREN

As with adults, the first task for children in this therapy is to try to understand that what they think about their world can affect how they feel:

*Therapist:* "What would you think might have happened if you were lying in bed at night and heard a crash in the room next door?
*Child:* Maybe the cat has knocked something over
*Therapist:* What would you do?
*Child:* Just turn over and go back to sleep
*Therapist:* How do you feel?
*Child:* Don't know, maybe cross, because I'll have to tidy it up?

An alternative explanation is then discussed.

*Therapist:* What if you don't have a cat?
*Child:* Maybe someone has broken in.
*Therapist:* How would you feel now?

*Child:*     I'd be scared . . . or worried.
*Therapist:* What would you do now?
*Child:*     I'd hide under the covers.

This helps children to begin to see that they can think different things about an identical situation, and that what they think will make them feel and behave differently.

## Thinking things through: Thought diaries

Keeping diaries of thoughts, behaviours, and feelings is an important part of CBT with adults (Hawton et al., 1989; Kendall, 1991). For children, however, there are many reasons why this is not effective. The first difficulty for many children is being able to keep the diary during the school day. Problems at school may get missed or altered by memory if they do not manage to remember what they wanted to write. Children can also forget to keep track of problem thoughts that are attached to difficult feelings. They may also feel unable to write down things that might get read by their parents. They may have learning difficulties and be unable to write sufficiently well to keep the diary. Another difficulty may be an inability to conceptualise the difference between thoughts and feelings.

> Felicity, 10, kept a diary for two weeks. Her thoughts were "I'm sad" and her feelings were "I'm sad" every day.

Young and Faneslow-Brown (1996) have described a more child-friendly thought diary using a cartoon format that is more easily completed by children. It allows them to choose the most important event of their day. The drawings also provide material that can be used in the therapy sessions. The cartoon attempts to distinguish between the thought bubble that is things you think inside your head ("I thought I'd get told off", "I thought I'd be sick") and the speech bubble, which is the feeling you might say out loud ("I feel scared, worried, sad"). It is clear for many children that this is a difficult distinction to make. A slightly modified version of the diary sheet completed by a child with food avoidant emotional disorder is shown in Fig. 11.1.

## Completing the diaries

CBT with an adult requires the patient to act in a collaborative manner with the therapist. Many children with eating disorders, particularly those with anorexia nervosa, are at best ambivalent about the need to change. The eating disorder can be thought of as *their* answer to *their* problem. As they have solved their problem, why should they want to change either their behaviour or the way they think about it. How will that change their experience of the world?

FIG. 11.1 Lucy (FAED) was 80% weight for height. She became very distressed when she talked about not being able to eat as much as her brothers and sisters. The large figure in the centre in the family is Lucy.

Motivation and commitment to change also varies depending on the type of eating disorder:

- Children with anorexia nervosa do not want to carry on being unhappy, but neither do they want to change their calorie intake under any circumstances. They are unlikely to want to write down—with any honesty—what they have eaten on a daily basis.
- Although children with FAED report that they would like to eat more, they often struggle to complete any behavioural tasks outside the therapy sessions. The nature of CBT allows this difference between what is said, what is done, and what is felt, to be examined and worked on in the therapy session.
- Children with selective eating often seem to want to increase the range of foods they can eat. However, the entrenched nature of the disorder means there is often a pervasive hopelessness about the possibility of change, which reinforces their restricted food intake. Those selective eaters who are determined to change will keep diaries with immaculate precision, whereas those who are unable to do so may have more entrenched underlying emotional difficulties that have not been made clear in the initial assessment.

The thought diaries can be used as part of the initial assessment or continued throughout the treatment phase. Generally, however, children begin to get bored with having to remember to keep the diaries after two to three weeks. The diaries offer a starting point and can be reintroduced as a way to monitor changes in the child's thinking patterns during therapy.

## WORKING WITH SILENCE AND WORRY

### Doing good: Feeling bad

One of the unifying or core features of all eating disorders is low self-esteem. Children with eating disorders may be "good" at home and "doing well" at school but "feeling bad". Many children with anorexia nervosa present as "perfect children". They are described as compliant, quiet, well behaved, top of their class (see Chapter 4). In contrast they *feel* bad, sad, hopeless, and worthless to such a degree they want literally to disappear.

> Jane, 15, described how when she was about 11 years old children always wanted to be her friend at school and would fight to sit next to her. She found this distressing: "I didn't deserve to have people like me so much."

A response to this lack of self-worth is to try to become as small as possible —to disappear. Many *actively* attempt to achieve this through starvation, whereas others are less consciously aware of their self-imposed progressive malnutrition. One of the aims of therapy, therefore, should be to help the child feel comfortable about herself. Children rarely need to learn to eat but they do need to learn to like themselves. For many children this may involve being given permission to not "do good" all the time in order to "feel good". Beginning this process can take a long time. Many children with anorexia nervosa are furious with their parents for having brought them to therapy, and with the therapist for forcing them to sit through what they see as pointless (and painful) discussions. In our experience anger, conflict, or assertion are often discouraged in families of children with anorexia nervosa. The only way such children can structure their experience (see Beck, 1967), i.e. impose some control over their environment, is to stop eating. To impose similar control over the therapeutic experience may require them to be silent. Sitting with a child in silence for an hour feels extremely persecutory and may also "replay" the angry silences that parents might have used to "punish" their refusal to eat. An inability to think in an abstract way may also make it hard for the child to talk about her problems.

## All about me

"All about me" is a board game with a numbered path through a jungle scene (Hemmings, 1991). A set of cards with questions or incomplete sentences are used to facilitate movement around the board. The way the game is played is limited only by the inventiveness of the therapist and the child's willingness to answer the questions honestly. The cards contain uncompleted sentences which can be pre-selected to focus on a specific aspect of the child's life:

- Family (a brother is . . . ? a father is . . . ?)
- Emotions (I feel happy when . . . , I feel sad when . . . )
- Experiences (My favourite joke is . . . )
- Behaviour (I like to eat . . . ).

The format of the game is non-threatening and can help test hypotheses generated in the initial formulation about underlying issues, e.g. which questions can the children answer and which do they say "don't know" to. The emotional content of the cards can be mixed and matched according to the needs of both the therapist and the child. It can also create a link between sessions. If nobody gets to the end of the path through the jungle, places can be marked for the following session. The cards can be saved and sorted into categories for discussion in other sessions. The therapist's participation in the game also provides a model that talking about feelings can be safe. The only rule is, there are no rules!

> Sarah, 14, had anorexia nervosa. She was so furious with her therapist that she played the game on her own, reading the cards to herself and refusing to allow the therapist to throw the dice.

Karen, 14, had suffered from anorexia nervosa since the age of 8. She would ask to play the game whenever she became so anxious that she wanted to leave the room. Playing the game allowed her to defy the "anorexia" by staying and talking.

Pauline, 13, had anorexia nervosa and only ever spoke to her therapist when they played the game.

## Emotions wall

Children who are able to keep the thought diary for only a few days, or who struggle to write anything more than a few words, clearly indicate that they are unable or unwilling to identify and describe their feelings. If they're not "upset" they are "fine", with no in-between. Such children present with two emotional conditions: "OK/not OK". They seem unable to differentiate or describe distressed, angry, sad, worried, happy, thrilled, etc. They may have very little contact with either their own emotional state or that of others, and find it hard to differentiate and describe emotions in others, particularly their parents.

The first step towards finding a safe way to think about these things is to build a list of words that *describe* emotional states, e.g. happy, sad, angry, cross, lonely. These "feelings" are things that are inside us. The child is encouraged to write these on a piece of paper. The therapist then gives the child a piece of paper that has a wall drawn on it. This is stuck over the emotions, blanking them out. The next task is to cover the wall with graffiti. The "graffiti" represents the various ways that people can act and behave: crying, laughing, smiling, shouting, hitting, eating, not eating . . .

The aim of the exercise is to think how what is *on* the wall can be connected to one or more of the feelings *behind* the wall. The therapeutic task is to try and think about how to connect what we see on the wall and what lies behind it. Paradoxes can be explored, for example crying with sadness or happiness, smiling when happy or angry but not wanting to hurt someone's feelings. The multiple links between feelings that are "inside" and expressed emotions can be explored both for the child and those around her. How does she know what her mum is feeling about her not eating? What does she think when her parents are shouting at her? Moving the wall down to show both the behaviours and feelings at the same time will allow the child to make physical connections with felt pens, or string, as the ideas are explored.

## Worry bag

Binnay and Wright (1997) have described a technique, used primarily for assessment, called "the bag of feelings". The child is given a drawn outline of a bag and encouraged to draw her worries inside it. Sometimes "worry" seems such an overwhelmingly large concept it feels as if it will consume the child. The idea that worry is normal is discussed, but also that some people have more than others. The aim is to help the child to externalise "the worry" (White, 1985; also see Chapters 9 and 12). Defining the worries and making them seem more "real" or concrete, helps the child believe they are easier to manage. The therapist offers various pieces of paper to the child and suggests that these could be used to represent all the worries she has at the moment.

> let's pretend that this sheet here is your biggest worry. Can you think how the big worry might be made up of worries about all sorts of different things. For example, can you colour in, or mark off, how much worry is about school?

This first part of this process gives the child explicit permission to have the worry. Each worry is subdivided into smaller and smaller sections until the paper is all used up. The paper can be cut up (like a jigsaw). All the pieces are then put into a big envelope which has been decorated and labelled as "My worry bag". At different sessions a worry can be taken out of the bag and discussed. Each worry can be further broken down into even smaller parts both verbally and concretely, by cutting it in half again and again and again.

> Samantha (FAED), 10, chose to subdivide her big worry about school into worries about finding her way around, not being able to carry her bags, not being able to make friends, not getting her homework done, no-one speaking to her. Each worry was assigned an appropriate amount of space and then returned to the worry bag, except for the one piece (or worry) to be discussed.

Problem-solving strategies can then be used to think about how to resolve the worry, or tasks can be set to challenge negative thoughts about what *might* happen.

> Michelle (BN), 13, made a list of all the people who spoke to her at school during the week and brought it with her to the next therapy session. She was then able to take "people might not speak to me" out of the worry bag and throw it in the bin.

This symbolic way of disposing of problems is a powerful reinforcing technique, particularly for young children. The process can be repeated as sometimes resolving one problem makes other linked problems disappear. Children can also decide how much of their worries they want to face at any time.

> Lucy (FAED), 10, and Josh (SE), 6, always liked to empty out the worry bag to see how much was in there.

Children can also choose where they want to keep the worry bags. If they feel that their parents are unable to cope with their worries, they may decide to keep the worry bag in the therapist's room.

After two weeks Josh (SE), 6, decided he would take the worry bag home with him so that he and his mum could get rid of the worries without having to wait for his therapy sessions.

The worry bag can be completed with silent children who are able to communicate by writing or drawing, although they may not wish to speak.

## Role play: Being a detective?

This technique requires the adoption of a new identity, which is "acted out" in between sessions, often without telling friends and relations. The impact of changing behaviour and how this affects thoughts or feelings and how it changes other people's responses can then be explored in the therapy session. Children can use this technique too, although it requires careful explanation and practice. In the first part of the session the child is asked what she thinks would happen if she were to behave in a different way (i.e. eat more).

- How would *she* feel?

Then other people's reactions are discussed:

- Who would notice you were eating more?
- What would they say?
- Who in the family would be the most surprised?
- Would your friends at school notice?

The next step is to discuss the idea that coming to therapy is like being a detective, looking for clues to why there are worries and problems.

- What would happen if you were a detective all week, not just in this room?
- What would happen if you went home and ate more than normal (e.g. took a second piece of toast at breakfast)?

Children are asked to keep a secret diary and to try to record people's reactions and how she felt when, or if, she did things differently. Parents are not told that their child is going to try to do this. This technique produces several kinds of information that can be incorporated into the assessment and treatment. First, it is a way of establishing the child's engagement in the process of change. If she has not been able to complete this task then focusing on self-directed change may not be helpful at this stage. If she *has* been able to eat a bit more, the parent's response (if any) can be discussed with the parents via the family therapist or parental counsellor as well as with the child.

Lucy, an 11-year-old girl with FAED, was 80% weight for height. The thera-peutic team felt that her parents were not taking an active role helping her eat more. Lucy was able to ask for more breakfast on a few occasions but reported that only her older sister and brother noticed this and made any comment. There was no reaction from her parents at all. The week after this "experiment" she lost 500g. Work with the parents was intensified to encourage them to acknowledge their role in helping Lucy to gain weight.

## Relaxation and guided imagery therapy

Relaxation is a well-documented technique used to counteract physiological symptoms of anxiety (Peveler & Johnston, 1986). It is often coupled with a list of anxiety-producing images of increasing intensity, where the relaxation is used to reduce the anxiety associated with each image. Involvement in fantasy or other thoughts is a normal process, especially in children, which has often been harnessed to bring about behavioural or somatic changes (Olness & Gardner, 1988). These techniques are variously referred to as "guided imagery", "relaxation with mental imagery", or "cognitive reconstruction", and sometimes reference is made to "hypnosis" or "hypnotherapy". The state of mind achieved can per-haps be best described as an intense imaginative involvement on the part of the subject, combined with belief in what is happening. After the session, subjects are often so relaxed that they may feel inclined to go to sleep. Even quite young children can be helped by hypnotherapy, and results on gender differences have suggested that there is a tendency for girls to respond better than boys (LeBaw, Holton, Tewell, & Eccles, 1975; Sokel, Christie, Kent, Lansdown, & Atherton, 1993).

Guided imagery or relaxation therapy can be used with a wide range of childhood problems. The most important component is a comprehensive assess-ment and formulation of the problem. The idea that being more relaxed and calm will help the child feel less worried is explained. The child is reassured that she will be in control at all times and must therefore work with the therapist to decide where she wants to be in her "story". Children can also be encouraged to choose someone to help them in the story. This can be a real person or a fantasy figure. The way the process is explained to children is also determined by their interests and age. The first stage is to explain that the therapist is going to show them how to use what goes on inside their head to help with their symptoms. For younger children (and some older ones) the term "magical thinking" can help to engage them. Computer-literate children are attracted to the idea that they can use their mind like a computer to search through directories to find the pro-gramme that controls "worry". There is no standard text or perfect story. Each child writes her own script including where she wants to be, who will be there, and what she wants to do when she gets there. The therapist uses this informa-tion to construct a story that involves images and ideas that help to reduce or control symptoms.

The following story was composed with a 10-year-old girl (Kate) with a life-long history of faddiness and selective eating. She retched every time she tried to eat a new food and would only eat peanut butter sandwiches, cheese and tomato pizza, and apples. In the initial assessment she had talked about how much she enjoyed horse-riding. She decided that she wanted to be on a horse in her story. She was asked to close her eyes if she could (although this was not essential). She was then asked to make herself comfortable and to concentrate on the therapist's voice. She was told she would have to remember the story so she could tell it to herself when she was at home.

> Imagine you are standing at the top of a flight of stairs. As you go down the steps take a big breath in through your nose and then blow out slowly.

The therapist models this while they are talking and then counts slowly from 1 to 10 breathing with the child, using the tone of voice (low) and speed of delivery (slow) to regulate and slow down the respiratory rate.

> At the bottom of the stairs there is a large, heavy door in a wall. Slowly put out your hand and push the door. It slowly opens. Through the door you can see a field. You start to walk through the door and feel the soft grass below your feet. The grass is a beautiful green and up above the sky is as blue as blue can be. Beside you there is a pretty little stream which is tinkling over the pebbles. You look around and feel the warm sunshine on the back of your neck. There is a gentle breeze blowing. You start to walk through the field following the stream and notice all the flowers. As you slowly breathe in you can smell the beautiful perfume of the flowers. The sun is as warm as can be and is beginning to make you feel a little sleepy. You hear the sound of a waterfall and start to walk towards it. As you walk into the clearing you see a beautiful brown horse standing by the waterfall. He paws the ground as if he has been waiting for you. You slowly get up on to the horse and he starts to walk, slowly at first. The wind is blowing in your hair as the horse starts to canter, getting faster and faster as you ride across the meadow. You ride and ride feeling free as a bird. The wind blows away all the tension and worry in your shoulders and your arms . . .
>
> . . . As he returns to the stream, you slowly slide off his back and sit down beside the stream. You feel calm and relaxed and decide to sit in the warm sun listening to the sound of the water trickling through the rocks, just to sit and rest for a while. The horse stands beside you gently breathing in and out. It's as if you can understand him as he pushes your hand gently towards the water encouraging you to take a drink of the water from the stream. You slowly lean over and put your hand into the crystal clear water lifting out a handful of water. As you put it to your lips the water runs down your throat. As it goes down your throat and into your tummy it starts to make your stomach feel warm and relaxes your throat all the way from the top to the bottom. You know that if you were to eat anything new you would have no feelings of sickness. Your throat and stomach feel relaxed and able to try anything new. The horse helps you to understand that if you come here

anytime before you have your meal you'll be able to try new foods without feeling sick. You put your hand round the horse's neck and let him help you up. You slowly walk away from the stream back through the meadow towards the gate. You can come here anytime you want, to this special place. When you reach the gate you turn around and see the horse is waiting for you guarding the stream for you. You push the gate and go through waving goodbye to the beautiful horse . . .
. . . slowly you begin to climb back up the stairs.

The therapist counts the child back up the stairs explaining that when she gets to the top she can open her eyes, if she needs to, and come back into the room.

A simple linear scale can be used to help children indicate how nervous, or anxious they felt before they began listening to the story and how they felt after it. Kate was asked to practise the story every night for 10 minutes before her evening meal, and then try a small taste of new food from her mother's plate. Her parents were asked to make sure she was given privacy to complete the relaxation. They were not asked to monitor or encourage her to complete the relaxation. The children are completely in charge of doing or not doing the task. This is partly because there is nothing quite as unrelaxing as being told to relax, but also that failure to practise is a motivational issue that can be worked on in other sessions. For some children it may be helpful to record the story on tape so that they can listen to it on a personal stereo. The therapist can also stop as the story develops, to check on details, like the colour of the sky, who they have met, and what they want to do next in their adventure.

Despite being reportedly desperate to change her eating habits, Kate had been unable to stop feeling anxious and distressed when she thought about trying new foods because of the anticipatory retching. After the first session she was given food diaries to keep. She was asked to practise the technique every night for a fortnight. The next session she reported that she had been able to try a wide range of new foods with no retching, nausea, or discomfort. Once she had desensitised herself to "new foods" she was able to stop the relaxation before mealtimes. 12 months later, Kate was eating a wide and varied diet and had become increasingly confident and outgoing.

## TOKEN CHARTS WITH A DIFFERENCE

As discussed in the earlier section on learning theory, behaviours are likely to increase when they are rewarded or reinforced. Rewarding successes with attention and tokens on charts are both well-documented reinforcement tools. Despite this, many parents report having tried, and failed, to use token charts with any success. This is usually because the goals that have been set are often too big to be achievable, e.g. asking a selective eater to eat a new meal every day to get a token. Another problem is that the token chart may be visually unrewarding, particularly for pre-teen children. The child may find it hard to link the behaviour with the chart or have beliefs and feelings about the behaviour that make the token insufficiently "rewarding". Images that can be incorporated into the therapeutic process can be used as the "chart" with the picture built from components that are the "tokens" the child achieves. These images can have a meaning associated with the symptoms: flowers that grow as the child attaches petals, caterpillars that get longer and longer until they become a butterfly, and mountains that are difficult to climb alone.

## Growing a flower

Felicity (FAED), 9, was given the goal of eating a small teaspoon of something she hadn't tried before, from her mother's plate, before eating her regular meal. She was to sit and eat with the family, regardless of what she was having. She was asked to keep a diary of each new taste and say whether she did or didn't like it. She was told that it was possible that there would be things that she wouldn't like. The "task" was to *try* things, with no expectation that she would like everything new. Her parents were encouraged to help her select one small teaspoonful but were not required to either encourage or argue with her. As before Felicity was asked to take responsibility for completing the task.

The following session the list of tried foods was discussed. For each new food that was considered to be "OK" the name of the food was written on a paper petal made from sticky paper (in lots of colours). She was then given a large "petal-less" flower, which she then stuck the new petals on around the centre. This flower then became her food menu. She used this to help her move onto the next stage, which was to choose one of the foods on the petal and have a small portion of it as part of her normal meal as well as continuing to try new teaspoonfuls. Larger outer petals were used to record the "OK" foods eaten as part of a meal, and small petals for new foods were added to the growing flower (Fig. 11.2).

## The hungry caterpillar

Young boys may find the idea of making a flower unappealing. A caterpillar can be used as a metaphor for growth and change with the sections of the body or feet used as the "tokens". The child can make the caterpillar as long and curvy as he wants to.

## Enhancing self-esteem

Children with eating disorders have low self-esteem. Both the flower and caterpillar can be used to identify, and positively reinforce, successes and achievements. The child and therapist explore things that the child is good at. For a child preoccupied with shape and weight the positive and functional aspects of her body can be discussed instead of the reported negative physical aspects, e.g. "my legs are *fast*" instead of "my legs are *fat*".

FIG. 11.2 Felicity was able to add these petals to her food flower over a three-week period. The inner petals were small tastes. The outer petals were increasing portion sizes of different foods.

The process of thinking of what they are good at can be difficult for children who cannot think of anything good about themselves. Even this difficulty, however, can be incorporated into a homework task, in which the child has to find out what each member of her family thinks are her "good points". The therapist can then discuss with the child what she agrees with, and see if there is evidence to support the child's refusal to accept positive self-attributes.

## Climbing the mountain: An incredible journey?

Negative attributes about the future are often articulated by children who have had a problem so long they cannot believe that it will ever change. This is discussed with them and it is suggested that they could think of the problem as if it were a mountain that they had to climb.

> Trying to get better sometimes feels like trying to climb a very, very high mountain, so high you don't feel you will ever get to the top. Being here is the beginning of a journey. The journey has a beginning—the bottom of the mountain (which is today), and an end (which is where you want to be when we don't need to see each other any more).

As CBT is a collaborative process children are encouraged to define their own ending (what they want to achieve or change). The child is not required to think about how she has got to the bottom of the mountain. The therapist is someone who is coming with her on the journey but the child is going to have to do her own climbing. We can use this model to explain the need to make steady progress. The child is not expected, nor should *she* expect, to run up all the way. Parents and children can also see that there may be times when they will need to stop and have a rest. The mountain can be represented in any medium the child wishes. It can be drawn as a homework task and then figures can be made to represent the child. These can then be stuck onto the mountain as the child progresses through the treatment programme. Older children may prefer the therapist to draw the mountain for them and just point to where they think they have reached. Other family members can be drawn, cut out, and attached if they have contributed to the achievement of a particular goals. Lack of progress or non-completion of a homework task can be formulated as stopping for a rest, rather than failure which helps to maintain motivation and engagement.

The mountain can be adapted for any programme of change:

• For the silent and distressed child with anorexia nervosa the journey represents the therapeutic relationship. The child may want the therapist to stand in front and help pull her along, or may prefer the therapist to stay behind to "catch her" in case she starts to slip backwards. The way the "anorexia" is holding up the journey, setting traps or obstacles, can be discussed.

• For children with FAED, the thoughts and feelings can be considered as luggage, an enormous heavy bag that makes it difficult to even begin the journey. This then allows the therapist to introduce the idea of looking inside the bag and trying to sort out which thoughts are connected to which feelings, and those that might be discarded, instead of bringing them along on the journey to the top of the mountain. This can be combined with the worry bag technique.

• For children who eat a limited range of foods, the mountain becomes a three-dimensional token chart with *their* progress toward *their* targets clearly visible.

Melanie, 9, began treatment for functional dysphagia and engaged quickly completing diaries and drawing her mountain. After a few sessions (both individual and parental), it became clear that rapid behavioural change had been easily achieved in the past but this was always followed by relapse. Changes in the treatment plan were explained to Melanie and her parents by saying that the difficulty wasn't climbing the mountain but the tendency to keep slipping back down. Rather than trying to achieve specific (behavioural) goals and climb the mountain, we were therefore going to work together to "tunnel through" the problems and worries and get to the other side.

## CONCLUSION

Cognitive behavioural therapy involves the examination and re-evaluation of dysfunctional thoughts that are driving problem behaviours and emotional responses. This rather sophisticated, and at times complicated, task can be beyond even adults, and certainly for children the work involved is unachievable if caught in the grip of a life-threatening eating disorder. It may also be difficult for the child who is overwhelmed by her own inability to eat more than a handful of food types, albeit in sufficient quantity *not* to be life-threatening.

The techniques presented in this chapter are resources that allow therapists to make contact and engage with children even though they are being asked to think about their difficult and painful situations. For these children, many of their "negative thoughts" may be based in reality (e.g. abusive families, poor living circumstances, difficulties at school). It is a difficult task to acknowledge reality without being drawn into the child's hopelessness. Certainly a therapist who fails to acknowledge what is real will lose credibility.

Unlike many adults, young children rarely have moments of intense "insight". They are unable to come up with "rational reframings" of abusive experience and don't like to be told that the way they think is "dysfunctional". Very few are comfortable being asked to write a record of their misery. However, children do seem to think about what is talked about in sessions and make connections between their thoughts and feelings. The aim of therapy is to achieve changes in behaviour accompanied by changes in the way the child thinks. The process is open and the child is acknowledged as the change maker using a model which is collaborative and empowering.

Therapy is a long, often tiring, and always incredible journey. The child cannot climb the mountain alone and needs the therapist to be there to hold her hand, catch her when she slips or falls, and help her see that she can get to the top. At times there will be discoveries that may help the child, like a well-cared-for flower, grow and blossom. We must believe that eventually it is possible for all children, like the caterpillar, to emerge as beautiful butterflies.

## SUMMARY POINTS

Therapy is a set of tools and techniques that is used to help children unlock their worries and unhappiness.

- Learning theory uses the principles of stimulus association, and the reinforcement of behaviour to provide a theoretical framework, which helps to both explain and modify behaviours. Behaviours *increase* when they are rewarded (or avoid punishment). To *reduce* an undesirable behaviour, ignoring (non-attending) and helping the child to find an alternative behaviour can be effective.
- Functional analysis allows the behaviour therapist to formulate events that are triggering, maintaining, and providing reinforcement for the behaviour.
- Measures of the severity of an eating disorder include:
  - weight-height ratio
  - behaviour ratings
  - descriptions of body image, shape, and weight.
- Cognitive behaviour therapy is successful for the treatment of adult eating disorders by:
  - making the relationship between thoughts and feelings explicit
  - focusing on the here and now.
- Cognitive behaviour therapy with children:
  - helps them see the link between thoughts and feelings
  - finds ways to help children who are silent
  - makes worries concrete and manageable
  - shows the impact of different behaviour on others.
- Relaxation and guided imagery help reduce anxiety associated with eating.
- Child-appropriate images can be used to motivate the child to resolve her eating difficulties and enhance her self-esteem.

# REFERENCES

Beck., A.T. (1967). *Depression: Clinical, experimental and theoretical aspects.* New York: Harper & Row.

Bell, L., & Vetere, A. (Eds.). (1996). Eating disorders [Special issue]. *Clinical Psychology Forum, 92.*

Binnay, V., & Wright, J.C. (1997). The bag of feelings: An ideographic technique for the assessment and exploration of feelings in children and adolescents. *Clinical Child Psychology and Psychiatry, 2,* 449–462.

Fairburn, C.G. (1997). Eating disorders. In D.M. Clark & C.G. Fairburn (Eds.), *Science and practice of cognitive behaviour therapy* (pp. 209–241). Oxford, UK: Oxford University Press.

Fonagy, P., & Target, M. (1996). Should we allow psychotherapy research to determine clinical practice? *Clinical Psychology Science and Practice, 3,* 245–250.

Hawton, K., Salkoviskis, P.M., Kirk, J., & Clark, D.M. (1989). The development and principles of cognitive-behavioural treatments. In K. Hawton, P.M. Salkoviskis, J. Kirk, & D.M. Clark (Eds.), *Cognitive behaviour therapy for psychiatric problems* (pp. 1–12). Oxford, UK: Oxford Medical Publications.

Hemmings, P. (1991). *All about me.* London: Barnardos.

Kendall, P.C. (Ed.). (1991). *Child and adolescent therapy: Cognitive behavioural procedures.* New York: Guilford Press.

LeBaw W., Holton C., Tewell K., & Eccles, D. (1975). The use of self hypnosis by children with cancer. *American Journal of Clinical Hypnosis, 17,* 233–238.

Meyers, A.M., & Craighead, W.E. (Eds.). (1984). *Cognitive behavior therapy with children.* New York: Plenum Press.

Mowrer, O.H. (1960). *Learning theory and behaviour.* New York: Wiley.

Olness, K., & Gardner, G.G. (1988). *Hypnosis and hypnotherapy with children.* New York: Grune & Stratton.

Pavlov, I. (1927). *Conditioned reflexes.* Oxford, UK: Oxford University Press.

Peveler, R., & Johnston, D.W. (1986). Subjective and cognitive effects of relaxation. *Behaviour Research and Therapy, 24,* 413–420.

Roth, A.D., & Fonagy, P. (1996). *What works for whom: A critical review of psychotherapy research.* New York: Guilford Press.

Sokel, B., Christie, D., Kent, A., Lansdown, R., & Atherton, D. (1993). A comparison of hypnotherapy and biofeedback in the treatment of childhood atopic eczema. *Contemporary Hypnosis, 10,* 145–154.

Target, M., & Fonagy, P. (1997). Research on intensive psychotherapy with children and adolescents. *Child and Adolescent Psychiatric Clinics of North America, 6,* 39–51.

Thorndike, E.L. (1898). Animal intelligence: An experimental study of the associative processes in animals. *Psychological Monographs, 2*(Whole No. 8).

Vitousek, K.B., & Orimoto, L. (1993). Cognitive-behavioural models of anorexia nervosa, bulimia nervosa and obesity. In K.S. Dobson & P.C. Kendall (Eds.), *Psychotherapy and cognition* (pp. 191–243). San Diego: Academic Press.

White, M. (1985). Fear busting and monster taming: An approach to the fears of young children. *Dulwich Centre Review, 29*–34.

Young, J., & Faneslow-Brown, P. (1996). Cognitive behaviour therapy for anxiety: Practical tips for using it with children. *Clinical Psychology Forum, 91,* 19–21.

# CHAPTER TWELVE

# Individual psychotherapy

**Jeanne Magagna**
*Great Ormond Street Hospital for Children, London, UK*

All repressed feelings accumulate inside and become more and more threatening as time goes on. The error is to ignore them. They may be huge, blood-thirsty, and glow in the dark . . . they lose their power as soon as they have been . . . painted, danced, sung, or spoken.

*Cameron (1996, p. 148)*

## INTRODUCTION

Marie, a 12-year-old with anorexia nervosa, was asked in her individual assessment, why she felt no one liked her.

She answered: "Because I'm fat."

"Would you like to draw a picture of yourself?", I asked. Marie hesitated for a moment and then drew the picture shown in Fig. 12.1.

"Yes, you feel very fat indeed," I said.

"I am very fat", she replied.

And now how do I respond? I thought.

Despite her experience of being fat, Marie is outwardly very thin and emaciated. No matter how often people tell her she is thin and not fat, her reality is that she is unlikeable because of "fat".

The focus of psychodynamic understanding is to listen while constantly being attuned to everything that is happening. A sense of "fatness" when actually emaciated is linked with a child's lack of an inner mental structure. Ordinarily, such structure gives meaning to emotional experiences and so puts them into some manageable psychological form. Instead of an inner mental structure, the child with anorexia nervosa "holds herself together" through attachment to a

227

FIG. 12.1   Marie's self-portrait.

"pseudo-autonomous self". With this pseudo-autonomy, she barricades herself against accepting nurture, both emotional and physical (Goodsitt, 1997).

Marie illustrates her dilemma through a drawing in which a locked door imprisons her and also barricades her against a relationship with her mother (Fig. 12.2) (Rey, 1994). Marie's hands are used to control herself so she is also not allowed to eat food on her plate. Palazzoli (1974) suggested that the child with anorexia nervosa, through her symptom of starving, is trying to negotiate control and autonomy with her family. The "pseudo-autonomy" of a child or adolescent with anorexia nervosa should not be confused with the desire for autonomy of a child who has internalised good experiences with understanding parents, and has thus matured sufficiently to struggle for more autonomy and control over her own life. The more mature child gradually enters relationships outside the family. The child with anorexia nervosa is basically unable to achieve dependency in an intimate relationship. Her control is used as a defence against intimate relationships with people (Rosenfeld, 1987). It leaves an inner self starved of understanding and support. For example, suicidal impulses or even suicidal attempts can be hidden from the parents in alliance with this "pseudo-autonomous" controlling self.

Gradually in psychotherapy, linking Marie's inner and outer reality creates a path towards understanding herself and the feelings which have accumulated inside her, becoming bigger and uglier with time. Consequently her sense of herself is developed. But while Marie's sense of self developed, her sense of her body being "fat and ugly" was fully maintained. This was her reality which needed to be deeply understood (Farrell, 1995).

FIG. 12.2    Drawing of a girl barricaded in a prison cell.

Much later in her therapy, when I asked, "What else about you besides your 'fatness' makes you unlovable?" Marie was able to give a fuller answer: "I'm shy, quiet, scared other girls won't like me. I lack confidence. I'm less clever than the others. I have different hobbies from them."

With the acceptance of her bodily "ugliness" by myself, Marie was gradually able to believe that I could tolerate disagreeable experiences. She writes:

There is a sadness inside
That is not able to go out.
It makes me feel bad
In my throat
In my head
There are tears in my eyes
Crying in my voice
Creating confusion in my heart.
But slowly
The cry inside me
Becomes a scream which comes out.

Through providing a regular, frequent and consistently timed therapy sessions as well as a listening and thinking place in my heart, which is the essence of empathic listening. Marie slowly found that the protective door to her inner experiences opened so that she could slowly share as much as she was capable of feeling at one time.

Marie arrived for treatment having suffered from anorexia nervosa for eight months, during which she had an unsuccessful hospital admission. She had an early childhood history of obsessional behaviour dating from around age 5. This seemed linked to the arrival of a baby sister that promoted extreme jealousy and hatred, which was probably controlled by Marie's obsessional rituals. Marie retreated to her bedroom when distressed. At school she performed well academically and become excellent in gymnastics. The main problem as she perceived it was that she was superficially liked, but had no real friends. At 12, when she arrived for therapy with me, Marie complained that she was being teased at school. Her parents were also experiencing marital conflict accompanied by denying difficulties both for themselves and the children.

The unfolding process in the therapy was primarily led by Marie. As a psychodynamic therapist I could give depth of meaning to her words, thus holding her emotionally so she could tolerate some of the pain of knowing herself and her relationships with significant others. Primarily though, Marie's journey was one in which she was free to explore as much or as little of herself as she felt able and willing to get to know. Her "protective door", which I call her "pseudo-autonomous self", served as her method of preventing too much psychic pain. The "pseudo-autonomous self" is felt to be superior to the adults, independent of human needs, and in control. The child's healthy self is dominated by it. Marie was attached to her "pseudo-autonomous self" rather than being able to depend on others. "Anorexia is my best friend," Marie says. "I don't want to lose that!"

The development of a dependent, trusting relationship with the therapist, and a sufficiently secure and containing external environment to allow Marie to "open the door" to her suffering took time. She had to be physically nourished far sooner than her emotional self could be sufficiently healed.

What is complicated, though, is that the decision for the child to have therapy is a parental one, often precipitated because of the life-threatening aspects of the eating disorder. Coming into the therapy room, therefore, can initially feel like being force-fed. For this reason it was essential to point out that, whereas Marie may not have had a choice about coming to therapy, she did have a choice about whether she spoke or did any work in the therapy through thinking alongside me, even if she was silent.

Sensations, emotions, and perceptions are often not encapsulated in words when a child with an eating disorder child begins therapy. For this reason it is helpful to provide puppets, dolls, toy animals, drawing material, building blocks, cars, and fences. It is striking how often an older adolescent may take an interest in these "children's things" as a means of enacting some not yet unformed verbal thought. It may be simply the force or gentleness of a gesture in handling the toys that conveys a sense of persecution, hurt, or anger.

In one therapy session a 12-year-old boy, with selective eating, said, "I'll never play with those toys. They are for younger children." However, he frequently began sessions by rolling a train over the body of several bodies of the dolls or knocking the dolls' heads together. As is often the case, his hands were able to "speak" first and lead the way for me to explore how going to sleep was difficult for him, because at night he was continually haunted by nightmarish creatures in his dreams, which he had kept private throughout much of his life.

Communication is always taking place in therapy. It is a luxury for the therapist to have communication through words from the child. Much of what needs to be understood is first put into words and given meaning through the therapist's physical and emotional experiences felt when anticipating the child's arrival for therapy, or sitting in the room with the child during the session, or pausing after the child has departed. This is the therapist's "countertransference" which is the primary fulcrum for making a timely interpretation, sensitively attuned to the child's current emotional experience and capacity to tolerate mental pain.

"Transference" and "countertransference" represent two components mutually giving life to each other and creating the relationship between the child and her therapist. Marie's therapy demonstrates this clearly and I shall be giving full illustrations later, but for the moment I would like to discuss these two concepts in a little more detail.

The "transference" of the child refers to her behaviour toward the therapist and her work. The child transfers both positive and negative aspects of her parental figures—both internal and external—onto the personality of the therapist, and the nature of this transference then determines how the child relates to the therapist at any moment in time. "Gathering the transference" implies scanning all the stories the child brings about experiences outside the therapy as well as the child's dreams, while focusing on the emotions that are most immediate and pressing in the child at that moment. Psychoanalytic practice is still often misunderstood as focusing on reconstruction of historical events, rather than dealing with the child's experience in the here and now. However, the primary tenet of current psychoanalytic thinking is that internal change can best be facilitated through interpretations that meet anxiety at the moment at which it is being experienced. The material that Marie brought involved consideration not only of the content and mood of her communications but also precisely how this provided clues to what was happening between us in the session. Her remarks were also given meaning through their chronological sequence in the session. Often reading notes of a session from end to beginning enables one to more fully understand the transference anxieties the child has in relation to the therapist in the beginning of the session. I also attempted to ask myself, "What does this story about the past or the future, this story about something outside the therapy room, unconsciously tell me about the nature of Marie's current preoccupations in relation to the therapeutic relationship with me?"

It is mainly through the "countertransference" that the therapist feels and can understand what the child feels and does in relation to the therapist. For this reason understanding the countertransference is the central focus of psycho-analytic psychotherapy (Hinshelwood, 1994). Often children with eating dis-orders cannot find or will not share words with their therapist. Marie was no different. At times in the silence I would feel frustrated and impotent. This was particularly true when I was having difficulty attuning to my countertransference. But what is the countertransference really? It consists of various levels of emo-tional experience. First, countertransference is based on a connection with the child's impulses and defences and also an identification with her currently present internal parental figures transferred on to the therapist.

As well as this, the child's transference to the therapist is a response to therapist's real and fantasised countertransference (Racker, 1974, p. 131). For example, the child's unconscious is quite skilled in seeing and projecting into problematic aspects of the therapist's personality. The child can project into the therapist's wish to be all-knowing, or her wish to be a mother, or into the therapist's aggression and defences against it (Brenman-Pick, 1985). In particu-lar, the child often projects into the therapist's guilt about not being a loving or adequate person in some way. If I, as a therapist, can be still and in the silence listen to what is going on deeply within myself in the presence of Marie, then there is no need for me to question her penetratingly in order to extract some words from her.

Problems in making progress in therapy are often viewed by therapists as the child's difficulties. But the child wouldn't be coming to therapy if she didn't have problems in facing psychic pain and putting her emotions into a symbolic form. Hence, however defended or hostile a child is in relation to therapy, I view the primary problem as being a problem of how I, the therapist, work on my countertransference in relation to the child. Having a capacity to dip into the riches of my own emotional experience is essential. Some people are natural therapists, but many people require the rigor of personal psychotherapy or psycho-analysis to tap the reservoir of pent-up confused emotions. Left unrecognised, such emotions can distort communication between the child and the therapist. For example, a therapist lacking self-esteem may feel she deserves to be disliked by the child and fail to understand the child's fear of personal awareness and intimacy with others. Alternatively, needing reassurance that she is a "successful and loved therapist", the therapist may be placatory and charming to the child and fail to acknowledge the child's latent hostility in the transference. This can often lead to a therapist's over-identification with the child and hostility to the parents for not being adequate in meeting the child's needs.

Working on the child's transference to the therapist and the therapist's countertransference responses is the essence of psychodynamic psychotherapy (Money-Kyrle, 1978). In eclectic weekly psychotherapy seminars with colleagues, who have cognitive-behavioural, cognitive-analytic, Jungian, Freudian, Kleinian, as well as other individual and family therapy orientations, we have found that it is essential to embody these concepts of transference and countertransference in each of our different kinds of therapy. What differs is the particular style with which we use our understanding of these concepts.

As the focus of this chapter is on working in individual psychodynamic psychotherapy such as Marie's, I shall briefly refer to a range of crucial therapeutic issues regarding this kind of work. In fact, throughout the chapter I shall be returning to Marie's story to illustrate many of the issues and concepts central to psychodynamic work with children and young people who have eating disorders. Some of the crucial therapeutic issues include:

- the treatment frame
- duration of treatment
- suitability for psychotherapy
- assessment for psychotherapy
- aims of psychotherapy and the therapeutic method
- using dreams for initial assessment and ongoing assessment of therapeutic progress.

## THE TREATMENT FRAME

The context of individual assessment and therapy for children is crucial. Anyone treating a child with an eating disorder must be closely allied with a physician. A doctor should take medical responsibility for the ongoing evaluation of the patient's physical condition. The psychotherapist needs to have a clear set of guidelines for the minimum weight for the child's age and height and degree of physical ill-health that warrants hospitalisation.

It is likely that during difficult moments in therapy, and during the therapist's holidays, the child with an eating disorder may wish to diet and discontinue therapy. This is part of her style of dealing with the psychological pain of separation. For this reason, it is irresponsible for a therapist to embark on individual therapy without ascertaining that there is an effective therapeutic link between the parents and a colleague who will assist the parents at difficult times. It is not uncommon for a child to stop therapy, engage in starving or bingeing, using laxatives, and exercising while at the same time fostering the parents' denial that the child has a problem warranting therapy. Sometimes the child may also hide weights or overload on water to conceal her true weight from the parents. It is, of course, essential to accompany individual therapy with some on-going work with the family or parents.

The most effective therapeutic frame I have encountered has involved:

(1)   At least two family assessments to ascertain strengths, weaknesses, and patterns of relating.

(2)    An individual assessment with the child to ascertain the individual patho-logy underlying the eating disorder, bearing in mind that both anorexia nervosa and bulimia nervosa have typical behavioural patterns that conceal a wide range of emotional difficulties.

(3)    A medical practitioner to monitor weight changes regularly and to liaise with the parents and child regarding the child's physical health.

(4)    Parental or family work accompanying the individual therapy. This provides support for the child and enables the parents or family to find a safe context in which they can explore the problematic aspects of their relationships and develop their capacities.

(5)    Consideration of possible hospital provision in case the child's health deteriorates. This is particularly important for those children with severe dif-ficulties, when they are faced with the initial holiday separation from the therapist.

## DURATION OF TREATMENT

Accepting the need for an adequate duration of treatment is very important. More than one eating-disordered child has expressed her fear, "When I look all right on the outside, I am afraid no one will now notice how bad I feel inside." In saying this, she expresses her fear that she must continually display her "starvation" for fear that other people will do as she does, that is, deny inner emotional states and focus only on weight gain and pubertal development. The therapist needs to reassure the child that she will be able to receive therapy until it is no longer needed. A minimum of two years is generally required to assist a child to develop a stable psychic structure; however, this may not always be possible. Family therapy accompanied by a briefer period of individual coun-selling can also be useful to enable a child to experience feelings in a more mature way and remain emotionally linked to others.

## SUITABILITY FOR PSYCHOTHERAPY

Because of the limited resources for individual treatment, and the efficacy of family therapy, individual therapy is often provided for children who cannot develop their capacities for owning and containing their emotions through family therapy alone.

It is common for someone with an eating disorder to have disturbed psychic functioning involving the denial of painful emotions. This denial impedes taking care of the infantile parts of the self and thus prevents the development of emotional maturity. For this reason, individual therapy is potentially suitable for all children with an eating disorder, as long as the child is willing to come regularly to the sessions and the external network of professionals and parents can support the treatment. The more crucial questions are:

(1)   Is the therapist suitably qualified to work with this child's particular difficulties as well as having a compatible personality willing to tolerate the full brunt of the child's projections of mental pain (Meltzer, 1967)?

(2)   Does the therapist have the willingness and capacity to work on the countertransference experiences to meet the needs of a child who has not yet transformed bodily experiences into emotions suitable for language—for example, the silent, negative, or borderline-psychotic child?

(3)   What help can be provided for a child who "closes her mind and mouth" to psychotherapy, as she transfers her starving and bingeing impulses for food to a rejection of the therapist or to a very demanding wish to be with the therapist all the time?

(4)   Is inpatient treatment initially necessary to support the child in undertaking the burden of working through her difficulties?

## ASSESSMENT FOR PSYCHOTHERAPY

As I approach an assessment interview, I bear in mind three patients: One is an adolescent with anorexia nervosa who told me that she had never told the doctors who had treated her for several years prior to seeing me, or me in two years of therapy, about repeated experiences of sexual abuse in her early childhood. When asked why not, she said, "No one has ever asked about sexual abuse. I felt awkward in bringing it up myself." She said she feared both I and her parents would blame her for the abuse taking place. The second patient told me she had never told anyone about "her voices". When asked why this was, she said she was afraid people would think she was "crazy" and anyway she liked her voices because they kept her "company". She said she was "afraid of losing them". The third patient, when asked about different suicidal impulses said she had none. However, when I asked her to describe a dream, it conveyed such a picture of hopelessness and despair, that I pressed her further. She then did say that she had secretly recently taken an overdose but didn't want her mother to know.

Beware of the "mask" of the child with anorexia nervosa or bulimia nervosa! An eating difficulty, whether it is bulimia or anorexia, involves the use of "pseudo-autonomy" and projection of feelings. The pattern of eating difficulties may appear similar in many children while masking a variety of psychiatric symptoms. A child with an eating disorder may be experiencing vivid auditory or visual hallucinations or ever-present "imaginary friends".

Because of the anorectic child's use of "pseudo-autonomy" to feel and appear "normal", such pathological phenomena are frequently concealed. For this reason, it is important to provide an individual assessment of approximately an hour for each child with an eating disorder. It is helpful to have at least one free-flowing assessment interview, in which the child is encouraged to use the opportunity to think about herself rather than supply information. Factual information can be gained in a subsequent interview and in other therapeutic settings. Fortunately, through her drawing, Marie was able to vividly portray the isolation of her inner self behind the protective cover of the locked door (Fig. 12.2). Even if family therapy is the treatment of choice, each child with severe problems also deserves the right to a private space apart from the family to think about her life and those issues that initially may be difficult to share with the family.

In individual assessments I have found it helpful to ask the child to draw a picture of a person. Then I ask the child to tell me about the person and create a story for that person. Subsequently, with the assistance of the child, I try to find similarities and differences between the person in the story and the child I am meeting. The rest of the session is used as a space for the child to explore issues of her choice. Spontaneous play and drawings are used for the assessment of a younger child. When the child has difficulty in speaking about herself, I discuss her difficulty in meeting a stranger, her fear of my criticism and of me. I find it helpful to give her a family set of small cloth dolls and ask her to speak from the perspective of various family members, as I interview the doll family regarding "their picture" of the child's life in her family. I also encourage the child to tell me a dream, any recurring dreams, and dreams from her past. In this way I gain access to the child's psychic structure.

Figure 12.3 illustrates how I consider the child's psychic structure. The key components are a maternal figure, a paternal figure, sibling figures and the infantile self. These paternal and maternal figures are typically used by children to represent the nurturing, procreating and regulating roles of each parent.

An examination of the maternal figure reveals the quality of nurturing and physical comfort and security provided, the capacity to receive distressed aspects of the infantile self and the ability to modify pain.

Evaluation of the paternal figure includes noting the capacity to regulate emotion so that feelings are neither too intense nor too restricted, to differentiate good from bad, to provide limits and also an ethical code out of concern for the self and others.

An assessment of the nature of the relationship with siblings and peers includes looking at the way in which conflicts between love, jealousy, and anger are expressed in these relationships, and also noting the capacity to acknowledge the existence and needs of siblings. I find that often hostility of the child with an eating disorder towards the parents is displaced onto the siblings.

My primary question during an assessment is: What capacity does the child have, in identification with internal figures, to look after her own infantile self? In empathetically listening to a child, I hear the child's stories and tone of voice, as well as noting my emotional responses to the child's predominant attitudes to her experiences. I then develop a picture of the current relationships between the parental figures and infantile self in the child's internal world. Evaluation of the child's relationship to the parents involves the place of emotional and intellectual nurture in the child's life and her attitude to discipline by school

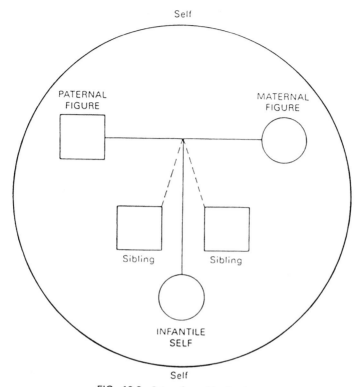

FIG. 12.3   Internal psychic structure.

figures. I also consider the child's capacity to allow the internal parental figures to be together in various creative ways, including procreation and the care of the siblings. This can be shown through scenes in dreams in which a couple are co-operatively doing something worthwhile.

The nature of the internal parental figures will be influenced by the qualities of real parents and by the child's own feelings towards them. A stable sexual identity is based upon acknowledgement of one's gender, as well as identifying with both internalised parental figures performing their task of looking after the infantile self and joining together in creative ways. The child's experience of her own body is influenced by these identifications and reflected in her sense of physical security and physical movement, as well as in the themes of her play, dreams, and stories.

Here are some remarks of Marie, which illustrate her internal configurations.

My mother isn't able to understand me. There is no point in talking to her, she justs gets upset.

My father vents all his anger on me, not on anyone else.

My sister is a "greedy pig". She gets everything she wants.

If I had to depend on my parents, I'd commit suicide.

Marie was explicit in showing that at that moment in time she was dominated by internal parental figures who could not be depended upon, who did not understand. She projected her own feelings into her "angry" father, "greedy" sister, and "non-understanding" fragile mother. The parental figure takes little responsibility for potentially overwhelming feelings such as greed, jealousy, anger, and the incapacity to understand feelings in herself. The child-part of the personality feels so antagonistic to the parental figures that she would prefer to manage without them rather than face the frustrations of depending on them. Perhaps most striking was the inability of Marie to face the problems of relying on her parents.

Marie was reliant on her own "pseudo-autonomous" methods of taking care of herself. By this I mean she was reliant on controlling activities involving concrete activity such as dieting, counting calories, and exercising, rather than relying on either her parents or an inner capacity to have empathy and tolerance for her own emotional experiences.

The psychotherapist needs to assess the severity of the self-protective structure represented by the child's belief: "I can take care of myself through physical and emotional dieting or through bingeing." The stronger this defence, the more likely that, in the initial part of therapy, there will be problems during separations and holidays. I have earlier highlighted how vital it is to have a supportive therapeutic team of parents and professionals.

## AIMS OF PSYCHOTHERAPY AND THERAPEUTIC METHOD

A psychotherapist's task is in many ways similar to that of parents. For this reason, psychotherapy is not a mode of treatment in which children must have good verbal capacity or intelligence. Equivalents of the parent–child relationship include a focus on the child's inner and outer experiences, consistency of care, specific and defined boundaries, and acceptance of the child even when she is destructive or rejecting. Also, a reliable and regular framework of meetings allows the child to develop trust in the therapist.

In these meetings, the therapist needs to be attuned to the emotional experience of the child, to give meaning to her communications. This is similar to a mother using her own emotional experience, coupled with her thinking, to make sense of the baby's expressions of physical and emotional states. This is particularly important to remember for a child with an eating disorder who often lacks integration of her physical and psychological experiences (Winnicott, 1958).

Because such lack of integration may be linked to a mismatch in communication in her primary experiences with her parents, a child with an eating disorder needs the therapist to consider her very early infantile experiences expressed in the child's demeanour, including sensations and movements of the body. The therapist must do this before the child can put her experiences into a symbolic form for communication. Only then can an integration of the physical and psychological self occur (Farrell, 1995).

Particularly at the beginning of therapy, the child often projects unbearable emotion and physical experiences onto the therapist before being able to feel, let alone verbalise, the experience. For example, hunger, nausea, tiredness, physical discomfort, anger, and sadness may often be first experienced by the therapist. The therapist then uses her own physical and emotional experiences felt in the presence of a child to understand these projections. The essential therapeutic task is to share the entire experience of the child, empathising with as much of the child's inner feelings as she will allow. Rather than intruding with questions or comments to the child, it is often appropriate for the therapist to speak "with the child's voice" suggesting that the child's non-verbal communication has been understood. For example:

> Marie was silent, face turned sideways with her hair hiding her eyes. She briefly glanced at me before retreating to look at the picture on my desk. I described the debate inside her: a debate about whether she talks with me or stays quietly alone. I also discussed how it seemed as if I were expecting something from her, and that she had told me she didn't want to talk with me. "Yes", Marie said in a dismissive way. I said she spoke as though I really was a nuisance. I added, using a loud and angry intonation, as though I was speaking with Marie's voice, "Things are all right. Let them be. Don't upset me by talking about something. It just causes problems."
>
> Then Marie began talking about how the maths teacher always shouted at the children. Only later was she able to admit being angry with me. I described how Marie wished that I would simply listen to what she was saying and think about it. Then I commented on how she had experiences that she felt unable to put into words, and that she wished I could experience her depth of feeling without her having to put it all into words for me. Marie nodded affirmatively in response.

Healthy psychological development can be ensured only through the presence of an effective inner psychic structure, functioning as parents understanding the emotions of a child and inspiring hope for the future. Through the therapist's work of bearing feelings and giving them meaning, the child can begin to experience being understood and accepted. This experience and further experiences of being helped in this way can then be internalised into the inner world of the child to form a resilient mental structure for transforming unbearable sensations into feelings suitable for thoughts. The structure is designed to "hold in mind" these intense and/or unbearable loving, hating, and conflictual feelings until thoughts about them can emerge.

# USING DREAMS FOR INITIAL AND
# ONGOING ASSESSMENT

Regardless of their underlying difficulties, children with eating disorders tend to progress through similar phases of emotional development in the course of therapy. This is well-illustrated by the dream-life of the child, which functions as a kind of internal theatre with internal family figures entering into emotional relationships and conflicts with one another (Meltzer, 1987).

Stable developments and growth of inner strengths in the personality structure of the child are most reliably traced through assessing her dream structure and her emotional relationship to her dream experiences. At present, the study of psychic development as observed through the dream process is a poorly researched area, yet the dream and the child's relation to it potentially presents one of the clearest pictures of the child's developing emotional capacities.

The dream structure of child in therapy suggests a fluctuation in the of psychic development. The child's developing sense of responsibility for the feelings expressed in the dreams suggests the same. One can view the dreams as unconscious thinking, equivalent to the action and play of young children. As the child discusses her dream, the therapist can focus on how the mind copes with emotional experiences, and how it deals with the distortions formed by the conscious self during the day (Meltzer, 1983). The focus of the therapist's interpretative work is to help the child look once again at her relationship with the parental figures as re-enacted in the relationship with the therapist. There is a gradual demarcation between the infantile feelings of the child and more mature parts of the child's personality. Maturity is characterised by having responsibility for thinking about emotional experiences and a growing, loving concern and sense of responsibility for destructive feelings and actions.

The phases of the eating disordered child's dream-life reflecting psychic development seem to follow this sequence.

(1)    There is difficulty in remembering dreams and/or difficulty accepting they are meaningful. There is a sense of rigid barrier between rational thoughts and the spontaneous expression of feelings. This should change during the course of a successful therapy of any theoretical orientation.

(2)    Dreams are described in which the child is overwhelmed with feelings that take over her sense of self. Examples might be:

> The child dreams that she is a Porsche. She has completely lost her own physical identity as she becomes an expensive racing car.

Or

> The child awakens from dreaming that she is disintegrating while falling off a cliff.

(3)   Dreams are described in which the child uses "pseudo-autonomy" as a means of caring for her distressed self. For example:

> When the therapist is ill, the child dreams that she is in a hospital with the therapist's face appearing and then disappearing. The child is then left in a room in which big, fat cats and rats, as well as black, furry monstrous creatures, are coming out from cages. She is terrified. She then pets a black creature and says: "Isn't it nice!" She has turned to a part of herself which gives her protection, but this is a false sense of safety, used to deny difficulties with separation from the nurturing therapist.

(4)   Dreams have more human figures in them and unwanted feelings of the child are projected into these figures so that they, rather than the child, become the owner of these feelings. Meanwhile, the self is experiencing a sense of hating, disowning, and/or being frightened of these feelings in others. The child, in describing the dream, has not yet begun to acknowledge these disowned parts of herself. For example:

> She dreams there is a teacher scolding all the other children in the class for being noisy and wanting too much attention.

(5)   Dreams are described in which the child projects her vulnerable feelings into others and, identifying with a parental figure, she takes care of her feelings located in others. At this point, the parental figure has developed the capacity for understanding and concern, but the child has not yet fully owned her dependent, vulnerable feelings located in "the others needing care". For example:

> She dreams that a baby is falling off a cliff, but she has adequate life-saving equipment and is able to rescue the baby. She had previously reported the dream of falling off the cliff.

(6)   The dreams suggest a more open acknowledgement of feelings in the self, but they are still uncontained and often seem to be on the verge of being enacted in the child's external life. For example:

> She dreams of getting into her parent's bed with a boy and then having a huge feast prepared by her aunt. Here she is confused between the wishes for physical comfort, sexual intimacy, and food. However, she has been able to dream, rather than act out these confusions as she had in the past.

(7)   The dreams suggest that not only is the child more openly able to acknowledge her own feelings and locate them in herself, but also she is able to accept responsibility for her destructive feelings and show inklings of maternal concern both for herself and for her siblings. The feelings seem more contained, as though there is the possibility of thinking before acting on the feeling. For example:

> She dreams she is shouting at her mother while her mother is talking to one of the younger children in the family. Then she decides she can join in the conversation too. She doesn't need to interrupt it by shouting. Later she is playing on the beach with her baby sister.

(8) In the dreams there is a fluctuation between dependence on parental functions in herself and the therapist (representing understanding parental figures), and the use of "pseudo-autonomy". For example:

> She dreams she is in a snowdrift. She is cold and being pushed down by the weight of the snow. She keeps going, but then she sees a light and she struggles to reach it. In this dream there is a hint that turning towards insight, in herself and in her therapist, might help her with the depression she feels as she acknowledges her loneliness.

(9) In the dreams there is more frequent evidence of a developing capacity to acknowledge feelings, think about them and take responsibility for what they imply. There is a sense that the internal capacity to parent oneself, in identification with good parental figures, is being established. For example:

> She cries in the dream, feeling sad when she quarrelled fiercely with her mother. In speaking to the therapist about the dream, she realises that she has been feeling more kindly towards her mother and treating her with more consideration. As she talks about this dream she is able to show responsibility for the punitive way she handles arguments with her mother. She describes how she is trying to reach some resolution of the conflicts.

By the termination phase of therapy the child is able to move from the egocentric position of thinking only of her needs, to a position of concern for her "baby self" as well as her internal and external siblings and parental figures.

In this stage of therapy there is a continual struggle between loving feelings and angry, jealous feelings. However, the loving feelings tend to dominate the child's relationships with others as well as her relationship with her "baby self". She no longer regularly treats her body or her feelings in a "pseudo-autonomous" way, but rather she attempts to take seriously her emotional and physical needs. She is able to truly "parent herself".

## THE INITIAL PHASE OF THERAPY: THE TOTAL TRANSFERENCE

Although it is essential for the psychotherapist to continually evaluate not only internal psychic development but also ongoing external relationships with family, school and peers, the scope of this chapter is limited to describing psychotherapeutic progress and impediments to growth present in either therapist or child. These developments or impediments emerge and are understood through transference and countertransference communications present in dreams, drawings, verbal, and non-verbal communication during the various phases of therapy.

Although as a therapist I am filled with willingness to offer hope and understanding to Marie, she arrives being cajoled by her parents into coming to the Eating Disorder Clinic. She feels "too fat". Her parents haven't told her she is too fat, but she is aware that there are girls thinner than her in the gymnastics class. She outwardly appears angry that she has been brought to the clinic, but I am aware that this anger conceals fear of intrusion by the entire inpatient and outpatient eating disorders' team.

Psychodynamic psychotherapy is characterised by a focus upon the total transference of the child to the entire institution, rather than solely to the individual therapist. By this I mean that the whole of the child's current emotional response to the setting, staff, and institution procedures—such as physical examinations, weighing, and dietary advice—are gathered into the transference relationship to the therapist. In this context, "gathering into the transference relationship" (discussed earlier) implies that the psychotherapist holds herself as representative of all clinical activity in relation to the child and her family (Janssen, 1994). In gathering the transference with Marie it was also essential to look at her previous relationship with the paediatric unit where she had had an unsuccessful admission. While there she had been isolated from friends and the team attempted to offer social contact as rewards for eating, a task that she didn't accomplish and perhaps found impossible. This led to an increase of resentment towards both her parents and the hospital. "The problem is that I am fat and my parents and the nurses want to make me fat", said Marie.

Understanding her total transference to the institution meant understanding that Marie felt threatened by the whole pattern of treatment—the intrusions through physical examination, family therapy, and refeeding in the inpatient unit, as well as the threat of intimacy and understanding provided by individual psychotherapy (Magagna, 1998). Marie desperately needed me to understand that her "delusion of fatness" was a bodily experience, which felt terrible. She had "fat", which she knew spoiled her self and needed to be controlled and eliminated. Marie also equated thinness with the possibility of feeling beautiful and being liked by friends rather than isolated at school.

Like many of the boys and girls with eating disorders, Marie did not fear getting tall. In fact, she wanted to be taller. I felt Marie equated tallness with an inner bone structure holding flesh. She also did not mind having hard bulging muscle because her flesh would be structured by the muscle. It was the "fat" without any inner structure that bothered her. And she feared we were all trying to make her "fatter".

## Dreams in the initial phase of therapy

Marie brought several nightmares, typical of this first phase of therapy. These included the following:

> Marie awakens at night because of a nightmare consisting of a horde of people banging on a wall to come in. She sees a crack in the wall appearing as though they may be successful.

and

> In her nightmare, the shadow of a huge man is falling on the wall and she
> can hear footsteps as though he is about to enter her bedroom. Marie
> awakens and cannot get back to sleep.

These dreams suggest that Marie has a physical sensation of occupying a space
that is being intruded upon by sinister, destructive forces or people. She depicts
herself as being vulnerable and weak, while being devoid of any hostile emotions.
There is a sense that she sees herself as good and the horde as a malevolent
intrusion.

## Countertransference issues and making an interpretation in relation to the total transference of the child

Marie is fixedly holding on to "I am fat. The only problem is that the hospital
wants to make me fatter and that makes me feel terrible."

As a therapist, I am wanting to share understanding of how I think the
problem is much more complicated than simply "feeling fat". I believe that her
repressed rage and anger at people closest to her, for not being exactly as she
wants them to be in relation to her, creates a sense of being filled with internal
parents who are damaged by her rage and anger. Her body, a woman's body, is
identified with that of her mother's. Hence, she occupies a body that is damaged,
not able to hold feelings or sensations in a manageable form, and is therefore fat
and lacking a solid internal structure. I also think that in her dream she has projected her destructive feelings onto the sinister invaders. I wonder if she has also
been sexually or physically abused, since about 30–40% of children with eating
difficulties have also experienced physical violence or sexual abuse. This needs
to be addressed as soon as some trust emerges in relation to some member of the
team. However, Marie is saying: "The hospital wants to make me fatter." My
countertransference is that she needs help and I wish to help by lending further
insight into the symbolic meaning of her dilemmas. But this would simply lead
Marie to feel I am making her "fatter", with more unmanageable feelings.

I thought then of Moreno (1914/1977, quoted in Goldman & Morrison, 1984,
pp. ix–x) who, when he was responsible for looking after very distressed refugees
in a Austrian camp, wrote:

> A meeting of two:
> eye to eye, face to face.
> And when you are near
> I will tear your eyes out
> and place them instead of mine,
> and you will tear my eyes out
> and will place them instead of yours,

then I will look at you with your eyes
and you will look at me with mine.

I realised that the "exchange of eyes" in which I would look at myself and the hospital through Marie's eyes would involve inhibiting my countertransference wish to rescue or nurture Marie through providing insight beyond that which she had already shared with me. So, I simply said to her, "You feel you need to be in control. This control of fatness makes you feel safe. You feel you need to be in control of the situation here."

"Yes," said Marie. "I write down every calorie that I eat."

In this initial phase of therapy Marie could only bear to hear descriptions of the ways in which she tried to protect herself from feeling anxious.

Originally, when I offered what I felt were more insightful interpretations, I felt that when they were rejected, they were simply incorrect. However, when I see with Marie's eyes, I realise that in my therapeutic zeal I provided too much understanding which was simply threatening her "pseudo-autonomy", which she needed to hold herself together. She needed to barricade her "crying self", for she felt I was a threat to her safety. I am reminded that in the picture Marie drew (Fig. 12.2) there is a big lock closing the door to her mother, as though her mother was a threat.

The main problem in the countertransference at this stage is that while wanting to feel helpful and potent as a therapist, one is being imprisoned, restricted, and rejected as a result of barricades erected by her "pseudo-autonomy" exerting control through restricting food intake and the experiencing of difficult feelings and pleasurable moments in the intimacy of a relationship. Anger and frustration are often present as one gets rejected and imprisoned by the slowness of pace required by the child.

If a therapist needs to be liked by the patient and cannot tolerate the experience of being a bad persecutory figure, there is a tendency to "split the transference". This can lead to terrible acting out by the patient in relation to the inpatient staff and parents. This problem is more fully explored elswwhere (Magagna & Segal, 1990). Gathering the positive transference and allowing the negative transference to remain split off can occur for a variety of reasons. These include the following.

(1)    The therapist has too great a need to feel loved by the patient or vice versa.

(2)    Either due to a transference of a weak, damaged parental figure onto the therapist or because the therapist is not sufficiently strong, the patient feels the need to protect the therapist from her destructive feelings.

(3)    The patient is afraid of the therapist and afraid of what will happen if she is destructive to the therapist.

(4)    The therapist has not sufficiently integrated her own latent destructiveness and thus is blinded to the hostile, destructive aspects of the patient in the session.

Assessment of the patient for borderline psychotic features is particularly important before treatment emerges, for it is particularly with this kind of patient that split transferences can lead to severe treatment difficulties with even the most experienced psychotherapist, regardless of her theoretical approach.

When I hear stories of the patient giving presents to the therapist early in the treatment while giving hell to the inpatient staff or parents I become alarmed that the patient is latching on to the therapist in a very primitive "skin-to-skin" way. This means that separation from the therapist leaves the patient feeling torn away, thrown away by the therapist. Many eating disorders can be rooted in early infantile rage about separations from the primary parental figure. A mother may be weaning the baby from the breast, having another baby, separating in order to have time for sleep, work, or another person, like the father. Rage about unmet needs, but also a possessive rage and panic about separation, are often some of the fundamental issues to be addressed in working with a child with an eating disorder.

In therapy the issue can be acted out by the patient who feels she has a good experience in the session with an idealised therapist but then goes out of the sessions with an internal image of a therapist who cruelly abandons her. During the interim between sessions, all inpatient staff or parents are then seen as representatives of the cruel therapist and are treated miserably by the patient. It is for this reason that any kin of regular therapy requires that the therapist fully prepare the child for separations and gather in the transference the variety of feelings about ends of sessions, holidays, and the ending of the therapeutic work.

"Gathering the transference" in this way is necessary throughout therapy, not only in relation to crucial issues of separation, but also in relation to all the other themes the child brings in her stories. The therapist's task is to ask how the theme of the story may be relevant to the therapeutic relationship at that imme-diate moment in the session.

For example, when Marie described how her mother always made her wait for 10 to 30 minutes to be collected after her gymnastic class, I became aware that I was being invited to identify with Marie and criticise her busy, but thought-less mother. (How much easier it is to identify with a child's grievance towards her mother, rather than oneself!) However, gathering the transference meant that I noted I was two minutes late for that day's session and she had had to wait three days since the previous session. I said, "I seem a therapist who does not think of you, your waiting, when I arrive several minutes late, and walk by you in the unit, not offering you a session, but talking to the nurses instead."

The transference interpretation is a primary method of psychodynamic work, but by no means the only one. I also wondered with Marie how she might talk more directly to me and also her mother. I tried to explore her anxieties about talking directly about a conflict she was experiencing. I noticed that repetitive discussions regarding food intake and weight control, needing to lose or gain weight, often occurred at the very moment Marie and I were talking about conflictual issues which really mattered to her. I silently noted that when you depend on another person and need them to be available, one of the worst things is that you cannot control them. That is the problem with depending on another person. On the other hand, food intake and weight gain can be controlled. Obsessional control of the body often occurred when Marie was most frustrated and hopeless about working out conflicts with an important person upon whom she depended.

Boredom in the countertransference often occurs when food issues are being examined yet again. I discovered that at times Marie existed only in the world of food and dieting with the recurring "pseudo-autonomous" fantasy of being in control of "a body". This was how she emptied her mind of intense emotions and conflicts in relation to me, whom she could not completely control during the session. Gradually we jointly developed some way of describing how Marie safely went back to her attachment to "food talk" as a method of moving away from something difficult. For example, on one occasion, when we tried to explore together why the "food talk" had emerged, Marie said, "I tell you something insignificant and you make a mountain out of a mole-hill. You make my problems bigger than they were in the first place."

## MIDDLE PHASE OF THERAPY: COMPLICATIONS IN THE INTEGRATION OF SPLIT-OFF PERSONALITY ASPECTS

. . . Let us pause from thinking
and empty our mind. Let us stop
the noise. In the silence let us listen to our
heart. The heart which is buried alive. Let
us be still and wait and listen carefully. A
sound from the depth from below. A faint
cry. A weak tapping. Distant muffled
feelings from within. The cry for help.
We shall rescue the entombed heart. We
shall bring it to the surface, to the light
and the air. We shall nurse it and listen
respectfully to its story. The heart's story
of pain and suffocation, of darkness and
yearning. We shall help our feelings to live in
the sun. Together again we shall find relief
and joy.

*Leunig (1990), pp. 31–32*

The middle phase of therapy is characterised by the child developing some trust in the capacity of the therapist to understand and accept her emotional experiences. The therapist's ability to do this is greatly influenced by her own willingness to remain emotionally alive to her won feelings and bear the psychic pain

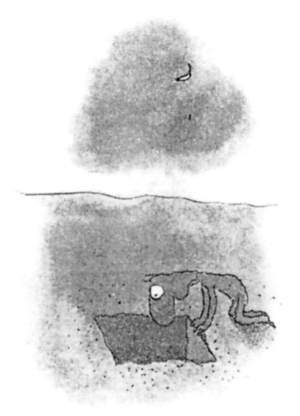

FIG. 12.4   "... Let us listen to the heart" (Leunig, 1990). © Copyright Michael Leunig 1990. Reprinted with permission.

of accepting intuitive insights that the child consciously and unconsciously highlights in the therapist's personality. For example, Marie said, "I have defeated a famous consultant and I will defeat you." Here she was aware of how her exploration of her own motivation was interfered with by my anxious wish to facilitate a successful therapy.

A psychoanalytic psychotherapist is required to have an extensive personal therapy herself, to develop access, through dreaming and free associating, to both loving and destructive aspects of her personality and the capacity to integrate such parts of her self that may previously have been projected. Yet, however much psychotherapy a therapist has, there remain deeper conflicts and buried hurt (Fig. 12.4), which can easily be projected into the child or simply split off from the central core of the therapist's personality. I believe that the need to repair this buried part of the personality and become what one truly can be is part of the unconscious motivation for people choosing to work psychotherapeutically with children having eating disorders.

The child's unconscious messages to the therapist provide the most penetratingly honest and helpful supervision to the therapist in facilitating repair of internal damage both in the child and in the therapist herself. The best psychotherapy is a "duet for two", in which buried and undeveloped parts of both the child and the therapist's personality are resurrected through neurotic and psychotic transferences of the child. Healing becomes possible through the way in which the therapist with considerable patience listens carefully, works on her countertransference to the story of the child's story of pain and yearning (Leunig, 1990), and lends insight on the basis of understanding the countertransference. If the therapist does not develop in the course of being with a child in therapy it seems likely that the child will reach some kind of impasse in the therapy.

It is a fallacy to assume that I can truly change another human being. In any case, my primary psychotherapeutic aim is to modify my countertransference responses which ultimately inform all that I am and do with Marie. I shall now delineate some recurring experiences in the transference and countertransference that have initially created an impasse but, through work in the countertransference, have facilitated development of Marie's internal psychic structure.

## Six recurring problems

I have already mentioned that the underlying nature of various eating disorders varies and reveals a multiplicity of pathological states of mind. Despite this, there are some common challenges in the middle phase of therapy with a child with an eating disorder. They are often present at different phases of the therapy, but it is in the middle phase of therapy, when the child has become more fully known to the therapist, that the underlying pattern can be seen more clearly. I shall illustrate these six challenges to therapeutic progress with clinical vignettes. The challenges include:

- silence
- hostility, fear, and revenge
- rivalry
- obsessionality and intellectualisation
- eating difficulties forming part of the transference
- placatory external progress masking inner difficulties.

### Silence

I have only twice had the experience of treating a child with an eating disorder without moments or hours of silence. There is always communication taking place between the child and the therapist, but when the child is silent the therapist is particularly impelled to understand the prevailing mood derived from the child's attitude to the therapist and the therapist's conscious and unconscious responses to the child (Magagna, 1996). If I, as a therapist, can be still and in the silence listen to what is going on deeply within myself in the presence of Marie, then there is no need for me to penetratingly question her (Leunig, 1990).

During Marie's silences I have always felt that she required some silent space, lasting 3–4 minutes. I have never felt that I should be quiet for longer than that. She needed to feel that I was able to continue to reflect on the relationship between us and wasn't completely controlled by her silences. If Marie arrived and was silent, I often reviewed our previous meeting aloud, trying to focus on ways in which she may have felt understood or not understood by me. I also looked at her experience of the ending of the previous session as well as how it may have affected the space between the sessions. Most importantly, I have needed to decide carefully whether or not I spoke directly to Marie, or whether she required that I spoke in the third person, wondering aloud, not looking at her directly, creating a stage to the side of her, where I could explore the meaning of her emotions through a story or discussion with myself, with her choosing to listen or not listen. She needed to feel that therapy was not a recreation of being "force-fed" by a controlling figure.

Because my countertransference responses to Marie's silence could seriously impede Marie's progress, it was essential to probe the depth of my own emotional response before venturing to speak. Outside the session, I would review the day in case my own issues or issues within the team were dominating and interfering with countertransference work of the therapy. If I did not monitor my own countertransference experience, I was unwittingly scripted into a counter-therapeutic role.

With Marie, it was useful during the silence to ask myself: Who is Marie being? What am I feeling? What am I supposed to be feeling in the role in which Marie has cast me? What is the meaning of Marie's drama into which I am being invited to participate?

By using my countertransference responses, involving understanding Marie's feelings projected into me in the silence, I was able to give her the experience that unbearable feelings could be contained and thought about. Gradually she was able to give her own experiences a symbolic form, sometimes first in a drawing and then giving them a name. Only later was she able to consider them.

There were three main problems in my countertransference responses when Marie was silent, as follows.

(1)   I could feel too hurt and despairing about my ineffectiveness as a therapist, forgetting that I needed to use that sense of ineffectiveness to understand Marie's inner experiences.

(2)   I could become over-protective, worrying that she wouldn't even come to the session if I didn't find some way of becoming just exactly the way she wanted me to be. This often stemmed from not sufficiently owning my hostile feelings and elaborating on them as part of what she was trying to communicate to me.

(3)   I could get angry that she was not speaking and making my work easier for me, thus allowing me to feel I was in a helpful therapeutic situation with her. My wish to be "a good therapist" was dominating the need simply to try to help her understand her emotions and integrate them within her personality.

These countertransference experiences created an impasse in Marie's therapy until I could transform them through understanding.

To expand on and illustrate these points, here are some vignettes of repeated countertransference and transference problems occurring between therapist and child in the silences. They include:

- overprotectiveness
- fear
- uselessness, rejection, and despair
- need for primitive communication—heart-to-heart without words
- allowing separateness.

*Overprotectiveness.*

Marie arrived and was silent. She had missed the previous session without calling to let me know she was not coming. I decided to ask her delicately why she had not come to the session. Marie responded that sometimes she did not come because she had other engagements, while at other times she simply did not feel like coming. I didn't say any more. It seemed to me she didn't want to discuss the matter further; her head was bent as though she was on the point of falling asleep and she did sleep momentarily. I remained quiet.

In this instance, I became too gentle and ineffective, over-anxious about hurting Marie's feelings in the course of therapy. Further examination of the counter-transference made me realise that my gentleness was a counterreaction to my anger that Marie never bothered to phone and cancel the session or phone after the session to explain why she hadn't come.

*Fear.*   The child's need for the protect armour of "pseudo-autonomy" must be respected. For Marie, too much deep insight put too forcefully, or too "emotionally intimate" interpretations, would often lead me to become frightening. Overcome and threatened by powerful feelings Marie would stop speaking as a way of protecting herself. She was holding herself together through silence. She didn't trust me. When I talked about her feeling that she had to have the protection of silence and respected her silence, Marie would sometimes spontaneously speak: "You are always acting as though you know what I feel", or, "I feel miserable". But when I attempted to speak with too much comprehension of underlying feelings, Marie would say, "I don't want to know about my feelings! I am sick of them!"

*Uselessness, rejection, and despair.*    I have to admit that at times I am simply useless when I keep on saying the same old interpretation using the same imagery. It inspires neither curiosity nor interest in the child and certainly does not foster progress. But the child's silence is a real test of whether or not the therapist will accept projections of helplessness, inadequacy, and rejection. I had to differentiate between Marie's powerful "pseudo-autonomous self" actively attempting to reduce me to impotence by silent, supercilious contempt and another process when by rejecting me she was actually trying to communicate an unbearable experience of being rejected herself. How can one tell? Bodily language gives a partial clue, but it is only through the emotional tone in the silence, heard in the countertransference, that one can really tell. A different relationship, coloured by more loving, trusting feelings, needs to exist before there will be a projection of a painful sense of being rejected.

> After one silence lasting for over five minutes (during which I spoke part of the time), Marie told me that she really thought that I wouldn't have gone on a mid-term holiday just when she was worried about returning to school. She thought that was a clear indication that really I just cared about myself.

Here, the quality of Marie's silence made it obvious that she felt rejected by me.

*Need for primitive communication—heart-to-heart without words.*

> Marie was sitting in the waiting room with her mother. She had her back turned to her mother and tears on the brim of her eyes. When she came in she was silent. She sat with her legs dangling over the chair, in a slightly sideways position in relation to me. It seemed that she was alive with painful emotions, not suggesting that I should keep out. In this situation I waited in silence.

Marie needed a safe quiet space before tears fell from her eyes. It was important for me to be there experiencing the depth of her feeling. I did not assume that crying meant sadness, because it could hide a multiplicity of feelings. In fact, later when I described how tears could have so many meanings, Marie said she was sad because she was always angrily pushing her mother away even when she wanted her mother near her. She didn't understand why that was. I realised that this was also a common feature of our therapeutic relationship and later I mentioned this.

*Allowing separateness.*    Because of the seriousness of Marie's underlying emotional disturbance, sleeping difficulties, and serious eating disorder, her mother and father had become more and more overprotective. At the time of her referral she was often either sleeping in her parents' bedroom or having one of the parents sleep near her bed in her room. Because of her own anxiety, mother watched her "like a hawk", and when Marie was on the ward there were times that she required close supervision. Her enmeshed relationship with Marie had prompted mother to searching her diary and drawers.

It was important for Marie, therefore, that therapy not be a re-creation of an intrusive relationship. She needed to know that I could be different from her and tolerate not knowing what she felt. Plying her with too many questions would also encourage her to be passive, waiting for me to take responsibility for the sessions. She might need to answer questions to please me, to allay my anxiety about her. I found that allowing some silence for a few minutes and exploring what I was wondering about, without a question-mark ending my sentence, was often a more helpful way to be working in the session. This allowed me to think about Marie's experiences without pressuring her to feed me her thoughts at that very moment.

### Hostility, fear, and revenge

Minuchin's aim of helping staff and helping parents to work together (Minuchin, Rosman, & Baker, 1978) to provide firm boundaries and rules for the child is suitable for many children with eating difficulties if compassion and sensitivity to the child's terror is present in the parents. However, I have discussed how the more vulnerable, helpless, chronically starved, or emotionally disturbed child may feel almost addicted to "pseudo-autonomous self" as a protection against an intense fear of losing a sense of herself. Without the firm psychic boundary provided by psychic manoeuvres of behaviours such as starving, dieting, exercising, vomiting, and the use of laxatives, the child could feel as if she is exploding into fatness or "falling into bits".

When behavioural procedures, including staff supervision of exercising and vomiting, were prescribed for Marie, she responded by cutting her stomach at night, hurling abuse, and hitting the staff. She also made an attempt to run away from the ward.

It was easy to notice Marie's violence, but much more complicated for staff to maintain a containing emotional stance experiencing not only her anger, but also her extreme terror. Marie was terrified because her entire protective armour was being broken into. As a result she felt her sense of self was being destroyed by the regime that said she must eat and not vomit. In other words, Marie's feeling was that her "pseudo-autonomous self", struggling like a soldier in a combat field, was being destroyed by external authoritarian controls and that nothing would be left of her. Death, or superficially cutting herself, seemed to be the last weapons to which she could resort to win the battle of who was in control. Her attempts to die or harm herself not only symbolised her sense of her self being destroyed, but also portrayed her view that death was a wonderful relief from the terror of psychic fragmentation.

As I said, when Marie hit out, it was easier to be in touch with her aggression rather than her terror. There was an enormous need for the team and her parents to unite and bear anger, despair, fear, and other uncomfortable countertransference feelings. When we were not successful in doing this, our rage with Marie for making us virtually impotent to help her was redirected to other staff members and the parents.

In the therapy the focus was on Marie's collusion with her "pseudo-autonomous self"—the self that was fighting us to stay alive as her "body-guard", but was actually cruelly taking away her life along with any hope in me and the staff. When I said this to Marie she responded, "At last—it took long enough for somebody to see this."

The "pseudo-autonomous" self was felt by Marie to be her only protection until she developed an inner psychic structure that was more helpful to her. At the same time she was terrified that it was forcing her to lose a helpful rapport with me and the adults who were trying to help her. Aggressive encounters provoking the danger of revengeful responses from me and the staff were an exciting camouflage for this primitive terror of the death of her physical and emotional connectedness to life.

### Rivalry

As the child settles into the group-life of a ward, or develops a more dependent relationship with the therapist seen on an outpatient basis, rivalry with "the other children" being treated by the therapist may propel her towards being "the illest child". Unlike school, where the teacher notices achievement, the child may feel that the therapist is only interested in problems and therefore the aim of being singled out by the therapist may consciously or unconsciously involve trying to cause the most worry and concern. This pathological need to be "the illest" in competition with the other patients can lead to chronic difficulties, particularly when the child is an inpatient.

As the relationship with Marie developed, I became increasingly aware that, although I perceived her to be less depressed and to be experiencing more intimate relationships with friends and her family, she continually complained, "Things are as bad as ever . . . I'm always a loner at school because no one likes me. I didn't do as well as the others on my school project . . . I am not ever able to talk to my mother as long as I would like, because she is always busy."

As I began to review the sessions in this context, I became aware that each time Marie noticed a child more ill than her, the intensity of her complaints about "things being as bad as ever" tended to increase. One day, she laughed with embarrassment as she told me that while at the entrance of the newspaper shop she had "accidentally" knocked over a younger, iller child whom she had previously seen with me. Marie then told me, "It's your job . . . from morning till night. You have patients, one after the other . . . until you are fed up . . . I wonder what I should tell you to get you involved . . . so as not to bore you . . ."

I realised then that Marie had to be "a very ill child" to keep me as worried about her as an outpatient as I had been when she was the newest and illest child admitted to the inpatient ward. She was continually consciously or unconsciously in competition with "the others". No matter how much better and livelier she felt, I was to know she was "miserable". This was done to maintain the position of "the most important child", gaining most of my concern for her difficulties. She described it as her need "stick to me like ivy".

## Obsessionality and intellectualisation

with a heart caked with cold past the brunt of feeling

*Crowe Ransom (1991, p. 37)*

Control through dieting is used to stop eating impulsively, in an out-of-control way. Phobias of certain foods may be present along with excessive dieting. Accompanying these symptomatic behaviours are underlying fantasies which, when understood, lend meaning to problematic eating or vomiting patterns and the use of laxatives. The child's mind functions in a way similar to that of the child's eating style. When there is no adequate mental structure for "digesting" intense emotions through lending thought to them and integrating them within the psyche, the child seems to be on a "mental diet" in which she avoids getting emotionally near certain crucial issues. An instance of this is the fact of Marie's sexual abuse. It was clear that unless Marie had brought a particular dream, I might never have begun to talk about the sexual abuse by her older neighbour occurring over a two-year period. Marie said she felt too guilty to discuss that situation.

I also became aware that, in order "to please me", Marie brought issues about her relationships with family members and dreams in which she knew I was interested because of the light they shed on her inner psychological situation. However, the reality was that once her feelings were more obvious to her, she resorted to being emotionally distant from what she was describing. Alternatively, she blunted the emotional relevance of what she was saying, by running through a variety of topics without wanting to stop and think about what she was saying.

Cold intellectual control was used to protect her from a torch of burning emotions which threatened her equanimity. So, for example, she reported with great calmness how she had been in an argument with her father in which he had lost his temper, pushed his fist right near her face and said that he would bash it into pieces and throw her out of the house if she didn't start being more obedient to her mother. I was to imagine the scene and experience the feeling of terror and horror she regularly experienced at home.

"A heart caked with cold, past the brunt of feeling" (Crowe Ransom, 1991) is a necessary protection for a child to retain her sanity when she is overwhelmed by emotions which she cannot psychically contain. When I prematurely tried to look at Marie's emotional responses to her father, she simply spoke in a flat, detached way to me saying, "I love him. This is the way he is and I have to accept that." I learned from this that the child's fear of some internal catastrophe leads to a distancing of emotions by projection and "intellectual control". Until the inner structure of the child is ready to hold intense emotions, she can only gradually allow herself to be freed from the cover of cold intellectualisation. Meanwhile, the therapist must hold and explore the intensity of emotions within herself (Kennedy & Magagna, 1994).

### Eating difficulties forming part of the transference

If you spit in the air, it will fall on your face.

Midrash Rabbah (*Ecclesiastes 7:9*)

I have already outlined "the treatment frame" for psychotherapy and high-lighted the role of parents who are usually asked to work together to help their child to eat. But it can often be easy for the therapist to forget that, in the course of treatment, changes in the child's eating difficulties are linked to the transference consisting of the developing relationship with the therapist, who is now representative of the child's internalised parents. My primary task as a therapist was to gather Marie's infantile feelings into the transference relationship with me and free her from some of the unmanageable intensity of feeling that interfered with her eating and psychological functioning. This was extremely important because Marie's mother would simply have felt too attacked and shattered if she had been on the receiving end of all Marie's feelings that had become liberated during her therapy.

A consequence of "gathering feelings into the transference" is that the therapist has to accept the child's growing dependence on her as well as the brunt of the child's hostility. At times this involves the therapist feeling guilty letting the child down. It is often difficult for therapists who have not had psychotherapy themselves to realise just how vulnerable the child is once she appreciates her relationship to the therapist.

In the first phase of her therapy, although Marie began eating with slightly less difficulty, she had days when she approached me as though the moment I opened my mouth I was going to scold her or make her feel terrible. Occasionally I had the sensation at times that my face was being transformed from Little Red Riding Hood's grandmother into the devouring wolf. There were days when the inpatient staff and later Marie's parents had to work strenuously to assist her to come to her therapy sessions. I had prepared them for the fact that "terrible food" often gets transferred onto "the terrible therapist" and that persecutory anxieties about food, now directed towards the therapist, could be understood in the therapy. But it was very uncomfortable to accept being transformed into a monster—very easy to believe that I was being viewed as bad because I was an intrusive, inadequate, unloving therapist.

I realise now how important it is for me, and new therapists in particular, to accept that, although we do make therapeutic errors by not understanding or being too intrusive, part of the child's negativity invariably stems from the situation itself. The point made earlier that children with eating disorders tend not to choose therapy but are required to have it by their parents is significant here. In addition to this, some of the negative feelings once projected into the food are transferred into particularly the eyes, mouth and words of the therapist. Such words are equated with "fattening food", making the child feel worse. The therapist's eyes are often felt to be sending rays of hate or depression into the child to shatter her. Understanding is felt to be like "dieting" which becomes addictive, controlling the child's mind and taking it over, so understanding also becomes dangerous.

The thought that if you spit in the air, it will fall on your face was helpful in describing Marie's transference relationship to me during the middle phase of therapy. Having made significant progress during the first term of therapy, I was shocked that during my first three-week holiday Marie lost several kilos. Later I realised that this is typical in the middle phase of therapy.

When the child has developed a good therapeutic alliance with the therapist, however much the therapist discusses a change in the rhythm of sessions, the child's response to separation from the therapist is, either consciously or unconsciously, generally one of feeling unsupported and unloved. Marie said, "You just don't care about me. I always try to make my best efforts to please you, but then with you, like with everyone else, things always end like this . . . in being rejected." Her "spitting on me" for leaving her created an image of my being a bad, uncaring therapist. This bad therapist was relocated in the food, which then became more noxious to her during the holiday, "the spit falling on her face". Hence she lost weight.

But it was not only a therapeutic holiday that could create a significant fluctuation in Marie's acceptance of food. When she was cross with me for saying "the wrong thing" she would say, "Right, I'm not going to eat now." She would leave the session keeping her mouth closed to food for hours and sometimes longer. Just as mother's food is equated with mother, so too does emotional food eaten during the course of therapy become associated with the therapist representing the child's relationship to her internalised mother. I gradually became confident that if Marie felt adequately supported by me internally, she would attempt to eat food no matter how difficult her experiences were. In doing this, I felt she would be identifying with "a good mother" who felt her child needed to eat, no matter how unhappy or lacking in hunger the child was. Certainly Marie's experience was that when she was filled up with anger or jealousy or unhappiness she both felt "full up" and also that the food was "horrible, tasting like cardboard".

Gradually Marie and I developed "a common metaphorical language" in which it was understood that her relationship with food was linked to her relationship with me, her therapist, representative of the "parents-in-her-mind", the internalised parents. As we did this, I gradually stopped silently criticising the parents for not adequately helping her to eat when there were "blips" and instead began understanding the meaning of her not eating. I now realise that Marie starved for many reasons including when she was angry with me. She starved to be in control of uncontrollable feelings experienced when outside the session, starved in identification with me starving her of therapy, starved instead of mourning the loss of different earlier developmental stages of our therapeutic relationship, starved because that was her routine way of facing a problem when I or a parent wasn't around to help her with an emotional conflict.

### Placatory external progress masking inner difficulties

... It is only with the heart that one can see rightly.
What is essential is invisible to the eye.

*St. Exupery (1995, p. 68)*

I have seen many children who have eaten to get out of hospital as quickly as possible and free themselves from the eyes of the nurses. Their aim in getting out was to lose weight again. The book *Anorexics on Anorexia* gives many accounts of feeding programmes without psychotherapy, which leave the patients feeling like this: "What really surprised and shocked me was the fact that the focus was on feeding me up to produce a change in my body, but never once did they take my mind into consideration. The way I was feeling did not seem important to them. I received very little in the way of counselling" (Shelley, 1997, p. 3). Although this may be partly a projection of the child's state of mind onto hospital staff, a treatment programme that does not have stated therapeutic aims beyond that of weight gain promotes a distorted picture of psychological development both to the children and their parents. Likewise, children can quickly work out what they feel is "the right attitude" to get discharged from hospital. For those of us, parents or clinicians, who are prone to rely on the child's comment: "My weight is right now, everything is fine, now I should stop therapy", it is essential to remember that this is but the surface. Before making a decision to end Marie's therapy, I needed to understand her inner reality through listening "with my heart" to her mood in describing her feelings. It was through the countertransference, accompanied by looking at her dreaming process, that I was able to ascertain both Marie's capacity to struggle with and ultimately integrate the destructive aspects of her personality, motivated by her love for others and for herself and also her capacity to bear rather than deny frustrations in the achievement of her personal goals.

When beginning work with Marie, I found myself unwittingly involved in the content of what she was saying about not wanting to eat, feeling everyone was controlling her, making her eat high-calorie food, and so on. At that time it felt essential for me to have the support of a supervision group. The emotional support of this group facilitated listening with "a third ear" to the emotional tone—a kind of accompanying music—in Marie's communication. This kind of listening then allowed me to begin to describe:

- how she was speaking
- how I felt before, during, and after she was speaking
- what my feelings revealed about her current inner state, often projected into me.

Recognising a placatory tone and discussing it openly can often bring great relief to children in therapy. One creative way of exploring a countertransference sense of "placatory pretence" on the part of the child has been shared with me by a supervisee (Neil, personal communication):

> I try to simply discuss the feeling of pretence directly with the child. On one occasion then I tried to explore this, the child said that the feeling was almost always there and that it spoiled everything for her. I suggested to her that the feeling of pretence might be linked to the angry feelings she tried to keep at bay. Using the image of a theatre set, I suggested to her that, every time "Anger" sees "enter stage right" in the script, the director (her) pushes "Anger" stage left and buries it in a box behind the set. Other feelings come and go, but without "Anger" the play is lacking. "Upset" and "Tearful" try hard to understudy but they are just not good enough. Not only that but "Pretence" (who is really "Anger" in disguise) insists on rubbishing everything else that goes on so the director, no matter how hard she tries, is left feeling awful inside. The child laughed at this, but I felt that she understood what I was getting at. She joked at the end of the session that she would think of ways of letting "Anger" have a few lines now and then.

No matter how many years of experience as a therapist I have, it is necessary for me to continually notice a child's immediate response to my comment or interpretation, as did the therapist in the example. I say this because Marie's responses provided a means of ongoing supervision of my work with her. I could use her response to my words to answer questions beginning with "Has my interpretation enabled her to feel:

- accepted rather than criticised?
- understood rather than penetrated with insight?
- interested in further exploration of her emotional life rather than in control, which prompts retreat to superficial intellectual levels or attack on my interpretations?"

Working well together as a clinic team creates an emotional climate fostering a shift from intellectual exercises with the child to a mutual exploration of crucial issues. When the team is experiencing too much conflict, I find that either I or other team members can get stuck as therapists because our attempts to understand the child change to criticising the child and parents for various reasons, including "not working" or "not co-operating". At these moments I realise that, just as parents sometimes direct unexpressed frustration onto the child, so too does the clinic team. Therapeutic impasses are quite likely to occur just at this time. When I or another therapist decide to discuss a session with a child in our small supervision group, we are frequently surprised by how just the thought of working together with colleagues in this helpful and supportive way promotes a shift in our relationship with the child so that strangely the next therapy session is "not as stuck" as the previous one.

## THE ENDING PHASE OF THERAPY

Termination of Marie's treatment reawakened old issues she had in elation to her parents. She had become dependent on the understanding provided in the twice-weekly therapy sessions. At the end of therapy there was the problem of her rage with me for not being "an everlasting therapist", like her "everlasting food machine", which she drew earlier in the therapy (Fig. 12.5).

In contrast to the therapist, the everlasting food machine can be a possession under Marie's control. She could choose when to take or reject food. But Marie's future stability was dependent on how she internalised the therapeutic relationship, a relationship never totally under her control. It would depend on how she continued the process of discovering and thinking about aspects of herself that emerged in her relationships by day and were portrayed in her relationships with internal figures in her dreams at night. I suggested to Marie that she continue an ongoing structured inner dialogue by self-analysis done through a journal written at intervals similar to her therapy sessions. This process assisted her mourning for the therapy space, which ultimately she had been able to use. Two follow-up sessions, at a time of her choice in the following several years, were part of the termination plan.

Marie returned for a follow-up appointment some years later. She had maintained a healthy weight and was eating normally. Finding pleasure in her studies as well as her friendships, she was able to communicate much more openly both with her parents and her boyfriend. However, Marie said she was always aware of the pressure on women "to be thin and beautiful". I felt that Marie's therapy had been helpful to her.

Successful therapy involves the child taking responsibility for looking after herself while remaining intimately connected to others upon whom she depends. It involves the development of concern for the feelings of others. There is a frequency of dreams in which supportive figures are able to meet distress in others. For example, Marie had a dream that she was looking after a little girl who was crying. She also described the dreams discussed earlier. Most particularly though, a successful outcome in therapy involves forgiving the parents for not being "perfect" but rather being human with frailties and problems of their own. However, it may also involve separating, at least temporarily, from parents whose problems grossly interfere with the child's psychological development.

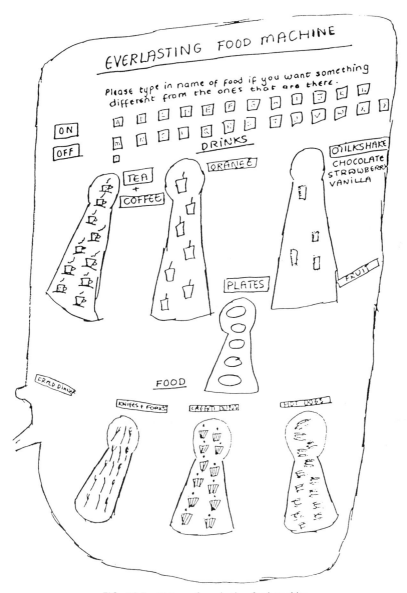

FIG. 12.5  Picture of everlasting food machine.

## CONCLUSION

Individual psychodynamic psychotherapy is costly in the short term because, with a child with a severe eating disorder, it is not something that can be successfully completed in six months. However, if the therapist and child are able to sustain a good therapeutic alliance to work through some of the child's central conflicts, psychotherapy provides a substantial base of security for the psychological well-being of the next generation of children. When a child leaves therapy I regularly ask myself: "What kind of a parent will this child be?"

My therapeutic endeavours with Marie were to enable her to own rather than project parts of her personality and unresolved emotional conflicts on to her child. Without therapeutic help it would certainly be very difficult for Marie to bear the intensity of her own possessiveness, hostility, and intense love in years to come. Left untreated, mothers who have suffered from anorexia nervosa of necessity can predominantly resort to denial of conflict and "pseudo-autonomous" methods rather than containment of anxiety when raising their own children. And so we see another generation of difficult lives (Stein, 1994).

A good outcome for Marie, or any other boy or girl having psychodynamic psychotherapy, would be a realised capacity to become an adult able to deal both with her own love and hate and that of her children. Most important, though, is the development of a capacity for concern both for oneself and for others as well as forgiveness of the parents for not being "perfect". Through identifying with more healthy internal parents by the end of therapy the child is beginning to develop a good sense of self and self-esteem.

## SUMMARY POINTS

The key issues addressed in this chapter are:

- recognising the inner world reality of children with eating disorder, which leads to acute emotional conflict and fierce protective defences against too much psychological pain
- assessment and treatment of children
- the therapeutic use of the concepts of "transference" and "countertransference" in psychotherapy, both in their wide application to institutions and in their personal application to the working life of the individual therapist
- the role of dreams in understanding the development of the inner world of the child towards psychological health
- some specific complications and impediments to growth during the beginning, middle, and ending phases of psychotherapeutic treatment.

## ACKNOWLEDGEMENTS

This is written with gratitude to the eating-disordered children and who have shared their dreams, drawings and feelings with me and to other colleagues who have shared their work for use in this chapter, particularly Nicky Harris, Staff Nurse on the Mildred Creak Unit. I would also like to thank my colleague Sarah Gustavus-Jones for her help on this chapter.

# REFERENCES

Brenman-Pick, I. (1985). Working through in the counter-transference. *International Journal of Psychoanalysis, 66,* 157–166.

Cameron, J. (1996). *The vein of gold: A journey to your creative heart.* New York: Putnam & Sons.

Casement, P. (1985). *On learning from the patient.* London: Tavistock Publications.

Crowe Ransom, J. (1997). In Winter remembered. *Carcanet selected poems.* Manchester, UK: Carcanet Press.

Farrell, E. (1995). *Lost for words: The psychoanalysis of anorexia and bulimia.* London: Process Press.

Goldman, E., & Morrison, D. (1984). *Psychodrama: Experience and process.* Dubique, IA: Kendall-Hunt.

Goodsitt, A. (1997). Eating disorders: A self-psychological perspective. In D. Garner & P. Garfinkel (Eds.), *Handbook of treatment for eating disorders* (2nd ed.). London: Guilford Press.

Hinshelwood, R. (1994). *Clinical Klein.* London: Free Association Books.

Janssen, P. (1994). *Psychoanalytic therapy in the hospital setting.* London: Routledge.

Kennedy, R., & Magagna, J. (1994). The aftermath of murder. In S. Box, R. Copley, J. Magagna, & E. Moustaki Smilansky (Eds.), *Crisis at adolescence* (pp. 203–221). London: Jason Aronson.

Leunig, M. (1990). *A common prayer.* North Blackburn, Victoria, Australia: Collins Dove.

Magagna, J. (1996). Understanding the unspoken: Psychotherapy with children having severe eating disorders. In *Psychosomatic problems in children* (ACPP Occasional Papers No. 12). London.

Magagna, J. (1998). Psychodynamic psychotherapy in an in-patient setting. In J. Green & B. Jacobs (Eds.), *The child psychiatry in-patient unit* (pp. 124–143). London: Routledge.

Magagna, J., & Segal, B. (1990). L'attachement and les processus psychotiques chez un adolescente anorexique. In R. Broca (Ed.), *Psychoses and creation* (pp. 121–137). Seuil, France: Diffusion Navarin.

Meltzer, D. (1967). *The psychoanalytic process.* London: Heinemann.

Meltzer, D. (1983). *Dreamlife.* Scotland: ?.

Meltzer, D. (1987). *Studies in extended metapsychology.* Reading, UK: Radavion Press.

Minuchin, S., Rosman, B., & Baker, L. (1978). *Psychosomatic families.* Cambridge, MA: Harvard University Press.

Money-Kyrle, R. (1978). Normal counter-transference and some of its deviations. In D. Meltzer & E. O'Shaughnessy (Eds.), *The collected papers of Roger Money-Kyrle* (pp. 330–342). Perth, Scotland: Clunie (Original work published 1956).

Palazzoli, M. (1974). *Self-starvation.* London: Jason Aronson.

Racker, H. (1974). *Transference and countertransference.* London: Hogarth Press.

Rey, H. (1994). Anorexia nervosa. In J. Magagna (Ed.), *Universals of psychoanalysis* (pp. 47–75). London: Free Association Press.

Rosenfeld, H. (1987). *Impasse and interpretation.* London: Tavistock Publications.

Shelley, R. (1997). *Anorexics on anorexia.* London: Jessica Kingsley.

Stein, A. (Producer) (1994). *Formerly anorectic mothers and their young children* [Videotapes]. London: Tavistock Clinic.

St. Exupery, A. (1995). *The little prince.* London: Mammoth Press.

Winnicott, D. (1958). *Collected papers: Through paediatrics to psycho-analysis* (pp. 243–254). London: Tavistock Publications.

# CHAPTER THIRTEEN

# Inpatient management

**Peter Honig**
*Phoenix Centre, Cambridge, UK*

**Wendy Sharman**
*St George's Eating Disorders Service, London, UK*

Children and adolescents with anorexia nervosa and related eating disorders sometimes require a period of inpatient treatment. Indications for admission include:

- severe malnutrition
- serious medical complications, such as cardiac arrhythmias, myocardial decompensation, electrolyte disturbance, and haematemesis
- other forms of self-destructive or suicidal behaviour, which parents feel unable to manage
- signs of another mental health problem requiring inpatient treatment, such as severe depression
- the need for a more comprehensive assessment
- poor or no progress during outpatient treatment.

## THE INPATIENT SETTING

There is probably no inpatient setting that ideally suits the treatment of eating disorders in children and adolescents, although obviously some are more suitable than others. It almost goes without saying that the specific needs of young people require admission to paediatric, as opposed to adult services. If admission to adult services occurs, perhaps because of a lack of bed availability, it is of paramount importance to transfer the young person to a paediatric centre as soon as possible. Depending on the aims of the admission, children and adolescents can be treated in general paediatric wards, child or adolescent psychiatric units taking a mix of patients (some with and some without eating disorders), and units that specialise solely in treating young people with eating disorders. Each will have its own advantages and disadvantages.

Paediatric wards have the advantage of readily available expert medical care. Any medical complications can be swiftly diagnosed and treated, and nursing staff will be skilled at managing artificial feeding, should this be required. However, it will probably be difficult for the nurses in this environment to provide important milieu therapy and they may lack the skills or confidence to engage in psychologically oriented work and with the children and their parents. Unfortunately, although there is much talk about the need for holistic care, paediatric nurse training (at least in the UK) continues to pay only lip service to child mental health issues. However, steps can be taken to overcome some of these obstacles. A consistent group of staff who care solely for children with eating disorders could provide the necessary attention, level of supervision, and consistency that these children require and go some way towards creating a therapeutic environment. Perhaps most importantly, there must be consultation and collaboration with child mental health colleagues, in order to enable a comprehensive understanding of these disorders and provide holistic treatment. Professionals skilled in parental counselling, family therapy, group work, and individual psychotherapy must form part of the team working with these young people and their families. Space is often a problem in the paediatric setting and, if young people with eating disorders are to be routinely admitted, it would seem sensible to redesign part of the ward for this purpose. A room for individual work, meeting families, and space for group activities are all important.

Admission to a paediatric as opposed to a psychiatric ward may be less distressing to the young person and her family because of the stigma associated with mental illness. Parents may also feel understandably concerned that, on a psychiatric unit, their child might adopt the disturbed behaviour of others. In addition, families who deny any psychological difficulties may be more willing to accept admission to a paediatric ward and gradually agree to participate in psychological treatments.

Those young people with more severe or persistent eating disorders, who have additional mental health problems and/or demonstrate more extreme challenging behaviour probably do require the milieu of a psychiatric unit. An increasing number of units specialise in eating disorders, but young people may also be admitted to mixed child and adolescent units. An advantage of admission to mixed psychiatric units, is that the young people with eating disorders can socialise with those who are not obsessively concerned with their body image and weight. In addition, peer pressure at mealtimes is likely to be greater and can be more helpful.

The main problem which mixed psychiatric units present relates to the level of supervision that these young people require. On the one hand, nursing staff on units that have a preponderance of behavioural disturbance will find it extremely difficult to provide a high level of attention. On the other hand, where high levels of attention are provided, those without an eating disorder may feel neglected and angry; this anger then being focused on the youngsters with eating disorders (Garfinkel, Garner, & Kennedy, 1985). Those with eating disorders will undoubtedly already suffer from a low self-esteem and, if criticised by others, their recovery from ill-health is likely to be impeded. The young people with eating disorders may go on to form strong, but unhelpful alliances, whereby everyone else becomes excluded, including clinicians and parents. It is important that nursing staff sensitively address such issues in order that they do not impinge on the effective treatment of all the young people.

Units that specialise in treating children and adolescents with eating disorders have the advantage of skilled staff who have the experience and training to manage the physical and psychological care of these young people and their families. The young people can receive the level of supervision that they require and generally have the benefit of peer support and understanding. Nevertheless, since each individual will be at a different stage in recovery there may also be feelings of neglect and anger similar to those described on mixed units. Garfinkel et al. (1985) have pointed out that one of difficulties that these units will experience is the competition that may arise between individuals to be the "most ill" and in need of most attention. Again, staff must openly and sensitively address such issues in group meetings and ensure that healthy behaviour is reinforced.

Whatever the type of inpatient setting, the approach to treatment should be one that recognises the multifactorial aetiology of eating disorders and essentially incorporates sensitivity, firmness, and consistency. Most young people with eating disorders will be in a state of denial and go to great lengths to avoid weight gain. Clinicians need to show the child understanding, while also demonstrating their determination to fight the eating disorder. Parents and clinicians must work together and be consistent in their approach.

## A MULTIDISCIPLINARY APPROACH

There is universal acceptance of the need for a multidisciplinary approach to the treatment of eating disorders in childhood and adolescence, for as our understanding of eating disorders develops, a more complex and multiple-layered picture emerges. Consequently the ideal model for the treatment of eating disorders in children and adolescents will be one which intervenes at a variety of levels in the child's life. This approach can be likened to the creation of a painting, where layer upon layer of acrylic can be applied with different tools/brushes in order to create depth as well as breadth. Perhaps the most crucial component of such an endeavour is the attention that is paid to the interaction of these layers. The inpatient component of treating eating disorders can similarly be seen within this model—one layer amongst many, needing blending with the other layers, and not to be thought of as a finished "work of art" in itself.

Anybody involved in the treatment of patients with eating disorders will be familiar with the following descriptions; "the manipulative patient", "the patient that *splits* the staff team". We can accept or reject these descriptions, or we can reflect on the processes that recur in the interactions between patients suffering from eating disorders and the staff treating them—it is these repetitive processes that lead to the creation of such descriptions and that call for our understanding. As Garfinkel et al. (1985) have suggested, these "countertransference issues" are ones that a well-functioning inpatient team are ideally suited to address. In this section we consider the structures required in order to create a well-functioning team so that the maximum benefit can be derived from any inpatient admission.

As mentioned earlier, we recognise that many children and adolescents will be treated in settings that are not ideal and that do not have the resources of some specialist eating disorders services. However, in describing structures that we have found to be useful in our setting we hope to highlight some general principles that could be useful elsewhere.

## ORGANISATIONAL STRUCTURES THAT ENHANCE GOOD COMMUNICATION

The need for good communication between those involved with a patient is so fundamental that it can, paradoxically, be overlooked. Inpatients become involved in a complex system that includes:

- the parents/family
- the nursing team
- the non-nursing team, comprising of other clinicians who contribute to treatment (e.g. psychotherapist and psychiatrist)
- the referral network—those clinicians involved at an earlier stage who have referred on, but who may well be involved in the longer-term treatment plan. Further discussion of their role will take place later.

Creating channels for communication between these people is a prerequisite to good practice. According to Vandereycken (1985, p. 418), "the cohesion of the therapeutic team is the cornerstone of an efficient inpatient treatment programme". A number of possibilities can be suggested here, but each setting is a unique context and readers will need to consider what is applicable to them and what alternatives are practical in their circumstances.

### The weekly multidisciplinary discussion— "ward-round"

On a weekly basis the *internal* multidisciplinary team should meet to discuss every patient. We have found that a highly structured format works best for these meetings, as their primary function is to establish treatment goals for the following week. On average, approximately 15 minutes discussing each patient should be sufficient.

Focused chairing of the meeting is necessary to ensure that all relevant information is covered and that discussion of one patient does not monopolise the time available. Such a monopoly of team discussion usually reflects the extent of the team's anxiety about a patient.

Karen was a 13-year-old child with a five-year history of anorexia nervosa, who evoked strong and conflicting feelings amongst staff. After several weeks it was observed that team discussions about her would often overrun. A decision was reached that she should be discussed last in the ward-round. This had the effect of ensuring that all patients received an equal share of staff attention and to some extent alleviated the team's unproductive belief that if only they talked for long enough they would come up with the *correct* solution.

The format should include the opportunity for feedback from all the key professionals so that the following information is gathered:

- review of the previous week's recommendations and decisions
- update of the patient's physical state (weight, results of any medical investigations, observations/alleviation of any symptoms)
- observation of the patient's relationships with peers, staff, and family
- patient's capacity to function in an educational setting
- parent's interaction with staff and child
- feedback from the patient's therapist and/or key worker regarding the patient's perceptions
- clarification of key dates/meetings in the week ahead.

Gathering so much information in such a short time requires that staff learn how to summarise and present concisely. Although it is clearly not helpful for staff to feel that their view has not been heard, it is equally unhelpful for too much detail to be reported. It may therefore be worthwhile for individual staff members to undertake some planning before the meeting in order to be con-fident that the main points are covered. Information should be available even from those who cannot attend; brief written summaries are better than silence or third-hand reporting. Once all feedback is taken, a period of discussion ensues. This is the part of the process where a variety of perceptions comes into being, where the different theoretical frameworks held by the different disciplines are subsumed within a broader and—as in the painting analogy described earlier—a deeper description. Ultimately from these discussions arise a number of action points.

In addition to the enhancement of good communication the ward-round has another function. It is an ideal setting for identifying *exceptions* to the problem, recognising the patient's areas of strength, and moving treatment forward into a "virtuous cycle" as described by White (1984, p. 115). The underlying theory of this approach is that patients/clients are seen by mental health clinicians at a time when their situation is described only in problem-language. A "vicious cycle" has become entrenched and taken over the context—rather like a baby cuckoo in another bird's nest. Because of this, attention is drawn, like a magnet, to the problem behaviour. A virtuous cycle is commenced when exceptions to the problems begin to be identified, for once they are observed they can be amplified, built upon, and encouraged. In the inpatient setting so much more information is available than in an outpatient context, that it is not usually hard to locate an exception, provided that the team is on the look-out.

> Susan, a 10-year old girl, had a nine-month history of pervasive refusal syndrome, which had required in-patient treatment on a paediatric ward. She was very withdrawn, non-communicative (eyes closed and not talking for several months), and was fed by naso-gastric tube as she refused to take food by mouth. While watching a creative dance class she was observed to be tapping in time to the rhythm of the piano music, which was being played on the other side of the room. The pianist, aware of Susan's interest, gradually involved her in the making of the music despite the fact that she refused to participate in the dance lesson. Feedback into the ward-round resulted in a number of suggestions aimed at amplifying this positive development. Outside of the lesson the other children were encouraged to involve Susan more and more in their spare-time activities of listening to tapes and collecting pictures of pop idols. Susan became an accepted and central member of the peer group and her mood improved dramatically— as eventually did her eating.

One final point concerning the time allocated for ward-round: It should be sacrosanct. Even if there is no time for any other of the structures that ensure a good flow of communication, the opportunity offered by the coming together of all team members should not be undermined. For the treatment of early onset eating disorders, where strongly held feelings are evoked and where different views are an inevitable consequence of the illness, it is an essential forum.

## The "mini-team" system

We have found this to be a useful model as it can compliment the ward-round described earlier. The mini-team in our setting consists of all the key members within the inpatient team who are involved with the patient and family. Usually this means: a key nurse/care worker, the child's therapist, and the member of the team who is working directly with the parents/family (this person usually acts as the case-manager, taking responsibility for guiding treatment and liaising with others including outside agencies). The mini-team meets for approximately half an hour each week (it is helpful to include older patients in these meetings; the decision as to what age is appropriate should be left to the clinical judgement of the team, as specified ages are not necessarily helpful). This forum can therefore provide a slightly more reflective context than the ward-round. The focus is to ensure that ward-round recommendations are carried out and to decide which points need to be highlighted in the next ward-round for fuller discussion. This is particularly useful when there are differences that cannot be resolved within the mini-team.

Mini-teams are clearly time-consuming and rely on the team having sufficient members of staff to make the division of roles meaningful. It is also a system that works best when most staff members work full time. It can be very difficult trying to organise regular mini-team meetings for all patients when nursing staff work a shift system and non-nursing staff are only available a few sessions per week. However, it is a system that we recommend for patients with particularly severe eating disorders where previous treatment has been unsuccessful.

Another potential advantage of the mini-team system is that it can be a useful forum for the joint planning of treatment with the patient. The patient must be included in the process of decision making even if the decisions reached are not ones with which they would happily concur. Similarly, it is a much more reasonable environment in which a young person can begin to practise newly acquired skills of assertion than would be the option of attendance at a ward-round. If one of the underlying issues for those with anorexia nervosa is a sense of having little control over their destiny and of being marginalised, then structures that support inclusion and amplification of the individual's voice are of themselves likely to be therapeutic (Sesan, 1994).

## Review meetings with parents

As well as counselling parents, it is crucial to involve them in all aspects of their child's treatment. There are many ways in which we attempt to achieve this (see later for details). One important way is to ensure that a review meeting takes place on a regular basis (every 4–6 weeks) where the key staff members, plus the consultant psychiatrist and the parents meet to evaluate progress, and review aims and objectives. Again this can provide a model of treatment which is more collaborative than prescriptive—but only if the team is genuinely open to feedback and the possibility of relinquishing some of its "expertise".

## WORKING WITH FAMILIES OUTSIDE OF FAMILY THERAPY

Family therapy is one component of treatment, but it should not necessarily be seen as sufficient family involvement to promote recovery. Working with families outside of family therapy sessions should be fundamental to any approach, but it is most crucial in the treatment offered on inpatient settings. Essentially it is an approach that requires staff never to forget that the parents are responsible for their child whether or not they are living under the same roof. Accordingly, it is crucial that parents are consulted regularly and in particular when staff are faced with decisions that put them in conflict with the child, if the child is an inpatient. This way of working is built on the belief that for the successful treatment of eating disorders in childhood and adolescence the cornerstone of any programme should be the inclusion and empowerment of parents. This will mean that throughout the process those involved in treatment should maintain the perspective that parents need to be informed, consulted, and encouraged to reach decisions that are in the interests of their child. Of course there may be plenty of work required in order to help the child express their dissatisfaction with their parents and support for the parents in finding new ways to approach old family problems. However, as Le Grange, Eisler, Dare, and Hodes (1992, p. 190) found, the critical factors in successful family interventions appear to be "lowering blame and enhancing family problem solving".

An example of parental involvement in day-to-day decisions on an out-patient basis would be whether or not their child should continue to attend school. Certainly parents require some guidance regarding medical state and for this reason all information should be shared with the patient and their parents. However, as there is rarely a definite answer to these medical judgements it can be useful to share these decisions and to encourage a sense of agency on the part of the parents. An example of partnership when the child is an inpatient would be to consult with parents if their child is refusing to participate in parts of a ward programme once they have been admitted, rather than staff battling directly with the young person.

At times like these, telephone liaison between staff and parents can be crucial. This will help the parents to feel a continual sense of involvement and may overcome the inevitable splits from developing. In this way the telephone can become an essential part of a developing, dynamic relationship and not just a tool for imparting information following the weekly ward-round.

Practising meals within the supportive context of a ward environment can be another useful way of involving the families of inpatients. Careful planning and negotiation should take place between staff, child, and parents to establish the most useful context for these meals (e.g. who should be present, who will serve, how the mealtime will be structured). The nursing task is to facilitate the process, helping the family to reach compromises and allowing them the opportunity of reflecting on the event afterwards, paying close attention to what was and was not successful.

Early integration back into family life is another area where a family approach extends way beyond the confines of the family therapy consulting room. Contact with families should never be used as an incentive/reward, as is the case with some adult treatment programmes. Unless there are clear child protection concerns, regular contact should be encouraged, with a view to the young person returning home at weekends as soon as possible. Weight restoration is not necessarily the primary criterion here. Rather, consideration should be given to the young person's ability to eat with her parents. It is for this reason that family meals should take place on the ward early in the admission. Once a degree of confidence between parents and daughter has been established in this area, a gradual reintegration can be attempted.

Sibling relationships also require attention and can be considered in discussion with the patient and their family. Finding opportunities for maintaining these relationships, or for working through any difficulties, can be part of a general discussion held early in an admission. This discussion should address how a treatment programme can best meet the needs of the particular family and all of the family's members. Occasionally, meeting the siblings to discuss the impact of the patient's illness upon them, and to offer some psychoeducational information can provide one such opportunity. Another involves arranging visits by siblings, when the patient has been admitted.

Different settings are likely to establish their own repertoire for intergrating families into a comprehensive treatment approach. The examples described here are far from a definitive list, but they are an attempt to highlight a way of working that is inclusive of family involvement.

## MILIEU THERAPY

Milieu therapy is the provision of a therapeutic environment in a clinical setting, which aims to build on an individual child's strengths and encourages the child to examine her own behaviour, recognise and name distressing feelings, and find alternative ways of expressing these (Crouch, 1998). Milieu therapy is an essential component of inpatient treatment for eating disorders. Specific areas that must be addressed within the therapeutic milieu include:

- *fear of losing control*—Other areas of the young person's life may seem out of her control, but weight control is within her grasp and gives her a clearer sense of self.
- *low self-esteem*—The young person is likely to believe that her self-worth is directly related to her ability to remain thin.
- *striving for achievement*—Young people with anorexia nervosa tend to set themselves high goals and are constantly striving to achieve them.
- *competition with others*—Young people with anorexia nervosa are likely to compete to be the thinnest and to demonstrate the most self-control.
- *denial*—A denial of illness is common and an important defence mechanism.
- *categorising significant others as "good" or "bad"*—The young person is likely to see each parent and individual staff member as "good" or "bad" and nothing in between. This behaviour seems to be an attempt to make sense of the incongruous positive and negative feelings that she experiences.

The young person's need to control her weight must be relinquished, and often children and adolescents experience some relief when parents and staff take over what has become an addictive control of weight.

Mark, 14, was admitted to an inpatient unit in a severe state of malnutrition, with pressure sores on his ankles and the initial signs of gangrene. In a family therapy session some way into treatment, Mark, angry and in tears, looked at his parents and shouted: "Why didn't you notice and do something about it?" His parents had of course noticed him leaving food and losing weight, but had decided that it was in Mark's best interest for them to play the situation down. At one family mealtime when they had openly addressed the issue, Mark had angrily left the table and eaten nothing.

In the initial stages of treatment it is essential that adults take charge of food and fluid intake. Dehydration and electrolyte imbalance obviously need to be treated immediately to preserve life. Regaining a healthy weight is not only important to promote physical health and development, but may also lift depressive symptoms, making the child or adolescent more accessible to psychological treatments. The young person is likely to mistrust the motives of her parents and staff and believe that she will be made fat. Adults must acknowledge these fears and attempt to reassure the young person to the contrary.

Establishing a target weight is a somewhat arbitrary exercise as the optimal weight for health will differ between individuals. However, it is helpful to have a goal in mind even if this must be regularly re-evaluated to allow for these differences and growth of the young person. A target weight range should be based on information derived from paediatric growth charts, body mass index, and cultural factors. It must be explained to the child at the outset that as she grows the target will have to increase (this may help to prevent a sticking point later in treatment). A weekly goal for weight increase of between 750g and 1kg perhaps provides a more tangible goal for the young person, her parents, and professionals.

If a young person is dangerously malnourished or dehydrated and refusing to eat or drink, it will be necessary to feed her artificially, ususally via a nasogastric tube. When children refuse to be fed, careful consideration must be given to the ethical and legal problems presented and indeed the team may need to seek the judgement of a court. Sometimes, the fact that clinicians and parents are working together to care for the child seems to help eating to recommence and court proceedings can be avoided. The weight chart in Fig. 13.1 is from a case seen by the authors which demonstrates this phenomenon. The sharp incline in the child's weight correlates with the parent's eventual agreement to seek court approval to enforce naso-gastric feeding. Court approval was never actually required.

The young person with an eating disorder such as anorexia nervosa or bulimia nervosa may exercise excessively in the hope of reducing weight gain, curbing appetite, and in order to avoid thinking about difficult or painful issues unrelated to food. Excessive exercise can exacerbate the physical complications of eating disorders, such as cardiovascular problems, and may also lead to injuries. Therefore, it is important to restrict exercise in the early stages of treatment, but as

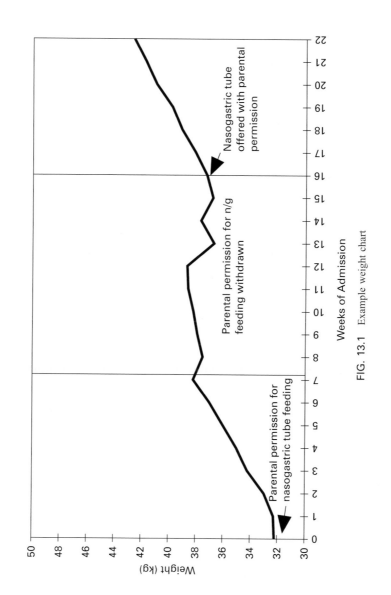

FIG. 13.1  Example weight chart

the young person progresses a moderate amount of "healthy" activity should be encouraged. Total restriction is unhealthy and unlikely to be successful, unless the young person is seriously malnourished. Exercise goals can be indicated on the weight chart so that the child or adolescent is fully informed and aware of what she is trying to achieve. As the young person gains weight she can be allowed to participate in more active pursuits. Again, young people talk about feeling safe when adults take control of areas that have become out of their own control.

Those young people with bulimia nervosa will need help to control bingeing. Restricted or supervised access to the kitchen will be important as well as supervision outside the unit, when the young person may visit the local grocers shop or hospital cafeteria (Cahill, 1994). Those with anorexia nervosa will also need limits set around food preparation or at least close supervision, as they will undoubtedly ration the use of butter or margarine, skimp on the size of servings, and so on. Children are likely to make staff feel as if they are being unjustly authoritarian. However, it is important to remember that taking control as far as weight is concerned is an essential part of treatment and caring for these children.

Vomiting repeatedly will not only reduce weight gain, but can also result in complications such as electrolyte imbalance (in particular hypokalaemia), ulceration of the oesophagus, and dental decay. In the initial stages of treatment, young people with anorexia nervosa or bulimia nervosa must be supervised immediately after a meal and at all times supervised in the bathroom. Nursing staff can stand outside the toilet door and flush the pan after use. It is helpful to distract the child after a meal thus allaying their anxiety about not being allowed to vomit. Laxative abuse, although not likely to affect weight gain, can possibly lead to an electrolyte disturbance and, in the longer term, to a dependence on medication to prevent constipation. Young people with eating disorders are likely to suffer constipation due to their poor diet and, if depression is evident, this will exacerbate the problem. Constipation is best treated with diet alone, but laxatives may need to be prescribed if it proves intractible. Children and adolescents with eating disorders must not be allowed to keep their own laxatives or go shopping alone, when they may buy medication over the counter. Nurses will need to check through the young person's belongings with her to remove any laxatives after any unsupervised outings. Gaining weight is so frightening for these children, that they will go to great lengths to prevent it. Talking openly about the problem, without reprimand, is important.

Since the young person is losing control of her weight, she is likely to challenge staff. This may take the form of disputing that a particular nurse is following the correct treatment plan (for example, insisting that another staff member had allowed her to exchange one food type for another), or more active behaviour, such as throwing food or hitting out at staff. Staff must take a consistent and firm, but sensitive, approach. There must be clear limits to behaviour, while staff continue to demonstrate their understanding of the child's predicament. It should also be possible to think of areas where the young person can have some control, perhaps being able to decorate her bedroom in her own style, being allowed some privacy, having some choice in how she spends her free time, and so on.

Young people with anorexia nervosa and bulimia nervosa base their self-evaluation on the thinness of their body rather than on their abilities or positive features in their personality. Creating an environment that values each child individually and focuses on individual strengths is essential. Positive reinforcement must take precedence over sanctioning inappropriate behaviour. It is usually possible to identify a skill that each young person possesses, which can be nurtured and developed further. The need of these young people to constantly strive for high achievement can have a devasting effect on self-esteem and must also be addressed. Nursing staff can model the acceptance of their own imperfections and will need to constantly remind these young people that it is alright to be only moderately good at something and find other things difficult.

Some young people may have such self-loathing that they attempt to harm themselves in ways other than starving, such as cutting themselves or taking an overdose of drugs. The management of self-harming behaviour will vary according to the age and state of mind of the child or adolescent. The ultimate aim will be for the young person to take responsibility for this behaviour, learning to recognise the feelings that precede self-harm and to seek help. During this learning process nursing staff must ensure that the physical environment is as safe as possible and that the child or adolescent has an appropriate level of supervision at all times. Initially physical restraint may be necessary to prevent self-harm and it may be considered appropriate to prevent the adolescent from leaving the unit alone (Sharman, 1997).

A proportion of young people with eating disorders will have been sexually abused (Palmer, Oppenheimer, Dignon, Chaloner, & Howells, 1990) and are likely to self-harm. These children and adolescents may also experience flashbacks. Nursing staff, together with the young person, may be able to identify particular sensations or events that trigger these flashbacks and so take action to avoid them until she is ready to confront such issues. The young person may also be taught coping mechanisms to reduce the anxiety aroused by the flashbacks. One way of achieving this is for her to take control of the flashback, using imagery, rather than the other way around. If, for example, the young person sees a scary figure during her flashback, with the help of a nurse, she could "push it out of the room and lock the door".

Competitiveness between children to be the thinnest and/or most ill, and therefore most needing attention, must be addressed openly and sensitively within the group. It should be acknowledged that all the young people need special help at this moment in their lives, although it may differ in the form that it takes. However, in addition, nurses need to ensure that they give time to those children who are further along the road to recovery and may be unwittingly neglected. Sometimes staff may have to resort to separating certain children if their competitiveness starts to seriously undermine their treatment and recovery. Although complete separation is impossible in the ward environment, ensuring that there are plenty of times in the day when each child mixes with other children should be feasible.

Denial must also be addressed and talked about openly. Staff can explain that they realise the young person does not believe she has a problem, which is bound to make it difficult for her to trust her parents and staff, who believe otherwise. However, staff can reiterate their experience of working with children with similar problems and their concern for the young person.

Parents and staff are likely to be categorised as either wholly "good" or "bad" by the young person. Good and bad feelings within the child tend to be projected onto separate individuals. The young person must gradually learn to accept that there is usually "good" and "bad" in everyone and find a way of coping with her own incongruous and confusing feelings. Parents may make mistakes but this does not mean that they are all bad or that they do not love their child. One of the most difficult positions to be placed in when caring for these young people is that of the hated person. However, usually it is the staff member with whom the child feels safest, that finds her or himself in this position. This nurse can help the child to learn that it is alright to express negative and aggressive feelings; the nurse will not stop caring for her.

> Fiona, 12, had anorexia nervosa. The unit that she was admitted to allocated two members of nursing staff to work closely with each child; the "key worker" taking primary responsibility for nursng care and the "shadow worker" providing support. Fiona experienced a feeling of extreme hatred towards her key worker, while believing that her shadow worker could do no wrong and was full of kindness and caring. Fiona had similar feelings in relation to her parents; seeing her mother as all good and father as all bad. Her parents had separated and each had new partners. Fiona lived with her mother and her brother lived with their father. Her father was unable to tolerate Fiona's hatred and anger and had withdrawn from having much contact. In contrast, her key worker was able to persist in demonstrating to Fiona that she could cope with this bombardment of strong, negative feelings and would not stop trying to help her. Towards the time of her discharge Fiona started to demonstrate her own affection and respect for her key worker and chose to continue outpatient work with this member of staff.

## MEALTIME MANAGEMENT

At mealtimes it is important to find a balance between being firm and consistent, but at the same time demonstrating empathy and flexibility. It is so easy to end up in a battle of wills, where someone must win and the other lose, or to find ourselves being punitive towards the young person. These children already have a low self-esteem and may at some level believe that they deserve to be punished. This belief must not be reinforced.

An individual diet sheet enables there to be a common goal at each mealtime, ensures that this represents an appropriate calorie value, and gives staff a baseline to compare daily intake. The calorie content should be decided along

TABLE 13.1

An example of a diet sheet to produce weight gain in a 12-year-old girl, weight 34kg, height 150cm, <85% weight for height

| | *kcal* |
|---|---|
| On waking: | |
| A glass of "Entera" (a fortified milk drink)* | 300 |
| Breakfast: | |
| 2 weetabix with milk (full fat) | 220 |
| A glass of fresh orange juice | 40 |
| Mid-morning: | |
| A glass of "fortijuice" (a fortified fruit drink) | 250 |
| A digestive biscuit | 80 |
| Lunch: | |
| A portion of meat, such as two chicken drumsticks, or vegetarian alternative | 350 |
| A portion of potato, rice, or pasta (4tbsp) | 200 |
| A portion of vegetable (3tbsp) | 50 |
| A dessert (if a piece of fruit is chosen, it must be supplemented with a biscuit) | 100 |
| A glass of water | |
| Mid-afternoon: | |
| A glass of "fortijuice" | 250 |
| A slice of toast, butter, and Marmite | 180 |
| Supper: | |
| A sandwich (1 round) | 350 |
| A yogurt | 100 |
| A piece of fruit | 40 |
| A glass of water | |
| Bedtime: | |
| A glass of "Entera" | 300 |
| Approx total: | 2800 |

* Fortified drinks do enable the young person to consume sufficient calories without having to struggle with enormous quantities of food in the early stages of treatment. As the young person progresses, the calorific value of meals will be reduced and these drinks can gradually be omitted from the diet or substituted for normal drinks. One disadvantage of using fortified drinks is that the young person may come to rely on them, rather than eating solid food, and after recovery may be tempted to slip back into taking fluid meals, designed for slimming.

with a dietician, but is likely to start at around 1500kcal, slowly building up to 2–3000kcal. Refeeding a starving individual too rapidly may lead to medical complications (see Chapter 8). An early sensation of satiety, feeling slightly bloated or even nauseous after meals is not unusual and has been associated with delayed gastric emptying (see Chapter 8; Ravelli, Helps, Devane, Lask, & Milla, 1993). To minimise this problem, the daily intake can be divided into moderate size meals and snacks (see Table 13.1). Yellowlees, Roe, Walker, and Ben-tovim (1988) found that patients with anorexia nervosa perceived portion size to be larger than it actually was and so small frequent meals may also reduce the young person's anxiety at mealtimes. The child should be involved in drawing up the diet plan and allowed some choice in food types. It is not advisable to discuss calories, but to talk in terms of a healthy diet. A diet sheet that indicates portion size rather than energy values can be given to the young person.

It is important to acknowledge that the child will find mealtimes difficult, and give reassurance that the staff will do all they can to make them easier. Initially, the young person may find it easier to eat separately from the other children with just one member of staff.

> Fiona would only take fluids on admission to the unit and this was extremely difficult for her. At home, when Fiona felt that she could drink no more, she would throw her unfinished glass across the room in desparation. Her key nurse explained that she would have to drink all her milk and so together they would have to find a way of achieving this goal. After discussion it was decided that Fiona would drink away from the other children with a nurse present. She was allowed to throw the plastic glass across the room after she had finished the milk. It was not long before Fiona was able to give up throwing the glass.

At mealtimes the child is likely to get upset and angry, possibly running away from the table. It is important to be firm but kind and perhaps think of a compromise that can be made. Perhaps at this point the child would prefer to sit elsewhere, one food type could be exchanged for another, or the goal for this mealtime be amended. This firm, but flexible approach demonstrates that staff care about the child (as they are not prepared to abandon the meal completely), but do not wish to get into battles or be punitive. Compromise can also provide a valuable face saver for the young person. Goals for mealtimes are negotiated with the child, which may be anything from touching their lips with food, to eating three-quarters of the meal. Limit setting must also include closely observing the young person during the meal and immediately after, in case food is hidden and then disposed of after the meal. The young person may hide food in her clothes, stick food under the table or simply spread it over the plate to appear less.

The exact sort of encouragement and conversation that each child will find helpful at mealtimes is likely to be specific to the individual. An eating disorder can be thought of as taking over part of the individual, so that part of the young person wants to maintain strict control of her eating, while another part, albeit small, wants to eat healthily and return to a more normal home and school life. Some children find this idea helpful and so can be encouraged at mealtimes to fight against the side of them with an eating disorder and give strength to their healthy side. In individual work the child can develop images for these two parts of themselves, which can then be used at the table.

Some children talk about a "voice in their head" that tells them not to eat. Helping to mobilise a young person's imagination may give her the strength to the fight against this voice. Some perceive the voice as coming from a "monster", which could be symbolically shut in a box during mealtimes.

Other young people with eating difficulties may respond to more straightforward verbal encouragement, prefer to talk about other things entirely, or may need the presence of an adult, but with little conversation. Peers can be extremely supportive to the young person and a certain degree of peer pressure to finish a meal so that an activity can begin may be helpful. However, care should be taken to ensure that this does not become punitive and/or prevent other children from joining in activities.

Staff must recognise how they are feeling during the meal. It can be helpful to communicate this to the child, so demonstrating an attempt to empathise with the young person. For example, "I'm sitting here feeling really stuck—I wonder if that is how you are feeling?"

Clinicians and parents must work together at mealtimes and any disagreement regarding food intake or mealtime approach should not be dealt with away from the table. The inability of adults to work together is likely to make it more difficult for the young person to eat and/or easier to avoid eating, and leave the young person feeling unsafe and uncared for.

As mentioned previously, some young people may need a period of artificial feeding, usually via a naso-gastric tube. It is helpful for these children to sit at the table with others, so that they can be a part of this social event and have the opportunity to start eating when they are ready. Bolus feeds of fortified milk, as opposed to continuous naso-gastric feeding, should ideally be administered after the meal to encourage eating at the table. Bolus feeding has the advantage of mimicking a normal pattern of eating, so that normal appetite patterns are encouraged. The use and value of naso-gastric feeding must be reviewed regularly, preferably daily, and as food intake increases the volume of the feeds should be correspondingly lowered. In extreme circumstances, where the child is not eating or drinking at all, naso-gastric feeding may be required overnight so that the child can be fully included in the ward programme during the day and will have more opportunity of benefiting from the milieu.

Mealtime management must be tailored to the specific needs of the individual child or adolescent. Each young person will find a different approach helpful as there is no "right approach". Nursing staff must continually evaluate mealtime management and regularly discuss and review their approach in the appropriate multidisciplinary forum.

## INDIVIDUAL WORK

It is important that each child or adolescent has one or two designated nurses with whom she can meet regularly. Nursing staff can play a key role in providing special individual time (which the authors refer to as "individual work") for young people with eating disorders. The nature of this work is based on normal/healthy parent–child communication, although may contain elements of cognitive and psychodynamic therapies (see Chapters 11 and 12). It must compliment other areas of treatment and clear communication amongst the multidisciplinary team is therefore essential.

Individual work may simply take the form of discussion; the young person or nurse bringing areas of concern or success to the meetings. It is an opportunity for the child to ask questions and vent feelings; both positive and negative. By allowing the young person this space, the nurse is conveying the message that it is OK to talk about feelings and indeed, more healthy than losing weight. Nursing staff can use their own clinical supervision to discuss the feelings that are aroused in themselves during the individual sessions. These feelings can give important clues as to how the child is feeling and can be usefully discussed in team meetings, and later communicated to the child to convey a sincere attempt to understand her.

The idea of an unhealthy and healthy part of the child, which was mentioned earlier, can be used visually in individual sessions. The young person could draw each part in whatever shape or form and then write down what each has to offer. Alternatively, balancing scales could be used to represent each part of the child and counters or weights to represent the advantages of each.

Individual sessions may also concentrate on specific topics, such as enhancing a healthy body-image, working on self-esteem, talking about issues related to growing up, and health education concerning diet and exercise.

## Exercises for enhancing body image

Using some ideas from a self-directed programme of body-image therapy for adults (Cash, 1991), these might include the following.

• Help the young person to identify when she feels most fat. Keeping a diary may enable her to establish particular activities, such as swimming, and thoughts, which increase her awareness of her body shape. In individual sessions the nurse and child can discuss the young person's interpretation of events. The nurse will be able to offer alternative ways of understanding events and so challenge the child's beliefs. For example, the young person may have noticed people staring at her at the swimming baths and assumed that they were thinking how fat she was. One alternative suggestion might be that they were staring because she had walked to the water's edge with a towel wrapped around her legs.

• Ask the young person to write a list of the parts of her body she dislikes and give each a rating of 1–10, where 1 represents a mild dislike and 10, total disgust. Alternatively, draw around the youngster on a large piece of paper and ask her to colour in the parts she dislikes. The young person creates a key to indicate her strength of feeling. Teach the child some relaxation techniques, which can then be used in desensitisation work, to reduce the tension associated with thinking about particular body parts. The child starts to relax and then thinks about the stressor for 15 seconds, followed by further concentration on relaxing. The time spent imagining the stressor is slowly increased to 1 minute. Desensitisation might also be used to reduce the anxiety associated with particularly stressful events, for example, swimming.

- The young person could also be asked to list the parts of her body she does like. There is a tendency to focus on the "hated" parts at the expense of the "liked". Look at the coloured body outline and compare the area of "liked" (not coloured) with the "hated" (coloured) parts. Although the "liked" parts may only cover a small area, such as the eyes, they may have great significance. The nurse could comment on the fact that we look at a person's eyes when we talk to them.

- Encourage the young person to use corrective thinking when she is exposed to triggers that spark negative and distorted thoughts, e.g. the child or adolescent might look at a magazine, see particularly thin models and think to herself, "why can't I look like that?". Corrective thinking would involve saying a word, such as "STOP", to herself, as soon as this negative and unrealistic thought came into her head. The young person must then come up with her own counterargument, e.g. "I don't need to look like a supermodel to be attractive". Corrective thinking work could be recorded in a diary, discussed in individual work, and rewards given for positive thoughts.

- Ask the young person to think of someone who is not thin that she admires. Explore what it is about them that she likes.

## Exercises to improve self-esteem

These might include the following.

- With the help of a nurse, the young person writes a diary at the end of the day, which identifies her achievements.

- Together with her parents and key nurse, the young person creates a "life book". This is a record of the child's life in the form of writing, pictures, documents, memorabilia, and so on, and aims to give the young person a sense of who she is. Life books are particularly useful for children who do not live with their birth families. They not only facilitate discussion about the past and present, but can also be used to help the young person think about her future and how to move forwards (Ryan & Walker, 1985).

- The young person draws a map to represent her life to date. The road, river, or railway starts in one corner of the picture and ends in another. Different buildings, trees, and so on, represent different people or events. The principle behind this exercise is similar to that of a life book, i.e. to promote a positive sense of self.

- With the help of her key nurse and/or a peer, the young person writes an advertisement for herself that highlights her strengths. This could be kept in a special file for self-esteem work.

- With the help of her key nurse, the young person writes a short questionnaire to find out what others think of her. One question might be: "What do you think my strengths are?" Together, the child and nurse approach different children, staff, and family members.
- The nurse draws around the child on a life-size piece of paper and together they write in the child's strengths, such as "big brown eyes" on the face, "neat handwriting" on the right hand, and "kind" on the chest. The young person can then stick the final work on her bedroom wall to act as a reminder of her positive attributes.
- Having discovered a particular skill that the young person has, the nurse could prepare her to teach others. This may take place on a one-to-one basis with the additional support of the nurse, or if the young person feels confident enough, group teaching could be arranged. Skills might include calligraphy, make-up, plaiting hair, and so on (Sharman, 1997).

## "Growing-up work"

Covering issues related to growing up should involve parents of the same sex if possible. "Growing-up work" would include areas such as independence and autonomy, as well as sex and sexuality. Sexuality includes gender identity, that is our self-awareness and expression of being male or female, and gender role, the behaviour that reflects our gender identity.

Before starting sessions with the child, the nurse must first meet with the parent who is to be involved, to prepare and plan the work. Having a discussion with parents about their thoughts and values is an important starting point for growing-up work. It enables the parents to help clarify their own views and wishes for their children, and, of particular importance, communicates these to the nurse. Different attitudes and perspectives are likely to occur within different ethnic and cultural groups and must be respected.

### Exercises for growing-up work

Possible exercises include the following.

- Issues of contention between the parent and young person, such as the time she should be home in the evening, could be discussed and resolutions made. A contract could even be drawn up between the young person and her parents. Areas of individual work such as these can be taken into family meetings for consolidation.
- Research into sex education suggests that using multiple channels of communication is more effective than using a single mode. The parent and nurse could select a television programme to view with the young person, which highlights particular growing-up issues.

• The parent and young person could choose a book on sex education to read together. Discussion should reflect age-related concerns and address questions and topics that the young person wishes to discuss, rather than what adults think she needs to know. Adults tend to place more importance on the long-term consequences of behaviour, whereas young people are guided by their present emotional state and the short-term consequences of their actions. Adults will concern themselves with abstract issues, whereas the child or adolescent will focus more on concrete realities. For example, parental concern about their teenage daughter not using contraception is likely to go beyond worrying about pregnancy and sexually transmitted diseases. An adult will also understand that pregnancy can limit educational opportunities, career development, and long-term financial independence (Campbell & Campbell, 1990). Parents will of course want to explain their concerns to the young person, but this should not negate the teenagers concerns and questions.

• The parent, nurse, and young person could look at magazines together and talk about the "ideal", but generally unrealistic, images of beauty that are portrayed. Perhaps from this session a "teenage" outing could be planned; the parent taking the young person to have a new hair cut, her ears pierced, to buy some new clothes, and so on.

• The parent could bring a recording of one of her best-liked songs from her teenage years and the adolescent, one of her current favourites. As well as discussing their understanding of the lyrics of each song, the more explicit nature of present-day lyrics could be talked about. This discussion may help to bridge the generational gap, helping the parent and child see each other's perspective on adolescence.

• Similarly, the parent and child could each bring an item to the session that has or had particular significance for them growing up, such as a pair of shoes, a particular book, an item of jewellery, and so on.

## Health education

The nurse can teach the child about healthy eating patterns and the dangers of vomiting and laxative abuse. Helping the young person to identify factors which lead to fasting, bingeing, or vomiting and laxative abuse may enable coping strategies to be found. For example, eating small frequent meals may reduce the craving to binge.

## THE ROLE OF THE EXTENDED PROFESSIONAL NETWORK

Anderson and Goolishian (1988) have described the way in which groups of people (often representatives of statutory agencies) gather together around a problem. They call this the "problem-organising" system, which is a "social-action system that is organised around [talking] about issues that concern and alarm those who comprise the system" (p. 379). This is a situation which is familiar to those working in the eating disorders field, particularly when the patient is a young person. Any effective treatment of a childhood eating disorder may need to consider the involvement of many different professionals all of whom have some significance to the child's life. These are most likely to include:

- school
- family doctor
- school health services
- local mental health services
- children's welfare services, when necessary.

If communication between members of the multidisciplinary team can be difficult to sustain, communication with the "external" network is often even more testing. Ideally the process should begin prior to an admission, with close liaison occurring following assessment. At this point, prior to the commencement of treatment, it is of particular importance to clarify who holds clinical responsibility for the patient prior to an admission, as confusion can inevitably pervade the system when more than one centre is involved.

Although many admissions need to take place as a matter of urgency, leaving perhaps little time for planning, a number can be identified where the central aim of the admission rests upon the successful involvement of outside agencies. When such a case arises, it is best to delay admission until a network meeting has occurred.

Sheila was a 12-year-old girl with a history of failure-to-thrive and poor school attendance. Her family were well known to the local health, education, and social service departments. She had developed a number of features of anorexia nervosa and had recently started to lose weight. At a pre-admission meeting, social services were alerted to the possibility that there were now increased concerns about Sheila (their involvement to date had focused primarily on the needs of Sheila's brother who had learning difficulties). Close liaison throughout the relatively brief admission ensured that social services were kept up to date with progress and were consequently in a position to offer appropriate alternative accommodation to Sheila, outside her family, once a recommendation to this effect was made by the treatment team.

## DISCHARGE PLANNING

It is clear that discharge planning should commence prior to admission. This is particularly the case where the inpatient service is unable to offer any significant outpatient treatment. As mentioned earlier in this chapter, we see an admission as only one part of a continuum of treatment—it is exceptional for patients to be discharged without the need for considerable follow-up work. It must therefore make good sense to involve local services in planning for discharge as early as possible. Such planning will need to clearly address the health and educational needs of the young person, so that community resources can be obtained to meet them.

> Paul was a 13-year-old boy with a scoliosis of the spine, severely restricted lung functioning, asthma, and anorexia nervosa. He was hospitalised for 18 months on medical and psychiatric wards, during which time a statement of his special educational needs was made and a number of network meetings with local professionals and parents were convened. Prior to discharge, his health, education, housing, and social needs were identified and a complex, jointly funded package of support was organised.

As a matter of course, we do involve parents in any network meetings that involve external professionals and would need to have good reason *not* to invite them, rather than the other way round. We believe that the bringing together of the various parts of the network, as described previously, can be one of the most powerful components of an inpatient admission as it can be another step towards creating a solution-focused context for the child and family. This can be achieved by each agency identifying what they can do to promote and to help sustain the child's health in the future. It is most unlikely that this will have taken place prior to an admission, as eating disorders are usually perceived as matters of concern only to health professionals, although the child's school may also have expressed some concern.

The whole thesis of our approach to the treatment of eating disorders in children and young adolescents is that it is a multidetermined treatment that permeates many different domains in a young person's life. Consequently, the involvement of parents and different agencies is required if the possibility of lasting success in treatment is to be maximised. Returning to the painting analogy may clarify our approach still further in this regard. In our view the relationship between the inpatient treatment team and the multidisciplinary group of external professionals is similar to that between a frame-maker and an artist—no matter how beautiful the painting, it is surely incomplete until it is set within a complementary frame.

## SUMMARY POINTS

- Children and adolescents may be treated in a variety of inpatient settings. If possible, the setting should be chosen according to the specific needs of the individual.
- The multifactorial aetiology of eating disorders requires a multidisciplinary approach to treatment.

- Milieu therapy is an essential component of inpatient treatment.
- Management of weight gain, including mealtime management, must be tailored to the individual child or adolescent and reviewed regularly.
- The unique therapeutic relationship that can develop between a young person and her key worker provides an opportunity for valuable individual work.
- An inpatient admission should be set within a context of close liaison with other professionals involved in the young person's life.

## REFERENCES

Anderson, H., & Goolishian, H. (1988). Human systems as linguistic systems: Preliminary and evolving ideas about the implications for clinical theory. *Family Process*, *27*(24), 371–393.

Cahill, C. (1994). Implementing an inpatient eating disorders program. *Perspectives in Psychiatric Care*, *30*(3), 26–30.

Campbell, T.A., & Campbell, D.E. (1990). Considering the adolescent's point of view: A marketing model for sex education. *Journal of Sex Education and Therapy*, *16*(3), 185–193.

Cash, T.F. (1991). *Body-image therapy—a program for self-directed change*. New York: Guilford Publications.

Crouch, W. (1998). The therapeutic milieu and treatment of emotionally disturbed children: Clinical application. *Clinical Child Psychology and Psychiatry*, *3*(1), 115–129.

Garfinkel, P.E., Garner, D.M., & Kennedy, S. (1985). Special problems of inpatient management. In D.M. Garner & P.E. Garfinkel (Eds.), *Handbook of psychotherapy for anorexia nervosa and bulimia* (pp. 344–359). New York: Guilford Press.

le Grange, D., Eisler, I., Dare, C., & Hodes, M. (1992). Family criticism and self-starvation: A stuudy of expressed emotion. *Journal of Family Therapy*, *14*(2), 190.

Palmer, R.L., Oppenheimer, R., Dignon, A., Chaloner, D., & Howells, K. (1990). Childhood sexual experiences with adults reported by women with eating disorders: An extended series. *British Journal of Psychiatry*, *156*, 699–703.

Ravelli, A.M., Helps, B., Devane, S., Lask, B.D., & Milla, P.J. (1993). Normal gastric antral myoelectrical activity in early onset anorexia nervosa. *Archives of Disease in Childhood*, *69*, 342–346.

Ryan, T., & Walker, R. (1985). *Making life story books*. London: British Agencies for Adoption and Fostering.

Sesan, R. (1994). Feminist inpatient treatment for eating disorders: An oxymoron? In P. Fallon, M. Katzman, & S. Wooley (Eds.), *Feminist perspectives on eating disorders* (pp. 251–257). New York: Guilford Press.

Sharman, W. (1997). Sad and self-harming. In *Children and adolescents with mental health problems* (pp. 29–33, 38–39). London: Bailliere Tindall.

Vandereycken, W. (1985). Inpatient treatment of anorexia nervosa: Some research-guided changes. *Journal of Psychiatric Research*, *19*(2/3), 418.

White, M. (1984). Pseudo-encopresis: From avalanche to victory, from vicious to virtuous cycles. *Family Systems Medicine*, *2*(2), 115–124.

Yellowlees, P.M., Roe, M., Walker, M.K., & Ben-tovim, D.I. (1988). Abnormal perception of food size in anorexia nervosa. *British Medical Journal*, *296*, 1689–1690.

CHAPTER FOURTEEN

# Physiotherapy and exercise

**Morag Close**
*Huntercombe Manor Hospital, Taplow, UK*

## INTRODUCTION

Anorexia nervosa, bulimia nervosa, and related eating disorders are complex illnesses involving physical, social, and psychological factors. Indeed, it has been said that in no other disorder is the complicated interplay between biological and psychological as well as sociocultural factors expressed so conspicuously as in the genesis and maintenance of anorexia nervosa (Vandereycken, Depreitre, & Probst, 1987). In an attempt to resolve as many as possible of the problems associated with eating disorders, it is now widely accepted that treatment plans need to involve several different types of therapy. These therapies may include individual psychodynamic psychotherapy, cognitive therapy, and family therapy. However, one therapy that is often ignored is physiotherapy. This chapter has been compiled by a UK physiotherapist based in a psychiatric hospital setting, attached to a specialist eating disorder service for adolescents. It is recognised, however, that the material covered in this chapter will not only be relevant to other physiotherapists, but also to occupational therapists, nurses, and anyone else working with eating disorder patients.

Anorexia nervosa, bulimia nervosa, and related eating disorders are so body-focused, with distorted body-image, fear of fatness, preoccupation with body weight and shape, and often excessive exercising, it is difficult to understand why it has taken so long for physiotherapy to be included in treatment plans. Physiotherapists are accustomed to using an holistic approach to treatment, and include in their range of treatment skills, exercise and movement, relaxation, massage, and breathing exercises. In childhood and early adolescence, eating disorders can pose particular problems for treatment as the child concerned may not have learned to use the language for describing emotions. Indeed, the behaviours of eating disorders can be seen as a manifestation of the difficulty in appropriate expressions of emotion. Yet most of the treatment available within an eating disorder service is verbally based. The non-verbal techniques of physiotherapy can successfully facilitate and reinforce the work being done by other members of the team.

The importance of dealing with the body experience (the thoughts and feelings a person has about being in their own body) and not just the mind has been acknowledged by eating disorder specialists. Vandereyken et al. (1987) wrote about the need to focus explicitly (and not just verbally) upon the body experience of patients with anorexia nervosa. A team in Sydney (Beaumont, Arthur, Russell, & Touyz, 1994) have reported positive results for including an exercise component in the treatment plan for patients with eating disorders, which includes both progressive therapeutic movement and educational elements. Another eating disorder team have recently produced an activity protocol handbook (Thomas, & Markin, 1996/97). It is of note that therapists working independently in different parts of the world have felt it relevant and appropriate to develop essentially similar exercise programmes.

In an inpatient setting, the support from members of the multidisciplinary team and from the other patients plays an important part in making these treatment plans both acceptable and workable. Some of the ideas in this chapter, however, can be successfully adapted for use on an outpatient programme, but will in most cases require the support of the young person's family. Early involvement of a physiotherapist or exercise therapist might help to reduce the need for hospital admission in some individuals as a greater understanding of the actual needs and function of the body can be reached.

Many of the young people on an inpatient unit are admitted because their health has become severely compromised. Although most of the patients have anorexia nervosa, some other eating disorders, e.g. bulimia nervosa and pervasive refusal syndrome, are represented and can respond equally well to physiotherapy techniques.

## EXERCISE

Excessive exercise and overactivity are common features of anorexia nervosa. By the time the child or young person is admitted to hospital these symptoms may have reached alarming proportions. Energy that should be channelled into linear growth, physical maturation, and sustaining vital functions is lost in overexercising. Many hours a day may be spent in the pursuit of thinness and much of this exercise may be done in secret. Children often set alarm clocks to get up early enough to complete exercise routines before anyone else is awake to notice what they are doing. This compulsion to exercise may have started as an attempt to lose weight but has spiralled out of control to become excessive. Any interruption to this covert routine will result in the child feeling the need to recommence the whole obsessive cycle. When prevented from exercising, anxiety levels rise alarmingly and all thoughts are concentrated on how to catch up and complete what is believed to be an essential routine.

Some bulimic patients may have a history of more chaotic exercising. They may over-exercise for days and then do nothing for weeks, resulting in feelings of guilt and failure.

Young people with eating disorders may have begun exercising in the pursuit of fitness and a healthy body, or for recreation or pleasure. This type of exercise often takes place with peers in a group situation, as in team sports, but as exercise becomes more demanding and compulsive it becomes concentrated into solitary activities, e.g. running or swimming, leading to social isolation. For some young people, exercising excessively may not only be aimed at losing weight but also acts as a defence against having to think about worries and fears. If the body is always on the move there is no time to think, and uncomfortable and worrying thoughts can then be ignored. It may also be an attempt to try and leave something bad or distressing behind.

> Belinda, 13, was in the school running team. She found that when she was actually running she no longer worried about her home problems. As her difficulties there increased, so her running increased, until much of her day was spent either in running or planning on how she could run. If she was prevented from running she became increasingly agitated and distressed, not only because it gave her time to think, but also because she developed feelings of guilt about not being able to run.

Over-activity presents itself as a restlessness, an inability to sit still, an aimless wandering, and a constant need to maintain movement. If asked to sit, the patient will start rocking, or leg-swinging, or constantly jiggling one part of the body. This seems to be most pronounced in the severely emaciated, and a common pattern is that the activity level increases as the weight decreases (Beumont et al., 1974).

## Physical problems that may develop with excessive exercise

There are many physical problems related to eating disorders, with many children and adolescents who are seen by eating disorder teams having serious medical complications. Any exercise additional to such normal activities of daily living as walking to the bathroom or climbing the stairs, may be contra-indicated until the child is medically stable.

Local joint problems are common in those patients who exercise excessively. The weight-bearing joints, particularly the knees, are most often affected. Restricted range of movement, pain and swelling, and occasionally hypermobility may occur. If not treated these can result in permanently damaged joints and early onset of osteoarthritis. The wasting of the muscles that support these joints results in a loss of the protective element of muscle control, and can leave a joint more liable to serious ligamentous damage.

> Belinda, prior to admission to the eating disorder unit, had been running for several hours each day, trying to run harder and faster each time. Both knees were swollen and tender to touch. They had restricted range of movement, with flexion deformities at rest, and both patellae were tethered.

Young people who include hundreds or, in some cases, thousands of sit-ups in daily routines may damage the skin over the spine. This type of damage, which can occur anywhere in the emaciated body that is subject to friction, e.g. toes or feet in running shoes, can develop into sores and ulceration. There is then a real danger of infection not only locally, but also systemically, as the weakened body struggles to cope with additional demands.

## Options for treatment

The problems of excessive exercise and over-activity, with resultant body damage, need to be resolved and the body allowed to repair itself. Various suggestions may be considered:

- rest
- full activity, provided weight is gained steadily
- a prescribed exercise plan allowing an agreed amount of safe exercise.

As a method of restricting exercise, prescribed rest has many disadvantages. Total bed-rest is only advocated for those patients with cardiovascular problems or other acute life-threatening symptoms. It is very difficult and time-consuming to enforce, and may need 24-hour supervision, as the young persom involved will still experience an overwhelming need to exercise despite her poor physical health.

Nursing staff are put in a particularly difficult position. On the one hand they are responsible for ensuring the child remains in bed, effectively policing activity, with the resultant battle of wills that this entails. On the other hand, they are trying to build up a supportive relationship and help the child overcome feelings of loss of control and dependence. For patients, it can be a time of acute anxiety as they worry about weight increase. Exercise may have been such an important part of their lives that its loss can be very traumatic. Exercise stimulates the release of endorphins and a subsequent "feel-good factor". This is similar to the "high" produced by drugs and alcohol, and to be totally deprived of it produces the same cravings and feelings of loss.

Osteoporosis is a real danger for patients with anorexia nervosa because of the loss of bone density (see Chapter 8). Bed-rest is followed by an efflux of calcium from the skeleton, which would further reduce bone mass (Rigotti, Nussbaum, Herzog, & Neer, 1984). Therefore, an early return to partial and then full weight-bearing exercise is advocated. The option of bed-rest should only be used if absolutely essential to stabilise a patient medically, and for as short a period as possible.

There are several disadvantages to the second choice of treatment, that of full activity provided weight is gained steadily. Until muscle bulk and strength have been increased to a satisfactory level, weight-bearing joints are unprotected. Excessive exercising can lead to damage to these joints with resultant osteoarthritic changes. Overload on bones with low mineral density can lead to stress fractures. Strain on the cardiovascular system may lead to serious medical complications. The energy being produced by increased food intake is being dispersed by excessive activity and not channelled towards repair and growth. Therefore, it takes much longer to regain a healthy weight. Too early a return to full activity can in this way prolong the time required to restore physical health.

The third option of a prescribed exercise plan is probably the most suitable in many cases. This is a plan of exercise, drawn up by the physiotherapist and the young person together, and is aimed at strengthening and toning muscles as weight is regained, maintaining flexibility of joints, and improving circulation. Muscles that have wasted because their bulk has been converted into energy will only be restored to normal size by exercise as well as food. Young people often seem to have an inaccurate understanding of how their bodies work, and have become absorbed in common misconceptions about exercise, e.g. the need to do several hundred sit-ups each day to strengthen the abdominal muscles. It is by challenging these false beliefs and providing accurate information that intellectual ammunition can be reinforced to overcome irrational and illogical fears. Physiological changes that take place during the illness need to be explained, and the young person has to be helped to accept the need for balance between energy input and output.

A prescribed exercise plan can of course be used with outpatients, provided parents or carers are willing and able to give sufficient support and supervision to make the plan workable.

## Prescribed exercise plan

Each patient should have individual time with the physiotherapist on a regular basis, if possible about once a week. The exercise plan should be agreed and time arranged when a daily routine can be supervised. If the concept of working together is developed rather than that of being told what to do, a relationship built on trust can be established gradually, i.e. therapeutic alliance (see Chapter 9). The agreed exercise plan will depend on the weight and physical condition of the patient. Any joint problems should be assessed and suitable treatments applied, e.g. ice, support, ultra-sound, etc.

In many cases the exercise plan will start with non-weight-bearing exercises whilst lying or sitting. Static contractions of various muscle groups can help develop a better understanding of how a muscle works. This is done by actively tightening a muscle group without producing joint movement. The muscle is seen to change its form from soft to hard and back to soft again. Often a young person is confused and convinced that a muscle that is soft and relaxed is not muscle at all but fat. This is particularly true for the muscles of the back of the leg (the hamstrings), and the muscles on the inside of the thighs (the adductors). When sitting, the patient will avoid sitting back on the chair as this causes the hamstring muscles to spread out and the adductor muscles are loose and relaxed. This is interpreted by a young person with an eating disorder as having fat and flabby thighs. By being shown how a muscle can change from soft to hard and being helped to understand why this happens, patients can learn to accept their bodies more readily.

It is important to treat each child or young person as an individual and allow a certain amount of controlled flexibility in the development of the exercise plan. This allows the young person to feel involved and means that particular personal concerns can be addressed.

It is usual to start with the larger muscle groups—the thigh, hip, gluteal, and abdominal muscles—as these are often the most wasted and are those that cause the most concern to the patient as bulk is being restored. These are the muscle groups that support the body in the upright position and relieve the stresses on the weight-bearing joints, so it is important that their strength is improved as soon as possible.

As physical improvements take place and strength is gradually restored, muscle control is regained and the non-weight-bearing exercises, e.g. straight-leg raises, knee rolls, etc., can be progressed to partial weight-bearing exercises. These can be performed sitting with the hands supporting some of the body weight, kneeling on all fours, or standing using a chair or wall for support. Such exercises involve gradual weight-bearing to the bones of the wrist, the hip, and the spine, which are the areas that seem to suffer the most from low bone mineral density (BMD) (see Chapter 8). Selective use of a static bicycle can be useful to strengthen thigh muscles and improve cardiovascular fitness, and is also a partial weight-bearing activity, but it needs to be well controlled lest it be misused.

Full weight-bearing exercises should be introduced when the patient is no longer in the wasting phase of the disorder. These should include strengthening exercises, flexibility exercises, and aerobic exercise. Examples of these are:

- strengthening exercises—using resistance of gravity, body weight, or apparatus
- flexibility exercises—stretches in standing positions
- aerobic exercise—dance or similar low-impact activity.

Graded partial and full weight-bearing exercise are important to prevent bone loss and reduce the risk of osteoporosis. The prescribed exercise plan is useful, as it fulfils the patient's need to exercise in a safe and controlled manner, and allows the body to repair and develop heathily.

## Group activities

As well as individual time spent with the physiotherapist, group activity sessions can also be helpful. Young people with eating disorders are often self-absorbed and isolated. They tend to lose the ability to move freely and expressively, and instead hold themselves in a tight, controlled way. Movement to music including dance is always popular and can be used to encourage freedom of movement. Working with partners or in small groups can reintroduce communication by touch, a skill that has often been lost.

Team games allow the naturally competitive spirit to be expressed. Ball games help to improve co-ordination skills that may have been affected by muscle weakness. Childhood games such as Grandmother's Footsteps, Dead Lions, and Musical Statues need an element of control (positions have to be held in a "frozen" mode), and are an enjoyable way of helping to develop a correct feeling for, and interpretation of, muscle state. "Rhythmic stabilisations" is a popular exercise for rebuilding trust and allowing proximity. Children work in pairs, one person puts her hands on the other's shoulders and tries to push or pull her out of position, while the other person resists the movement. It can be done with the eyes open and then closed. It helps to redevelop the proprioceptors of the joints (the sensory nerve endings which recognise position), and this allows patients to know where their bodies are in space, and to have a more accurate knowledge of their body shape. Most important of all is relearning how to have fun and enjoy physical sensations.

As freedom of movement returns and the understanding of how the body works increases, the need for periods of calm and stillness become more acceptable. Patients should be encouraged to realise that "doing nothing" is not a negative state. It is a positive state in allowing the body to rest, repair if necessary, and prepare for activity.

When a healthy body weight is regained it is time to move away from "exercise" towards more normal physical activities. The young person with an eating disorder would normally be participating in sports at school or college and needs to return to these. However, there is also a need to understand that when energy is expended it must be replaced. Young people can start learning how to achieve this balance during the recovery stages. Once they approach a healthy weight they can be encouraged to participate in such sports as swimming or playing badminton. This helps social interaction, and overcomes the hurdle of doing things again in front of other people, and of revealing their new shape to the world.

Young people often find it difficult to realise that ordinary activities like shopping, walking, and dancing all demand energy. It is by gradually increasing activities and learning to adjust the diet accordingly that it is possible to understand the balance that must be achieved for a healthy weight to be maintained. When plans to resume other activities are being made, advice should be given to join group activities such as badminton, swimming with friends, hockey, football, or yoga, as these are less likely to become compulsive, rather than participating in solitary activities like running or working out in a gym. It may also be necessary to suggest that patients do not restart activities that have previously taken over their lives.

## BODY AWARENESS

Low self-esteem is common in young people with eating disorders, and is often accompanied by poor posture. Typically the shoulders are held hunched up and pulled forward. The head is often dropped down and the arms are held across the body, even when walking. This position often causes aching muscles, persistant headaches, poor breathing patterns and constricted circulation. It also influences the way other people see the individual and, perhaps more importantly, how patients see themselves. It can reinforce the feelings of hopelessness and helplessness, and in some cases heightens the feelings of being a victim and unable to change anything. Improving a patient's presentation can be a positive step towards boosting self-esteem, but it does need to be handled sensitively or it might make matters worse by further eroding confidence. Giving support to a young person who is trying to make change will produce better results than just demanding change.

The first approach can deal with the side-effects of the slumped, hunched posture—the aches and pains. Once the problem areas have been identified, the young person can be shown how to change posture to relieve the symptoms and encouraged to do this regularly. The physiotherapist can indicate the changes that need to be made, using a mirror if the patient agrees. Exercises to strengthen the back and neck muscles can be included in the general exercise plan, and once confidence is returning group sessions can be used to reinforce the individual work. It is important to remind patients that the way they carry themselves may well reflect the way they feel about themselves, but continuing with old habits may perpetuate the feelings of misery once they have moved on in other ways. By making simple changes, distressing symptoms can be relieved, confidence gradually restored, and self-esteem improved.

Hilary, 16, had a long history of anorexia nervosa. On admission to hospital she presented a picture of total despondency. When sitting, her head was held down so that her hair fell across her face, her shoulders were hunched and her arms held tightly across her body. During her physiotherapy sessions she learned upper body stretches and loosening exercises. Gradually, inch by inch, she was able to lift her head and put her hair back away from her face. Initially this was only possible for short periods and in the privacy of the physiotherapy room. As her mood improved and she regained some self-confidence, she was able to transfer these changes to the unit where she continued to improve with the support of the nursing staff and other patients.

Discussion on posture and body awareness often leads quite naturally to the changes that occur to the body during puberty. Many young people complain that they have "never been this weight before" and that, as their clothes do not fit anymore, this must mean that they are fat. Helping them to understand pubertal changes can ease the transition from emaciation to health.

## Relaxation

Relaxation is more than a cessation of effort; rather, it is a positive change and refinement of activity (Keable, 1985). It is also a switch from an active mode of coping with stress to a rest mode of coping (Stoyva & Anderson, 1982). Young people with eating disorders can find this concept difficult to grasp. For weeks, months, or years they may have been coping with feelings of insecurity or fear by refusing to release their control over their bodies. The primitive fight and flight instinct is awakened as the body reacts to a perceived threat, and this is reflected in the classic posture of tension with the head held down and forward, the shoulders hunched, the arms held flexed and close to the body, and the fists clenched.

Under normal circumstances, once anxiety has passed, the muscles holding the tense posture relax, and body tension is released. When anxiety is prolonged there is no release, tension mounts, and the tense mode becomes "normal". Many young people with eating disorders have no concept or memory of how it feels to be relaxed. At stressful times they will curl up tightly. Even when sitting they will perch precariously on the edge of the chair unable to sit back and relax. Relaxation training assists by teaching how to recognise tension, helping to understand how tension can escalate, and showing how to release tension as it develops.

There are two progressive physical relaxation techniques that focus on changing the body's response to stress. The Jacobson method (Jacobson, 1938) teaches systematic contraction and relaxation of those groups of muscles particularly affected by tension. Attention is then paid to the changes that occur with these actions, so that the difference between a muscle that is tight due to stress and one that is relaxed can be distinguished. This method seems to be more suited to those patients with bulimia nervosa. This is probably because they do not continuously hold their whole bodies in a rigid, controlled manner, and therefore can recognise and feel muscle contraction followed by relaxation.

The Mitchell method of relaxation involves contracting those muscles acting as antagonists to muscles held tense by stress. This action results in reciprocal inhibition and decreases tension in tight muscle groups (Mitchell, 1977). For example, when the shoulder depressors are contracted, the shoulder elevators are released. Using this method to work through different joints, the body gradually changes from a position of stress—tight and closed—to a position of relaxation—loose and open. It is this method that seems to be most successful when working with patients with anorexia nervosa. Such patients often hold their bodies so rigid and "closed" that it is impossible to elicit any further contraction in the muscle groups that are tense, but by contracting the opposite muscle groups, reciprocal inhibition occurs and relaxation takes place.

Whichever method is used, the aim is to help the young person become aware of physical tension and develop some self-control in reducing it. These practical physical methods of relaxation can be easily explained and understood. They allow the patient to feel more in touch with the body and the changes that occur as tension rises. It is important, however, to start slowly and be sensitive to the difficulties that the young person may have in making changes. The old, seemingly comfortable and comforting ways are being put aside, but the new ways do not feel immediately safe. It may be some time before major change can be made.

Initially, it is probably better to teach relaxation in an individual session. The patient may find the "letting go", quite frightening, and needs to be able to stop if the feelings of loss of control become too great. Allowing the young person to choose a starting position that feels comfortable, e.g. curling up in a ball, and covering with a blanket to reduce the feelings of vulnerability, may help to overcome some of the early resistance. At first, it may only be possible to work at reducing tension in one limb, e.g. the arm, or a part of a limb, e.g. the hand, but, as trust is established and confidence returns, it is usually possible to incorporate the whole body. It is important for the patient to understand that it is a skill that is being learned, and that practice will be needed to improve, in the same way that it is necessary to practise riding a bicycle or playing a musical instrument.

Once the fear has abated, relaxation can be incorporated into group sessions. Slow, gentle, stretching exercises with appropriate music can start a relaxation session and may help to encourage those who are reluctant to participate. It is also helpful to try the relaxation techniques in different positions, e.g. lying and sitting. Once they are comfortable with their new skills, the young people are encouraged to adapt the methods they have learned to use in particularly difficult situations. This can be done by focusing on relaxing those muscle groups that react most to tension, e.g. the shoulder elevators, the finger flexors, and the muscles that clench the teeth. Releasing the tension in these muscles can significantly alter tension levels. It can also be seen as good training for the future, for school or college examinations, or a driving test.

## Massage and touch

Touch, a very simple form of communication, is used in many ways in every-day life, e.g. shaking hands, putting an arm around someone, holding hands, or stroking. Patients with eating disorders have often become isolated within their families, and the normal expressive touching between the family members may have been lost. Caring, reassuring touch for someone who is confused can make that person feel wanted and valued (Montague, 1971). Touch can be used as a form of communication to reach those who feel alienated or disturbed in order to help them understand their world (Pratt & Mason, 1981). Those who are confused and bewildered by what is happening to them, and those who no longer understand the meaning of words, have to rely on tactile and other forms of non-verbal communication (Poon, 1995). For some patients, however, particularly those who have been physically or sexually abused, touch has unpleasant connotations and may revive painful memories. It is particularly important, therefore, that therapeutic touch is presented in a sensitive way. It should be introduced in a calm, unhurried manner with respect for personal boundaries.

Tactile experiences can provide feelings of safety and assurance (Mason, 1985). Physiotherapists are privileged in being authorised to touch, not only in the form of treatment for specific ailments, but as a means of communication. For young people with eating disorders, massage can help to re-establish pathways of communication, release some of the tension they find so difficult to release themselves, and help them become more positively aware of their bodies.

Before starting massage, a clear explanation of the planned treatment should be given, permission obtained to procede, and an understanding reached that it should stop whenever the patient so requests. Starting by working with a hand or a foot can be a way of introducing massage to a young person who is apprehensive or unsure about the treatment. As trust is developed, it is usually possible to include massage to the neck and shoulders to release the tension that is so often present there. Experience has shown that for those patients suffering from tension headaches, massage to the neck and shoulders followed by a forehead massage can bring great relief.

Some young people are reluctant to remove their clothes for massage, and this problem can be overcome by covering the area to be treated with a towel and massaging over this. Hopefully, as they become more comfortable with the treatment, they can be encouraged to dispense with the towel, and when they become confident enough, to remove their clothing from the area to be massaged. Some enjoy massage with oils and taking part in the selection of those which are suitable for treatment.

During the massage, the therapist should be constantly alert to feedback, whether visual or verbal. Emotions not expressed may be suppressed and one of the mechanisms of suppression is muscle tension (Thornquist & Bunkan, 1991). Massage and relaxation can enable the patient to get in touch with deep feelings in the subconscious that need to be aired (Davison, 1995). The physiotherapist may not have the counselling skills necessary to deal with this but, by involving the other team members, a way of working together can be evolved to the benefit of the patient.

Those young people who are initially the most withdrawn and hesitant in expressing themselves verbally often become the most responsive to the therapies of massage and touch. They have come to understand that touch can be pleasurable, and that it can be used to communicate when words are difficult or impossible. Young patients have often been seen giving massage to anxious or distressed friends when together in an eating disorder unit.

## Breathing exercises

Young people with eating disorders are usually very anxious, with high levels of body tension. They may have experienced panic attacks in the past or currently be experiencing them as a result of the additional stress of being in treatment for an eating disorder. Panic attacks are very frightening and distressing, both for the patient, and for family and friends. The physiotherapist can explain the mechanics of a panic attack and then work with the young person to help her learn techniques to control it.

A concise explanation of how tension and anxiety can affect the body should be given, with simple diagrams illustrating breathing patterns, if necessary. It is the breathing pattern that changes most as tension levels rise. Many patients have breathing rates that are two or three times faster than that of normal. The normal respiratory rate of 10–15 respirations a minute may increase to 25–35 per minute. This change has probably taken place over a period of weeks or months, and because breathing is an automatic activity may not have been noticed.

Overbreathing, by eliminating too much carbon dioxide, results in respiratory alkalosis. This can produce many symptoms including palpitations, chest pain, dizziness, faintness, headache, numbness, pins and needles, excessive sighing, tremors, depersonalisation, sleep disturbance, sweating, and lack of concentration. Many of these symptoms are familiar to patients with anorexia nervosa or related eating disorders. Once they understand that these symptoms are normal physical responses to an abnormal level of anxiety they can be helped to learn how to control them. There need to be both short- and long-term aims of treatment, and the patient needs to understand that it will take time and effort to make the necessary changes.

The short-term aim, until a new breathing pattern is established, is to help patients recognise the situations that trigger the onset of symptoms, and to teach them how to control their breathing at those times.

The long-term aim is to decrease the breathing rate so allowing the carbon dioxide levels to rise and reduce respiratory alkalosis. This reduction in respiratory rate may take weeks or even months to achieve.

The patient should be seen alone and encouraged to listen to herself breathing. This can prove quite difficult and may result in breath-holding or the breathing of excessive volumes of air. With gentle encouragement, however, most people are able to do this. They then try to listen to the rhythm of their breathing. There are various ways of making this easier. Young children seem to like the idea of picturing the pendulum of a clock and identifying whether their breathing is like a cuckoo clock—very fast—or a grandfather clock—very slow—or somewhere between the two. Older children can use the idea of music rhythms to pick up their own breathing pattern and to feel comfortable with listening to it. Once they can do this they are asked to "listen in" several times a day and to notice what causes change. As well as noticing the speed of their breathing, they are also asked to be aware of where they are breathing. They do this by putting one hand on the upper chest and the other hand on the abdomen, just below the ribs at the front. They can then feel the actual movement that is taking place. Once the habitual pattern of breathing has been established, it is possible to work towards change.

When learning to control breathing the patient is encouraged to recognise that the inspiratory phase of breathing is the active part of breathing. In this stage the young person learns to contract the diaphragm and to keep the work of the chest muscles to a minimum. This gives the feeling of the "tummy" filling up with air and, if the hands are in place, pushing the lower hand up. In patients with eating disorders this needs to be carefully explained or they become distressed by seeing their "tummies" becoming "fat". The expiratory phase of breathing is passive, with the diaphragm relaxing and the natural recoil in the lung tissue allowing the lungs to collapse down. It is this phase that seems to be the cause of most of the problems for patients. They may have been forcing the air out or not allowing complete relaxation of the lungs to take place, resulting in rapid expiration and a consequential excessive loss of carbon dioxide.

> Susie was acutely anxious with a respiratory rate of 35 per minute. She was constantly pacing and when persuaded to sit was unable to keep still. Diaphragmatic breathing was started to help to reduce her anxiety levels. At first she found this difficult as she worried about her tummy looking fatter when she was breathing. Gradually, however, she was reassured and started to find the breathing control exercises helpful. She was able to slow her respiratory rate, and, as her anxiety levels started to fall she became less agitated and her need for constant activity reduced.

It may take some time before the change in breathing pattern feels comfortable, and encouragement should be given to practise for short periods throughout the day until it becomes easier. Coloured stickers can be given to children to put in their rooms, or on their pencil-cases or books to help them to remember to do this. New breathing patterns are easier to learn when lying down with the knees bent as this allows the most freedom for the diaphragm. However, it is often in sitting that the most stressful situations occur, e.g. mealtimes, or in school, so the new breathing skills should also be practised in sitting.

Once a smooth pattern of diaphragmatic inspiration followed by a relaxed phase of expiration is established, it is possible to slow further the breathing rate. A short pause, during which the patient consciously relaxes, follows the expiratory phase of breathing. The pause may be very short initially, but gradually lengthens as the patient becomes more confident. Some patients are eventually able to insert a further pause after the inspiratory phase, and consequently lower even further their breathing rate. Regular practice is encouraged as this is the only way that permanent change will occur. Many patients find that these breathing control exercises, combined with the relaxation techniques, are very helpful if they are having trouble getting to sleep.

In the short term, the patients have to be reminded that they may still experience some of the symptoms brought on by hyperventilating. Until their new skills are established it may be difficult to control their breathing when anxious, and at these times they should be encouraged to think about breathing "slower and lower" until they regain control.

Breathing exercises can be introduced into group relaxation sessions, and it is often useful for young people to monitor each other's breathing patterns. This can lead to interesting discoveries about their own breathing, and can be used in a positive way as they learn how to help each other when distressed. As patients with eating disorders become more sensitive to change in their bodies they learn to recognise tension as it is developing. They can deal with it earlier, and can take control of it before it takes control of them.

## HELP AT HOME

The family or carer of a young person with an eating disorder has a vitally important part to play in her continuing recovery. The work with the physiotherapist can be done on an out- or inpatient basis, but the family should be involved early, so that the techniques can be learned by parents. Support can then be given to the patient, both in practising new skills and in overcoming problems as they arise. Returning to school after a period of ill-health can be a troublesome time; friendships have moved on and the feeling of being left out is quite common. Difficulty in concentrating and pressure to catch up can raise tension levels.

Time should be set aside on a daily basis to practise relaxation techniques, and charts or diaries can help this to be organised. Avoiding activities that have previously become compulsive is advisable, and new activities that might replace them should be carefully planned. Families that are very involved in sport and exercise may need help to understand how other less demanding activities can be beneficial, or how more of a balance can be maintained. Solitary activities should be avoided and family and friends encouraged to be supportive of this. A family trip to the swimming pool, rather than a solitary visit, is less likely to turn into compulsive length swimming.

Dancers present particular problems when looking for change. Many ballet schools require their dancers to be thin, and some will only accept children with a weight/height ratio that is known to cause unwelcome and damaging changes to the body. The adult dance world is beginning to realise that low weight can produce more problems than advantages, and more attention is being focused on the importance of a healthy diet and a healthy body for dancers. This message should be conveyed to ballet and dance schools. Meanwhile, parents should be encouraged to consider a school's attitude on these matters when making decisions with their children about which school to attend.

## CASE STUDIES

As a means of illustrating the use of the techniques described in this chapter, two case illustrations follow.

### Case 1

Victoria, 14, was admitted to hospital following sudden rapid weight loss. She was unhappy at boarding school and admitted to worrying a lot. She loved sport including horse-riding, skiing, and all school team sports, but had also been exercising secretly and confessed to doing 2000 sit-ups each day. An exercise plan was drawn up with her, and within a day or two of starting this she managed to stop doing her sit-ups. Massage was given to release the tension in her shoulder and neck muscles and the Mitchell method of relaxation taught to give her the skill to release the tension herself.

On admission, her breathing rate had been 24 per minute, so diaphragmatic breathing exercises were started. Three weeks later, as she started talking about some of her problems with her psychotherapist, her breathing rate escalated to 30 per minute and she felt increasingly restless and agitated. Massage was increased to twice a week, and she was helped to control and slow her breathing rate by using the diaphragmatic breathing she had been learning. Relaxation practice was agreed for a set time each day. Over the next two weeks she regained control of her breathing and was able to release tension before it overwhelmed her.

Once a healthy weight had been regained, physical activities were gradually reintroduced, and Victoria started horse-riding for an hour each weekend. Through trial and error, and lots of discussion about the need to balance energy output and input, Victoria realised and came to accept the need to increase her diet as she increased her level of activity. Prior to discharge from hospital she planned ways to do this when she returned to school, and decided on times each day she could continue to practise her relaxation and breathing control exercises.

## Case 2

Eileen, 14, was admitted to hospital with an 18-month history of anorexia nervosa. She had been exercising frantically in her bedroom and had become isolated from her peers. She admitted to being a worrier and suffered from tension headaches. Her posture indicated her inner tensions with her shoulders held up, her head held down, and her arms wrapped tightly around her body. An exercise plan was agreed and, apart from some secret exercising soon after admission, Eileen was able to follow her plan. She was very quiet and rather isolated on the unit, often curling up and sucking her fingers. She was an inpatient for some months and always attended her physiotherapy sessions. She asked for and enjoyed massage to her neck, shoulders, and head, and she reported great relief from her tension headaches.

Eileen struggled with talking about her problems, and was often withdrawn from the other young people on the unit. However, she appeared to draw strength from the non-verbal treatment of massage and therapeutic touch. She gradually became more involved in the movement sessions, and at the end of these she could be seen to be less tense as she moved more freely and her posture improved. By the end of her stay she was joining in the football session with great enthusiasm.

## CONCLUSION

Physiotherapy and controlled exercise can play an important part in the treatment of anorexia nervosa and related eating disorders. Together, they aim at developing an awareness of the link between the mind and the body. Without this knowledge, it is difficult to see how a full understanding of an eating disorder can be achieved. Physiotherapy reinforces and compliments in practical terms the work being done by other members of the team, and can be both educational and supportive. To be successful, however, it needs to be presented as a positive aid to recovery, rather than a negative restriction on activity. The emphasis is on working with young people to help them to recognise and interpret correctly their body experiences. With this knowledge, it is possible to work with them to solve some of the problems presented by their illness. As a greater awareness develops, they are able to work constructively to make the changes that are necessary to break out of the self-destructive cycle that has developed. This allows the young person to move on towards improving both physical and mental health.

## SUMMARY POINTS

- Physiotherapy, relaxation, and exercise programmes play an important part in the management of early onset eating disorders.
- The focus is on the body experience.
- Communication can be both verbal and by touch.
- The parents (and other family members) should be involved.

# REFERENCES

Beumont, P.J.V., Arthur, B., Russell, J.D., & Touyz, S.W. (1994). Excessive physical activity in dietary disorder patients: Proposals for supervised exercise programme. *International Journal of Eating Disorders, 15,* 21–36.

Davison, K. (1995). Eating disorders. In T. Everitt, M. Dennis, & E. Ricketts (Eds.), *Physiotherapy in mental health* (p. 309). Oxford, UK: Butterworth-Heinemann.

Jacobson, E. (1938). *Progressive relaxation: A physiological and clinical investigation of muscle states and their significance in psychology and medical practice* (2nd ed.). Chicago: University of Chicago Press.

Keable, D. (1985). Relaxation training techniques—a review—Part 1: What is relaxation? *British Journal of Occupational Therapy, 48*(4), 99–102.

Mason, A. (1985). Something to do with touch. *Physiotherapy, 71,* 167–169.

Mitchell, L. (1977). *Simple relaxation.* London: John Murray.

Montague, A.M. (1971). *Touching: The human significance of the skin.* London: Harper & Row.

Poon, K. (1995). Touch and handling. In T. Everitt, M. Dennis, & E. Ricketts (Eds.), *Physiotherapy in mental health* (p. 94). Oxford, UK: Butterworth-Heinemann.

Pratt, J.W., & Mason, A. (1981). *The caring touch.* London: Heydon Press.

Rigotti, N.A., Nussbaum, S.R., Herzog, D.B., & Neer, R.M. (1984). Osteoporosis in women with anorexia nervosa. *New England Journal of Medicine, 265,* 601–660.

Stoyva, J.M., & Anderson, C.D. (1982). A coping-rest model of relaxation and stress management. In L. Goldberger & S. Breznitz (Eds.), *The handbook of stress—theoretical and clinical aspects.* New York: Free Press.

Thomas, A.B., & Markin, D. (1996/97). *A proposed activity protocol for individuals recovering from eating disorders, St Pauls Hospital, Vancouver.* Unpublished manuscript.

Thornquist, E., & Bunkan, B.H. (1991). *What is psychomotor therapy?* Oslo, Norway: Norwegian University Press.

Vandereyken, W., Depreitre, L., & Probst, M. (1987). Body oriented therapy for anorexia nervosa patients. *American Journal of Psychotherapy, XL1*(2), 252–259.

CHAPTER FIFTEEN

# Group work

**Shelagh Wright**
*Southampton Eating Disorders Service, UK*

## INTRODUCTION

This chapter focuses on the process and practice of group work for young people with eating disorders. Group work, like other forms of therapy, can be conducted in a variety of settings, with outpatients, day-patients, and inpatients. In children and adolescents, group work should always be seen as one component of a more comprehensive treatment package, as involvement of parents is essential to the effective and appropriate management of eating disorders in young people.

## General considerations

For many years group work has been a popular form of treatment for a number of reasons: (1) groups are generally seen as cost effective because they enable more people to receive treatment at any one time; (2) they can help reduce waiting times between assessment and starting treatment; (3) those participating in groups can benefit from being able to meet other people who are struggling with similar problems, and share experiences and solutions; (4) groups can offer each person the benefit of exploring a number of possible ways of tackling their specific difficulty; (5) groups can demonstrate that it is not necessary to get it "right" first time; (6) groups can reduce feelings of loneliness and isolation, helping to develop a more cohesive sense of identity, and providing a sense of accomplishment from co-operating with others within the group; (7) groups help explore action of one's effect on others, and vice versa; (8) groups encourage the direct expression of feelings.

## Group work with children and adolescents

Groups for young people are often designed to focus on some of the tasks of growing up, within an environment that offers more structure and specific feedback than a naturally occurring group. Such groups may be experienced as a safe place to try out different behaviours, while at the same time being challenging to unacceptable behaviours. This can be achieved by the group members and the therapist actively acknowledging and reflecting on a behaviour and the impact that that behaviour might have outside the group. The young person is encouraged to change her behaviour in a "face-saving way". The group then becomes a place where it is possible to make mistakes, without the fear of exclusion.

Young people often find it easier to communicate through play or activity. Activities are used to elicit the child's characteristic role responses or behaviour patterns, and to introduce the individual to alternative responses through the modelling of others. More recently the use of activities and games has been developed for specific therapeutic purposes (Schachter, 1986).

## Group work for young people with eating disorders

It is well established that individuals with eating disorders can benefit from group work (Polivy, 1981; Polivy & Garfinkel, 1984). Many of the early applications of cognitive behaviour therapy to bulimia nervosa involved group treatment (Kirkley, Sneider, Agras, & Bachman, 1985; Mitchell, Pyle, Eckert, Hatsukami, Pomoroy, & Zimmerman, 1990).

The literature on groups for young people with eating disorders is limited and mostly based on patients within an inpatient setting (Gardner & Nissam, 1987; Lieb & Thompson, 1984). Gardner and Nissam (1987, p. 185) found that "the cohesive and competitive 'anorexic subculture' significantly changed for the better. The difficulties within the group had been replaced by a positive sharing in the group leading to increased awareness not only of themselves but of others also." Lieb and Thompson (1984) have cited the benefits of group therapy as helping to reduce the sense of loneliness and isolation, assisting in the development of a sense of identity and promoting a sense of achievement in the co-operation with other group members.

## GROUP COMPOSITION

### Age and maturity

It is best not to mix children and adolescents in the same group, because the different age groups have quite different developmental needs and tasks. Similarly, adolescents and adults should be treated in separate groups.

Behr (1988) has described the main differences between adolescent and adult groups as arising from the greater impact of boundary issues, which seem to impinge more on the group process. Adolescents are much more likely to test out the boundaries in a group situation by competing for talk time and pecking order. The style and the pace of communication reflect that of the adolescent membership: namely, rapidly changing themes, volatile moods and a tendency toward action (Behr, 1988). This will tend to be different in groups of younger children, and too wide an age range may be intimidating for younger members.

## Gender

In group work with young people, there is usually a mix of male and female. However, with young people with eating disorders the group composition is likely to be predominantly female. The therapist needs to be aware of how distracting is the presence of a member of the opposite sex. In addition, there is a need to be sensitive to how difficult it might be for an adolescent boy to be placed in a group of adolescent girls. Groups for children and adolescents with eating disorders can include both boys and girls, but there should be a willingness to recognise and discuss any gender issues that may arise.

> Joe, 14, announced how difficult he found it to be "himself" in a group full of girls, because when with other boys he found he behaved differently. The group helped him to explore the reasons why he might behave differently with different groups of people. Joe had been worried about his sexual orientation and thought that this was why he behaved differently.

## Size

The optimal size of any group differs according to its type and aims. If the group is too small, it can be difficult to generate ideas to encourage change. This can be particularly noticeable when the group members are withdrawn or depressed and unable or unwilling to contribute positively. However, one advantage of a smaller group is that it can enable less confident members to be more open, trusting, and willing to take risks in self-expression.

Young people with eating disorders can be emotionally immature and their social development may be delayed. They may become over-stimulated and confused in a group that seems large.

Large groups have both advantages and disadvantages. It can be more difficult in a large group to develop cohesiveness, as well as being harder to ensure that each member has enough opportunity to participate. However, an advantage of a larger group is that it can make it easier to integrate new members. It is also easier for group members to have the opportunity to listen to or observe others taking part, without being expected to contribute themselves. It becomes easier to participate as one matures (Northen, 1970).

## Presenting problems

When starting a group, it is important to consider which young people should be included, in terms of their differing needs. There are costs and benefits of having young people with different problems together in one group. In inpatient units, the groups might include young people with eating disorders as well as those with a wide range of other problems. The focus of such groups may be far more general than the concerns specific to eating disorders.

Within groups of young people with eating disorders there are also potential advantages and disadvantages of having people with different types of eating disorder together in one group. A frequently expressed concern regarding mixed groups is that this will encourage learning how to be "better" at anorexia nervosa or bulimia nervosa, or that group members might catch or copy other self-destructive or pathological behaviour. However, experience has shown that the benefit of being with people their own age with similar problems has such a powerful positive impact that any "bad" habits they might pick up will generally be discarded as they recover.

The effects of mixing adolescents with different types of eating disorders depends on the balance between them. For example, when there are only one or two young people with bulimia nervosa, it may be very difficult for them to feel part of the group. They may feel envious of those with anorexia nervosa, believing them to have achieved the control for which they are striving. Those with anorexia nervosa may become scared of becoming bulimic. They may feel they are coming face to face with their own nightmare. The benefit of having the two groups mixed is that both realise that neither one actually achieves that control.

## GROUP STRUCTURE

### Open and closed groups

In closed groups the membership remains constant, whereas in open groups the membership changes. Either type is applicable for young people with eating disorders, but it is difficult to run closed groups on inpatient units. Open groups can continue on a weekly basis until the demand for them diminishes, their therapeutic value runs its course, or the members of the group move on. Closed groups can be designed to have a time limited framework with a specific focus.

### Timing

Group sessions generally last for 60–90 minutes: Longer groups tend to be too demanding and become unproductive. The length of each group should be known in advance, and the group should occur at a fixed time.

## Leadership style

Dies (1983) and Leiberman, Yalom, and Miles (1972) have identified positive dimensions of therapist style which include: having a caring, supportive approach, promoting an understanding of group events, establishing a meaning for behaviour, and ensuring moderate levels of control. Therapist style that might negatively influence group work includes: being too controlling or not having clear boundaries, appearing uninvolved or apathetic, and relying on charisma to coerce the group.

In working with young people with eating disorders, it is helpful for the group facilitator to have a sound practical knowledge of group work and to be skilled in separating eating disorder behaviour from healthy adolescent or pre-adolescent behaviour.

> Rebecca, 16, and Chrissie, 14, from an inpatient unit were having a quarrel outside of the group and continued it once the group had started. The other group members found it difficult to tolerate the atmosphere that this quarrel had created. Rebecca and Chrissie were given positive feedback from the group facilitator for being brave enough to show how they felt, and encouraged to discuss the quarrel in the group so that the other group members could help them come to a resolution.

The success of a group depends on the facilitator having a positive attitude and building a good rapport with each group member. It is important to promote a climate of acceptance, respect, understanding, and honesty. As the group becomes established the role of the facilitator becomes less pivotal and the group members do more of the work.

> In one session of a relapse prevention group that had been running for several months, Zoe, 16, who had been steadily losing weight, stated clearly that it was not okay to challenge her regarding her weight until after she had sat her exams in 3–4 months time. After the conversation had moved on, Julie, 17, said that she could not sit and watch someone she had known and cared about continue to destroy herself, without saying something. This gave other members of the group the confidence to support both Zoe and Julie. At the end of the session, Zoe thanked the group for confronting her because although it had been difficult it showed that she was important enough for them to risk offending her.

Although the group facilitator takes overall responsibility for the group, the group members and facilitator are jointly responsible for defining the tasks of the group. However, the facilitator can take part in the tasks, and can be the first to feed back to the group. This can demonstrate the adult's belief in the usefulness of the task and can help to overcome the trivialising, embarrassment or withdrawal that the young people may display. It also shows the group that a working alliance is necessary to confront and explore their difficulties. The sense of working together, collaboration, and mutuality, strengthens the motivation and the support of the group therapy sessions.

One of the most valuable therapeutic tools is that of the group learning through each other, including from the group facilitator, who can model listening, acknowledging, accepting, empathy, successful conflict resolution, and non-defensive disclosure.

## Rules

In order for young people to feel free to express themselves, appropriate rules are necessary. It is important for them to feel involved in the ownership of group, as this enhances their feelings of being connected and sharing control. This can be achieved by encouraging group members, at the beginning of the life of a new group, to participate in developing the group rules. This places the locus of control with the group members, leaving the role of the facilitator as one of ensuring that the rules are adhered to. A set of group rules might include: everybody participating (listening and paying attention will do); everybody being given time and space to express themselves; no side conversations; and laughter is permissible (if it is shared).

The first session might be used for establishing group rules, and including discussion of boundary issues such as group confidentiality. For example, a joint decision may be made that members are only allowed to discuss their own contribution to the group with people outside of the group, not anything that any other member has contributed. Another example relates to punctuality: The group may agree that members can arrive late for groups but can not leave before the group has finished.

## GROUP DYNAMICS

In this section, some of the interaction and relationship issues both amongst the group members and between the group members and the facilitator will be highlighted. These group dynamics can have a significant influence on how the group functions, and how comfortable the group feels for each person present.

### Peer acceptance

There are powerful issues of personal development that have to be taken into account by the group facilitator while simultaneously addressing the symptoms of disordered eating in children and adolescents. Groups of young people with eating disorders can be experienced as quite a competitive environment. Peer acceptance and identification within a group are important concerns for young people and the group facilitator will need to be sensitive to how this affects the individuals' ability to express independence and separateness. Given that peer acceptance and self-esteem are closely related, and low self-esteem is a core feature of an eating disorder, forming satisfying peer group identity may be a crucial developmental process for these young people.

## Dependency

Some young people attending groups may have been in more intensive treatment or may for other reasons develop dependent relationships with particular staff. In this circumstance continued dependency and even regression can occur. The facilitator must be constantly aware of the fine line between support and dependency, and be able to help group members to use the group as a place where they can "test out" and move on to greater autonomy and independence. The promotion of autonomy and independence can reduce dependency, for example, by encouraging group members to return to school or to be involved in activities with friends. This may help individuals to realise that their eating disorder is preventing them from doing what they would like to be doing, and to see that it may not be the most effective way of managing their problems. However, younger patients, who are still highly dependent on their parents, can find this process more difficult.

## Resistance

Groups constitute an excellent context for challenging body image distortions. However many young people find this very difficult, and so try to avoid situations where their beliefs and ideas might be challenged. When the group members challenge a behaviour or belief within the group, this can be far more powerful than the therapist or parent challenging the same behaviour or belief.

> Lisa, 16, refused to come to a community group meeting, instead lying on her bed with her face to the wall. She stated that there was little point in her attending as nothing she had to say was of any importance, and no one really wanted her to be there anyway. The therapist explained that Lisa was part of the group and so had an important role as a group member. The community group was held around Lisa's bed, and despite keeping her face to the wall she listened to what was being said and contributed at the end. Lisa voluntarily attended the next community group.

## FEEDBACK AND SUPERVISION

Feedback to other members of the clinical team and supervision for the facilitator both require consideration. Feedback can be provided at ward rounds or clinical review meetings. Such information can then be integrated with feedback from other therapeutic contexts to provide an integrated picture. Supervision for group facilitators should always be available to ensure that the facilitator has an opportunity to reflect upon the complexities of the group process and explore strategies for dealing with problems.

# POSSIBLE TYPES OF GROUP

## Psycho-educational groups

Psycho-educational groups can cover a variety of topics, for example assertiveness, anger management, life skills, growing-up issues, nutrition, and self-esteem. In this chapter, psycho-educational group work is described by considering groups with a focus on assertiveness, anger management, and self-esteem.

*Assertiveness group.* An assertiveness group can address such issues as the need for assertiveness, basic assertiveness skills, and the difference between assertion, aggression, and passivity. These topics can be addressed through practical work using scripting and role-play.

Situations requiring assertiveness can be elicited from group members and will most usefully reflect peer group culture and pressures. For example, the group could role-play how to say "no" to peer group pressure to smoke, or use illegal substances. The situations vary depending on the age range and cultural background of the group members. Occasionally, situations within the group itself can be used for role-play or discussion.

> Rebecca, 16, told the group, that when at home over the weekend, a boy from her class at school had asked her to go to the cinema with him. She had never been asked out before and did not know how to respond. Some of the other group members had teased Rebecca about her lack of knowledge. The facilitator encouraged the group to role-play this situation to help her. The girls that had been teasing her were then able to be supportive.

*Anger management group.* Many young people with eating disorders feel very angry but are unable to express this directly. Anger is often a natural response to hurt; if it is directed inward it can present as depression and more dangerously as self-harming, which all too often feature in the eating disorder. People can use groups to recognise their anger and its origins as a prelude to finding healthier ways of expressing it.

> Sharon, 16, had always in the past stormed out of groups when the topic or situation became too difficult for her. When this happened the facilitator encouraged the rest of the group to negotiate with Sharon how much time she felt she needed, before she could return to the session. In later sessions she began to request a break instead of leaving and eventually was able to stay and say why she found the groups difficult.

*Self-esteem group.* Groups are a useful context for working on poor self-esteem, particularly because of the opportunity for instant feedback. The process of setting group rules and agendas, together with the therapist ensuring that each member has opportunity to voice her opinion, can enhance each person's sense of self-worth. Work focusing on enhancing self-esteem might also include exploring how self-esteem develops, with the resultant self-depreciating thoughts, developing strategies for breaking self-destructive habits by positive thinking, reframing, affirmation, and assertion.

> Susie, 17, who was particularly negative about herself, brought in a video recording of herself many years previously when she had appeared on a children's television programme. The group watched the recording and gave Susie many positive comments, which helped her to feel good about showing them the recording and better about herself. Looking back at a child who was obviously happy, sociable, and confident reminded Susie that she had not always felt so badly about herself.

## Activity groups

The regressed emotional state of many youngsters with eating disorders presents a considerable challenge to the therapist to find a route into their closely guarded inner world and then to find a helpful way to respond. Many are unable to access and express their emotions verbally.

Activity groups make use of specific activities to facilitate conversations and explore particular issues. The activity might help the group members to work on difficult issues in a non-direct and sometimes non-verbal way. They can offer an opportunity to gain greater insights and new awareness using a creative approach. Such groups can facilitate and unleash the persons' power of creative expression in a safe environment. This can be achieved by allowing her to choose her own medium and to explore issues at her own pace. The group facilitator should not analyse or interpret the work but offer a supportive role, in order that the young person can interpret her own work. Examples of activity groups might include: art therapy, drama therapy, dance therapy, and music therapy. For the purpose of this chapter, there will be descriptions of a music group and an art group using a combination of activities.

*Music group.*   Nolan (1989), in his work with people with bulimia nervosa, has described a formal therapy using traditional music with the client's own compositions. He discussed music's ability to elicit "extra-musical associations". Through these associations the emotions expressed in spontaneous improvisations can be brought to greater consciousness. Sloboda (1993, 1994), in her work with people with both anorexia nervosa and bulimia nervosa, has described the immediacy of the experience of creating music as having helped clients to become more conscious of their emotional state, and with free improvisation the client can develop confidence and strength of expression (Sloboda, 1994).

Most people have a particular favourite tune or song or one that has a particular meaning for them. In the same way that the singer tells a story through the lyrics, young people may find it easier to begin to tell their story through the words of popular songs. A session can be started by inviting the group to choose a song that describes their mood that day, or describes the way they may be feeling. Each person might take their turn to play their song and then say what they want about the song. The facilitator may also take a turn. Young people tend to enjoy such groups and in our experience seem particularly to enjoy the facilitator participating.

With a newly formed group, the members might play songs that do not have a particular meaning for them. As the group becomes more established and its members begin to feel safer in each other's company, the songs might become more descriptive and emotional. As the young people start to see this group as a means of talking about themselves, so the culture of the group can become one of sharing and solidarity. It can become a forum for them to share particularly important experiences.

> Joanne, 16, used Madonna's "Live to Tell", a song about a girl who has a secret and is trying to decide whether to tell it. Joanne had disclosed that she had been abused sexually by her father and was working through this with her therapist.

> Kelly, 14, played Sade's "Stronger than Pride", a song that describes the dilemma between love and hate, living and dying. Kelly had repeatedly taken overdoses, and had previously been unable to share with anyone what was driving her self-destruction.

> Ali, 14, played 4 Non Blondes' "What's Up?" a song that describes an uphill struggle, and has been popular with young group members as a way of describing their uphill struggle with weight gain.

Sheryl Crow's "Strong Enough" song, which describes the uncertainty of whether to trust in someone else's ability to be there, has been very popular. One of the most frequently played songs is REM's "Everybody Hurts", which describes emotional pain. The songs played are not all sad; many of the patients play hopeful, happy songs—for example M People's "Hero Inside", Labi Siffery's "Feelings So Strong", songs which describe people overcoming difficulties through inner strength.

Obviously there are many other songs and pieces of music, but these examples demonstrate the variety of issues that can be addressed through song lyrics.

> One of the most emotional groups was when Beth, 17, chose to play Tasmin Archer's "Ripped Inside", then said, "that's what happened to me". Archer sang about feelings of powerlessness, personal intrusion, and betrayal, suggestive of a sexually abusive nature.

There are many ways to structure a music group. A popular technique involves setting a theme for the week such as picking a song that is reminiscent of summer, or creates a feeling of happy/sad/safe/lonely. Group members then encourage each other to talk about the song.

*Art group.*    Children and adolescents find creative groups particularly useful because of the non-verbal component.

Shaw (1981) has suggested that art gives form to chaos and provides a means of productive functioning, a way to work through the struggle. Fleming (1989) has proposed that the use of art materials can satisfy developmental needs. Pleasure can be obtained from the tactile, visual, and olfactory qualities of paint mediums, which can be squidged or smeared using hands or tools and sometimes even feet, to the heart's delight.

> In one session the theme was a "dream holiday". Images of a day at the beach were invoked; some of the group recalled their memories of family holidays. The group facilitators provided a large sheet of plastic on to which they emptied a sack of sand. A paddling pool of water was placed by the sand together with a quantity of plastic sand and water toys, buckets and spades. Art materials, writing equipment, and musical instruments were available. The members of the group were invited to express themselves in any way that they wanted, while the facilitators withdrew to the side of the room, not wishing to inhibit the group members. A couple of the members drifted towards the sand and water and started to make sand castles. Others watched and then joined in, while initially a few remained aloof. Shortly all of them were paddling, playing, laughing and squabbling. It was interesting to observe these young people playing independently, side by side. We were reminded of toddlers in a playgroup, playing in parallel, not interactively. There was evidence of pleasure, and a sense of them losing themselves in the simple sensory experiences of sand, water, and the fun of playing with the toys.

Wurr and Pope-Carter (1998) have described a drama therapy group for adolescents with eating disorders using the metaphor of a journey. The group was used in the context of other therapy that the group members were receiving. They noted that simply being part of a group of people facing similar issues and who would not accept bluff or denial enabled the group members to face up to their eating problems. The authors hoped that the group members' feeling more comfortable in the drama-therapy exercises by the end of the group represented a degree of increased comfort with their own bodies. The metaphor of a journey provides a thread of continuity throughout the life of a group and is a useful metaphor to explore both verbally and using drama-therapy, as well as other creative techniques.

Elliott (1998) has described a dance therapy group for children, that was part of the education programme at a child psychiatric inpatient unit. It highlights the successful and innovative collaboration between artists, teachers, and unit staff. Elliott has stated that dance, along with other creative and expressive subjects, is an important activity for children experiencing feelings of hopelessness and self-destructiveness. Dance uniquely combines thinking, feeling, sensing, and doing. It has strong effects on physiological and psychological well-being, combining the benefits of physical exercise with heightened sensory awareness, cognitive function, creativity, interpersonal contact, and emotional expression.

## Other groups

*Community groups and ward milieu.*   Hospitalisation automatically places people into a treatment group. It is inevitable that they will be involved in both planned and unplanned group processes and interactions. Crouch (1998, p. 115) has stated that the key elements of a therapeutic milieu are "maintenance of a safe and containing environment, a highly structured programme, physical and emotional support, collective involvement of the child, family and staff in the unit regimen and continuous evaluation of all therapeutic interventions". The role of the nursing staff within the ward milieu is important, because the young people will spend the majority of their time in the company of the nurses. It is the behaviour and attitude of the nursing staff that the young people will be influenced by.

*Relapse prevention group.*   The purpose of this type of group is to offer support and solidarity from peers, to help toward relapse prevention. Such a group offers a forum to discuss group member's struggles with maintaining healthy attitudes and healthy weights. It can also be a place where negative thoughts and feelings can be discussed openly.

A common problem occurs when the young person appears to be putting on a "mask", that is, appearing to have recovered, in that they are of normal weight, but still experiencing many of the eating disorder thoughts. Shelley (1998) has described a stage in which the individual continues to have distorted thinking but maintains a normal weight. The focus of the group could be to explore what might happen if they discussed thoughts and feelings more openly and what might happen if they did not. One fear may be that they were placing unnecessary burden on other people. Group members will tend to be at different stages of recovery and so have different views on this, so the debate can be very constructive. It is helpful to have the group open to people at all stages of recovery. The aim is to help individual group members to find a way of getting the support that they need from the people that they need it from, without using their eating disorder.

Leanne, 16, described how her mother could not tolerate her saying that she still thought about losing weight. Sometimes Leanne could not keep her feelings in and would tell her mother that when she felt unhappy she would sometimes still think about her weight. Her mother would panic and accuse Leanne of vomiting again. The group helped Leanne to explore different ways of letting her mother know that, although she still had these thoughts, she was not acting upon them.

*Parent support group.* The literature on parent support groups is very sparse (Jeammet, 1984; Lewis & MacGuire, 1985). Nicholls and Magagna (1997) have described a parent support group as part of the overall treatment package for children with eating disorders. They felt that despite having different presenting symptoms the basic needs of the young people were the same, namely, "to be able to eat an adequate amount to grow and develop, and to be able to express emotional difficulties through a medium other than food and eating" (p. 566). It is the parents' responsibility to meet these needs, a task that they can find very difficult. Having a forum to be able to explore their own vulnerabilities and feelings of inadequacy or failure can enable them (through the process of discussion) to regain their mastery of parenting. The task for clinicians is to provide a safe place for the parents to explore the difficulties in meeting the tasks that their children set them (Nicholls & Magagna, 1997).

The purpose of such a group is to offer support to parents of young people with eating disorders. The support comes from the group facilitator and the other parents. A particular advantage of parents' groups is that parents are at different stages of the treatment process, so can see some hope of progress from their existing position. Nicholls and Magagna (1997) commented on the feelings of guilt, demoralisation, defeat, and decreased skill that many parents feel, and suggested the need for parents to come together to share knowledge and skills and to learn from and support each other. They emphasised the differences between how each individual responds to the eating disorder, and noted that it was important to be aware that each parent reaches his or her turning point at a different time and in a different way. It is important to allow time and space for parental self-reflection within the group (Nicholls & Magagna, 1997).

Like many, Nicholls and Magagna experienced a shortage of fathers' input to their parent group, and considered this to be a result of the group being inaccessible to the fathers, rather than the fathers being inaccessible to the group.

A first session might begin by asking the members to say what they want to use the group for. It might be that just having the space to talk to other parents, who are experiencing or have experienced the same or similar difficulties to themselves, is helpful in itself. Parents may welcome the opportunity to meet with different members of the team to ask them questions specific to their expertise. Sometimes parents may want to offer support to new members by way of a telephone list of people willing to be called. One of the times when parents seem to need the most support is when their child has just been admitted to or discharged from inpatient treatment.

At one parents' group, the mother of Clare, 12, who had just been admitted, became tearful when she described her feelings of failure. She felt that she should have been able to make Clare better herself. The parents of Rosie, 15, who had been successfully maintaining progress outside of hospital for over a year, reassured Clare's mother, by suggesting how important it was for her daughter to see her ask for help in such a difficult task. Clare's mother, by asking for help, was giving her daughter the message that it was also okay for her to accept help from the unit.

It can also be useful for parents/carers to recommend books to each other. They can comment on what they have found helpful and unhelpful and why. The group facilitator may challenge also some of the less helpful ideas in these books. Understandably, parents have a need to obtain as much information as they can. This hunger for information can sometimes lead them to be less discerning about what they are reading than they might otherwise be.

Parents groups can help the communication between the parents and the clinical team and can have a positive effect on the number of minor complaints received from the parents.

On one occasion when the inpatient unit had been particularly unsettled, one of the group outings had at short notice been re-arranged for another time. Some of the parents felt that their child had been let down. They brought the issue to the parents' group to explore ways in which situations like that might be handled differently.

There will always be issues about which parents and staff differ. Having a forum to discuss these helps to promote a collaborative relationship, as well as modelling problem solving to the young people. Nicholls and Magagna (1997, p. 561) found that staff and parents meeting together in the group had the effect of "enabling the staff to feel more empathic towards parents, less identified solely with the child and more united overall".

## CONCLUSION

The sharing of concerns between young people with eating disorders can be an invaluable means of support. Groups provide an atmosphere of mutual support while creating an environment where confrontation and pressure can be tolerated. The intensity of relating is diffused by the presence of group interaction, so increasing the likelihood of independence and autonomy. Within the atmosphere of mutual sharing and support, people can feel more comfortable with talking about some of the behaviours generally felt to be degrading and humiliating (bingeing and purging). This sharing helps patients acknowledge their illness.

## SUMMARY POINTS

Group work appears to have the following advantages:

- Group work brings people together to share experiences, and possible solutions.
- Groups are a place where ideas and beliefs can be challenged in a gentle and supportive way.
- Group work is cost effective.
- Group work is a way of involving families in the treatment process.
- Groups are a place where relationships and interactions can be modelled.

## REFERENCES

Behr, H. (1988). Group analysis with early adolescents: Some clinical issues. *Group Analysis, 21*, 119–133.

Crouch, W. (1998). The therapeutic milieu and the treatment of emotionally disturbed children: Clinical application. *Clinical Child Psychology and Psychiatry, 3*(1), 115–129.

Dies, R. (1983). Clinical implications of research on leadership in short term group psychotherapy. In R. Dies & K.R. Mackenzie (Eds.), *Group therapy*. New York: International Universities Press.

Elliott, R. (1998). The use of dance therapy in child psychiatry. *Clinical Child Psychology and Psychiatry, 3*(2), 251–265.

Fleming, M. (1989). Art therapy and anorexia: Experiencing the authentic self. In L. Hornyak & E. Baker (Eds.), *Experiential therapies for eating disorders* (pp. 279–304). New York: Guilford Press.

Gardner, M., & Nissam, R. (1987). Group work with adolescents: Is it worth the bother? *Educational and Child Psychology, 4*, 180–188.

Jeammet, P. (1984). Le groupe de parents: sa place dans le traitement de l'anorexie mentale. *Neuropsychiatrie de l'Enfance, 32*, 299–303.

Kirkley, B.G., Sneider, J.A., Agras, W.S., & Bachman, J.A. (1985). Comparison of two group treatments for bulimia. *Journal of Consulting and Clinical Psychology, 53*(1), 43–48.

Lewis, H.L., & MacGuire, M.P. (1985). Review of a group for parents of anorexics. *Journal of Psychiatric Research, 19*, 453–458.

Lieb, R.C., & Thompson, T.L. (1984). Group psychotherapy of four anorexia nervosa in-patients. *International Journal of Group Psychotherapy, 34*(4), 639–642.

Lieberman, M., Yalom, I., & Miles, M. (1972). *Encounter groups: First facts*. New York. Basic Books.

Mitchell, J.E., Pyle, R.L., Eckert, E.D., Hatsukami, D., Pomoroy, C., & Zimmerman, R. (1990). A comparison study of anti depressants and structured intensive group psychotherapy in the treatment of bulimia nervosa. *Archives of General Psychiatry, 47*, 149–157.

Nicholls, D., & Magagna, J. (1997). A group for the parents of children with eating disorders. *Clinical Child Psychology and Psychiatry, 2*(4), 565–578.

Nolan, P. (1989). Music therapy improvisation techniques with bulimic patients. In E. Baker & L. Hornyak (Eds.), *The handbook of techniques in the treatment of eating disorders* (pp. 167–187). New York: Guilford Publications.

Northen, H. (1970). Size of groups. In T. Douglas (Ed.), *Groupwork practice* (pp. 84–95). London: Tavistock.

Polivy, J. (1981). Group therapy as an adjunctive treatment for anorexia nervosa. *Journal of Psychiatric Treatment and Evaluation, 3,* 279–283.

Polivy, J., & Garfinkel, P.E. (1984). Group treatments for specific medical disorders: Anorexia nervosa. In H.B. Roback (Ed.), *Helping patients and their families cope with medical problems* (pp. 68–78). San Francisco: Jossey-Bass.

Schachter, R.S. (1986). Techniques of kinetic psychotherapy. In C.E. Schaefer & S.E. Reid (Eds.), *Game play: Therapeutic use of childhood games* (pp. 95–107). New York: John Wiley.

Shaw, J.A. (1981). Adolescence, mourning and creativity. In S. Feinstein & P.L. Giovachinni (Eds.), *Adolescent psychiatry* (pp. 60–77). Chicago: University of Chicago Press.

Shelley, R. (1998). The journey is as important as the destination. *Signpost, The newsletter for The Eating Disorders Association, UK,* Feb., 4–5.

Sloboda, A. (1993). Individual therapy with a man who has an eating disorder. In M. Heal & T. Wigram (Eds.), *Music therapy in health and education* (pp. 103–111). London: Jessica Kingsley Publishers.

Sloboda, A. (1994). Individual music therapy with anorexic and bulimic patients. In D. Dokter (Ed.), *Art therapies and clients with eating disorders* (pp. 247–261).

Wurr, C., & Pope-Carter, J. (1998). The journey of a group dramatherapy for adolescents with eating disorders. *Clinical Child Psychology and Psychiatry, 3*(4), 621–627.

CHAPTER SIXTEEN

# Schooling

**Anna Tate**
*Mildred Creak Child and Adolescent Psychiatric Unit,*
*Great Ormond Street Hospital for Children, London, UK*

## INTRODUCTION

Parents often nostalgically describe school days as the best days of their life. Although in retrospect this age-old aphorism may be true, it ignores and under-rates the demands of school work in our complex industrial and technological society, and adults should recognise this. The push from governments throughout the developed world to increase standards of attainment in schools has resulted in a corresponding demand on pupils to achieve (Green, 1993) and, possibly, greater competition among peers as well as a wider gap between success and failure.

Education at the close of the twentieth century is extremely demanding. A typical school day is academically, physically, and emotionally challenging. Pupils need to be healthy and psychologically robust in order to maximise their intellectual and social development at school, and, furthermore, they will require the understanding, security, and support of adults both at home and in the school community.

What then when a pupil develops an eating disorder, begins to lose weight, lacks energy, or becomes frail? How will this affect learning and relationships at school? To what extent might school work and related experiences be con-tributing to the child's psychological condition? And what role can teachers play in helping the child recover?

The causal factors for childhood onset eating disorders are multiple (see Chapter 5). They will, inevitably, either involve or eventually affect the child's school work. Therefore, school has a key role to play in multidisciplinary inter-ventions providing it can be harnessed to complement and reinforce treatment aims.

Ideally, teachers should work with the treatment team to accommodate and meet the child's particular individual needs at school. However, this is not always possible in some schools, particularly those that give precedence to academic excellence at the expense of the pupil's healthy psychological and emotional development. It may be necessary for some children with eating disorders to change schools, and a few may be able to benefit from treatment interventions without the support of their school.

## Positive school factors

School can play a positive role in recovery when teachers work with the parents and the treatment team in order to prioritise:

- enhancing the child's self-esteem
- facilitating and encouraging the child's interaction with peers and adults at school
- targeting ways in which the child can demonstrate strengths at school
- meeting the child's individual educational and emotional needs.

## Negative school factors

The school may hinder recovery when it has inflexible, rigid expectations, does not join with the treatment team, and pursues aims that:

- value academic achievements over and above individual endeavour
- encourage competition between peers
- require pupils to be extremely independent of adult support
- do not prioritise the child's individual educational and emotional needs.

## EATING DISORDERS AND SCHOOL

The school attainment of children suffering from eating disorders will vary enormously as will their individual academic potential. The stereotypic picture of a middle class, high-achieving, adolescent girl suffering from anorexia nervosa disregards the complexity of childhood onset eating disorders, which affect both sexes, all social groups, and the full spectrum of intellectual ability including some children with learning difficulties.

Mary, 12, was from a working class background. She had specific learning difficulties in mathematics, spelling, and reading, resulting from poor abstract reasoning, and poor ability in the rapid processing, long-term storage and recall of visual information. These difficulties had been identified and were being well managed by her school until the onset of anorexia nervosa, when they were compounded by Mary's low self-esteem, negative mood, and sense of ineffectiveness. She began to compare herself unfavourably with peers even when producing good work, saying, for example, "I can never be as good as other kids" and "I do badly in subjects I used to be good in".

Generally, children with eating disorders are polite and obedient pupils who present no overt behavioural difficulties at school. However, they are frequently solitary children who have become isolated from their peers. Teachers often describe them as vulnerable, or shy, and, sometimes, as if they need looking after. It is not uncommon for teachers to feel sorry for children with eating disorders, or to be over-protective of them, disregarding or excusing their poor interaction with peers.

Usually, the secrecy and control involved in the child's self-starvation or restricted eating precipitates a gradual withdrawal from social situations and eventually leads to isolation at school. However, a marked lack of self-worth and an inability to be assertive, which precedes, or develops as part of the eating disorder, may heighten and reinforce the child's sensitivity to personal criticism.

Some children with eating disorders are perfectionistic; they are overly critical of their own work, even when it is very good, and copy it out until it contains no mistakes. Such behaviour may be associated with the obsessive compulsive component of eating disorders, or with poor self-esteem, or may be a means of blocking out other painful thoughts including those concerned with eating; or it may be a combination of one or all of these. It is important for teachers to understand that, whatever others may think, the child's subjective perception of her own performance is very poor, and the experience of persistent hard work carries no intrinsic rewards for the child.

Peers and teachers sometimes misunderstand children with eating disorders because they do not associate their behaviour with feelings of inadequacy.

Sarah, a 12-year-old girl suffering from anorexia nervosa, was considered to be very bright and always achieved good grades. She appeared to be self-assured and seemed rather haughty, belying her innermost feelings of worthlessness, which she successfully projected into others. Consequently those around her, including teachers, often felt stupidly inept in her presence but afforded her little sympathy because she appeared to be so superior. In fact, she was teased by peers for being a snob.

Many children suffering from eating disorders report incidents of verbal bullying at school. Sometimes such experiences predate onset or may have acted as one trigger in the onset of the disorder. There are many examples of dieting that result from children being called "fatty" or similar names at school, or being intentionally or unwittingly humiliated in sports lessons for being unfit, clumsy, or slow.

Other forms of verbal bullying might occur once pupils become aware that a peer is losing weight. Children suffering from eating disorders have the capacity to evoke in others powerful feelings of envy or fear, which often generate verbal bullying and rejection by peers.

Occasionally, children suffering from eating disorders will attach themselves to the periphery of a group of children with whom they appear to have little in common, but who seem to possess attributes which they, themselves, would like.

Anna, 13, attached herself to a high-achieving group of confident and stylish girls, although she herself could only aspire to their fashionable dress and academic attainments and was completely unassertive.

Nancy, 12, had been sexually abused. She attached herself to a group who presented anti-social behaviours at school by flouting conventional expectations and openly challenging authority. This group may have appeared particularly attractive to Nancy, who could only turn her anger in against herself. Alternatively, the group may have confirmed Nancy's sense of worthlessness and being an outsider. Whatever the attraction, this alliance put Nancy further at risk of abusive situations.

Children suffering from anorexia nervosa usually have good school attendance and often continue to attend even after significant weight loss. In contrast to this, children suffering from food avoidance emotional disorder may manifest school-phobic features.

Samuel, 12, had poor school attendance because he was always tired due to extremely restricted food intake. In addition, he was actively avoiding both social contact with boys who frightened him because they were physically bigger and stronger than he was, and the maths lessons, which he found difficult and hated.

## IDENTIFYING PUPILS WITH EATING DISORDERS

Teachers may not find it easy to identify children with eating disorders, as they are usually good at concealing both their eating habits and their weight loss. However, often teachers who have become concerned about a child's eating and well-being, may not know the best way to help and support that child at school. Teachers' need for guidance from clinicians should never be underestimated.

The signs to look out for may not be specific to eating disorders but include a pupil who:

- wears layers of baggy clothing whatever the weather
- feels the cold
- refuses to undress in front of others for Physical Education classes
- has withdrawn from friendship groups

- presents exceptionally neat work, which contains no crossing out or corrections
- is persistently self-critical of good work
- seems unable to accept praise
- avoids eye contact
- fails to engage in oral work in the classroom
- works rather than socialises during breaks from class, especially during the lunch period.

## PROFESSIONAL BOUNDARIES

Sometimes a teacher, who suspects that a child has an eating disorder, will try to help the child without involving another appropriate person in the school establishment. Furthermore, there are a number of situations where teachers, who themselves have had or still have an eating disorder, become the child's confidante at school.

Both these circumstances demonstrate poor professional boundaries on the part of the teacher and are unhelpful to the child. The teacher should make a trusting relationship with the pupil, this is a prerequisite to supporting the child, but the teacher should always balance professional responsibility with the limitations of the professional role. Any teacher who becomes aware that a child has an eating disorder should inform a line manager as soon as possible; and any individual teacher support given to a child with an eating disorder should be part of a programme agreed by other staff within the school, the parents and, if the child has been referred for treatment, the specialist team. Teachers who have had or who are suffering from eating disorders should not be given pastoral responsibility for a child with similar difficulties and may require clear guidelines regarding the limitations of professional responsibilities.

## EDUCATION AS PART OF A MULTIDISCIPLINARY ASSESSMENT

An educational assessment is required in order to establish whether there is a relationship between the child's learning and the eating disorder. The child may have some specific learning difficulty in addition to an eating disorder or may be striving to fulfil unrealistic expectations.

Irene, 14, a girl of average ability, was attending a selective, fee-paying school with a reputation for academic excellence. Her teachers reported a sustained improvement in Irene's attainment, which was thought to be the result of her considerable hard work. Irene was working through school break times and spending an increasing amount of time at home working on school assignments. The Headteacher felt that it was Irene, rather than the school, who had set rather unrealistic and ambitious expectations, although the Headteacher did emphasise that the school expected extremely high standards from all its pupils. In such a school environment, Irene would always be under pressure to perform at her very best and yet her attainment might never be outstanding in comparison with other pupils. She first presented with eating difficulties when beginning this school at the age of 11, and the treatment team felt that school pressure had been a factor in the onset of anorexia nervosa when Irene was 13.

The following questions should always be addressed as part of an educational assessment.

- Is the child anxious about work and/or relationships at school?
- Does the child spend unnecessarily long periods of time on homework at the expense of other age-appropriate and more sociable activities?
- Is there undue pressure on the child to achieve and, if so, from whom?
- Are any difficulties the child experiences understood by the parents and the school?
- Is the school suitable to meet the child's educational and emotional needs?
- What can the school do to meet the child's educational and emotional needs?

Psychometric assessment is not essential, but can help to clarify the sometimes complex and puzzling cognitive discrepancies presented by some children suffering from eating disorders.

Sheila, 13, was underweight and failing to grow. She was from a disorganised family that had not responded to the support offered by statutory agencies. Her attendance at school had dropped from 70% to 52% and the school was concerned that many of these absences were unauthorised. Furthermore, the school believed these absences were adversely affecting Sheila's general progress. She had particularly poor literary skills. On the other hand, Sheila's mother was concerned that Sheila had some form of cognitive delay, which was not being addressed at school. Teachers from the treatment team felt unable to clarify Sheila's actual potential because, in the classroom, she presented as both immature and depressed.

Psychometric tests indicated that Sheila's ability was in the average range although her scores on literary tests were some four to five years below her chronological age. This discrepancy was accounted for by a lack of consistent educational and environmental stimulation rather than by a specific learning difficulty. Although the test results were thought to be a reasonable approximation of Sheila's level of functioning, depressed mood may have resulted in an under-representation of her actual capabilities.

In this case psychometric assessment was helpful to teachers because the results clarified the importance of regular school attendance for Sheila, and her need for intensive remedial help in literacy skills, rather than any other specialised educational support. By clarifying Sheila's actual potential, the results indicated that Sheila's parents were not providing the necessary level of support required for her to attend school regularly and progress well there, and this information helped inform the future plans for Sheila made by clinicians.

## LIAISON BETWEEN THE TREATMENT TEAM AND THE SCHOOL

The specialist treatment team should identify one of its members to be responsible for liaison with the child's school. If it is at all possible, a school visit should be made, as this often produces information not contained in written reports. The purpose of such a visit is to collect information about the child's cognitive ability, performance, and general health, and, in addition, their relationships and behaviour in school. The visit provides insight into the child's daily physical environment, the size and layout of the school site, and the number of stairs inside the building.

If a school visit is impractical, this information will need to be obtained by other means, as it may be relevant to precipitating or maintaining factors in the disorder. A teacher could be invited to meet the treatment team or its nominated representative. At the very least, telephone contact should be established, and a representative from the school should be invited to any professionals' meetings.

## THE ROLE OF TEACHERS IN THE TREATMENT TEAM

The team should include one named teacher from the child's school. This might be, for example, the Head or Deputy Head, the Special Needs teacher, a teacher with pastoral responsibility, or the child's personal tutor. The named teacher is usually a member of the teaching profession but it could be a school counsellor or nurse.

The named teacher will be a representative of both the school and the treatment team, responsible for providing relevant information to the team and for disseminating information to teachers at the child's school. This role establishes a circular loop, which involves all the teachers being properly briefed so that they can consistently implement appropriate management strategies at the school, and pass back to the named teacher relevant observations and information about the child.

In this way, the named teacher can establish an up-to-date, well-informed picture of the child at school, which can be communicated to the treatment team. Many teachers' concerns about children with eating disorders are non-specific and, therefore, never get reported. One common concern, for example, is that the child is reluctant to contribute to class discussions. Not only do many children with eating disorders avoid drawing teachers' attention to themselves, but frequently teachers are unaware of the support and management that will help them. Having a named teacher responsible for collecting and disseminating information should counteract both these difficulties.

> Annette, 13, was recovering from pervasive refusal syndrome and was reintegrating into a high-achieving school after a year's absence. The teacher from the treatment team recommended that, during Annette's first term back, academic attainment should not be prioritised, and Annette should not be entered for any examinations, as this would enable her to settle into the school routine and begin to mix with her peer group.
>
> During one of her first school visits, a teacher gave Annette the choice to try a past examination paper which the rest of the class were sitting as a test. The teacher suggested that Annette might just like to "try" the paper and stressed that Annette's performance would not be recorded. As far as the teacher was concerned, she was not pressuring Annette, who could have refused to do the examination paper and therefore the teacher felt she was respecting the guidelines set down for Annette's reintegration into school.
>
> Given this choice, Annette felt extremely nervous. She became worried about how well she would cope with the paper, thinking about how much work she had missed during her year's absence and comparing her knowledge with that of her peers. Also, she was angry that the teacher had placed her in the position of having to choose when the agreed management was for her not to sit examinations. However, she felt unable to refuse and reluctantly sat the examination paper.
>
> When Annette reported this incident to the teacher in the treatment team he discussed it with the named teacher in Annette's school who, in turn, clarified the management with teaching staff. Weekly meetings were set up between Annette and the named teacher, so that Annette had a forum in the school where she could discuss such problems as they arose.

The close monitoring of agreed plans by the named teacher can prevent the swift escalation of small difficulties as they arise.

## ARRANGING A SCHOOL MEETING

It is difficult to discuss and agree school management plans for a child with an eating disorder unless all the involved parties are present. Therefore, it is usually helpful to arrange at least one school meeting. The meeting should include the parents, a representative from the treatment team, the named teacher, and any other members of the teaching staff whom it may be appropriate to invite.

Decisions should be recorded in writing and circulated to all involved in order to eliminate misunderstandings that might hamper their implementation. Further school meetings may be necessary to review and change school management plans or to discuss difficulties as and when they arise.

# HOW MUCH SCHOOL?

Childhood onset eating disorders affect all aspects of life including school work and attendance. Retaining a link with school is beneficial, even when the child has become quite seriously ill. The child will have to cope with the demands of school life on recovery, and treatment should address the issues that will facilitate this, while, at the same time, monitoring the child's capacity to cope at school during the crucial period of regaining and maintaining a healthy weight.

Careful consideration will have to be given to the balance between proper physical care, and the maintenance of some normal, age-appropriate expectations, such as attending school. Every possible attempt should be made to minimise the disruption to a child's life caused by any illness. However, it may become necessary for some children suffering from eating disorders to attend school on a part-time basis or, in some cases, to study at home on work set and marked by their school teachers, while working towards reintegration into school. Three factors influencing this decision are:

(1) the child's health
(2) the availability of adult supervision at home during the day
(3) the school's flexibility in supporting arrangements which meet the child's needs.

These three factors are interrelated. The extent to which it is safe for a child to be physically active will depend on their general nutritional status and will be determined by clinicians. Having taken this into account, clinicians, parents, and teachers may be able to design a school programme that is individually tailored to meet a child's needs; the same plan would not work for all children. This plan should consider the family's capacity to cope at home as well as assessing the contribution that school can make to the treatment programme.

## Part-time school programmes

Limiting a child's attendance at school is one aspect of a treatment programme designed to facilitate recovery, and is not punitive. It helps the child, family, and school staff confront the consequences of the eating disorder that eventually disrupt everyday life and, in so doing, it counteracts the possible collusion with any denial regarding the severity of the child's condition.

Part-time school programmes can sometimes be designed to suit both the needs of the child and the availability of parents to provide supervision at home. For example:

• attending only morning or afternoon school may provide a good opportunity for the child to eat lunch at home with proper parental supervision

- attending school only to pursue certain subjects may be relevant for adolescents preparing for public examinations
- if a parent works parttime, attending school when the parent is at work may be more convenient for family life.

Inevitably, parents will need to provide an income for their family and may not be able to supervise their child at home during the day; and schools, which have the interests of the majority of pupils to consider, may be unable to accommodate the particular needs of an individual child. There will be occasions when compromises and sacrifices produce only the best available arrangements.

## REINTEGRATION INTO SCHOOL

Those children who have been too frail to attend school may find returning to face peers and teachers a daunting prospect. They may need support to think about what they will say about their absence and how they will cope with the expectations that may be made on them. Teachers will need to think about the best way of preparing the class for the return of one of its members. A preliminary, "ice-breaking" visit can be helpful prior to a programme of part-time reintegration.

For some children, working towards increasing school attendance can be used successfully as a motive for weight gain and, for others, it can be a face-saver. If a child particularly wants to participate in a school activity, she may be sufficiently motivated to gain some weight in order to do so. Equally, linking school attendance with healthy eating enables the child to justify weight gain by saying "I had to put weight on so that I could go to school".

The pace of reintegration into school must be matched to the child's ability to cope. In some circumstances, it may be appropriate to have a prearranged, step-by-step plan which is linked with targeted weekly weight gain. However, for some children, such a plan will be too threatening, as it involves accepting some responsibility for weight gain and acknowledges a steady progression towards recovery with the possibility of less support from the treatment team.

Mary, 12, had been maintaining a healthy weight and had expressed a wish to begin reintegrating into school. However, once she started to attend for one lesson a week she began to lose weight. The treatment team suspended the school reintegration programme and intensified work with Mary and her family. This brought about an improvement in Mary's physical condition and in her mood. When considering school reintegration in the light of this improvement, the treatment team decided that Mary should attend school for one day each week, for three consecutive weeks, prior to her recommencing school full time. This plan was agreed because it was not dependent on Mary's weight so she did not have to prove to the treatment team that she could maintain a healthy weight. The plan communicated to

Mary the tacit belief and confidence that she was well enough and would cope with normal school expectations.

## Allocating a buddy

It may be helpful to identify one buddy, a peer who will act as a friend and support the child suffering from an eating disorder during the school day. This is a delicate task because the well-being of the buddy needs to be considered in addition to that of the child with the eating disorder. Many children have been drawn into hiding food and keeping secrets about the eating habits of children suffering from eating disorders. The role of buddy is not for the impressionable or unassertive child, and the buddy should always have a named teacher to turn to if his or her role becomes difficult. A teacher who knows the child with the eating disorder should be responsible for selecting an appropriate buddy and for monitoring the relationship in the best interests of both the parties involved.

Despite potential problems, the advantages of allocating a buddy usually outweigh the disadvantages. Basically, the buddy takes an interest in, gives support to, and provides company for the child with an eating disorder, and by accepting the onus for socialising, the buddy prevents the child with an eating disorder from being isolated at school. Buddies often create social interactions, which the child with an eating disorder enjoys but might not initiate, and the company of a buddy distracts the child with an eating disorder from drifting into an internal world dominated with thoughts about food.

## Emotional support at school

In addition to the support of a buddy, the child suffering from an eating disorder should have the support of a named teacher in the form of regular, individual meetings. Initially these will need to be structured, for example on a daily or weekly basis, but once the child builds, a trusting relationship with the teacher, the meetings may take place less frequently and more spontaneously.

Usually, the greater the concern there is about the child at school, the more frequent the meetings will need to be held. The agenda will vary according to the needs of the child, but the teacher should encourage the child to talk about positive experiences at school in order to acknowledge strengths and the ability to cope. However, the meeting may also need to explore the child's difficulties at school and the teacher must help the child to develop strategies for dealing with these, if necessary drawing on the ideas and support of colleagues from within the school system and the treatment team.

## EATING AT SCHOOL

When a school plan is made for a child suffering from an eating disorder, it must give clear guidelines regarding eating arrangements. There is no easy method whereby teachers can supervise a child's eating at school. Teachers have neither the parental nor the professional authority to insist that a child eats, or to supervise the child in the lavatory to check for purging or vomiting.

On the whole, it is probably best for teachers to target areas of intervention other than eating, such as the child's low self-esteem and interaction with peers, as it may not be helpful to the child if the relationship with the teacher is associated with battles over eating. Nevertheless, many teachers wish to help and, in the child's interests, agree to offer encouragement at mealtimes, either sitting with the child through lunch, arranging for the child to sit with sensible peers, or checking the contents of a packed lunch box to see what has been eaten. Such arrangements may well be inadequate. In the end, only regular monitoring of the child's weight will indicate whether the child has sufficient calorific intake during the school day.

## THE VOLUME AND CONTENT OF SCHOOL WORK

School is part of the normal, everyday life of the child and, therefore, continuing with school work will help the child suffering from an eating disorder to keep in touch with everyday life. However, the purpose should be to maximise the use of potentially positive, therapeutic, school factors which will encourage self-expression, raise self-esteem, and facilitate interaction with others, while, at the same time, minimise the influence of potentially negative school factors such as rivalry among peers and the pressure to succeed academically.

Therefore, the volume and content of school work, including participation in sports activities at school, should be carefully matched to the child's physical and psychological condition. Children suffering from eating disorders may not be well enough to continue studying the entire curriculum even if they are attending school full time. Some children of low weight will experience concentration difficulties and may become harshly self-critical of their own inability to think and achieve. Others will continue to work diligently and pressure themselves to maintain their own personal standards of achievement as well as their usual volume of work.

The amount of school work a child undertakes should be manageable and should not impose unnecessary pressure or anxiety on the child. It should be quantified by both time and content, and agreed collectively by the adults (parents, teachers, clinicians) responsible; not decided by the child, parents, or teachers alone. The adults will need to decide how many subjects the child will continue to study and for how long each day. Limiting the amount a child studies communicates a clear message that the child is unwell, and demonstrates care and concern for the child's well-being.

Some children respond well to the harsh reality that by strictly controlling their eating habits, they are relinquishing control in other areas, such as the amount of school work they can do. Others will be unable to think so coherently. Most children will require close adult supervision to ensure that they are not working for longer than the prescribed time period as they may find it difficult to put aside unfinished work or be satisfied with the standard of the work they have completed.

School can be used to distract the child from ruminations about body image, weight, food, and eating. However, it is surprising how many school subjects involve these topics in some form or other. A modern foreign language, for example, usually contains a whole module about meal times, eating out and buying food. Food technology, biology, anatomy, and some sport education can emphasise topics relating to calories, food intake, fitness and body image; the very topics that morbidly preoccupy children suffering from eating disorders. If the purpose of school work is to provide distraction from the eating disorder, then the content of the child's curriculum may require some monitoring.

On the other hand, some aspects of the curriculum can be used positively as a forum in which to tackle issues related to eating disorders. For example, Personal, Social, and Health Education provides an excellent opportunity in which to discuss the image of beauty portrayed in the media, gender stereotypes and the importance of friendships, as well as other factors affecting self-image. It can also provide an opportunity for children to raise issues which worry them such as a friend's dieting, or keeping secrets.

If it has been decided that a child must work at home until regaining lost weight, she should be set school work that can be completed without the supervision or support of a teacher. However, tasks targeting research, analysis, and communication skills, which require the child to think and make judgements, should take precedence over repetitive, routine work. Any tendency to gravitate towards subjects that the child struggles with should be avoided; focusing on her weaknesses will reinforce her sense of inadequacy. Those subjects and activities that the child particularly enjoys should be targeted, encouraging her to capitalise on strengths to gain confidence and improve self-esteem.

Drawing and painting, together with pictorial or diagrammatic formats, are preferable to lengthy, factual written explanations. An illustrated, personal project will provide a means to increased knowledge as well as self-expression. The child may be unable to complete imaginative writing assignments until reaching a healthy weight, although reading, critical writing, and writing poetry could be encouraged.

Teachers and parents should understand that, in most cases, it will be necessary temporarily to suspend ideas of improving the child's standard of achievement until she has retained and is maintaining a healthy weight. Furthermore, some of the most successful strategies for actively targeting self-esteem, and facilitating interaction with others may result, temporarily, in a lower standard of academic work. Parents and teachers should be prepared to accept this.

## CREATIVE ACTIVITIES IN THE
## SCHOOL CURRICULUM

Creative activities provide children suffering from eating disorders with a positive outlet for self-expression. This can act as a natural counterbalance to the powerful self-destructiveness of starvation, as well as a means of communication that initiates social interaction with others. Yet many children limit their involvement with creative subjects at school, often restricting them to out-of-school activities, and opting for more academic studies. Furthermore, it is not at all uncommon for their creative talent to be entirely associated with attainment rather than personal expression

> Sarah, 12, was an accomplished pianist. She had only ever played classical music, but with minimal encouragement found an outlet for her developing personality and individuality in a confident improvisation of the song which was currently at the top of the pop charts. This impressed peers and consequently brought her both an improved image and greater acceptance. It sidestepped verbal communication, which Sarah found difficult, yet conveyed her interests, her talent, and the fact that she could be fun, presenting a stark contrast to the image of Sarah as a hard-working snob. Sarah enjoyed her new image and subsequently took up playing the guitar, progressing to play an electric guitar in a rock band.

Some children suffering from eating disorders have been interested in ballet prior to the onset of their illness but have only ever experienced the rigid and perfectionistic side of dance, which focuses on technical excellence and is highly competitive. Creative dance and movement requires no verbal communication but engages participants in interacting with and responding to each other. It can be creative, sociable, and fun, and, at the same time, help children develop a more realistic, positive, and integrated sense of their bodies. It also provides a method of moderate exercise that improves cardiovascular fitness and physical strength (Elliott, 1998).

Other children suffering from eating disorders are accomplished artists or good at drama. They are perceptive observers of others and are often surprisingly good mimics, or cartoonists with the ability to portray critically or humorously the mannerisms and characteristics of those around them. All these creative attributes attract the attention of peers and usually stimulate spontaneous praise and admiration. Such skills may be the only source of pride for children suffering from eating disorders, and may be the one thing they really enjoy and for which they will accept praise.

These creative activities should not be confused with the disciplines of therapies, such as art or music therapy, but they are therapeutic in their own right because they provide an outlet for self-expression and a method of communication. They can be used imaginatively to engage children with eating disorders in peer interaction. Teachers may find opportunities to utilise them fully as part of classwork and within the school community, for example in magazine work or posters, in concerts, plays, and performances.

## PREPARING FOR EXAMINATIONS

Examinations can act as a trigger in the onset of an eating disorder or can impose an additional stress that may hinder recovery. However, parents may be concerned about reducing the extent of their child's examination course work, fearing that their child will fall behind and be in danger of having future life chances jeopardised. Withdrawing a child from examinations, or restricting the number of subjects studied, warrants careful consideration, and each case will need to be decided individually. However, experience suggests that reducing the number of subjects studied brings a corresponding increase in the child's ability to cope and succeed, and may, therefore, be successful in the long term. Moreover, many examination boards are sympathetic to, and will make concessions for, adverse personal circumstances such as ill-health. In addition, some educational institutions will waive their entry requirements in exceptional personal circumstances.

Parents' anxieties about school issues are sometimes easier to vocalise than concerns about the eating disorder, which carry so many confusing and uncomfortable feelings. However, it is imperative that the child's healthy physical and psychological development is given priority over academic attainments even when the child is studying for examinations, and clinicians will need to ensure that this is understood and respected. What happens to the child in the future can be decided once the child's eating and weight have become more stable and, therefore, less worrying.

## DEALING WITH WORRIES

School can be identified as a place where the child can successfully "take a break" from the eating disorder, although the teacher may need to remind, encourage, or enable the child to do this. It is not the role of the teacher to become involved in listening to or trying to sort out worries about eating, but to have an expectation that the child will set the worries aside and have a rest from them during the school day. The teacher might say, "you look a bit worried, I thought you were going to take a break from worrying during school time".

The aim is to help the child contain worries, but not bottle them up. Therefore, the teacher may need to acknowledge the child's feelings while, at the same time, helping the child to contain those feelings. It may help the child to have a worry book in school (Sharman, 1997). This involves the child in writing down her worries, either at regular times during the day, such as in lessons or breaks, or as the need arises. The entries are read and discussed later with an appropriate adult, other than the teacher. This helps the teacher to respect a proper professional boundary. The teacher may deal with school worries but other adults will deal with worries about food and weight.

## USING SCHOOL ACTIVITIES AS AN INCENTIVE FOR WEIGHT GAIN

When school activities are pleasurable, they may be used successfully as incentives that encourage weight gain.

> Mary, 12, was highly motivated to be with her peer group in school even when she was of very low weight. Therefore, consuming the required number of calories was made a condition for her participation in school activities and outings. Mary responded positively to this management.

The same management does not work for all children.

> Pauline, 14, seemed to derive little pleasure from school. She was solitary and uncommunicative, speaking only when spoken to, and giving the impression that creative work was unstimulating and babyish because it was not academically challenging. However, during the weekly dance session, she interacted well with other children and adults, spontaneously suggesting ideas and movements, appearing relaxed and happy. The only time during the week when she was seen to smile in school was during dance sessions. When Pauline's participation in dance became dependent on her finishing a mid-morning drink, she persistently refused to finish the drink, thus denying herself the opportunity to take part in the one activity she appeared to enjoy.

Pauline is typical of other children suffering from eating disorders who do not respond to incentives. It may be that these children will not allow themselves any pleasure in their lives and find ways to sabotage the very experiences they most enjoy. Such children present a dilemma because the use of punishments or restricting their repertoire of activities only serves to reinforce their cycle of self-denial and joylessness. For these children, school activities should not be associated with eating management. Pauline's management was changed so that she could participate in dance without any conditions related to food intake. Her pleasure in dancing was used to distract her from her preoccupation with food and weight, drawing her into healthier relationships with peers and staff, capitalising on her creativity, and enabling her to establish a role for herself as the oldest girl in the group.

## DEALING WITH PERFECTIONISM

Perfectionist tendencies are manifested through an inability to tolerate mistakes, repeatedly copying out work, painstaking neatness, often very small handwriting and the diligent use of corrector pens. Sometimes perfectionism is related to the other obsessive-compulsive symptoms of eating disorders, but is it also closely allied to the child's sense of not being "good enough".

Teachers will sometimes unwittingly encourage perfectionistic tendencies and praise pupils for meticulous, unblemished work. However, it is a painful irony that this praise does not appear to help the child suffering from an eating disorder to have a better self-image, but actually appears to reinforce the child's sense of inadequacy as well as the desire to produce even more perfect work in the future.

Conversely, challenging the pupil's criticism of the work and helping her to tolerate mistakes, assists her in developing more realistic attitudes and accepting both praise and criticism from the teacher. In order to give appropriate feedback, the teacher must listen to the child's self-criticism and aspirations and then engage in discussion about these. Instead of responding to the child's dissatisfaction by saying, "don't be silly, this is excellent!", the teacher can say "what is it about your work that you don't like?" or "what would you change to improve it?". The teacher might openly disagree with the child, saying, for example, "we have a different opinion about this, don't we?"; or the teacher might state that the pupil is not yet ready to give in work that contains mistakes. If there is a trusting relationship between the teacher and the child, and the child seems strong enough, the teacher might begin to take in work as finished even when the pupil would like to do more to it. Some children can only learn to tolerate the idea that work is not perfect by the teacher taking control over when the work is finished.

These kinds of interaction separate the child as an individual, with feelings, standards, and wishes, from the work, which is a product of knowledge, skill, and effort. The child with a poor self-image may only value herself in terms of her own academic achievements and may constantly strive for perfection in order to satisfy a need for approval from others. The child may see her school work as significant whereas she, as a person, remains insignificant and worthless, or she may believe that adults are only interested in the work produced rather than the person who produced it.

## DEALING WITH SOCIAL WITHDRAWAL

Children suffering from eating disorders, particularly those who have become perfectionistic and also those who have become withdrawn, often sit in class working throughout the lesson without talking or being spoken to by anyone.

George, 12, and suffered from food avoidance emotional disorder. He was of very low weight but attended school regularly because he was under pressure from his father to achieve. However, he never spoke to anyone while he was there, and would not ask for help from teachers even though he had considerable difficulty in coping with the work.

It is important for teachers to talk to such children in order to interrupt their self-enforced ostracism. Such a simple strategy might not even occur to a busy teacher. Yet the teacher's lack of direct, individual attention and communication may reinforce that child's belief that she is worthless, or her anger at being treated without care and respect. The child should believe that she has a voice, the right to contribute an opinion that will be listened to, an individual contribution to make to the group. Talking to the child once during the lesson will, over time, result in the child making spontaneous remarks. Moreover, actively seeking the opinion of the child, using her knowledge and expertise, will gradually facilitate her assimilation into class discussions and, eventually, into the peer group.

If possible, the teacher should find time to talk to the child about subjects other than the school work in hand, e.g. the weather or pop music, which, over time, encourages the child to initiate spontaneous conversations about topics other than school work. Small steps such as these will lead to increased self-confidence and improved self-esteem.

## COLLABORATIVE WORK IN THE CLASSROOM

Collaborative work with peers is beneficial to pupils suffering from eating disorders, because it requires the ability to compromise as well as assertiveness and communication skills. These attributes are usually the very weaknesses of children suffering from eating disorders, who therefore find it difficult to work co-operatively with other children.

Collaborative work should have a positive impact on the interaction among peers. What dictates the success of collaborative work in helping children with eating disorders is how they are matched by the teacher with the child or children with whom they are working. This match has to be carefully considered in each individual case.

Jo was suffering from anorexia nervosa. She was a withdrawn, intelligent 11-year-old who completed the work set without any flicker of emotion or interest. She was matched with Barbara, also aged 11, a lively and sociable peer who was interested in the work but did not always understand it and found concentration difficult to sustain. This was a successful match. Barbara made Jo laugh and demonstrated a lot of care and concern for her feelings. Jo explained the work to Barbara, which increased her enthusiasm and energy for it. When the work was completed Barbara acted as a communication bridge between Jo and the class, which drew in Jo and made her part of the peer group.

An unsuccessful match as that of Irene and Paul, both 14. Irene, suffering from anorexia nervosa, made good contributions to class discussions but always chose to work alone and presented her work to a high, perfectionistic standard. However, the content of her work did not correspond with the self-contained, scholarly image that Irene projected in class. Paul was quite unassertive but understood the work and needed to be allied with a confident partner. When set collaborative work in a practical science lesson, Irene took control, completing the experiment without including Paul. It was as if Irene were a demonstrator and Paul a spectator. There was no interaction between them and Irene's position in the peer group remained unchanged. In this case, the teacher had to intervene to facilitate and supervise a more co-operative working relationship between Irene and Paul, challenging Irene to seek Paul's opinion and to share decision making with him, while challenging Paul to be more assertive and demand a more active role in the shared tasks.

## PUPIL SELF-EVALUATION AND EVALUATION BY PEERS

Self-evaluation involves the child reflecting on personal performance as well as setting targets in school; evaluation by peers involves classmates appraising the performance of a peer. These forms of evaluation are internationally recognised as integral to good teaching practice because of their impact on improving pupils' self-esteem and social skills, and developing pupil autonomy (Gipps, 1994). Self-evaluation is particularly helpful to children suffering from eating disorders because it requires them to see themselves as objects of their own thought, and to verbalise their perceptions of their own performance in relation to the requirements of the task, their own personal best, and the performance of others. Therefore, it provides a forum in which the good teacher can encourage the pupil to realistically assess personal performance and the effort invested in it as well as comparing it to past performances.

Personal target setting creates a cycle in which the pupil's success fosters increased motivation and results in intrinsic satisfaction and a sense of personal achievement leading to a new target. Through these processes, self-evaluation can enable the child suffering from an eating disorder to shift from a harshly self-critical position, which results in the lack of any pleasure in the work undertaken, to one where the child can begin to acknowledge and enjoy success or progress. However, this will only be possible if the teacher carefully supervises the pupil's own target setting to ensure that the goals are appropriate, realistic, and achievable.

Peer evaluation brings the child suffering from an eating disorder into face-to-face contact with the reality of the opinions and judgements of peers. It also requires the child to consider the work of other pupils and communicate with them about it. Peers can successfully challenge the perfectionist's self-criticism and give work its due praise and admiration. The teacher must encourage the child to listen to praise as well as criticism, for if the child heeds the latter, they should also heed the former.

However beneficial self and peer evaluation may be in reinforcing the learning of the majority of pupils, it must be stressed that such work may be threatening for solitary children suffering from eating disorders and will always require the oversight of an experienced, skilful, and sensitive teacher.

## THE EFFECTIVE USE OF TEACHING STRATEGIES

All the strategies mentioned are fundamental to good teaching practice and are often an intrinsic feature of the school ethos. When this is the case, clinicians will only need to bring them to the attention of teachers, in order for them to be prioritised within an individual education programme for the child with an eating disorder.

These strategies are difficult to adopt in schools that place value on attainment over and above individual pupil need. In such circumstances, clinicians will have to assess whether the school environment is conducive to the healthy physical and psychological development of the child, and advise the parents accordingly.

Teachers will need to understand that any strategy that aims to engage the withdrawn child (suffering from an eating disorder) in everyday school interactions will take time. Teachers should not be put off by failure and will need to persevere with a positive belief that they will be successful and with the expectation that the child will respond. This is an important point, because children with eating disorders have the power to project into others, including teachers, feelings of complete inadequacy and failure. At times, teachers are likely to feel powerless, frustrated, and hopeless. When this happens, they should seek the support of colleagues, either in the school system or the treatment team, to discuss their feelings in order to understand and control them. Otherwise such strong feelings may interfere with the capacity to make objective decisions about the child's needs.

## WORKING WITH INPATIENTS

Children suffering from eating disorders who are admitted as inpatients are likely to present a wide variety of educational needs. At one end of the spectrum may be a child admitted to interrupt and reverse a pattern of weight loss. At the other end there are children with intractable conditions, children who have suicidal ideas, and those with pervasive refusal syndrome.

The hospital inpatient school should reflect such diverse individual needs, but also provide a sense of group cohesion, so that every group member, irrespective of their own needs, experiences a sense of belonging and contributing to the classroom group.

Educational assessment and school liaison will be required for inpatients as it is for outpatients, although it should be possible to ensure that educational aims are compatible with and complementary to the treatment aims. Moreover, the content of the curriculum can be organised to be beneficial for children with eating disorders, including creative activities to balance academic work. The work should be differentiated to meet individual need and planned to facilitate interaction between peers through collaborative tasks.

For planned, short admissions and for children studying for examinations, it may be appropriate for some work to be set by the child's home school (the school where the child is on roll and will return on discharge). This should be current, relevant classwork that other children in the home school are doing rather than work set simply to occupy the child in hospital. However, work from the home school should not provide the entire curriculum for the child in hospital, as this would prevent more collaborative work taking place with peers in the classroom.

## Making a record of achievement

When children are discharged from hospital, their personal achievements are often negated or minimised by references to what they have missed. This is especially true of school work. Children should not automatically be expected to catch up on school work; this may engender feelings of inadequacy, which should be avoided at all costs during the rehabilitation period. Furthermore, the child's school work, completed in hospital, should be valued and celebrated as a part of their scholastic achievements.

Any child who is in hospital for a month or longer should be involved in making a record of achievement, which presents samples of work and reports on the child's strengths. It should contain the child's own personal statement, which tells the reader something about them, their interests, strengths, and hopes. Writing such a statement can be linked to the process of self-evaluation. One model is to involve pupils in writing a diary in which they discuss their week in school. This gives teachers valuable insight into the child's experience of school perceptions of their performance. A rule can be made that any negative comments written should be balanced by positive ones, discouraging the pupil from dwelling on critical and pessimistic thoughts. The child can set a personal, attainable target for a particular time period, for example, a calendar month or the period up to discharge.

> Mary, 12, wrote that she would try to keep her feelings out of school, that she wanted to enjoy science lessons and think about returning to her home school. These were all difficult, yet attainable, targets against which Mary could evaluate her week in school and which teachers could help her to achieve.

Targets and diary entries may be used by pupils to assess how much they have achieved in school during a hospital admission, can feed into the child's personal statement, and at discharge may be used by the children to write their own school reports for inclusion in the record of achievement.

The record of achievement can contain photographs of school outings and activities as well as examples of the child's work completed in hospital. It should also contain reports from teachers. These should focus on the child strength's and the progress that has been made, because their purpose is to celebrate achievement. Concerns about the child's educational needs should be addressed in reports written for parents and other professionals.

The children who find it difficult to acknowledge their own progress may not feel that any work is good enough to include in their record of achievement. There will be times when the teacher must take responsibility for helping to collate the record of achievement. Experience suggests that children are very proud of these folders of work once they are completed, because they look impressive and represent tangible proof of their endeavours.

## PERVASIVE REFUSAL SYNDROME

Children with pervasive refusal syndrome are uniquely dependent on adults because they are so resistant to normal activities and expectations. They require particular consideration and management in order to ensure that the teacher has some expectations of them, while, at the same time, carefully nurturing and protecting them so that they feel secure and safe in the classroom.

Children suffering from pervasive refusal syndrome tend to be intelligent and observant. They continue to be aware of what is going on around them even when they give no indication that they are alert or interested. They should attend school but, as they make no effort to look after themselves, teachers must work co-operatively with nursing staff to ensure they receive proper physical care in the classroom. They should be placed in whatever position is most comfortable for them.

Annette, 13, lay on three bean bags because she would not sit in a chair.

Their clothing should be properly adjusted so that it is not twisted or uncomfortable and does not leave them exposed, and they should be neither too hot nor too cold.

Recovery from pervasive refusal syndrome is very gradual. In the classroom, such children, just like any others, require a programme in which they have some individual teacher attention, some attention from peers, some time working alone, and some time when they are required to be a member of the group. The individual attention should be uninterrupted time when teachers can focus their entire attention on the child, by reading a story, or doing an activity on behalf of the child, for example making a bracelet with beads. Other children can also give this kind of attention, or by giving a commentary as they undertake an activity, and by describing and showing the work they have completed.

It is important for children suffering from pervasive refusal syndrome to have time alone in the classroom, without the attention of teachers or peers. They can be given a choice either to have a break from the demands of individual or group work, or to listen to what is going on around them. Reports from children who have recovered from pervasive refusal syndrome suggest that they make good use of this time. Listening to what is going on around them has stimulated their interest in what is happening as well as in relating to particular children.

Children suffering from pervasive refusal syndrome can be helped to feel part of the group by the way they are positioned in the classroom, being asked rhetorical questions, and when they are recovering, being given a small task.

> Annette loved dance. First she had listened and then watched with interest. Gradually she progressed to a stage where she would take part passively, playing a role in which she did not have to move but where others danced around her. A breakthrough came in a session where dances were being made in small groups using the theme of fire. Annette was lying on three bean bags, everyone was still, dramatically she flicked up her thumb, the flame which started the fire, and the group dance began.

Children suffering from pervasive refusal syndrome need face-savers. Their complete refusal is so dramatic that the smallest improvement is noticeable and is likely to arouse a reaction from adults and children.

> The first known, independent classroom activity, undertaken by Susan, 10, was when she made a house from Lego, but no-one saw her do it. At the time, her teachers felt that she was ready to do something and were placing in front of her a different activity at different times of the day. On this particular occasion a tray of Lego was placed in front of Susan. She acknowledged that she had made the house and her teachers realised that she needed some privacy in which to begin to experiment with activities. They ensured that everyday objects such as a book stand and pencil pots were placed on the table to provide a shield behind which Susan could begin to work. They also ensured that other children gave her the space she needed.

## CHILDREN WITH INTRACTABLE EATING DISORDERS

Such children often seemed locked in a hopeless cycle of disappointment and failure and it is usually difficult to establish a good relationship with them. They sometimes sabotage any progress made in school by denigrating or destroying their work, and always compare themselves poorly to peers. It is difficult for the teacher to stay positive in the face of such negative behaviour. However, it is imperative for such a child that the teacher finds a strength which that child possesses, so that the child can use it to make a contribution to the class group.

Karen, 13, had a five-year history of anorexia nervosa, which had involved several hospital admissions. She was being fed by a gastrostomy as she had been unable to tolerate naso-gastric or intravenous feeding. She was too ill to concentrate on age-appropriate academic work but rejected other work as babyish and, at the same time, was fiercely self-critical of her own inability to cope. Karen was an excellent actress and, in addition, two interests gave her expertise in the peer group. These were her knowledge of pop music and her skill with make-up and nail varnish. These interests, and her talent for acting, were used to engage Karen and give her a role in the group. This was not sufficient to reverse her own entrenched, poor self-image, but it provided some fun and some moments of relief from the ordeal of her illness.

The maintenance of a positive and therapeutic milieu in the classroom can be threatened when the pupil group contains a child like Karen. The behaviour of her peers suggested that they experienced many confusing feelings. They appeared to want to please her, in order both to be accepted by her and to give her support. When other children were enjoying school activities and Karen was not, they seemed to feel guilty and disloyal, constantly looking over to her, as if seeking her approval or permission to take part in school activities. On many occasions, Karen's difficulties indirectly resulted in other children becoming disaffected and rejecting school activities. At times, her despair was so striking that it was difficult to ignore. Consequently, her mood adversely influenced the atmosphere in the classroom, and counteracted the benefit of school as a distraction from worries and preoccupations.

Teachers working with children like Karen, who project such hopelessness, may require the help and support of colleagues in the treatment team in order to remain positive and manage the pupil group objectively in the best interests of all the children.

## CONCLUSION

When assessing how children with eating disorders are coping in school, it should not just be their learning that is taken into consideration. If school management complements treatment aims, school can play a role in enhancing the child's self-esteem, facilitating relationships with peers and encouraging contributions to group activities. Children with eating disorders need to "find their voice" and place in the school community. Their experience of illness may change them. They may make new friends and take up new interests. Teachers should work with parents and the treatment team to supervise them during their illness and rehabilitation so that school makes a positive impact on their recovery and future well-being.

## SUMMARY POINTS

- School issues should be part of a multidisciplinary assessment and treatment programme.
- The child's physical and psychological well-being should take precedence over academic success.
- Effective communication systems need to be established between teachers and clinicians.
- The school can play a positive role in the child's recovery when it aims to improve the child's self-esteem and encourages interaction between peers.
- The child's curriculum may need to be modified, limiting the time spent on academic subjects in favour of creative activities.
- Teachers may need support from clinicians in order to understand the best ways of helping children with eating disorders.

## REFERENCES

Elliott, R. (1998). Creative dance and movement in child pyschiatry. *Clinical Child Psychology and Psychiatry*, *3*(2), 251–265.

Gipps, C. (1994). *Beyond testing, towards a theory of educational assessment*. London: Falmer Press.

Green, A. (1993). *Educational achievement in Britain, France, Germany and Japan: A comparative analysis*. London: Institute of Education, University of London.

Sharman, W. (1997). *Children and adolescents with mental health problems*. London: Bailliere Tindall.

# CHAPTER SEVENTEEN

# Ethical and legal issues

**Marianne Bentovim**
*London Child & Family Consultation Service, Harley Street,
London, UK*

## INTRODUCTION

There are few conditions in child and adolescent psychiatry that are potentially life threatening, and which may have serious or even fatal consequences
in the event of no treatment being offered or effective. It is therefore important
that there are guidelines based on ethical and legal considerations available to
practitioners and clinicians for reference when making difficult decisions in
respect of patient care.

Management of child and adolescent anorexia and bulimia nervosa is
often complex and difficult, not least because the wishes of the patient are
often in conflict with the goals of treatment. At the point of diagnosis many
children or young people either do not recognise or deny that they have an
eating disorder, and they are often reluctant to engage in treatment, whether
as outpatients or inpatients. Although it is possible in some cases to establish
a therapeutic alliance with the "healthy part" of the child, as opposed to the
"anorexic part", this is clearly not possible when the "anorexic part" is denied.
In all cases, a therapeutic alliance has to be established with the young person's
parents.

## PRINCIPLES OF GOOD PRACTICE

Generally speaking, when engaging children and adolescents in treatment,
attempts should be made to explain to them and their parents as comprehensively as possible:

- what an eating disorder is, with specific reference to the characteristics of the particular disorder
- what is entailed in treatment, both in terms of physical management, e.g. reinstatement of feeding, and what psychological help can be offered.

Care should be taken to elicit the young person's own perception of her illness, what she understands about it, and what her feelings are about treatment and what it entails. An opportunity should be given for her to ask questions, and have those answered as fully as possible.

After a period of self-starvation or severely restricted food intake, there is usually resistance to eating a balanced diet again, and sometimes a panic response ensues, with hostility and refusal to co-operate. On being asked to take responsibility for refeeding their child (certainly in outpatient treatment) parents too might be anxious, suspicious, and reluctant to risk being in conflict with their child by being firm and unequivocal in their expectation that the child will eat. It may be necessary to provide a clear explanation of the physical effects of anorexia nervosa, e.g. the effect on the body of starvation, accompanied by loss of menstruation and the increased risk of osteoporosis; circulatory failure; cardiac arrest; or even death. Thus, the need for effective therapeutic intervention needs to be established.

Interestingly, many patients subsequently reveal in therapy that, although diagnosis and the commencement of treatment were initially frightening and resisted, at the same time there was often a sense of enormous relief. Responsibility for eating and day-to-day life effectively became delegated to parents or others, since the child or young person's own capacity to assume responsibility had become significantly diminished. The very control they sought in respect of their eating may have been overtaken by a growing sense of powerlessness in the face of the illness. Alternatively, they may feel that supreme control over food intake represents their last vestige of personal autonomy with the fear that loss of control will result in emotional fragmentation and chaos. Often there is a reluctance to relinquish the association with anorexia nervosa, which may have provided a refuge in terms of the young person's sense of identity, and the social persona by which they are known. Thus, getting well may appear terrifying and the young person may feel driven to thwart the efforts of parents or clinicians in this respect.

## ETHICAL DILEMMAS

It is important to distinguish between the ethical dilemmas faced by those treating adults with eating disorders, and those treating children and young people under the age of 18. When adults with serious anorexia nervosa decline treatment, clinicians are faced with the dilemma of whether or not to seek permission or a mandate to treat the patient against her will, in order to preserve life. In the UK, an application may be made under the Mental Health Act 1983 for the patient to be compulsorily admitted to an appropriate unit or hospital for treatment. The opinions of two independent psychiatrists are required to establish a diagnosis, and give an opinion as to whether or not treatment is necessary; an approved social worker will conduct an assessment to determine whether or not it is in the patient's interests for hospital admission to proceed. The patient's rights will further be upheld within the tribunal system, which allows for regular review of her status and gives her the right to appeal against continuing treatment, with appropriate representation being made on her behalf.

There have been some controversial cases, both in the UK and abroad, involving young women who have claimed the right not to continue with treatment for anorexia nervosa, and who, as part of their right to self-determination, have requested non-intrusive management and their right to die as a consequence of self-starvation. In Holland, there have been some anecdotal reports of young women who have insisted on the right to die and effectively requested euthanasia, rather than to prolong their suffering, both from anorexia nervosa, and the gruelling process of treatment.

This raises serious ethical dilemmas for clinicians. On the one hand, they may wish to respect the rights of their patients, and they may well be sympathetic to the principles involved in euthanasia, or the right to self-determination. On the other hand they recognise the serious effects of starvation on cognitive functioning, which may render a sufferer's capacity to make a reasoned decision about her life seriously compromised. The depressive effects of anorexia nervosa are also recognised, accompanied at times by clearly expressed suicidal ideation. The fact that anorexia nervosa is a treatable condition, albeit with a rather guarded prognosis at follow-up, further adds to the pressure on clinicians to wish to intervene actively in their patient's life in order to preserve it. Furthermore, recovering sufferers often recall their despair during the acute phase of their illness, and their wish to die, or certainly to be left alone without any intervention of treatment being proffered. However, they report that with the re-establishment of normal weight, accompanied by an improvement in mood and therapeutic support, they were very glad, despite their ongoing struggle, still to be alive.

It seems therefore unethical to withhold treatment on the basis of the difficulty in engaging their co-operation, since their judgement is likely to be seriously impaired by their illness. Of those patients who, although recovered from the acute phase of their eating disorder, still remain suicidal, a small proportion may, and sometimes do, find alternative ways of ending their lives if they are intent on doing so. Although there are differences of opinion within the professional community concerning the ethics of treating an adult patient against her will, in respect of the treatment of children and adolescents there is generally a broader consensus in favour of treatment being provided, even where the young person herself does not want it.

# ETHICAL ISSUES IN RELATION TO CHILDREN AND ADOLESCENTS

Ensuring that children and adolescents are fully informed about the principles and implications of treatment for a variety of disorders is fundamental to our approach. In respect of whether or not to continue treatment for a serious medical disorder in very young children, consent or withholding of consent to treatment will be given on the patient's behalf by the parents, or those acting "in loco parentis", in consultation with the clinical team responsible. Thus, for example, parents' wishes in respect of maintaining the life of a terminally ill child or baby will be taken into consideration, although as has been upheld in the Court in Scotland (Edinburgh, July 1997) final clinical responsibility for providing or withholding treatment rests with the doctor.

In this case the parents attempted to sue a Consultant Paediatrician and his employing Health Authority for failing to intervene sufficiently to try to preserve the life of a baby born at 24 weeks gestation. The parents claimed that the doctor was in default of his medical responsibility to try to preserve life; the doctor and the Health Authority maintained that the chance of preserving life was so small and the danger of very severe disability so great that, together with current advice from the British Medical Association, it was deemed to be inappropriate to intervene invasively to try to preserve this baby's life. The autonomy of the doctor in making the final decision was upheld by the Court, and the parents' case was dismissed. Generally, however, such difficult ethical decisions are made by clinicians together with parents. Time and supportive counselling are made available to help parents to reach their decision, and similarly the clinical team will discuss very carefully the pros and cons of continuing invasive therapies.

In the case of older children, e.g. those with terminal illnesses such as cystic fibrosis or cancer, many of whom may have had long periods of ill-health, several hospital admissions, invasive treatments (e.g. chemotherapy, radiotherapy, or, in the case of cystic fibrosis suffers, heart/lung transplantation), the wishes and feelings of the child or adolescent will be taken carefully into account by the clinical team. On occasions, a child may be thought to be unreasonably withholding her consent to treatment, perhaps because of anxiety or fear, or because she has become depressed and lacks the motivation to continue. In those cases the parents may override the child's refusal to consent to treatment and provide consent on her behalf. However, with children who are facing yet another course of invasive therapy, for which the prognosis is poor or guarded, the clinical team, together with the parents and child, may come to the decision that the poor prognosis does not justify the discomfort or suffering that a further course of treatment would entail. They might conclude on balance that palliative care would be in the child's best interests, and that her wishes should be respected.

In contrast, when a child with anorexia nervosa expresses the wish not to be treated, and her health is seriously compromised, her refusal to consent to treatment may well have to be overridden. It is difficult to see how any clinician could feel sanguine about respecting the wishes of a child to die through starvation, when treatment aimed at re-establishing adequate nutrition would in itself be life saving. Also, given that anorexia nervosa is a treatable condition, and would not ordinarily be terminal, the right to die is a questionable option. In any event, most children and adolescents with anorexia nervosa who decline treatment do so not so much from an active wish to end their lives, as through a fear of food and of gaining weight. This may be accompanied by a difficulty in relinquishing control over the one aspect of their lives that they have.

## LEGAL ISSUES

Although legislation alters from one country to the next and it is not possible to make reference to its application outside the UK, the principles should be applicable in most countries and of assistance in guiding practice.

In the UK, the legal framework that provides for the welfare, interests and protection of children is the Children Act 1989. This stipulates in a general sense:

(1)  the need to place the needs or interests of the child as its paramount concern.

(2)  the need to consider the welfare of the child in accordance with the welfare check list. The welfare checklist should be taken into account by the Courts, Local Authorities, and other agencies when making decisions about a child. These include the following.

- his or her ascertainable wishes and feelings should be taken into account;
- his or her physical, emotional, and educational needs;
- the likely effect of any change in circumstances;
- age, sex, background, and any other characteristics;
- how capable his or her parents or other people are in meeting his or her needs;
- the powers available to the Court.

The welfare of a child is best ensured when there is a co-operative working relationship between parents and professionals, and it is important therefore that families are involved as far as possible in any decision concerning their child's welfare.

(3)  to ascertain the wishes and feelings of the child in any matter concerning him or her.

(4)  to balance the child's wishes against the determination of others, e.g. parents, professionals, and the Court, in deciding what course of action is in his or her best interests.

# REFUSAL OF TREATMENT

If a child or young person refuses to eat or actively avoids treatment in other ways, e.g. running away; removing a naso-gastric tube, etc., treatment may still be given provided that a parent or someone acting "in loco parentis" gives consent on her behalf. In practice, however, particularly in the case of a young person over the age of 16, guidance will often be sought from the Court. This ensures that the young person can express her views through a legal representative who is independent of her family or the treatment team.

The right of a child or young person under the age of 18 to consent to or withhold consent to treatment is dependent in the UK on whether or not the child is deemed to be "Gillick-competent" (Gillick v. West Norfolk & Wisbech AHA, 1986). The Gillick Principle highlights a child's right to self-determination, i.e. her right to decide what happens to her own body. The Gillick-competent child is one "who is of sufficient understanding to appreciate in general terms the nature of what [treatment] is involved, and the implications of it". However, in some recent cases the Courts have clarified that even when a child is deemed to have reached that level of competence, it is acceptable on occasions for adults to override the young person's wishes to stop her from suffering significant harm. Some cases brought the High Court highlight the need to set the right of determination within a context of cognitive and emotional development, with any impairment which results from a diagnosable eating disorder. Thus, if a child refuses consent to treatment, her parents retain the right to consent on her behalf; this is deemed to be sufficient to allow medical treatment to proceed lawfully, even though the competent child was refusing consent (Elton, Honig, Bentovim, & Simons, 1995).

In *Weekly Law Reports* (1992), a girl aged 16 suffering from severe anorexia nervosa, whom we shall call Deborah, had her right to withhold consent to further treatment in another adolescent unit overruled by the High Court on the basis that her illness (self-induced starvation which impaired her cognitive capacity) rendered her incompetent to withhold her consent to treatment). Deborah, an orphan, was being looked after by the Local Authority, and had been accommodated with foster parents. When she developed a serious eating disorder (anorexia nervosa), which could not be effectively managed on an outpatient basis, she was admitted to an adolescent unit. It was subsequently thought, by those treating her and the social worker, that she would receive more appropriate treatment at the specialist Eating Disorder Unit based at a London teaching hospital. The girl refused to consent to being transferred and, thus, the Local Authority sought directions from the Court. The Court, having heard representations from both the girl and the Local Authority acting in loco parentis, decided that its prevailing duty was to provide for her welfare and to protect her from harm, which would certainly have followed had further treatment not been instigated. Thus, the girl was moved against her consent to a new unit, and treatment continued.

This ruling, which was published as a precedent case, was commented on by Lord Donaldson (*Weekly Law Reports*, 1992, p. 82), who said, "It is a feature of anorexia nervosa that it is capable of destroying the ability to make an informed choice. It creates a compulsion to refuse treatment, or only to accept treatment which is likely to be ineffective. This attitude is part and parcel of the disease and the more advanced the illness the more compelling it may become."

In a more recent case, in March 1997 (*The Times*, 1997) a High Judge ordered a 16-year-old girl with anorexia nervosa whom we shall call Catherine to be detained at a specialist eating disorders clinic for treatment aimed at restoring her weight. The girl, who had a two-year history of anorexia nervosa, with previous admissions, discharges, and relapses, had actually given her consent to remain at the clinic and accept treatment. However, because of her history of "running away" and fasting, her doctors were not confident that she would continue to consent to treatment for the duration of the programme. In those circumstances, together with the fact that she had in the past made serious suicide attempts, they felt that she would be at risk of significant harm without a Court Order requiring her to complete her course of treatment and reach and maintain her target weight.

This ruling was significant in that the High Court used its inherent jurisdiction to compel the girl to be detained at the clinic as necessary, and allowed for her to be returned to the clinic should she run away. Thus, for the first time a Common Law Order was used to forcibly restrict a child's liberty for medical reasons. The Courts had ordered medical treatment against a patient's wishes in the past, but this was thought to be the first time that approval had been given to detain a child without using the Mental Health Act, or unless the child was in need of secure accommodation or a Care Order. The Judge stated that the Court had the power to order a minor to undergo medical treatment against her will, and that had been done before with children with anorexia nervosa. In this case it was not thought appropriate to invoke the Mental Health Act of England and Wales because the clinic concerned was not a psychiatric hospital, nor did it constitute secure accommodation, nor was there any question of Care Proceedings. The Judge concluded that detention was an essential component of Catherine's treatment, and the Court overrode the girl's instructions to her own lawyers to oppose the making of any Order.

Although concerns were raised by civil liberty groups in respect of the Court's dispensation with Catherine's consent, the judgment was welcomed by clinicians and practitioners in the field for giving such a clear lead in terms of:

•   recognising that anorexia nervosa is a potentially life-threatening illness
•   recognising that it can seriously distort a sufferer's perception and capacity for insight

- recognising that, in respect of children and young persons under the age of 18, the Children Act and the inherent jurisdiction of the High Court provides sufficient authority to detain a young person against her will if necessary, for the purpose of providing life-saving treatment.

An alternative would have been for application to have been made within the Mental Health Act 1983 for Catherine to be independently assessed by two psychiatrists and an approved social worker to see whether she was deemed to be in need of treatment, for which she was unable to unwilling to give consent, and whether or not, without that treatment, she would have posed a risk to herself or others. Use of the Mental Health Act should be considered when the parents are working in partnership with the clinical team, but the competent child and in particular those aged between 16 and 18 may be refusing treatment and suffering from a clearly diagnosable mental disorder. (Anorexia nervosa would meet these critiera.) When treatment warranting detention in hospital is thought necessary to prevent any deterioration in a patient's condition, the use of the Mental Health Act may be preferable. In addition, it may allow for a number of treatments to be given in addition to refeeding, e.g. the passing of a naso-gastric tube or, in more extreme cases, the surgical intervention necessary for a gastrostomy. Where patients actively refuse the medical interventions, care should be taken to avoid rendering an "assault upon the person" both for the patient's sake, but also to protect staff from possible charges of ill treatment. Thus, is it good practice to try and elicit the patient's consent to necessary medical manoeuvres, but failing that to either obtain the leave of the Court (within Children Act proceedings) or to invoke the Mental Health Act in order to gain necessary permission (Honig & Bentovim, 1996). The following two case examples illustrate the use of the relevant legislation.

## Case example—use of Children Act

Anastasia, 13, developed anorexia nervosa aged 12. As her weight dropped, she became lethargic, cold, and unable to attend school. Her mother and father, who were members of a fundamental sect, nursed her at home and, despite the attempts of health and education professionals, resisted outside intervention. The school staff communicated their concerns to the Social Services Department, who made several attempts to visit the family home but were rebuffed by the parents.

Eventually, an application was made to the Court within the Children Act for an Assessment Order requiring the parents to allow their daughter to be seen by a general practitioner and social worker. On examination, the girl was noted to be grossly emaciated, dehydrated, and she had bed sores. Her weight-height ratio was 67%. The parents refused consent to allow the girl to be hospitalised, stressing their belief that they could care for her at home. The Local Authority applied to the Court for an Interim Care Order within the Children Act on the basis that the girl had suffered "significant harm" to her health and development and was likely to suffer further harm if she remained in her parents' care.

The application was granted, the girl was hospitalised, and she gradually recovered. She was noted to have a number of other emotional, behavioural, and developmental difficulties associated with prolonged illness, social isolation, and lack of educational opportunities. Her parents remained implacably opposed to the treatment plan and her father refused to visit her in hospital.

The Local Authority was subsequently granted a full Care Order so that parental responsibility would be shared by the parents and the Social Services Department. It was thought that the prognosis for recovery was poor if the girl returned home and she was therefore placed in a specialist therapeutic and educational unit, where she continues to thrive.

In summary, the parental refusal to allow Anastasia to be appropriately treated led to clinicians having serious concerns for her health. As neither Anastasia nor her parents would consent to life-saving treatment, an application was made to Court on Anastasia's behalf, by the Local Authority. The Court agreed that Anastasia had suffered and was likely to suffer significant harm attributable to the care of her parents. A Care Order was made, giving the Local Authority leave to consent to treatment on Anastasia's behalf, even though her parents refused.

## Case example—use of Mental Health Act

Sophie, 16, who had a three-year history of anorexia nervosa, was admitted to an adolescent unit that specialises in the treatment of eating disorders. She was noted to be depressed, expressed suicidal ideation, and had seriously self-harmed (by cutting her arms). She disclosed having been sexually abused aged 11–13 by a music teacher.

Although Sophie's parents agreed that she should be in hospital and gave their consent for treatment, Sophie herself refused to co-operate. She would only drink water, refused to eat, and refused to have a naso-gastric tube inserted. She did not perceive herself as ill and expressed the wish and intention to die. She twice ran away from the hospital, on one occasion having bought and ingested 25 paracetamol. The hospital applied under the Mental Health Act 1983 for Sophie to be treated against her will. An independent assessment of her was undertaken by two psychiatrists and an approved social worker, as a result of which she was made the subject of an Order and compulsorily detained and treated, initially for one month and subsequently for up to a year.

In this case, Sophie's parents were in agreement with the hospital and its proposed treatment plan. They gave their consent to Sophie's treatment but, given Sophie's age and understanding, the hospital decided to seek the opinions of independent colleagues. The Mental Health Act gives permission to treat, in certain circumstances, against a young person's will. Details of the proposed treatment plan are communicated, in writing, to the independent assessors. The patient's interests are safeguarded by being legally represented and by having her case reviewed on a regular basis.

In general, the Children Act, which is particularly geared to address the needs and best interests of children and young people, is probably the preferred legislation to use where possible, not least because being compulsorily treated under the Mental Health Act may create a stigma for a young person, and affect educational or occupational opportunities in the future.

## CONCLUSION

In principle, management of young people should always proceed with the least invasive treatment possible, i.e. encouragement within a caring, supportive environment to re-establish normal eating, with naso-gastric feeding only resorted to in the face of persistent refusal to eat normally. Most programmes use some behavioural techniques to support the treatment goals (see Chapter 11). However, the so-called "strict" behavioural regimens, e.g. patients having to earn "privileges" such as contact with their families, are no longer acceptable practice for a number of reasons. First, it is difficult to determine what a young person experiences as a privilege, reward, or punishment (e.g. parental visits may be either desired or detested). Second, such regimens focus only on weight restoration and militate against the therapeutic alliance, so essential to the recovery process. Third, there is no evidence such approaches work. Finally, it is both unethical and (at least in the UK) illegal to deny a child's rights (e.g. to see her parents regularly).

Force feeding, i.e. placing food in the child's mouth and ensuring swallowing, is unacceptable both ethically and legally. It is preferable to pass a naso-gastric tube, which is often perceived as being less frightening than being forcibly made to chew and swallow food (see Chapter 9). Even where naso-gastric feeding has to be resorted to, it should be done within the context of having established a trusting relationship with the child, and having given her prior opportunity to eat normally. Care should be taken by the nursing staff not to use unduly coercive techniques to persuade children to eat. It should be remembered that a proportion of children and young people with eating disorders, as with a range of other emotional and or behavioural problems, may have suffered physical, emotional, or sexual abuse prior to the onset of their eating disorder, and may be particularly sensitive and aversive to being forced to do things against their will.

Thus, it is vital to ensure that the treatment team does not unwittingly recreate abusive dynamics within its treatment regimen. Ensuring that inpatients have therapeutic help from members of the team not directly involved in refeeding them is also very important. This provides them with the opportunity to discuss their feelings and difficulties about eating, gaining weight, and their fear of fatness with a therapist, who is there to support them and help them gradually resolve their fears and anxieties.

Good interdisciplinary communication and working together is essential to ensure optimal treatment, and avoid unwitting abuses of patients, and it is usually the role of the team social worker to ensure that young peoples' rights of determination are respected and upheld within the treatment setting, and to advise on the steps necessary within a legal framework that will balance the need for treatment with the patient's wishes or feelings.

Finally, inpatient units should have written policies and guidelines designed to promote and safeguard the interests of children and adolescents, in line with the requirements of the Children Act and, where relevant, the Mental Health Act in the UK, and their equivalent in other countries.

## SUMMARY POINTS

- Achieving a treatment alliance with children and young people with eating disorders can be difficult. It is essential to establish a strong alliance with the parents.
- Resistance to treatment should be recognised and respected, but it is unethical to withhold treatment when a young person's judgement is likely to be seriously impaired by illness.
- Difficult decisions about the implementation of treatment need to be made by clinicians together with parents, who can override the child's refusal to consent.
- The courts have ruled that, despite the competence of a young person to understand the nature of their condition and to refuse treatment, nevertheless such refusal can be overridden.
- The competent young person aged 16–18 may be considered to be suffering from a clearly diagnosable mental disorder, and therefore detention in hospital may be achieved by the Mental Health Act.
- If parents are resistant to ensure their children/young people are treated adequately, then their health may be significantly harmed and the Children Act may be used to secure adequate car and treatment.
- Treatment should always proceed with the least invasive approach possible, in a context of support and care.

# REFERENCES

Elton, A., Honig, P., Bentovim, A., Simons, J. (1995). Withholding consent to lifesaving treatment: 3 cases. *British Medical Journal, 310.*

Gillick v. West Norfolk & Wisbech Area Health Authority. (1986). Appeal Courts 112.

Honig, P., & Bentovim, M. (1996). Treatment of children with eating disorders—ethical and legal issues. *Clinical Child Psychologist and Psychiatry, 1*(2), 287–294.

*The Times.* (July 1997). p. 1.

*Weekly Law Reports.* (1992). Re W (a minor). *758.*

# Epilogue

The complexity and severity of the early onset eating disorders present a major challenge to the child's health, to the carers and clinicians, and to researchers. Much remains to be learned and understood, including the nature and interactions of predisposing, precipitating, and perpetuating factors, and what constitutes the most effective forms of treatment.

Little is known about the prevention of early onset eating disorders. Theoretically, it might be possible to reduce the incidence by discouraging children, other than the very overweight, from embarking on rigorous dieting. However, research to date on such approaches has revealed very disappointing results. Six school-based programmes have been evaluated (reviewed by Carter, Stewart Dunn, & Fairburn, 1997). Each had been designed to reduce the prevalence of common behavioural precursors of eating disorders, especially dieting. The programmes were all similar and focused on education about the nature and consequences of eating disorders, discussion about the adverse effects of dieting and other methods of weight control, and skills training for resisting social pressure to diet. None of the programmes led to a change in the target behaviour despite increasing knowledge.

Carter et al. (1997) built upon these findings by evaluating a school-based intervention programme for 13–14-year-olds, which included not only the components previously evaluated but also cognitive behavioural procedures. In particular, children were taught to identify and challenge problematic thoughts and beliefs about their shape and weight. Although there was an increase in knowledge following the intervention and a decrease in target behaviour and attitudes, these effects had disappeared at 6-month follow-up and there was an *increase* in dietary restraint, suggesting that the intervention had actually been harmful. A longer term follow-up may show different results but clearly there is a need to be cautious about focusing on dieting behaviour in this age group.

Given that self-esteem is so commonly based on weight and shape and that such cognitions develop so early in life (e.g. Hill, Oliver, & Rogers, 1992), a logical prevention programme would be focused on helping young children base their self-esteem on other facets than weight and shape. For example, parents and teachers could help children to place more value on their inherent skills and aptitudes and personality characteristics.

The role of the media must also be considered. The media's preoccupation with promoting slimness as an ideal and dieting as a necessity is a malign influence. This is compounded by the increasing exposure of young children to sex in magazines and newspapers, on television and videotapes. It is likely that some children find the intensity and explicitness sufficiently worrying for a subconscious avoidance mechanism to commence. It is perhaps a little optimistic to expect messages to be portrayed on screen and in the popular press in a more balanced way, and we may have to wait for current trends to be replaced by healthier ones. Parents can help by at least discussing with their children the values that are so vigorously promoted in the media, and helping their children to become more discerning.

Early detection of eating problems may help reduce morbidity by allowing for earlier treatment. The diagnosis of early onset eating disorder is often overlooked (Bryant-Waugh, Lask, Shafron, & Fosson, 1992), with consequent delays in the initiation of appropriate treatment (Bryant-Waugh, Hankins, Shafran, Lask, & Fosson, 1996). More education of primary health-carers is clearly necessary.

One promising area is that of biomedical research. Ever more sophisticated techniques are becoming available for investigating brain biochemistry and physiology (see Chapter 8) and abnormalities in cerebral functioning (not necessarily secondary to weight loss) are increasingly being identified (e.g. Gordon, Lask, Bryant-Waugh, Christie, & Timimi, 1997; Kuruoglu, Kapucu, Atasever, Arikan, Isik, & Unlu, 1998). The combination of brain imaging and neuropsychometry may be of particular value (e.g. Christie, Bryant-Waugh, Lask, & Gordon, 1998; Kingston, Szmukler, Andrewes, Tress, & Desmond, 1996).

Finally, we must remain aware of the continuing need to review and improve our treatment skills. The prognosis for many of the eating disorders in childhood and early adolescence remains poor, with a high relapse rate and prolonged morbidity. We need more treatment evaluation studies with lengthy follow-up periods (e.g. Eisler et al., 1997) that attempt to evaluate the effectiveness of specific treatments for particular populations. However, it is likely that the most effective approach for the treatment of early onset eating disorders will prove to involve a combination of treatments.

# REFERENCES

Bryant-Waugh, R., Hankins, M., Shafron, R., Lask, B., & Fosson, A. (1996). A prospective follow up of children with anorexia nervosa. *Journal of Youth and Adolescence, 25*, 431–438.

Bryant-Waugh, R., Lask, B., Shafron, R., & Fosson, A. (1992). Do doctors recognise eating disorders in children? *Archives of Disease in Childhood, 62*, 114–118.

Carter, J., Stewart, A., Dunn, V., & Fairburn, C. (1997). Primary prevention of eating disorders: Might it do more harm than good? *International Journal of Eating Disorders, 22*, 162–167.

Christie, D., Bryant-Waugh, R., Lask, B., & Gordon, I. (1998). Neurobiological aspects of early onset eating disorders. In H. Hoek, J. Treasure, & M. Katzman (Eds.), *Neurobiology in the treatment of eating disorders* (pp. 291–309). Chichester, UK: John Wiley.

Eisler, I., Dare, C., Russell, G., Szmukler, G., le Grange, D., & Dodge, E. (1997). Family and individual therapy in anorexia nervosa—a five year follow-up. *Archives of General Psychiatry, 54*, 1025–1030.

Gordon, I., Lask, B., Bryant-Waugh, R., Christie, C., & Timimi, S. (1997). Childhood onset anorexia nervosa: Towards identifying a biological substrate. *International Journal of Eating Disorders, 22*, 159–166.

Hill, A., Oliver, S., & Rogers, P. (1992). Eating in the adult world: The rise of dieting in childhood and adolescence. *British Journal of Clinical Psychology, 31*, 95–105.

Kingston, K., Szmukler, G., Andrewes, D., Tress, B., & Desmond, P. (1996). Neuropsychological and structural brain changes in anorexia nervosa before and after re-feeding. *Psychological Medicine, 26*, 15–28.

Kuruoglo, A., Kapucu, O., Atasever, T., Arikan, Z., Isik, E., & Unlu, M. (1998). Technetium-99m-HMPAO Brain SPECT in anorexia nervosa. *Journal of Nuclear Medicine, 39*, 304–306.

# Author index

# Subject index